Advanced Windows Deployments Using 1E Software

Dave Kawula

Émile Cabot

PUBLISHED BY
Deployment Artist
http://www.deploymentartist.com

ISBN: 978-91-87445-12-5

Warning and Disclaimer

Every effort has been made to make this manual as complete and as accurate as possible, but no warranty or fitness is implied. The information provided is on an "as is" basis. The authors and the publisher shall have neither liability nor responsibility to any person or entity with respect to any loss or damages arising from the information contained in this book.

Feedback Information

We'd like to hear from you! If you have any comments about how we could improve the quality of this book, please don't hesitate to contact us by visiting www.deploymentartist.com or sending an email to feedback@deploymentartist.com.

Foreword

I was quite taken aback when asked to contribute to this book by writing the Foreword. I've been a Microsoft MVP in the Enterprise Client Management (formerly known as Configuration Manager) expertise for over 11 years and an Industry Expert speaker numerous times. My personal experience dates to SMS2.0 RTM back in 1998/1999 when I deployed the initial SMS2 RTM installation in the United States in January 1999. I've known Dave and Johan for many of those years, and continue to be in awe of their knowledge and experience with this subject matter. I've also known Émile for a number of years via his partnership and collaboration with Dave. It is humbling indeed to be asked to contribute to this work.

I'm also a long-time employee of 1E, being hired as Employee #3 when the US organization was established nearly eight years ago. In my capacity as a Solutions Engineer, it is my role to deliver technical product functionality and education to our prospective customers in the pre-sales engagement. This is done in a variety of ways, including demonstrations, delivering a proof-of-concept (as illustrated in this book), as well as the (now more common) pilot-to-production method.

Reviewing this document it is readily obvious that the authors have put their collective *years* of operating system deployment (OSD) expertise into a thorough end-to-end walkthrough of the process of taking the System Center Configuration Manager engineer into every aspect of the powerful out-of-the-box Microsoft technologies, folded in the appropriate 1E technologies to augment that system, and clearly and concisely provided the *extremely powerful* **solution** that results from this combination of ingredients.

Make no mistake about it: OSD engineering is complicated! It is also something that will happen far more frequently than we have seen previously. Many years went by when one could get by with Windows XP, while maybe bringing Win7 into the company as old systems were retired. As Win7 replaced those XP systems, Win8 adoption is increasing and there is already talk of Windows 10 coming soon! Does this mean that the Configuration Manager engineer has to go through the WinXP migration nightmare every other year or so going forward? Absolutely not! Using the techniques and processes outlined in this document, and leveraging the significant value-added proposition that the 1E tools bring to the table, the reader will for the first time be given the knowledge and techniques to make the OSD process simply Business As Usual, using the existing Configuration Manager team! This previously daunting effort becomes hardly more complex that deploying security updates! No more will there be a need for months and months of planning, endless meetings, or outsourcing the entire effort at significant cost.

With this book as your guide, you have in your hands the collective wisdom and *real world experience* of some of the very best experts in the world. These individuals have not only "talked the talk," but "walked the walk," helping some of the largest organizations in the world to tame the OSD beast. You too now have at your disposal the means to accomplish the same thing for *your* company or business.

One last point: the authors are among the most visible and approachable people in the entire Systems Management community, whether through social media, individual blogs, myITForum, TechNet, or any number of major conferences around the world where they are often speakers. They are all here to help *you*, whether you bought this book, or are just looking for some straight answers to complex questions.

Now, turn the page, start reading and learning, and go get that lab built! You're in for a fun ride!

Ed Aldrich

Microsoft MVP, Enterprise Client Management (2003-2014)

Solutions Engineer | 1E | www.1e.com

Acknowledgements

From Dave

There are not enough words to say thank you to the "BEST Wife" in the world, Cristal Kawula. Christian, Trinity, Keira, Serena, Mickaila and Mackenzie, you kids are so patient with your dear old dad when he locks himself away in the office. You have been my source of inspiration and the ones that pushed me to finally write this book. Your constant encouragement makes it easier to put in all of the long hours.

My coauthor and partner in crime, Émile Cabot, has been there with me the whole way. He would come over to my home office and put in tireless hours working through concepts and ideas. His ability to write down our thoughts and make them legible so that you the reader can understand our concepts is unbelievable. I had a chance to see just how good he really was as we dug into the deep realms of products and processes.

To the whole team at 1E for helping with the technical editing and putting in so much extra after hours effort. You help and support has made this a book a reality. The beverages and steak are definitely on me next time we meet up.

Thank you, Oliver Bargetzi. You are the best friend anyone could ever want. Even when I thought I would never finish this book you were always there for my calls and kept pushing me along.

Thank you, Mom and Dad (Frank and Audry). You got me started in this crazy IT world when I was so young. Your efforts helping me review this book are truly appreciated.

Last but not least, Johan Arwidmark, you have been so supportive as we brought this book to life. You are empowering people like Émile and me to expand our horizons with awesome new opportunities like this book. I couldn't think of a better publisher to work with.

From Émile

When Dave and I first met Johan in 2011, he sparked the OSDWeek class and ultimately the idea to write this book. Your guidance and incredible patience throughout this endeavor has been worth its weight in gold, alleviating the complications of the publishing process to let us focus on the content.

Speaking of content, I've always been impressed with all the benefits that can be achieved by implementing 1E solutions, and have thoroughly enjoyed every single implementation. Transforming our "What worked best" implementations into this format would not have been possible without the assistance of the wonderful teams at 1E. Your late nights polishing our explanations, validating our statements, and correcting a grammar mistake or two (okay…maybe three) will not be forgotten, without which this book would not have come to fruition.

Mr. and Mrs. Kawula, words can't describe the appreciation I have for everything that you've both done for me over the past few years. From introducing me to the world of 1E, to the joys of mudding on a mini ATV, being a part of TriCon Elite has been the experience of a lifetime.

Mom and Dad, from my first VIC-20 to my first business, you've always been there to guide and support me. You taught me the value of integrity and ethics early on, and the importance of enjoying life to its fullest.

Laura, my love, without your unrelenting support and patience over the years, there's no way I would have made it this far. I've spent the better part of the past 18 months locked in the office while you tirelessly kept Tyson and Erick entertained and out of trouble. You're a wonderful wife and an amazing mother. I thank you from the bottom of my heart for being by my side.

About the Authors

Dave Kawula

Dave is a Microsoft Most Valuable Professional (MVP) with over 20 years of experience in the IT industry. His background includes data communications networks within multiserver environments, and he has led architecture teams for virtualization, System Center, Exchange, Active Directory, and Internet gateways. Very active within the Microsoft technical and consulting teams, Dave has provided deep-dive technical knowledge and subject matter expertise on various System Center and operating system topics.

Dave is well-known in the community as an evangelist for Microsoft, 1E, and Veeam technologies. Locating Dave is easy as he speaks at several conferences and sessions each year, including TechEd, MVP Days Community Roadshow, and VeeamOn.

As the founder and Managing Principal Consultant at TriCon Elite Consulting, Dave is a leading technology expert for both local customers and large international enterprises, providing optimal guidance and methodologies to achieve and maintain an efficient infrastructure.

BLOG: www.checkyourlogs.net

Twitter: @DaveKawula

Émile Cabot

Émile started in the industry during the mid-90s working at an ISP and designing celebrity web sites. He has a strong operational background specializing in Systems Management and collaboration solutions, and has spent many years performing infrastructure analyses and solution implementations for organizations ranging from 20 to over 200,000 employees. Coupling his wealth of experience with a small partner network, Émile works very closely with TriCon Elite Consulting, 1E, and Veeam to deliver low-cost solutions with minimal infrastructure requirements.

He actively volunteers as a member of the Canadian Ski Patrol, providing over 250 hours each year for first aid services and public education at Castle Mountain Resort and in the community.

BLOG: www.checkyourlogs.net

Twitter: @ECabot

Contributing Authors

Johan Arwidmark

Johan Arwidmark is a consultant and all-around geek specializing in Systems Management and Enterprise Windows Deployment Solutions. Johan also speaks at several conferences each year, including MMS and TechEd events around the world. He is actively involved in deployment communities like deploymentresearch.com and myitforum.com, and has been awarded Microsoft Most Valuable Professional (MVP) for more than ten years.

Allan Rafuse

Allan has worked as a senior member of the Windows and VMWare Platform Department at Swedbank. He took part in the architecture and implementation of multiple datacenters in several countries. He is responsible for the roadmap and lifecycle of the Windows Server Environment, including the development of ITIL processes of global server OSD, configuration, and performance.

He is an expert at scripting solutions and has an uncanny ability to reduce complexity and maximize the functionality of PowerShell. Allan has recently rejoined the TriCon Elite Consulting team again as a Principal Consultant.

Contents

Introduction

This book was created to take your operational knowledge of Configuration Manager (ConfigMgr) to the next level and show you how you can optimize your architecture and streamline your Windows 7 and Windows 8.1 deployments by augmenting industry-leading solutions from 1E Software. We guide you through architecting an efficient environment while reducing support costs by empowering the end-user community with some backend software and deployment automation.

ConfigMgr is one of the most complex of Microsoft's products. When implementing it in an organization, it is tough to build a stable solution while maintaining a small footprint. Dispersed organizations find this especially difficult due to limited interconnectivity, requiring servers to be decentralized and deployed to virtually every site in the enterprise. This book guides you through the architecture process of your ConfigMgr 2012 R2 design optimization strategy, the factors that determine role placement, and how 1E Nomad will further reduce the server footprint. We show you how to eliminate distribution/PXE and state migration points from your environment, and automate the delivery of applications during the deployment of Windows. We also show you how deployment success rates in excess of 99 percent are possible and make the network team your best friends in the process.

Say Hello (Possibly Again) to ViaMonstra Inc.

In this book, you optimize the ConfigMgr 2012 environment of a fictitious company, ViaMonstra Inc., and fully implement a Windows 8.1 operating system migration strategy. ViaMonstra is a mid-sized company that is undergoing massive growth and in the past year alone, increased employees from 6,500 to 50,000. The datacenter and head office are in New York, with a staff of 6,500. There are 200 other sites spread across the globe with sites ranging from 10–2,500 employees.

ViaMonstra has standardized on System Center 2012 R2 ConfigMgr across the enterprise. They have a single primary server in New York, with four management points, eight distribution points, and two software update points. There are ~200 secondary sites.

If you are new to the organization, the name ViaMonstra comes from *Viam Monstra*, which means "Show me the way" in Latin.

Structure of the Book

The first chapter of this book introduces you to the world of 1E solutions. We discuss 1E as a company, each of the products it offers, what they do, and how they can optimize your environment.

Chapter 2 goes through the ViaMonstra ConfigMgr 2012 infrastructure as it existed in previous books. We discuss the changes that have occurred in the organization and the new requirements presented to enterprise client management.

Chapter 3 outlines current operational constraints and the architectural efficiencies gained by implementing 1E Nomad.

Chapters 4 and 5 discuss in detail the products highlighted in this book, as well as the implementation of ActiveEfficiency, Nomad, Shopping, and AppClarity.

Chapter 6 looks into patching with ConfigMgr 2012 and how the standard process changes with the implementation of Nomad.

Chapters 7 and 8 start the deep dive into task sequence engineering. We follow Johan's practices in creating an ideal reference image in MDT that can be deployed using any medium. Then in SCCM we create a task sequence that can deploy operating systems over bare metal, as well as for OS refreshes and hardware replacements.

Chapters 9–12 cover utilizing Nomad for an operating system deployment scenarios. We outline the benefits of this design, and you then perform required task sequence injections and create additional task sequences purpose-built for pre-caching specific packages on Nomad clients. We then explain extending the sequence further, utilizing Nomad to deploy the sequence to bare metal workstations at locations that already provide Trivial File Transfer Protocol (TFTP) boot services. We also cover the implementation of PXE Everywhere, and how we use it to eliminate remote TFTP servers and PXE enabled distribution points from the enterprise. Finally, we wrap up the Nomad task sequence injection process to include PC replacements. This is implemented using 1E's Nomad's Peer Backup Assist feature to provide state migration functionality without the use of server/NAS storage.

We cover empowering the end-user community in Chapter 13, implementing Shopping and configuring it for self-service OSD.

How to Use This Book

We have packaged this book with step-by-step guides, which means you will be able to build your deployment solution as you read along.

In numbered steps, we have set all names and paths in bold typeface. We also have used a standard naming convention throughout the book when explaining what to do in each step. The steps are normally something like this:

1. On the **Advanced Properties** page, select the **Confirm** check box, and then click **Next**.

Code and sample scripts are formatted like the following examples, on a grey background.

```
DoNotCreateExtraPartition=YES

WSUSServer=http://wsus01.corp.viamonstra.com:8530
```

Code and commands that you type in the guides are displayed like this:

1. Install **MDT 2013** by running the following command in an elevated **PowerShell** prompt:

```
& msiexec.exe /i 'C:\Setup\MDT 2013\
MicrosoftDeploymentToolkit2013_x64.msi' /quiet
```

The step-by-step guides in this book assume that you have configured the environment according to the information in Chapter 2, "ViaMonstra Inc. and the Proof-of-Concept Environment." All prerequisites and component downloads associated with using hydration to create the environment are located in Appendix A.

This book is not intended as a reference volume, covering every deployment technology, acronym, or command-line switch known to man, but rather is designed to make sure you learn what you need to know to build advanced deployment solutions for your Windows clients.

Readers of this book should go through Johan Arwidmark's book *Deployment Fundamentals – Volume 4* as a prerequisite. There are core skill sets that Johan teaches that we build upon in this book with the advanced deployments using 1E Software.

Sample Files

All sample files for this book can be downloaded from http://deploymentfundamentals.com.

There are certain sample files that will require access to 1E Software for source binaries. These can be requested by going to the following site: http://www.1e.com/nomad-windows-software-deployment/request-trial/.

Additional Resources

In addition to all tips and tricks provided in this book, you can find extra resources like articles and video recordings on our blog http://www.checkyourlogs.net.

Topics Not Covered

This book does not cover Windows Server deployments, even though the tools, methods, and processes explained in it do apply for Windows Server. The book also does not cover other System Center 2012 solutions or the following products by 1E: NightWatchman, and Wakeup.

Chapter 1

Who Is 1E?

1E was founded in 1997 by three former Microsoft contractors, Sumir Karayi, Phil Wilcock, and Mark Blackburn. Today, Karayi leads the company as CEO, and to date 1E has sold more than 26 million licenses deployed across 1,700 organizations in 42 countries, ranging in size from 500–500,000 users. Its customers are drawn from public and private sectors around the world. To date, those customers have collectively documented $2.5 billion in actual hard dollar savings using 1E solutions.

The company's name is derived from a Windows NT computer error. Sometimes when NT servers crash, a blue screen containing "STOP 0x0000001E" appears. This name was chosen because the founders had the ambition that 1E could prevent this from happening to big companies.

The company's first hit, 1E NightWatchman, provides industry-leading energy savings across an organization's workstation environment, utilizing power profiles to manage unused equipment's energy usage. Since then, its product suite has been extended to include the following products:

- **1E WakeUp.** WakeUp is a product that allows computers to be powered on as required.
- **1E Nomad.** Designed to optimize network utilization for software deployment, Nomad is an enterprise grade peer-to-peer solution that uses unallocated HDD space on client workstations to store packages, rather than implementing costly distribution points.
- **1E AppClarity.** Addressing software licensing optimization, AppClarity enables organizations to discover exactly which software is being used, or not, within departments or on specific computers. It also dramatically reduces the complexity of reclaiming unused software.
- **1E Shopping.** A web-based app store, IE Shopping allows users to "shop" for applications, task sequences, and Active Directory security groups. It can act as a front end to a ticketing system, eliminating help desk and manual intervention from the software deployment and installation process.
- **1E ActiveEfficiency.** The newest solution in the 1E product suite, ActiveEfficiency is a framework solution designed to manage data and interconnectivity between 1E products, systems management solutions, and client devices.
- **1E MyWorkNow.** This is a cloud-based, virtual PC desktop solution that can be used on *any* Windows PC or Mac. MyWorkNow supports both online and offline use.

In this book, you implement 1E Nomad and Shopping in the ViaMonstra environment, so it is useful to look into each of these products a little further.

1E Nomad

1E Nomad's value is critical to organizations for a number of reasons. In simplest terms, Nomad is network protection technology, but it is also so much more. The patented Reverse QoS ™ technology intelligently uses unused network bandwidth to reliably and securely distribute packages/applications like operating system upgrades, software deployments, and patches to thousands of PCs, servers, and sites without disruption. "Intelligently" means that it dynamically adjusts to bandwidth usage conditions on the network, throttling itself accordingly. So, your network is always stable, always protected, and always available for servicing business critical traffic.

Nomad also reduces hardware and management costs by eliminating the need for dedicated branch distribution servers ConfigMgr. At its heart, the core functionality of Nomad is its agent-based peer-to-peer sharing model that ensures that content is ever downloaded only once to a location.

Nomad gets essential patches and updates delivered fast, *without* disrupting the business, vigilantly avoiding negative impact to user productivity. It provides reliable software delivery, even over slow or unreliable WAN links. Consider that the next time you groan over a request to deliver an Office 2013 upgrade to thousands of PCs by Monday.

Another key indicator of Nomad's brilliance is that it super-charges OS migrations. Deploying operating system upgrades can be done at any time—no need to wait until after hours for when the network is underutilized, paying overtime to IT. As an example, using Nomad, a large US telecommunications customer automated Zero Touch desktop software deployment across their entire PC estate, delivering annual cash savings of $5 million and an 80-percent reduction in deployment times. In another customer success story, a US financial organization was able to achieve 1800 OS deployments per day during their Windows 7 migration efforts.

Nomad is a MUST for any organization that:

- Has System Center ConfigMgr and branch offices
- Is deploying software, patches, and operating systems

1E PXE Everywhere

With the implementation of 1E Nomad into a ConfigMgr hierarchy, branch distribution points can be completely eliminated. However, now a requirement needs to be filled to provide a PXE boot point to any and all sites, as this role has now been combined with the Distribution Point role in ConfigMgr 2012. To provide a solution for this, 1E created a product called PXE Everywhere.

First released in 2006, PXE Everywhere was created to install on a branch workstation to provide PXE boot capabilities. During the typical PXE boot process with a ConfigMgr 2012 distribution point enabled with PXE, information is provided dynamically when a client request occurs. However, when workstations are used to provide this SCCM-enabled boot image, it is not capable of providing this data dynamically. Therefore, the boot image is manually injected with this configuration information, using a 1E utility called UpdateBootImage.exe. When a PXE client requests a boot image, a PXE Everywhere workstation first communicates with ConfigMgr through the PXE Central web service to validate whether an operating system deployment (OSD) task sequence has been deployed to the client's MAC address. If so, the PXE Everywhere workstation provides the boot image to the client via TFTP transfer, at which point the client boots into WinPE and is provided with any available/required task sequences.

1E Shopping

To reduce support and management costs of the application lifecycle, and to help organizations transition into a user-centric management platform, Shopping has become a popular addition to a company's solution suite. Providing end users with a familiar web-based app store to request new software and even schedule OS upgrades, it integrates directly with ConfigMgr (and AppClarity, if available) to provide automated software delivery to user workstations, even during operating system deployments.

When a user requests an application from Shopping, it creates a collection in ConfigMgr, adds the machine to that collection, deploys the requested software to the collection, and triggers a Machine Policy Retrieval and Evaluation Cycle on the client workstation. This provides a near-instant response to application requests.

Should a software installation be associated to a license cost, Shopping can be extended to automatically bill the user's business unit. If a software title requires approval prior to installation, Shopping sends an email notification request to a manager or list of approvers, providing them with a one-click option either to accept or deny the request.

When OSD task sequences are published to Shopping, users are provided with an intuitive interface to walk them through scheduling their migration to a new operating system. They can be provided with scheduling options, as well as visibility into any application variances that are presented during their migration. Shopping administrators have full control over the dates and time available to the end user for scheduling. Administrators also can limit the number of deployments that can be scheduled in a given time to avoid overwhelming infrastructure or support resources.

Integrating AppClarity into the solution is extremely powerful for operating system migrations, as pairing these two products creates the ability for workstations to have software titles removed or replaced during migration, all based upon usage history. For example, if a user rarely used Visio Professional, shopping can recommend installing Visio Viewer during the migration, instead of its more expensive counterpart. Similarly, software titles the end user no longer uses are automatically identified and deselected for reinstallation in the OSD Self-Serve Wizard.

Chapter 2

ViaMonstra Inc. and the Proof-of-Concept Environment

The environment that we work with throughout the course of the book is that of the fictitious company ViaMonstra, Inc. The original 6,500 user design was implemented by Kent Agerlund in *System Center 2012 SP1: Mastering the Fundamentals*. As ViaMonstra has rapidly grown, it has simply added secondary sites or standalone distribution points (DPs) to existing servers as new branches were acquired.

While implementing 1E solutions for advanced OSD, you also reoptimize the environment and implement some efficiencies through the 1E solution suite.

ViaMonstra's current ConfigMgr 2012 design is described in the following section, after which an expanded conceptual design is presented.

Conceptual Design – 6,500 Users (Before)

In case you have not been acquainted with the ViaMonstra environment before today, here is an outline of the environment, as it exists at the end of Kent's book.

Each branch office has a distribution point. Right now the current design has following:

Site Server Role	Location	Number of Servers
Primary site server + all roles	New York	1
Secondary site server + DP	Liverpool	1
Remote offices	Remote offices	30+

This is a familiar design that we see in many environments with subtle differences. It consists of a primary location and highly connected datacenter that serves as a centralized location for the majority of the organization's business application and infrastructure servers. Branch locations see no server infrastructure, with larger overseas sites housing region-specific application servers and limited infrastructure, such as directory services.

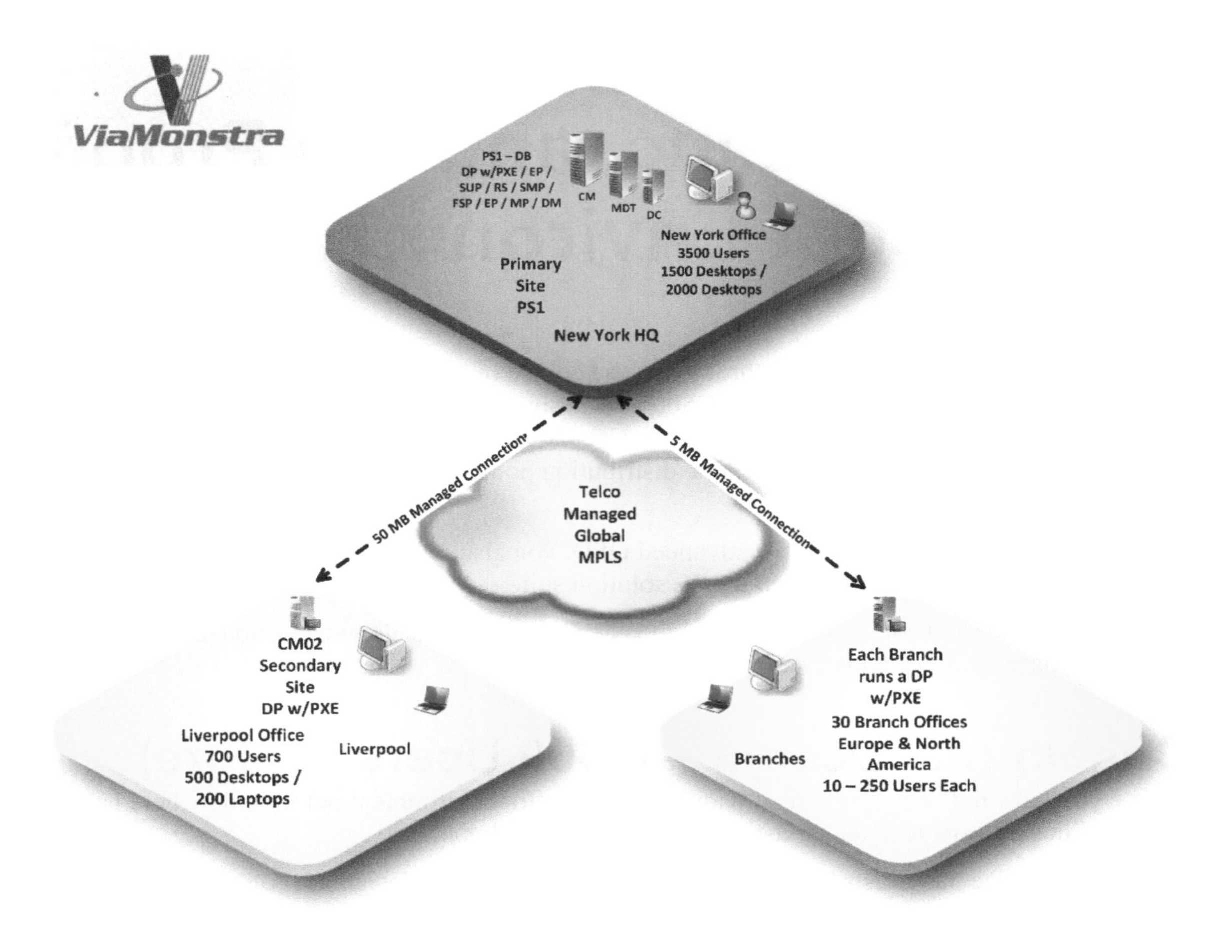

The ViaMonstra "Before" conceptual design.

Conceptual Design – 50,000+ Users (After)

ViaMonstra has entered into the fitness business and has acquired GloboGym, which has more than 1,300 locations and supports approximately 43,000 global users and devices.

In a traditional ConfigMgr world, the hierarchy would be sized to something like this:

Site Server Role	Location	Number of Servers
Primary Site ConfigMgr Infrastructure	New York	10–15
Secondary Site ConfigMgr Infrastructure (Including DPs)	Larger offices (250+) = 10	10
Remote offices	Remote offices—each has a DP with the PXE role	1,330

This may seem far reaching, but it is a very common scenario for many companies—especially those that go through a heavy cycle of mergers and acquisitions.

The unfortunate reality of a design like this is that it would require adding approximately 1,300 remote servers running as distribution points.

The following graphic shows what the typical ConfigMgr design might look like.

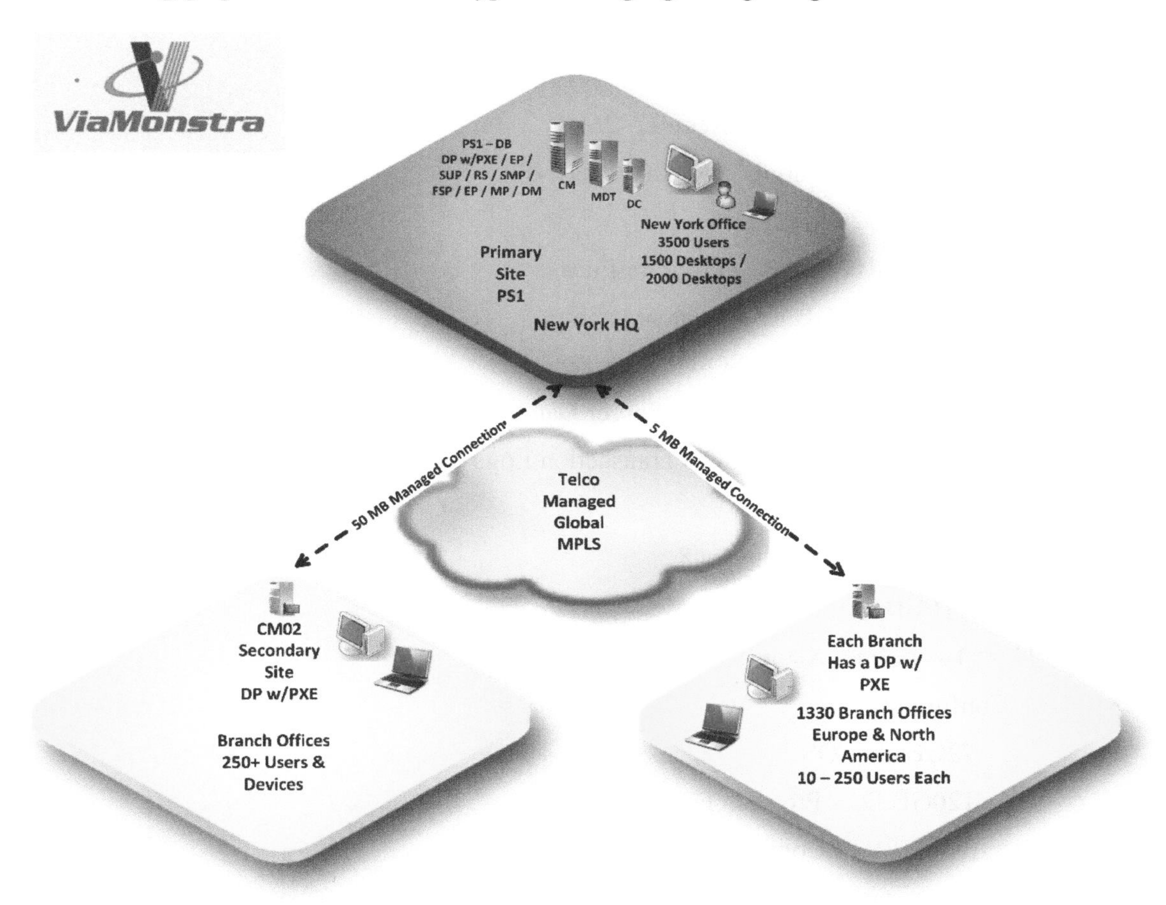

The ViaMonstra "After" conceptual design.

Site Server Design Physical Hardware

Primary site server:

- The single primary server hardware was designed to support 6,500 users.
- It has the following components and configurations:
    - Host: HP ProLiant DL380p Gen8
    - Memory: 32GB
    - CPU: 2x6-core Intel Xeon E5-2630
    - Disk Configuration: 5 RAID 10 LUNs
        - 72GB C:\ - OS
        - 100GB D:\ - Program Files
        - 300GB E:\ - Content Library
        - 50GB F:\ - SQL Server TempDB
        - 100GB G:\ - SQL Server Database
        - 75GB H:\ - SQL Transaction Logs

14 site system servers:

- Host: HP ProLiant DL380p Gen8
- Memory: 16GB
- CPU: 2x4-core Intel Xeon E5-2603
- Disk Configuration:
    - 72GB C:\ - OS
    - 120GB D:\ - Program Files
    - 300GB E:\ - Content Library

~200 secondary site servers:

Various hardware configurations added through acquisitions

~1,300 stand-alone distribution points

Various hardware configurations added through acquisitions

Servers and Clients for the POC Environment

ViaMonstra's lab environment was built using a process called *hydration*. This process uses task sequences in the Microsoft Deployment Toolkit to build a complete environment that can be deployed via lite-touch. You can use this hydration kit, provided in the book sample files, to build a fully-functional lab and follow along with the book.

> **Friendly Reminder:** Detailed step-by-step guidance on how to deploy the servers and clients used in the book, using the hydration process, can be found in Appendix A. Also note that the password for the accounts created by the hydration kit is P@ssw0rd (including the Administrator account).

The environment consists of the following systems:

- DC01
    - A fully patched Windows Server 2012 R2 machine
    - Configured as a Domain Controller, DNS Server, SMTP and DHCP Server in the corp.viamonstra.com domain
    - IP Address: 192.168.1.200
- CM01
    - A fully patched Windows Server 2012 R2 machine
    - Configured with WSUS
    - SQL2012 Standard installed
    - MDT 2013 installed and integrated into ConfigMgr
    - Contains the following ConfigMgr roles:
        - Management Point
        - Distribution Point
        - Software Update Point
        - Application Catalog Web Service Point
        - Application Catalog Website Point
    - IP Address 192.168.1.214
- MDT01
    - A fully patched Windows Server 2012 R2 machine
    - MDT 2013 installed
    - MDT monitoring database installed

  - Host for the following 1E components:
    - AppClarity
    - PXE Central
    - Shopping
  - IP Address 192.168.1.210
- PC0001
  - Windows 7 Enterprise SP1 x64
  - IP Address: DHCP
- PC0002
  - Windows 8.1 Enterprise x64
  - IP Address: DHCP
- PC0003
  - Windows 7 Enterprise SP1 x64
  - IP Address: DHCP
- PC0004
  - Windows 7 Enterprise SP1 x64
  - IP Address: DHCP

Software

Along with the previously mentioned systems, you need to download copies of the following software to populate source directories in the hydration kit. You can use either evaluation media or full version media:

- Windows Server 2012 R2 Standard
- Windows 7 Enterprise with SP1 x64
- Windows 8.1 Enterprise x64
- SQL Server 2012 with SP1
- System Center 2012 R2 Configuration Manager
- Windows Assessment and Deployment Toolkit 8.1
- Microsoft Deployment Toolkit 2013
- Microsoft Office 2013
- TechSmith Camtasia 8

- TechSmith Snagit 11
- BGInfo
- Visual C++ Runtimes
- .NET Framework 4.0 for Windows 7
- Required 1E software for Nomad, PXE Everywhere, and Shopping

Note: If you are an existing customer of 1E, you can download the software from supportportal.1e.com. If not, you can go to the following website to request a trial key and download: http://www.1e.com/nomad-windows-software-deployment/request-trial/. The 1E software is required to complete all lab work.

Chapter 3

Operational Considerations

Because ViaMonstra has grown so fast, the infrastructure team has not had the opportunity to properly scale up the ConfigMgr 2012 R2 hierarchy to support the large influx of machines. We start by addressing this from the primary site server level and work our way down the hierarchy.

Note: It is important to understand that the operational considerations discussed in this chapter largely reflect limitations of ConfigMgr 2012 R2 and not 1E products. The proposed design using 1E products overcomes many of these operational limitations.

The current design places the primary site server database on the same server as the Primary Site Server role. Microsoft recommends keeping the SQL Server instance local to the Primary Site Server role if it's supporting fewer than 50,000 endpoints, though this is a "soft" requirement; given appropriate hardware, we have seen much larger client counts with a local SQL install. ViaMonstra has about 50,000, so this part of the design will stay. However, with an increase of almost 45,000 clients, the drives will need to be resized. Factoring in the new client counts results in the following increases on the primary site server:

- The database will grow to 255 GB.
- TempDB grows to 75 GB.
- Transaction logs consume 80 GB.
- The content library is expected to grow up to 1 TB in size to support additional line-of-business applications for ViaMonstra's expansion into additional markets.

As a result of the dramatic increase in database sizes, we have come to the realization that the current disk configuration is insufficient; LUNs will have to be reconfigured to support the new capacity.

IOPS Are Your Friend

For most environments, the largest bottleneck on a ConfigMgr primary site server that also holds the SQL database is disk I/O (IOPS). Because you will optimize this environment and upgrade the disk configuration, you will replace the SAN storage with local enterprise-grade solid state drives. These drives not only drastically outperform traditional spinning disks with both read and write operations, but also have a much longer lifespan.

Management Points

Microsoft recommends that a management point (MP) be deployed for every 25,000 users. It is also recommended that management points be highly connected to the primary site server. Given this direction, you will decommission two of the management points to reduce the server footprint. This will leave you with two MPs to align with Microsoft recommendations and provide higher availability.

Distribution Points

Addressing distribution points (DP) is the point where the architecture efficiencies of 1E Nomad are introduced. It is recommended to have a distribution point deployed for every 4,000 clients, which can be geo-dispersed to reside closer to large offices rather than the primary site server. With the introduction of Nomad and Single Site Download (SSD) into the architecture, you can effectively have a distribution point serve up to 4,000 sites, thereby reducing the DP-client ratio for this 200 site environment. Introducing PXE Everywhere and Peer Backup Assistant to the Nomad deployment reduces the need for enabling PXE on the distribution point and state migration points (SMP).

DPs are intensive in network and disk I/O, where management points are intensive in CPU and memory utilization. These roles are designed to work nicely together. You will combine the Management Point and Distribution Point roles onto shared servers to optimize resource allocation within the site system. Ultimately, you will have two MP/DP servers residing in the datacenter, eliminating your single point of failure on the DP role. By using Nomad's adaptive bandwidth throttling technology, you will be able to deploy software globally from the datacenter without being concerned about affecting business traffic.

Software Update Points

The functionality of the Software Update Point (SUP) role in ConfigMgr 2012 is different from a stand-alone WSUS server. The only data that is communicated between the SUP and a client is update metadata; its main purpose is to synchronize updates between ConfigMgr 2012 and Microsoft Update. Microsoft guidelines state that one SUP can service 100,000 clients; however, this does not provide any redundancy. For an environment of 50,000 clients that utilize System Center Endpoint Protection (meaning definition updates are delivered three times daily), we recommend that a segregated SUP role be deployed to a server, having two standby SUP instances configured on the MP/DP machines in the event that the main SUP server is unavailable.

Although Nomad has deprecated the need for having DPs spread across the enterprise, under this design all clients now communicate with MPs that exist in the New York datacenter. This two-way policy-driven data is not optimized by Nomad and will ultimately cause strain over the slow WAN-links that exist between New York, Australia, and the Middle East. To alleviate this, you will deploy a secondary site server to Sydney and Dubai, as secondary sites will proxy upstream management point data and communicate with the primary site server via SQL replication.

The Proposed Design with 1E Software

ViaMonstra's new acquisition, GloboGym, has over 1,300 locations and supports approximately 43,000 users and devices globally.

The optimized 1E design for a large ConfigMgr deployment might look something like this:

Site Server Role	Location	Number of Servers
Primary site server + segregated site system roles	New York	5
Secondary site server + DP	Larger offices (250+) = 10	0
Remote offices	Remote offices—each has a PXE-enabled DP.	0

As you can see with the 1E optimized ConfigMgr architecture, we have been able to successfully eliminate more 1300 branch servers.

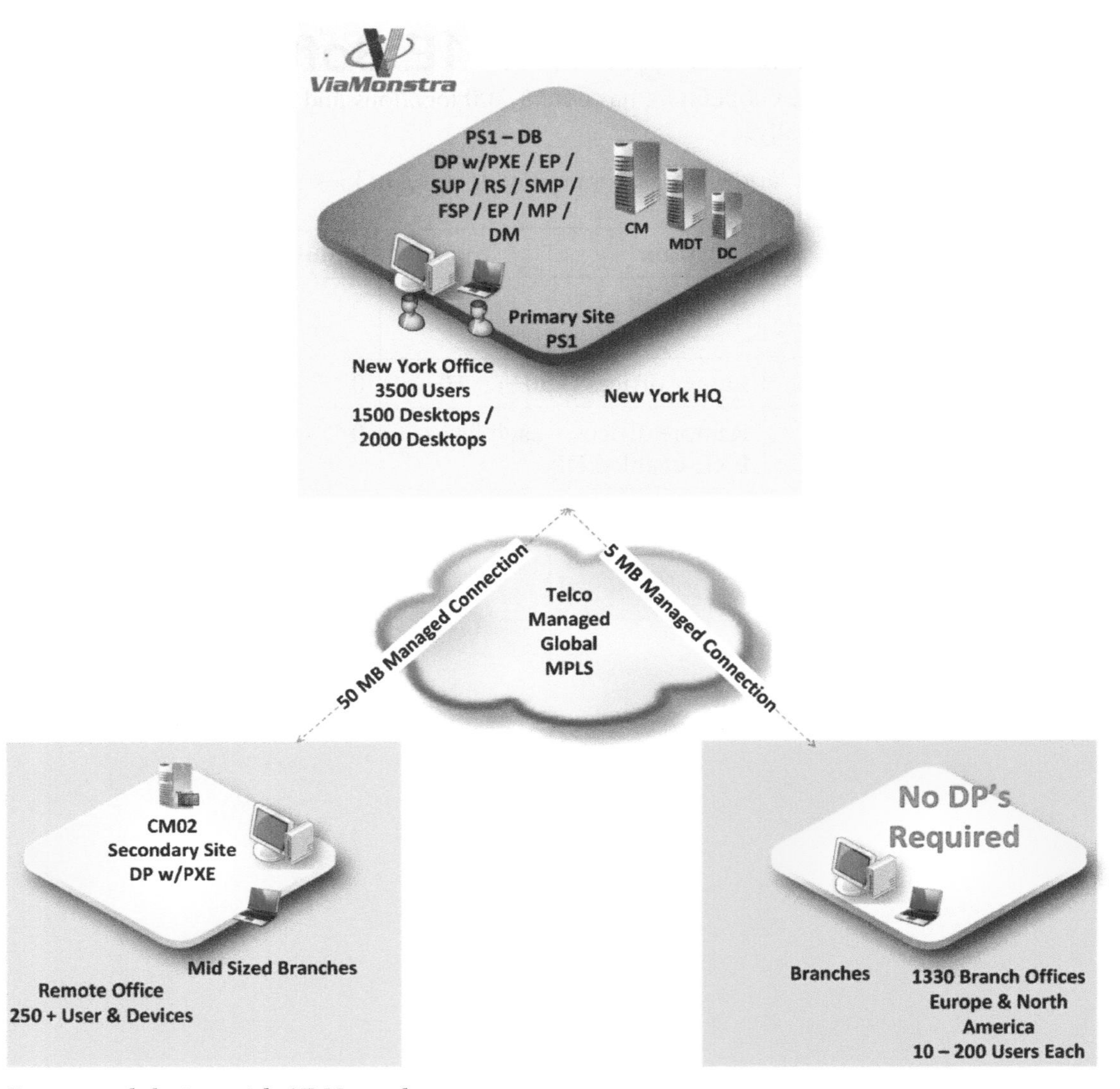

Conceptual design with 1E Nomad.

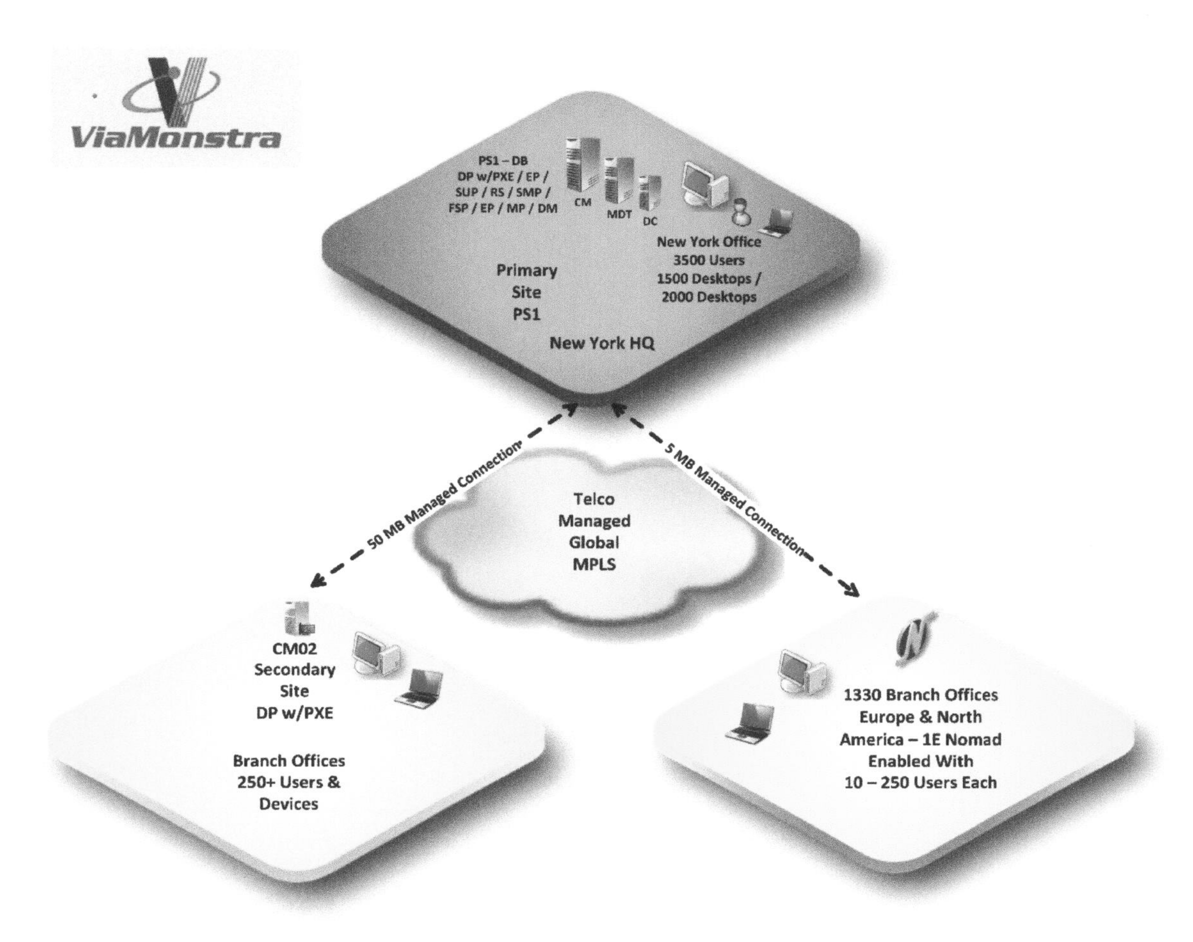

Proposed 1E design using Nomad.

One of the major requirements for the optimized 1E design is that you do not lose features or functionality.

Real World Note: It is important to understand that 100 percent of the native ConfigMgr features still exist while using 1E Nomad.

Chapter 4

ActiveEfficiency

As mentioned in Chapter 1, ActiveEfficiency is a framework solution that 1E developed to extend the functionality of its product suite. It is designed to retrieve and process information from various data sources and act as a centralized repository for 1E products. Based on the solution it is configured for, ActiveEfficiency can perform several actions that increase the versatility of one or all of its products. When ActiveEfficiency is configured to work with Nomad, for example, the per-subnet limitation is eliminated for peer transfers allowing content to be shared across an entire highly connected site.

ActiveEfficiency Key Concepts

As a framework solution, ActiveEfficiency has been designed to provide a communications hub for 1E activity. Comprised of a database and multiple connection options, it is a solution-agnostic tool that allows the integration of 1E products in highly complex environments, with or without an implementation of ConfigMgr.

There are five components that make up the ActiveEfficiency platform. Though all can be configured when ActiveEfficiency is implemented, not all components may be required for your specific implementation.

- **ActiveEfficiency Database**

  Stores all data that are used with other 1E products

- **ActiveEfficiency Web Service**
  - Provides client connectivity into the ActiveEfficiency Database (AEdb)
  - Allows administrators to view data that is stored in the AEdb

- **ActiveEfficiency Agent**

  A client-based application that collects and reports data about the host computer to the ActiveEfficiency server installed in the enterprise. This data can then be consumed by other 1E products.

- **ActiveEfficiency Cloud Connection**

  Provides functionality to receive automatic updates for product catalogs and other future data service offerings

- **ActiveEfficiency Scout**

  A tool that collects data points (such as ConfigMgr) for client data and retrieve pertinent data to be placed in the AEdb.

Design considerations when planning the implementation of the product are greatly affected by the solutions that it's supporting. In cases when ActiveEfficiency is used to enable Single Site Download and Single Site Peer Backup Assistant for Nomad, it has very light requirements because it's used only to maintain a database of machine, location, subnet, and content information. When configured to support AppClarity, however, ActiveEfficiency performs daily scouting activities to various data points, as well as communicates with the 1E Cloud, resulting in higher memory, CPU, and storage requirements.

ViaMonstra will eventually implement the entire 1E product suite, so it will require a dedicated server for ActiveEfficiency. It has the following components and configurations:

- Host: HP ProLiant DL380p Gen8
- Memory: 32 GB
- CPU: 2x6-core Intel Xeon E5-2630
- Disk configuration:

    Three SSD RAID arrays:

    - 72 GB C:\ (OS)
    - 240 GB D:\ (Program Files/SQL Server Database)
    - 120 GB E:\ (SQL Logs and Temp)

For the purpose of this book, we use MDT01 as an application server to host 1E web services such as ActiveEfficiency.

ActiveEfficiency Configuration (Registry Keys)

In case you haven't picked up on it by now, the implementation of ActiveEfficiency is highly dependent on what the product is going to be working with. For example, if it is being implemented alongside Nomad only, no default configurations are required. However, when implementing AppClarity, ActiveEfficiency is responsible for all communications between ConfigMgr and the AppClarity database, requiring several customizations, connections, and scheduled tasks.

Real World Note: If Single Site Download (SSD) is required for the 1E Nomad deployment, then updates must be made to AEdb tables to use this feature.

As with all of 1E's products, the configurable options during the ActiveEfficiency setup are performed by manipulating Windows registry keys. Here are the ones that were modified during the install at ViaMonstra:

Registry Key	HKEY_LOCAL_MACHINE\SOFTWARE\Wow6432Node\1E\ActiveEfficiency
Value Name	IISPort
Data Type	REG_SZ
Data Value	Configures the communications port for the ActiveEfficiency website

Registry Key	HKEY_LOCAL_MACHINE\SOFTWARE\Wow6432Node\1E\ActiveEfficiency
Value Name	Installation Directory
Data Type	REG_SZ
Data Value	Lists the local folder where ActiveEfficiency has been installed

Registry Key	HKEY_LOCAL_MACHINE\SOFTWARE\Wow6432Node\1E\ActiveEfficiency
Value Name	SQL Server
Data Type	REG_SZ
Data Value	Configured with the SQL server that stores the top-level ConfigMgr database

ActiveEfficiency Log Files

After ActiveEfficiency has been implemented, you want to confirm that all components were installed and configured correctly, and that communication is flowing between ConfigMgr and the respective 1E products. As with ConfigMgr, all actions are logged in a .log file and can be viewed using CMTrace.exe. Here is a list of all log files related to the implementation or operation of ActiveEfficiency for Nomad and Shopping:

- Scout.log
    - Logs all actions and results pertaining to the execution of Scout
    - Located in C:\ProgramData\1E\Scout
- Service.log
    - Main ActiveEfficiency log file. Provides configuration and operational information pertaining to the ActiveEfficiency log
    - Located in C:\ProgramData\1E\ActiveEfficiency
- WebService.log
    - ActiveEfficiency Website log. Provides information pertaining to inbound/outbound HTTP client connectivity information
    - Located in C:\Program Files (x86)\1E\ActiveEfficiency

ActiveEfficiency Conceptual Design (ViaMonstra)

In this book, you implement Nomad v5 and Shopping v5, both of which require ActiveEfficiency. You need to install the ActiveEfficiency Database and the website to provide connectivity, and configure Scout to connect to ConfigMgr. Cloud Connection, only used for AppClarity Catalog Sync at the time of this publication, will not be configured at this time.

Real World Note: Nomad v5 does not require ActiveEfficiency if features such as Single Site Download are not required.

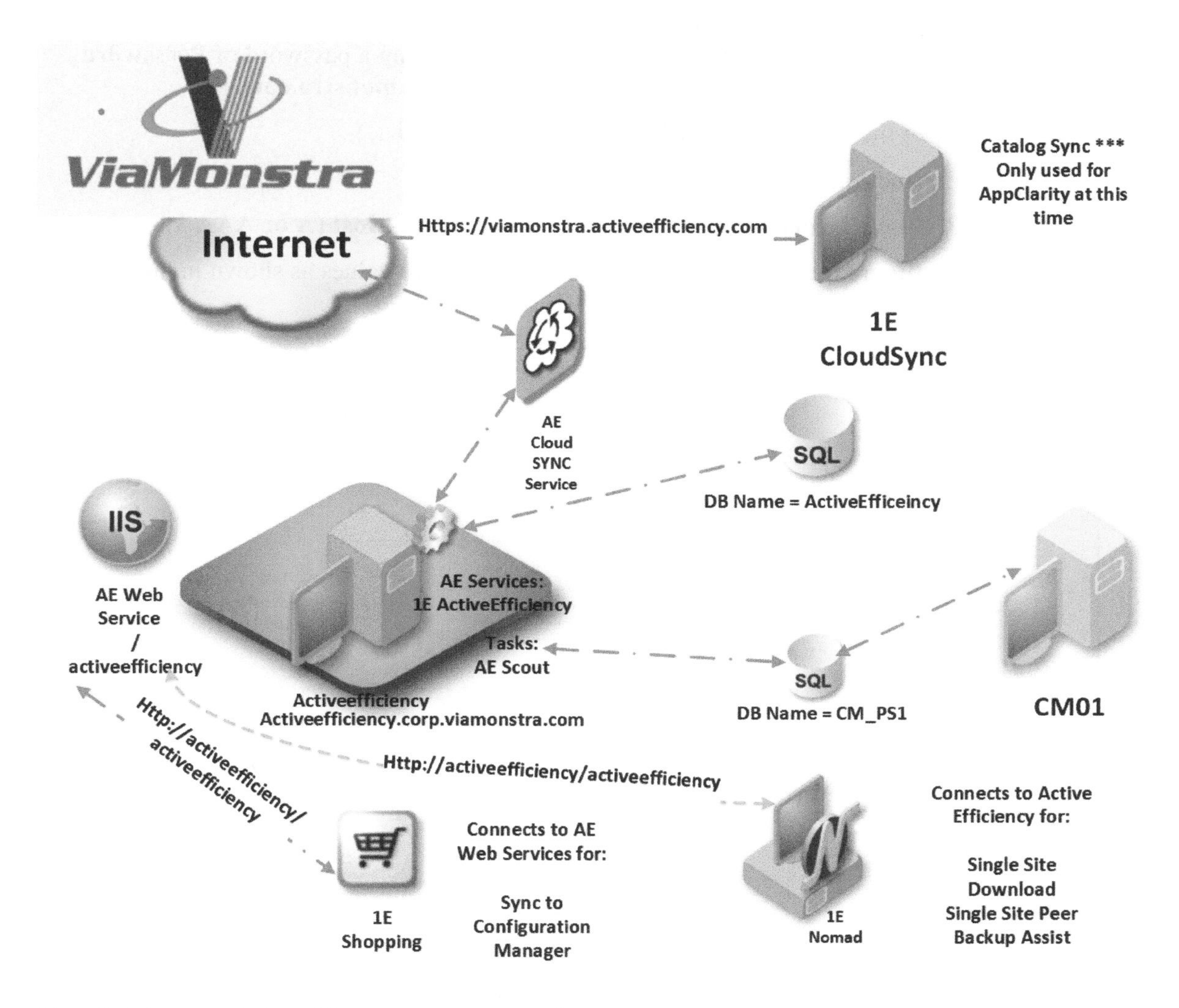

The ViaMonstra ActiveEfficiency conceptual design.

Install ActiveEfficiency

Prior to the actual installation of ActiveEfficiency, you need to ensure that some prerequisite configurations are performed. You install ASP.NET 4.5 and Message Queuing (MSMQ) on the server, and ensure that a DNS record is created for the host header that will be used to connect to the ActiveEfficiency Website.

In this guide we assume you have downloaded 1E ActiveEfficiency to C:\Labfiles on MDT01.

Note: In order to download the 1E media, you need to request a copy of 1E products directly from 1E. They are not downloadable from their web site without registration.

1. On **DC01**, log on as **VIAMONSTRA\Administrator** using a password of **P@ssw0rd**, and create a new host record for **activeefficiency.corp.viamonstra.com**:
    a. Open the **DNS Management** console (dnsmgmt.msc).
    b. Expand **Forward Lookup Zones**.
    c. Right-click **corp.viamonstra.com** and select **New Host (A or AAAA)**.
    d. Configure the **activeefficiency** and **192.168.1.210** values as shown in the following figure:

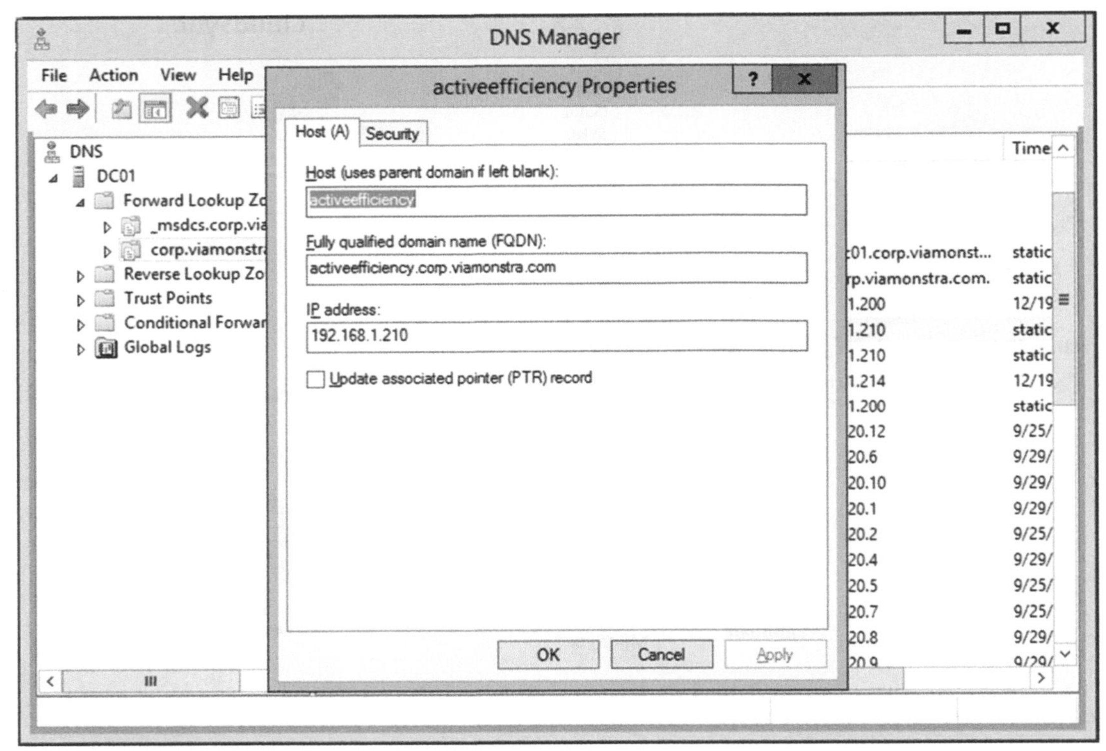

Adding DNS host records for ActiveEfficiency.

2. On **MDT01**, log on as **VIAMONSTRA\Administrator** using a password of **P@ssw0rd**.
3. Install **ASP.NET 4.5** by running the following command in an elevated PowerShell prompt:

```
Install-WindowsFeature -Name Web-Asp-Net45
```

4. Enable the **MSMQ** feature, by running the following command:

```
Install-WindowsFeature -Name MSMQ -IncludeAllSubFeature
-IncludeManagementTools
```

5. When the installation has completed, verify that MSMQ has been installed by typing:

```
Get-WindowsFeature MSMQ*
```

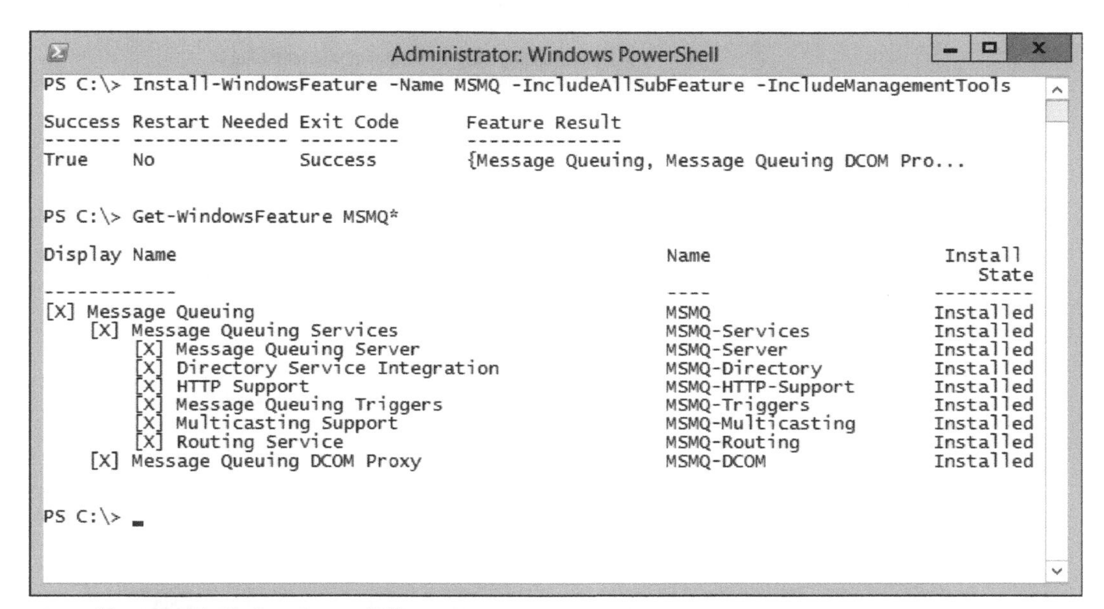

Installing MSMQ for ActiveEfficiency.

6. From you downloaded 1E media, copy the **ActiveEfficiency v1.5.100.5** setup files to **C:\Labfiles\ActiveEfficiency v1.5.100.5** (you need to create the folder).
7. Browse to **C:\Labfiles\ActiveEfficiency v1.5.100.5**.
8. Double-click **ActiveEfficiencyServer.msi**.

9. Use the following settings for the **ActiveEfficiency Server** installation:

   a. On the **Welcome** page, click **Next**.

   b. On the **License Agreement** page, accept the terms and click **Next**.

c. On the **Prerequisite Checks** page, click **Next**.

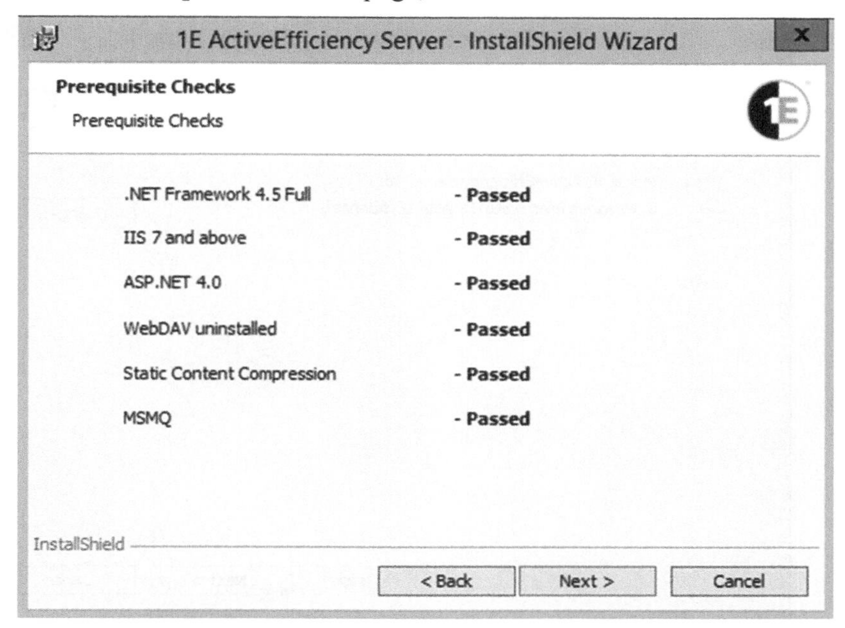

d. On the **Enable 1E ActiveEfficiency Cloud Connection** page, clear the check box for registering with 1E Cloud Services, and click **Next**.

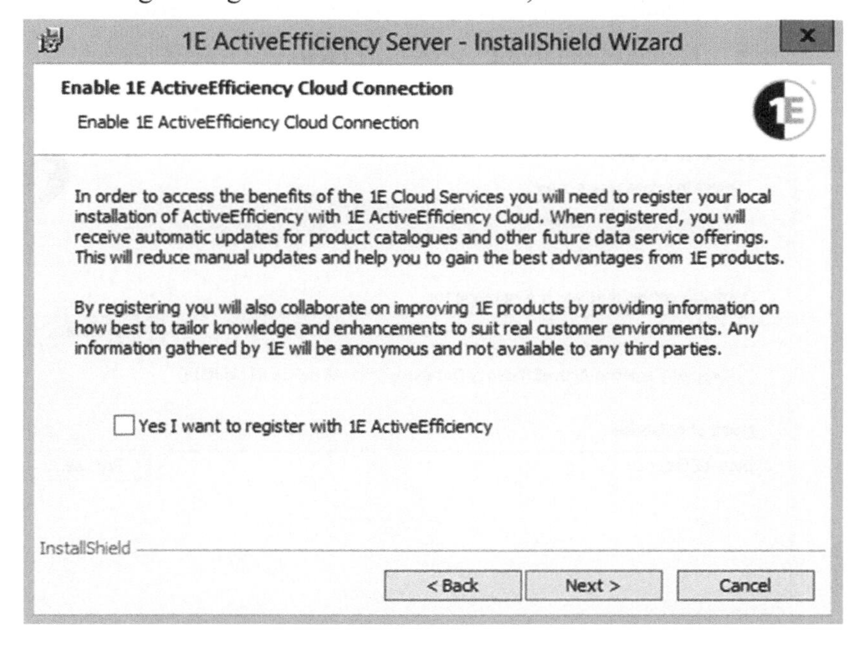

e. On the **Destination Folder** page, accept the default settings, and then click **Next**.

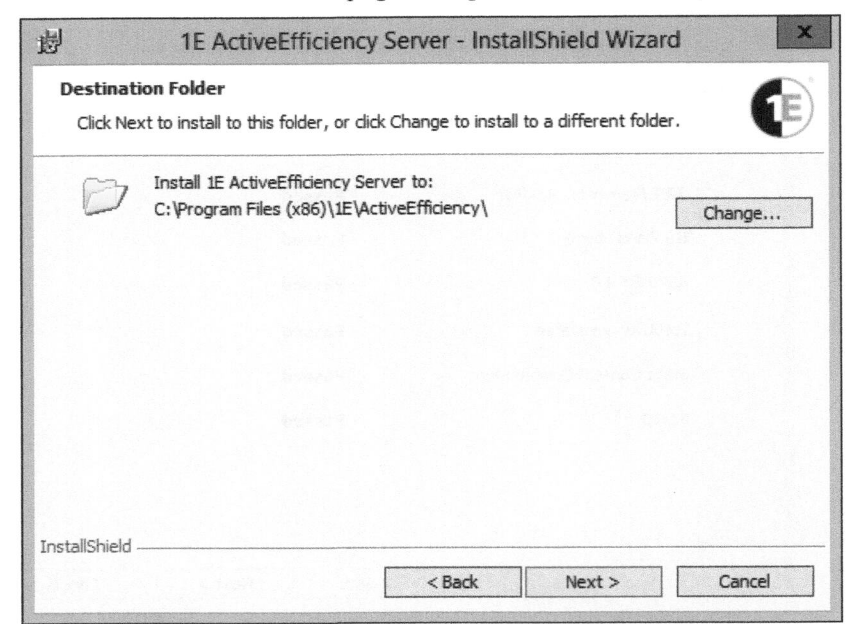

f. On the **Database Server** page, use the following settings and then click **Next**:

- Database server that you are installing to: **CM01**
- Name of database: **ActiveEfficiency**

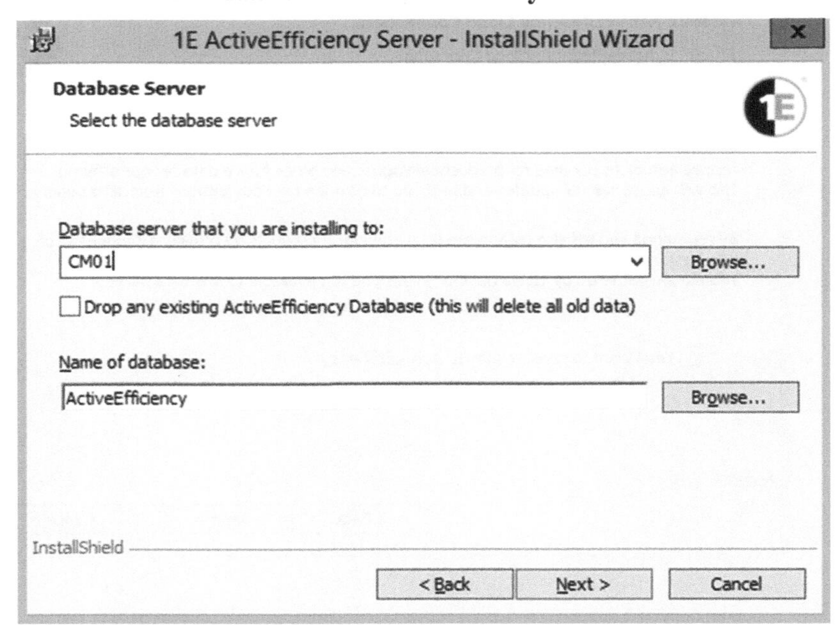

g. On the **ActiveEfficiency Website Settings** page, use the default settings and click **Next**.

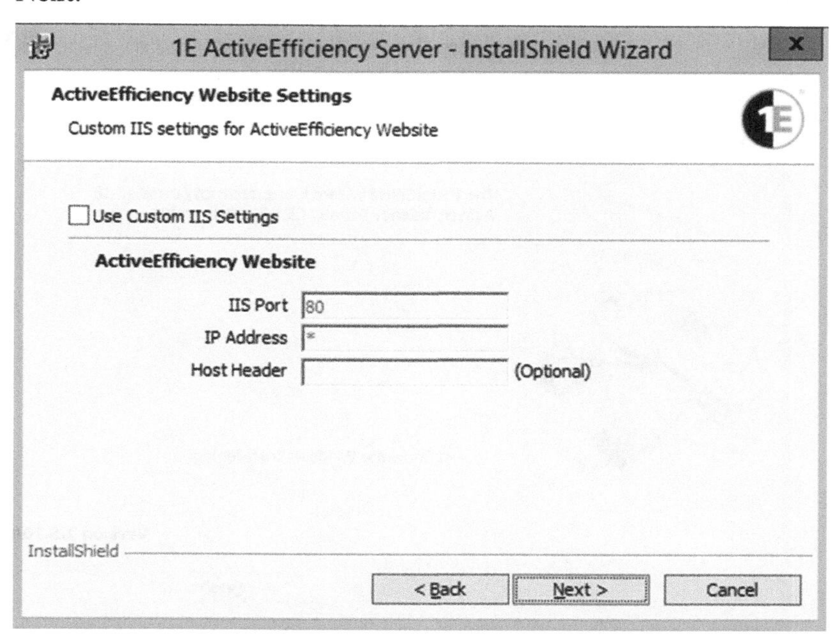

h. On the **Ready to Install the Program** page, click **Install**.

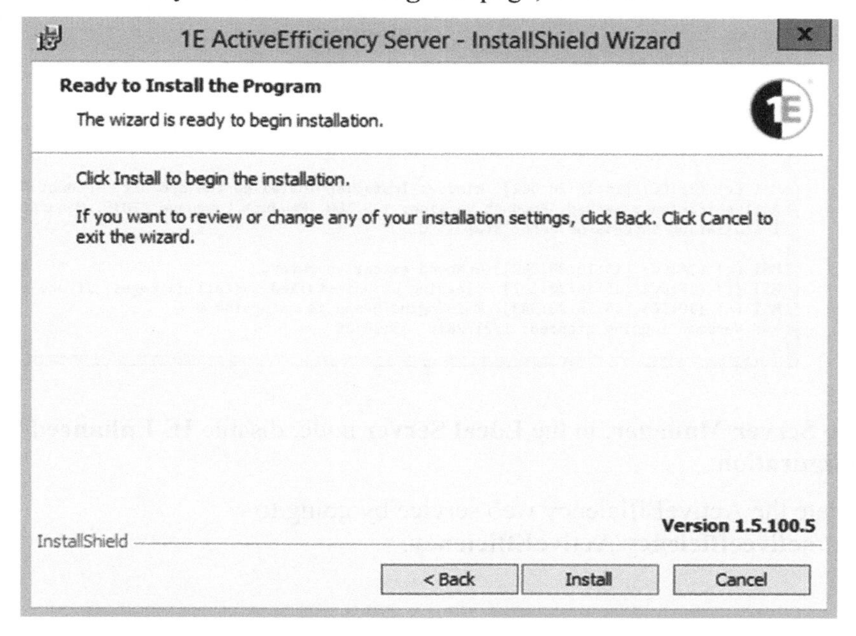

i. On the **InstallShield Wizard Completed** page, select **Show the Windows Installer log** and click **Finish**.

j. View the Windows Installer log to confirm a successful installation:

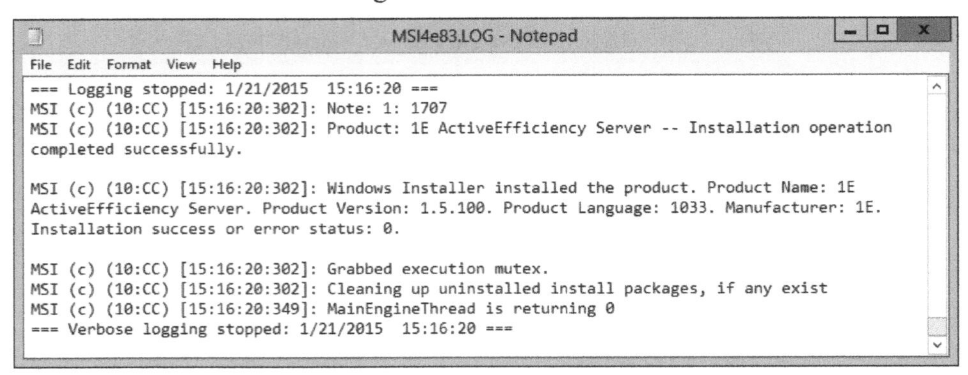

MSI4e83.LOG - Notepad

File Edit Format View Help

```
=== Logging stopped: 1/21/2015  15:16:20 ===
MSI (c) (10:CC) [15:16:20:302]: Note: 1: 1707
MSI (c) (10:CC) [15:16:20:302]: Product: 1E ActiveEfficiency Server -- Installation operation
completed successfully.

MSI (c) (10:CC) [15:16:20:302]: Windows Installer installed the product. Product Name: 1E
ActiveEfficiency Server. Product Version: 1.5.100. Product Language: 1033. Manufacturer: 1E.
Installation success or error status: 0.

MSI (c) (10:CC) [15:16:20:302]: Grabbed execution mutex.
MSI (c) (10:CC) [15:16:20:302]: Cleaning up uninstalled install packages, if any exist
MSI (c) (10:CC) [15:16:20:349]: MainEngineThread is returning 0
=== Verbose logging stopped: 1/21/2015  15:16:20 ===
```

10. Using **Server Manager**, in the **Local Server** node, disable **IE Enhanced Security Configuration**.
11. Validate the ActiveEfficiency web service by going to **http://activeefficiency/ActiveEfficiency**.

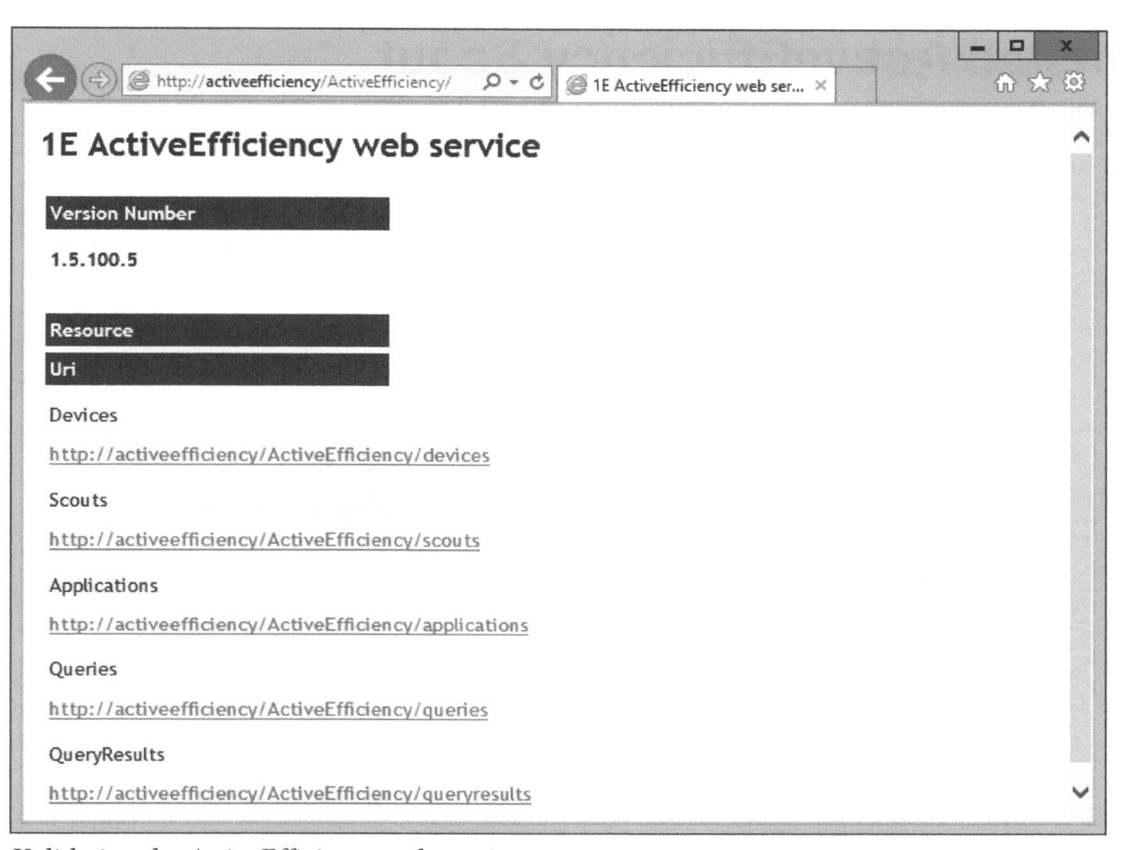

Validating the ActiveEfficiency web service.

Note: For the purpose of this lab, the ActiveEfficiency web service is to be co-located on the MDT01 server. In production, this should be configured as a separate workload and sized according to 1E's best practices.

You also can review the ActiveEfficiency Database on CM01 via SQL Server Management Studio. The ActiveEfficiency Platform is becoming a requirement for all 1E Product installations.

Install ActiveEfficiency Scout

Scout is a very important piece of ActiveEfficiency, as it controls the data acquisition process for its database. At ViaMonstra, Scout is connected to the ConfigMgr database to provide data connectivity between ConfigMgr 2012 and Shopping.

1. On to **MDT01,** log on as **VIAMONSTRA\Administrator**.
2. Browse to **C:\Labfiles\ActiveEfficiency v1.5.100.5**.
3. Double-click **ActiveEfficiencyScout.msi**.
4. Configure the installer with the following options:
    a. On the **Welcome** page, click **Next**.

b. On the **License Agreement** page, accept the terms and click **Next**.

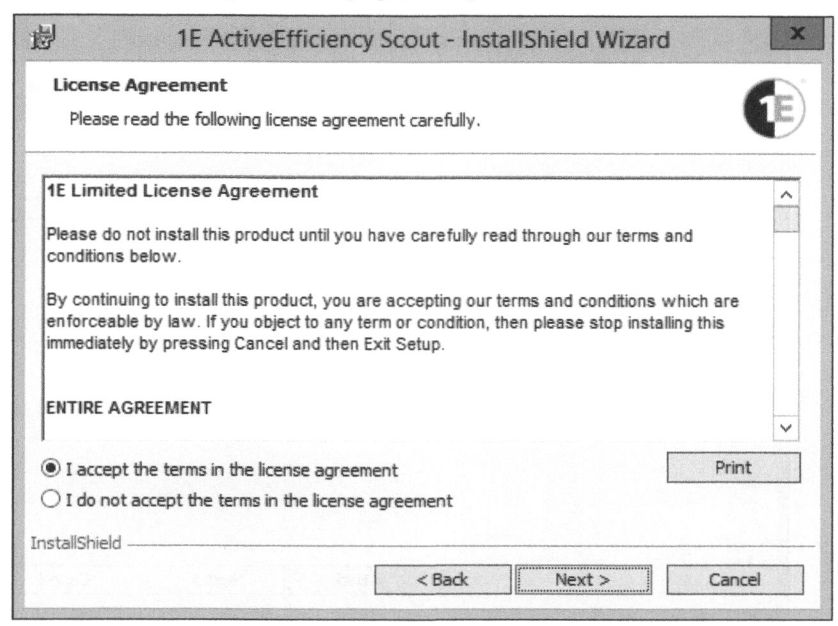

c. On the **Component Selection** page, use the default settings and click **Next**.

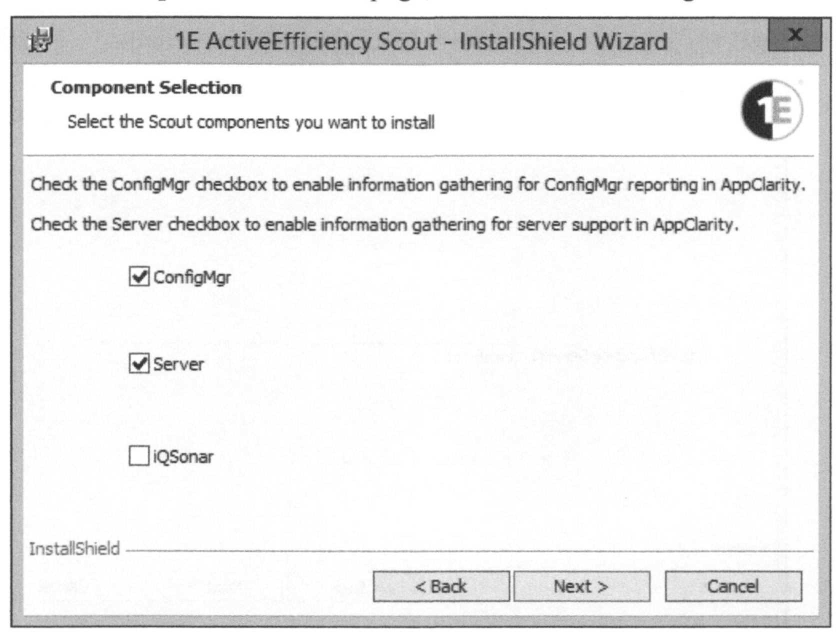

d. On the **Destination Folder** page, use the default folder and click **Next**.

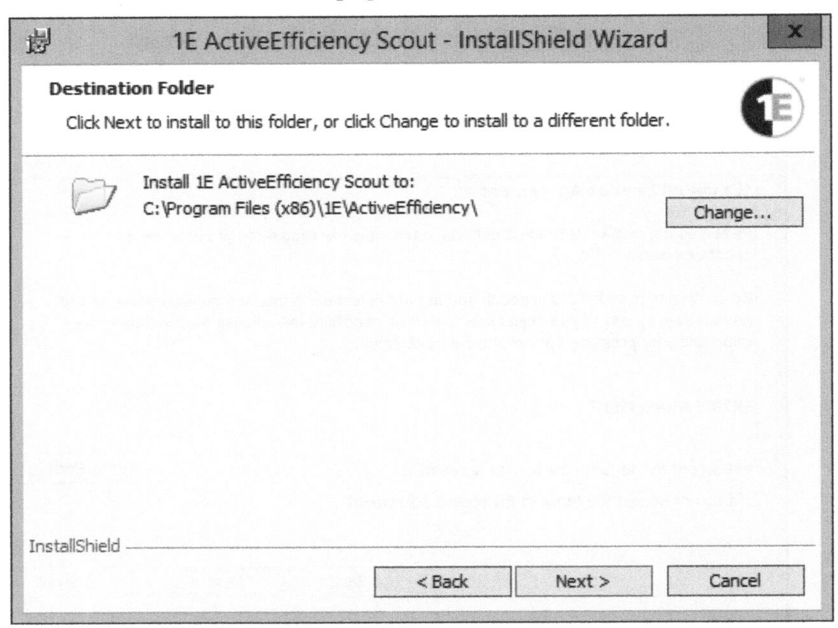

e. On the **1E ActiveEfficiency Server** page, use the default and click **Next**.

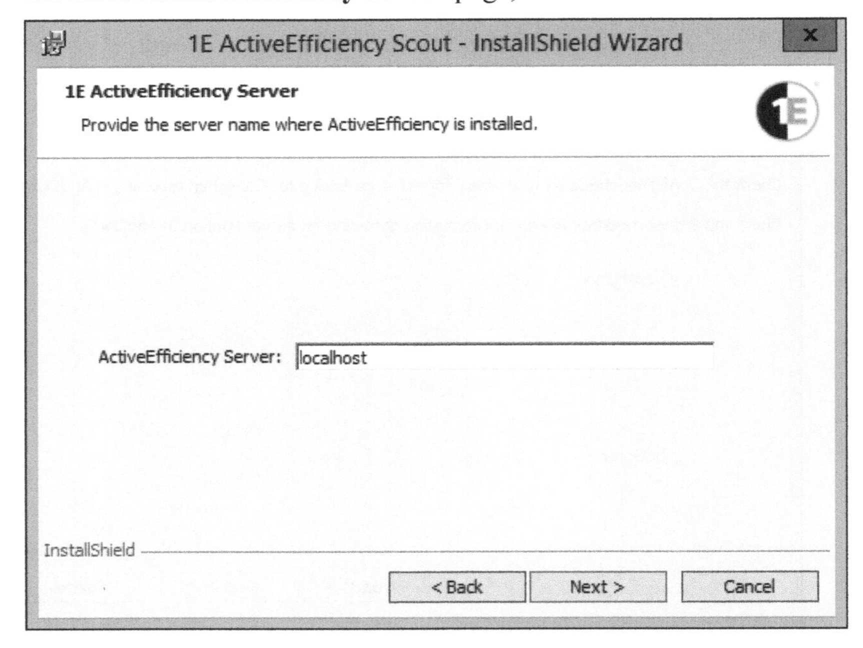

f. On the **ConfigMgr Database** page, configure the following and then click **Next**:

- ConfigMgr Database Server: **CM01**
- ConfigMgr Database Name: **CM_PS1**

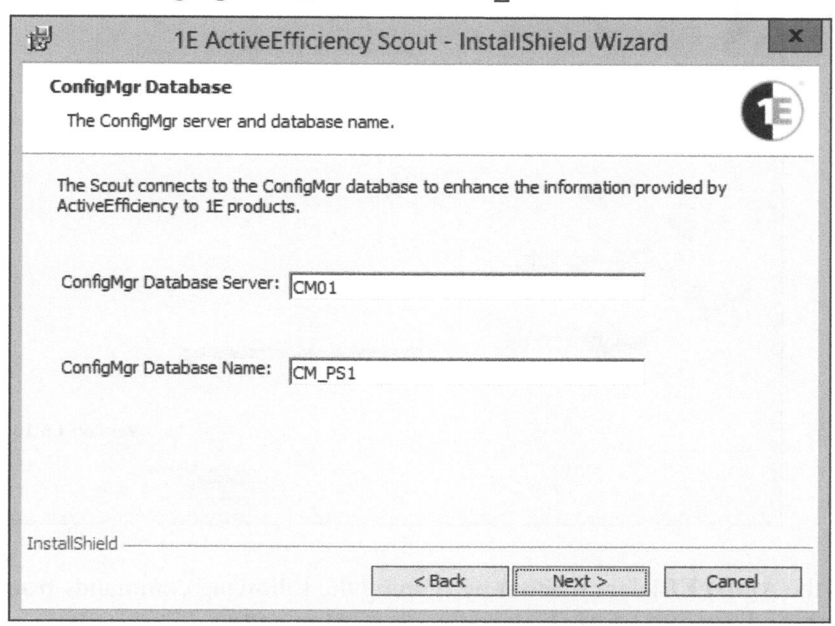

g. On the **Ready to Install the Program** page, click **Install**.

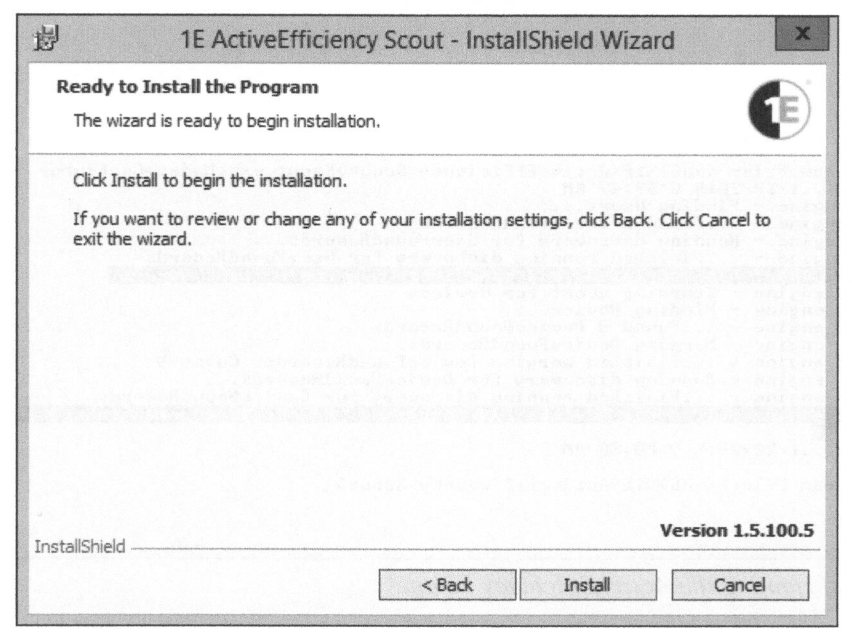

h. On the **InstallShield Wizard Completed** page, click **Finish**.

5. Run the **ActiveEfficiency Scout** by running the following commands from an elevated **Command prompt** (press **Enter** after each command):

```
cd "C:\Program Files (x86)\1E\ActiveEfficiency\Scout"
Scout.exe Modes=ConfigMgr
```

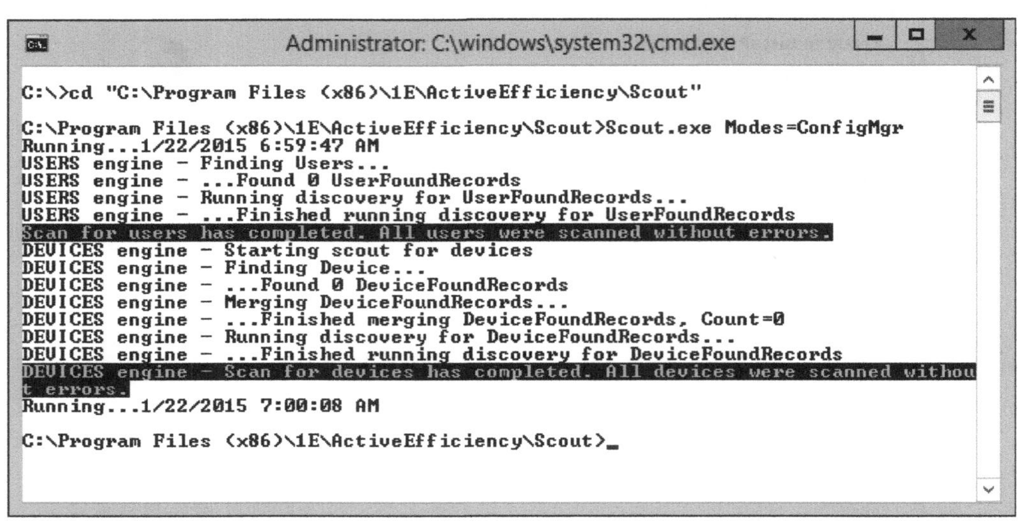

Output of running the ActiveEfficiency Scout.

6. Configure the Scout to run daily as a scheduled task:

a. In **Task Scheduler**, in the **Actions** pane, select **Create Basic Task**.

b. Name the task **1E AE Scout SYNC to CM** and click **Next**.

c. For **Task Trigger**, use the default **Daily** option and click **Next**.

d. For **Daily**, use the default settings and click **Next**.

e. For **Action**, use the default setting and click **Next**.

f. For **Start a Program**, use the following settings and then click **Next**:

- Program/script: **"C:\Program Files (x86)\1E\ActiveEfficiency\Scout\Scout.exe"**
- Add arguments: **Modes=ConfigMgr**

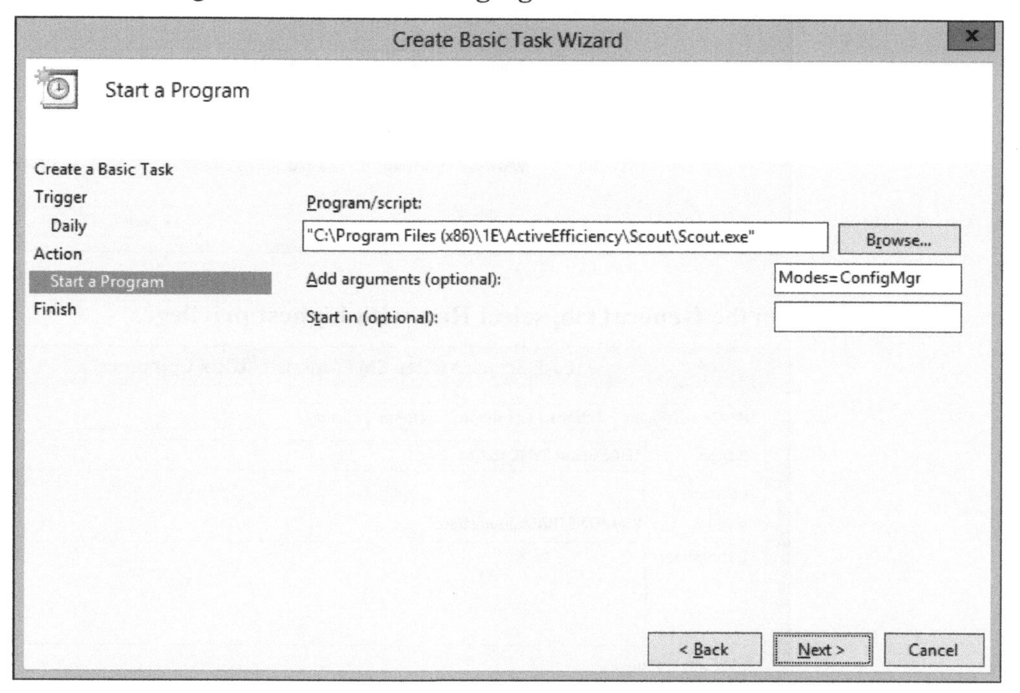

g. On the **Summary** page, select the **Open the Properties dialog for this task when I click Finish** check box, and then click **Finish**.

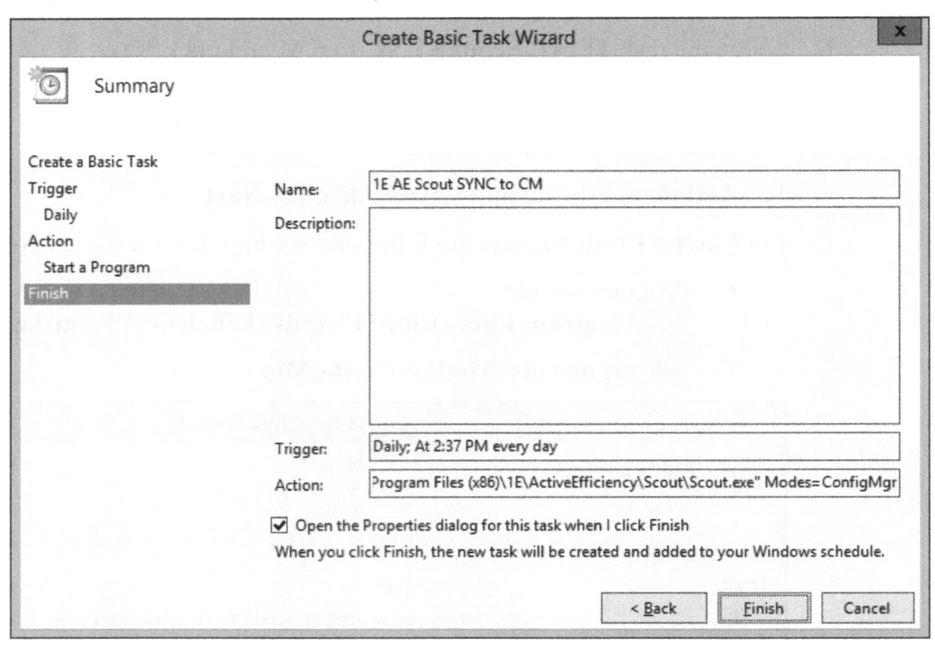

h. On the **General** tab, select **Run with highest privileges**.

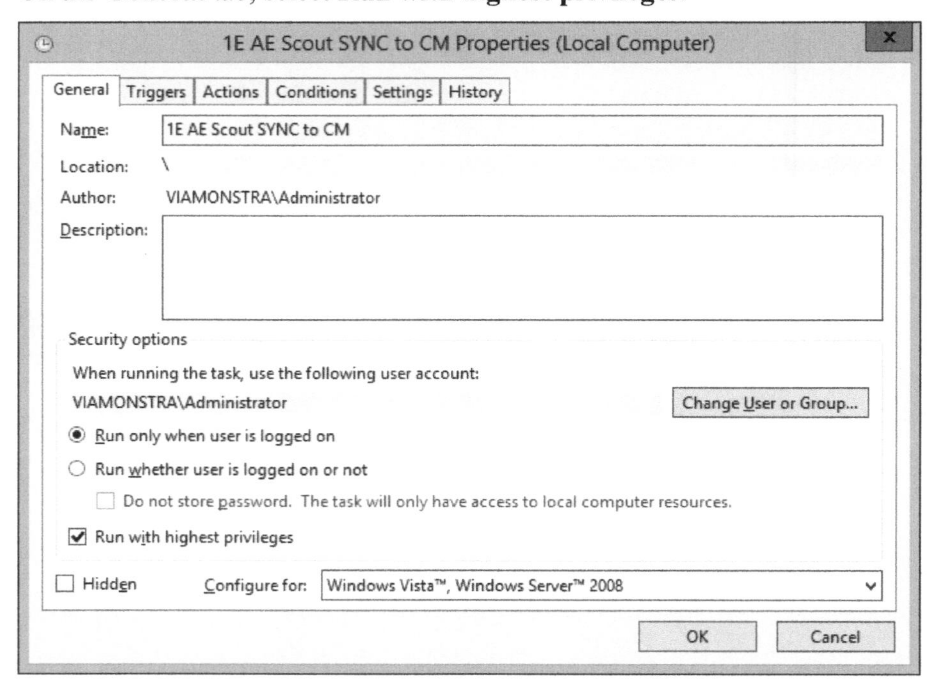

i. On the **Triggers** tab, select **Daily** and click **Edit**.

j. In the **Edit Trigger** dialog box, select **Repeat task every: 1 hour**. Then click **OK** twice.

Note: We are using this setting just for the lab. It is not recommended for production.

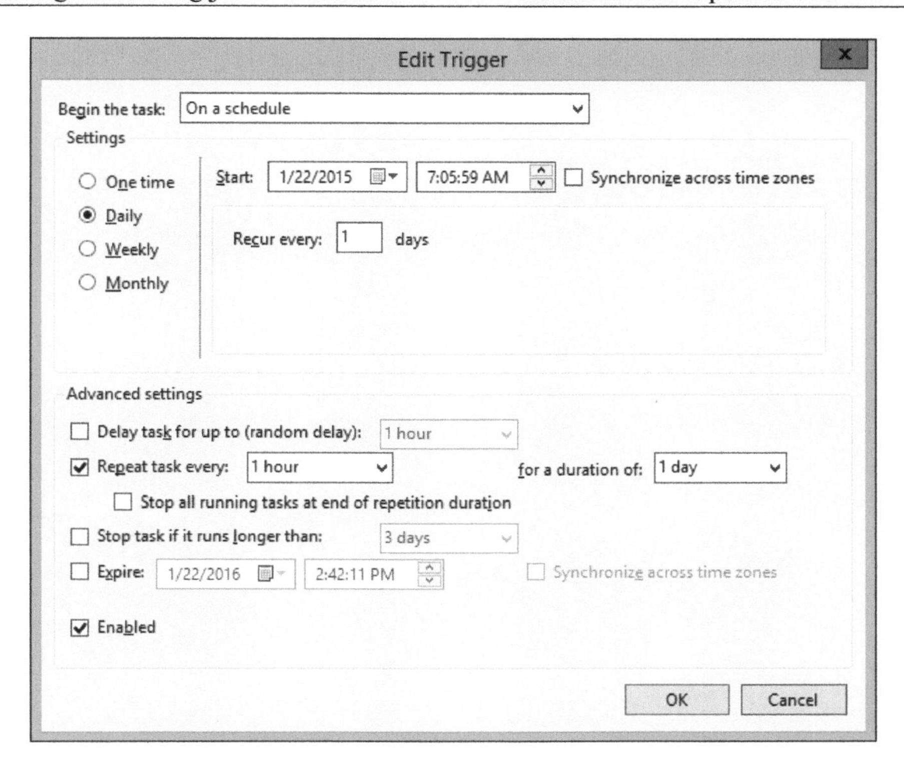

7. Right-click the **1E AE Scout SYNC to CM** task and select Run. Right now it is set up to pop up a window (command prompt) when it runs. You can always select to run it hidden if you like.

Chapter 5
1E Nomad

1E Nomad can greatly simplify an existing ConfigMgr infrastructure. With 1E Nomad, a typical customer can expect to see the following:

- A 95 percent or higher reduction in distribution points
- Simplified management
- Additional control over server to client software distribution
- Elimination of PXE functionality on distribution points
- Advanced extensions of the OSD task sequence engine from Microsoft
- Elimination of all SMPs for user state migration data

The goal of the re-architecture project at ViaMonstra is to minimize the ConfigMgr 2012 footprint while optimizing the end-to-end solution. The implementation of 1E's Nomad allows you to have an efficient hierarchy that is simple to manage and eliminates the risk of affecting business traffic, as you learned in Chapter 1.

Real World Note: Because this is still a single primary site, and distribution points are now centrally located, a single boundary group can be used for site assignment and content location.

Configuring protected distribution points is no longer required. This is a reality because of Nomad Reverse QoS™ technology which dynamically throttles system management content distribution traffic by "backing-off" when other traffic is detected on the network.

Nomad Key Concepts

At its core, Nomad is a network optimization solution for software distribution. When configured properly, a network simply cannot be crushed by an enterprise-wide deployment. Though a user's workstation is storing and sharing content, performance degradation will be negligible. 1E is able to do this with some pretty slick innovations that surround the Nomad product.

Bandwidth Management – Reverse QoS™

Reverse QoS™ is a method that looks at the complete round trip time that it takes blocks of data to traverse a WAN link, such as multiple network hops between the server and client. It is able to back off or speed up accordingly in a safe manner. This is special because it can actually take *everything* into account. This includes high CPU utilization of a client down to even disk read latency from the OS. This is hugely beneficial to businesses because network hardware, such as router queues, does not need to be accounted for as the solution is purely software based. It also means that Nomad is able to avoid using any kernel mode drivers that risk a blue screen of death as previously mentioned (Chapter 1) that could cause havoc to your organization and possibly require visiting every system if there is a problem.

Bandwidth Management – Work Rates vs. BITS

As part of the console extensions that are included with Nomad, there is an option to specify a work rate for specific deployments, or organization wide, which by default is set to 80 percent. The key difference between work rates and Background Intelligent Transfer Service (BITS) throttling is that work rates are configurable and *dynamic*. When BITS is configured to use, say 2 MB of a 10 MB connection, it will utilize the 2 MB of allocated bandwidth regardless of current utilization over that connection. BITS also can only identify the speed to the first network hop, for example to the edge router. Over the same connection, if Nomad was configured to use a work rate of 20 percent and the connection was over-utilized with business traffic, Nomad would throttle itself down to virtually nothing, allowing business traffic to take priority over the link despite the 20 percent work rate. Nomad dynamically rechecks after each 32 KB block transferred and makes adjustments accordingly.

Real World Note: With an 80-percent work rate as the default, Nomad has gone through rigorous development and tested over its lifetime, assuring customers that the default work rate of 80 percent provides the most efficient, safest, and highest performing value.

It is extremely rare for lowering the work rate from the default value of 80percent to provide any substantial benefit.

Dynamic Elections

When content is deployed to a machine (or group of machines), the Nomad client broadcasts an election request on its subnet to determine whether the content is available on a Nomad master:

- If content is not available on the subnet, the machine elects itself as a master and then sends a Single Site Download request to ActiveEfficiency to see whether there is a Nomad master on another subnet at the site/location. If there is not a Nomad master at the site (on another subnet), then the machine will become both a Nomad *site* master and Nomad *subnet* master (for the subnet it's connected to).
- Every 5 minutes during a download, an additional election process on the subnet occurs, checking to see whether another peer machine on the subnet has downloaded a *greater* percentage of the content already downloaded in its cache. The same reoccurring election process happens if and when the Nomad master goes offline or the network connection changes. The Nomad peers downloading from the master trigger the election and determine among themselves which will be elected as the "new" Nomad master for the content being downloaded.
- If content is available on the subnet, and it's only on one machine, that machine is elected as the master and provides the content to the client via SMB transfer.

- If content is locally available on multiple machines, the election process determines the best machine to offer up the content. It uses election weighting to determine the winner. This is performed by checking several factors on the machine:
    - Percentage of cached package
    - Current Nomad master
    - Time since the cache was last verified by Nomad
    - Uptime: Machines with a longer uptime receive a higher election weight.
    - Chassis type: Servers receive a higher election weight than desktops, which is higher than laptops.
    - Machine initiating the election
- If a master becomes unavailable for whatever reason, another master is elected and assumes the responsibilities of content provisioning.

Real World Note: When working with mobile clients such as service trucks with cellular-enabled devices, Nomad automatically forces a reelection process whenever a new connection is detected. For example, while returning to the depot location, a mobile truck comes within range of an 802.11 wireless access point and automatically connects, dropping the cellular connection. Nomad immediately forces an election and utilizes the wireless connection as the primary transfer medium.

Pre-Caching

A core feature with Nomad is the ability to store packages on client workstations for later use by same-site machines, a critical component to server-less OSD.

- Nomad peer-to-peer transfer is the basic method used to locally redistribute downloads on a branch network. It relies on the use of share connections to the locally elected Nomad master machine. To avoid any impact on the host, Nomad limits the number of connections to six.

Real World Note: This limitation applies to SMB connections to the Nomad share. However, Nomad also can operate in *connectionless* mode, which is a viable alternative when file and printer sharing is disabled on client workstations. Connectionless uses UDP download content from peers rather than SMB.

- FanOut
    - When a master has been elected for a content download, all other clients on that subnet will opt to download the content from a peer. The master that is downloading the package will share it out to six machines.

  - Nomad 5 introduced FanOut, a new distribution model uninhibited by the six-connection limit. When a peer system finds the master's six connections currently in use, instead of waiting, it requests the election of a "FanOut Peer." The content is downloaded from the FanOut Peer.
  - FanOut is not enabled by default.

Multicast

Though often requiring multiple changes to network infrastructure to accommodate the solution, multicast is a viable configuration for organizations that are performing large amounts of simultaneous deployments.

- If configured, multicast is automatic, which means that when enough systems are a part of the peer-to-peer process, Nomad will automatically switch from peer-to-peer to multicast.
- WinPE clients can consume content from other FanOut clients, but cannot share out content. Therefore, FanOut can be used for OSD.

Local Multicast

- Local multicast is designed to reduce LAN network traffic at the branch and reduce the load on the elected Nomad master machine.
- This option should be used in preference to central multicast if multicast traffic is prohibited over the WAN. Nomad local multicast utilizes all the functionality of Nomad, but after the download is at the branch, it is distributed locally using multicast.
- Local multicast improves the performance and efficiency of Nomad across the LAN, especially for branch offices containing hundreds of computers.

Real World Note: Although local multicast is an option, FanOut is typically always recommended for most customer engagements. This is because it is easier to implement because there are no network changes required.

Options for Mobile Clients

Nomad is aware when clients are connecting over VPN or DirectAccess and by default does not permit peer sharing with clients connected in this fashion. Not only is this option completely configurable, but 1E provides a plethora of other options to tailor the client experience when connecting over various types of mobile connections. As an example, if an organization utilizes multiple mobile carriers with different data plans, Bell users could have their Sierra Wireless DirectAccess connections restricted from content download, where Telus' Huawei SmartHubs could be configured to allow Nomad to download packages and clients to peer-share content, effectively operating as a typical branch.

Here are a couple of the configurable options in Nomad for mobile clients:

- KnownMobileDevices: Contains a list of mobile devices to restrict delivery of packages to only those that contain the -mobok Nomad switch
- SpecialNetShare bit 12: Grants clients the ability to become a Nomad master even when clients are on a VPN, wireless, or behind a firewall
- NomadInhibitedSubnets: Allows for subnets that do not require Nomad peer-to-peer transfers to be excluded using Reverse QoS™.

Cache Management

Another benefit of Nomad is that it takes up less than 10 MB on a ConfigMgr client. When Nomad is installed on the same drive as the ConfigMgr 2012 client, it uses hard links to manage the ConfigMgr cache. This has two main benefits:

- It does not consume any additional space outside of the CCMCache directory.
- Enabling packages for peer distribution is immediate.

Nomad Configuration (Registry Keys)

Unlike other 1E products, *all* configurations for Nomad are performed via registry settings. These settings can be performed via registry modification/import, or by command-line switches during installation. It is not uncommon to configure six or more non-default settings during installation, so as a result we like to script the install string and/or create a custom transform file.

Here are the registry settings you are configuring for ViaMonstra, what they define, and why they are important:

Registry Key	HKEY_LOCAL_MACHINE\SOFTWARE\1E\NomadBranch
Value Name	MultiCastSupport
Data Type	REG_DWORD
Data Value	0
Description	This setting disables Nomad support for multicast environments.

Registry Key	HKEY_LOCAL_MACHINE\SOFTWARE\1E\NomadBranch
Value Name	SpecialNetShare
Data Type	REG_DWORD
Data Value	0x00002050 (8272)
Description	SpecialNetShare is a rolled up value. At ViaMonstra, the following settings are implemented on the clients: • 0x00002000: Enables SMB and HTTP Connectivity. In ConfigMgr 2012, this setting configures Nomad clients to fall back to a legacy SMB package share if the HTTP content provider is unavailable. • 0x00000040: Enables Nomad FanOut behavior • 0x00000010: Configures the Nomad share to be hidden (NomadSHR$)

Registry Key	HKEY_LOCAL_MACHINE\SOFTWARE\1E\NomadBranch
Value Name	PlatformURL
Data Type	REG_SZ
Data Value	http://ActiveEfficiency/ActiveEfficiency
Description	This setting instructs Nomad to use the provided URL to connect ActiveEfficiency when Single Site Download information is needed to locate package content for download or to register content that has been downloaded.

Registry Key	HKEY_LOCAL_MACHINE\SOFTWARE\1E\NomadBranch
Value Name	SSDEnabled
Data Type	REG_DWORD
Data Value	3
Description	This configures Nomad to use SingleSiteDownload, both as a potential host and client for content download across local subnets.

Note: A comprehensive list of registry values for Nomad can be found at http://help.1e.com.

Nomad Log files

As with ConfigMgr, all actions are logged in a .log file and can be viewed using CMTrace.exe. Here is a list of all log files related to the implementation or operation of 1E Nomad:

Log Name	Description
MSI logs	All 1E products are installed via a Windows Installer package. When executing these installers from a command line, append /l*v C:\Temp\1ENomadInstall.log to the msiexec.exe string to log the installation process of a particular product.
NomadBranch.log	This is the main log file used by the NomadBranch client. It stores all information pertaining to Nomad configuration and operation. On distribution points, information regarding LsZ generation for server-side package validation is also stored here. Default location: C:\ProgramData\1E\NomadBranch\logfiles
NomadBranch.hist.log	This log contains a listing of all Nomad-activated content on the client. Default location: C:\ProgramData\1E\NomadBranch\Logfiles
CAS.log	This is the ConfigMgr 2012 Content Access Service log. This log is important to Nomad as it shows the client requesting content from a distribution point. A NomadBranch client will recognize this request and provide an alternate content location to the client, enabling download via Nomad. Default location: C:\Windows\CCM\Logs\CAS.log
ContentTransferManager.log	This ConfigMgr 2012 log is heavily utilized during traditional content delivery; however, when Nomad is in play, only a CTM started notification will be displayed, and that Nomad gets invoked as the alternate content provider. All other transfer information is viewable in the NomadBranch.log. Default location: C:\Windows\CCM\Logs\ContentTransferManager.log

Server-Side Log Files

Server-side log files are also very important in the troubleshooting process. There are several log files listed in this chapter that will be very useful for day to day operation and troubleshooting.

Real World Note: Failure to completely deploy Nomad on every required machine can have catastrophic consequences. A perfect example is if Nomad was not installed on ViaMonstra's secondary site, all Nomad functionality in that region would revert back to native ConfigMgr methods and cripple the already limited connectivity in the region.

Primary Site Server

On the primary site server, there are no operational roles pertaining to Nomad, unless it also is configured as a NomadBranch client or distribution point. However, after running NomadBranchTools.msi on the primary, you can confirm that future boot image creation will include the Nomad components by viewing <ConfigMgrInstallationPath>\bin\x64\osdinjection.xml.

Distribution Point

The distribution point, though underutilized in a Nomad-optimized environment, remains critical to software distribution with ConfigMgr 2012. It is also a critical component of the Nomad software distribution process, performing two main functions: providing Nomad-enabled content to a client when peer content is unavailable, and performing content validation for packages that are delivered from Nomad peers. Information for DP-client content delivery, as well as integrity and consistency checking, can be viewed in the NomadBranch.log.

Nomad Conceptual Design (ViaMonstra)

Implementing 1E Nomad into an organization drastically affects the ConfigMgr hierarchy more than any other 1E product. By removing the requirement for remote distribution points, state migration points, and PXE, 1E Nomad has eliminated the requirement for virtually all remote site server roles, providing more opportunity to implement the ideal ConfigMgr hierarchy: *centralized*.

With smaller organizations (<50,000), unless operating in a multi-hub and spoke WAN, there is no longer a requirement for any non-centralized servers. The caveat, what I like to call "The Australia Scenario," is when an organization has a second hub that's well-connected to a group of sites, however exists behind a poor connection to the central datacenter. Placing ConfigMgr secondary site servers in these regions provides proxy management and distribution point services to its well-connected sites, while providing additional network control for not only downstream distribution data, but also up/downstream management point data. Further compression of this data via SQL replication provides additional benefits over not deploying secondary sites to these types of regions.

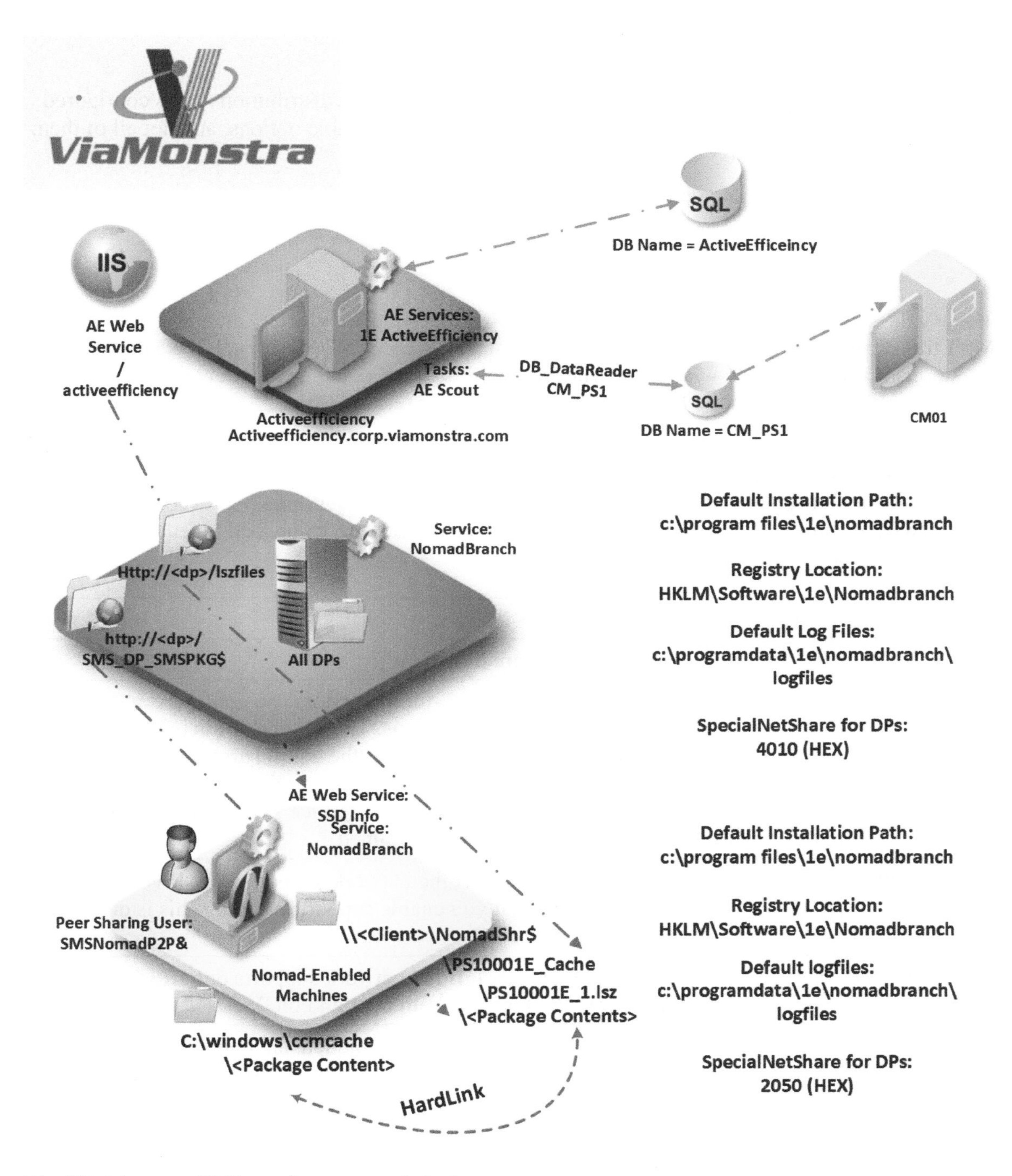

The ViaMonstra 1E Nomad conceptual design.

NomadSHR

NomadSHR is the default folder share that is used for peer content distribution and is configured via the *SpecialNetShare* registry key. This key has many configurable options, and not all of them relate specifically to the Nomad share.

For the purpose of this book, you use the following values:

- 2050 for your clients
- 4010 for your distribution points

These values must be configured when installing Nomad (typically via the command line or a MST transform). By default, Nomad creates a local user account (SMSNomadP2P&) that it uses to establish communication with peers. The password is complex and is uniquely generated for each client computer when the Nomad service is started or restarted.

SpecialNetShare

The following table contains a complete list of values for SpecialNetShare, excerpted from http://www.1e.com/help. To arrive at the ultimate SpecialNetShare value, add together all the required options.

Bit	Hex	Decimal	Description
	0x0000	0	No special features are turned on
0	0x0001	1	Custom Share Permissions. Administrators can configure and manage custom share permissions. The service doesn't create the share NomadSHR on startup so that the administrator can manually create the NomadSHR with required permissions. Also, the share NomadSHR is not deleted when the service stops and therefore existing share permissions are retained.
1	0x0002	2	Enable support for IPv6. If the network supports both IPv6 and IPv4, it is recommended that you enable support for both. This is done by setting bit 1 but not bit 2.
2	0x0004	4	Disable support for IPv4. If the network supports only IPv6, you should disable IPv4 and set both bit 1 and bit 2.
4	0x0010	16	Hidden Share. The Nomad share is hidden and named NomadSHR$. When using a hidden share, all Nomad installations must be configured to use this option. This cannot be used in conjunction with Custom Share Permissions ((0x0001).
6	0x0040	64	Enable Nomad FanOut behavior

Bit	Hex	Decimal	Description
7	0x0080	128	Use Machine Account. The machine account is used when connecting to a peer agent. The SMSNomadP2P& account is not created. This is only supported on Windows XP and above.
12	0x1000	4096	Allows a computer to become Nomad master even when the Nomad traffic has been inhibited by a VPN, a wireless connection, or a firewall.
13	0x2000	8192	SMB and HTTP Connectivity. Enables the Nomad agent to download content from the Distribution Point using HTTP or SMB depending on the content location provided by ConfigMgr. This parameter should be used on clients when the following setting has been enabled on the Distribution Point(S) in ConfigMgr: Allow clients to transfer content from this distribution point using BITS, HTTP, and HTTPS (required for device clients and Internet-based clients): Allow intranet-only client connections.
14	0x4000	16384	Web LsZ Generation. Enables the Nomad Distribution Point agent to handle LsZ file generation requests coming from HTTP/HTTPS-enabled clients. You should use this parameter on Nomad Distribution Point agents when either of the following parameters are enabled on the clients: (0x2000) – SMB and HTTP connectivity (0x8000) – Web Connectivity Only. On enabling this registry entry, the Nomad Distribution Point agent creates a virtual folder called LsZFILES. The permissions for this are copied from the ConfigMgr SMS_DP_SMSPKGX$ share. By default, it is assumed that access to the LsZFILES folder will require SSL to be enabled. This is the case for Internet facing scenarios where local client access certificates will ensure authentication. If you are using HTTP, instead of HTTPS, you will need to disable SSL manually on the LsZFILES web folder for the Nomad LsZ file generation process to work.
15	0x8000	32768	Web Connectivity Only. Enables the Nomad agent to download content from the distribution point using HTTPS or HTTP depending on the content location provided by ConfigMgr. The Nomad agent will not use SMB to download content from the distribution point when this registry entry is enabled. You should use this parameter on clients when either of the following settings has been enabled on the distribution point(s) in ConfigMgr: Allow clients to transfer content from this distribution point using BITS, HTTP, and HTTPS (required for device clients and Internet-based clients): Allow Internet-only client connections: Allow both intranet and Internet client connections.

Real World Note: SpecialNetShare values included as properties on the command line or as values in an MST must be converted to decimal and entered as such. The client value of 0x2050, for example, is 8272 in decimal and SPECIALNETSHARE=8272 on the command line, or entered as 8272 for the SpecialNetShare in an MST.

LsZ Files

When a Nomad client is elected as the master, it requests content from a Nomad-enabled distribution point. The Nomad service generates an .LsZ file for the client to download.

This file is a manifest which is used in validation of the content that has been retrieved.

On the client, it is normal to see files with an .LsZ extension in the Nomad cache. On the distribution point, there is a virtual directory created called LSZFILES that contains the originating copies created on the distribution point.

Alternate Content Provider (ACP) and Nomad

When a client initiates a software download request, it obtains a list of available distribution points from ConfigMgr. Stored within the package information is also a property called alternate content provider (ACP). Modifying ACP with Nomad information is how the solution operates at its core level and is what happens when the Enable Nomad option is selected in the package properties.

For example, when the client receives the content download instruction the Content Transfer Manager hands off content retrieval to the ACP (Nomad in this case) if one is installed. Nomad then dynamically identifies the list of content locations through the election process, retrieves the content from either a Nomad peer with content or a DP. It then notifies the Content Transfer Manager that content transfer is complete. When finished, it passes control back to the ConfigMgr client for execution of the policy.

The following image shows the Nomad Properties dialog box of the Adobe Reader XI package, which indicates that it is enabled for Nomad distribution and a work rate of 85 percent has been specified. This has been changed from the default recommended value of 80 percent for illustration purposes only.

Real World Note: All applications use Nomad when Nomad is enabled in the Client Settings policy of the ConfigMgr console.

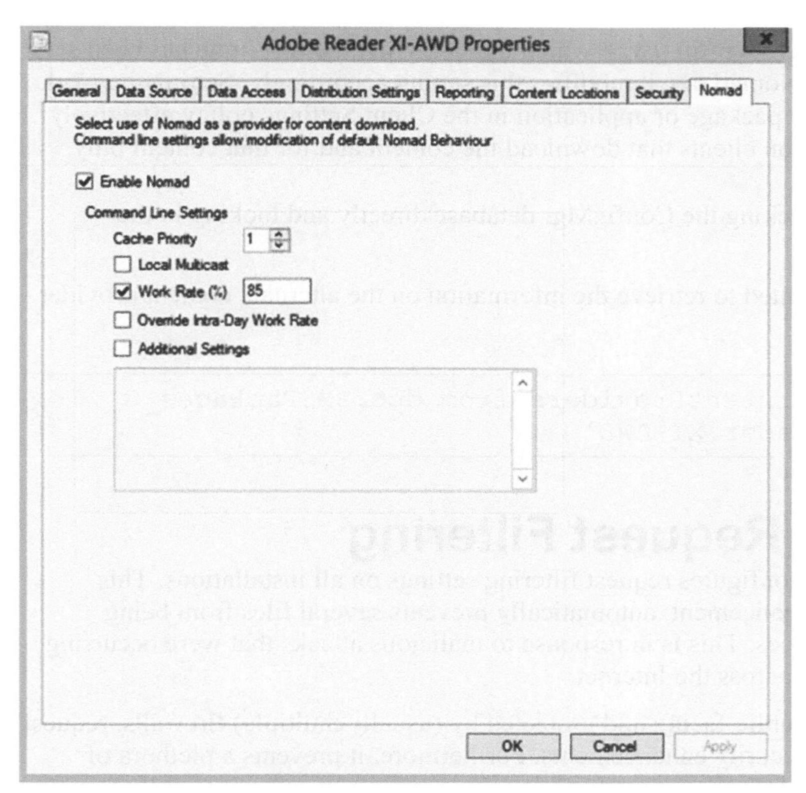

The Enable Nomad check box for making Nomad an alternate content provider.

The value for the alternate content provider can be viewed by simply opening a ConfigMgr PowerShell prompt and typing the following:

```
Get-CMPackage -Name Adobe*
```

```
Administrator: Windows PowerShell
PS PS1:\> Get-CMPackage -Name Adobe*

ActionInProgress              : 1
AlternateContentProviders     : <AlternateDownloadSettings SchemaVersion="1.0"><Provider
                                Name="NomadBranch"><Data><ProviderSettings /><pc>1</pc><wr>80</wr>
                                </Data></Provider></AlternateDownloadSettings>
DefaultImageFlags             : 0
Description                   : Adobe Reader XI 11.0
ExtendedData                  :
ExtendedDataSize              : 0
ForcedDisconnectDelay         : 5
ForcedDisconnectEnabled       : False
ForcedDisconnectNumRetries    : 2
Icon                          :
IconSize                      : 0
```

Listing the Adobe Reader package, including the alternate content providers.

Note: The value shown above has **<wr>80</wr>** which indicates that the work rate has been set to 80 percent. If you change the Nomad tab, it modifies this setting accordingly. Setting the work rate in the Nomad tab of a legacy package or application in the Client Settings policy effectively *overrides* the work rate property on clients that download the content and for that content only.

This can also be validated by checking the ConfigMgr database directly and looking in the SMSPackages_G table.

The following query can be executed to retrieve the information on the alternate content provider directly from the database.

```
SELECT Name,AlternateContentProviders from dbo.SMSPackages_G
where Name = 'Adobe Reader XI-AWD'
```

Configuring IIS Request Filtering

Starting with IIS 7.5, Microsoft configures request filtering settings on all installations. This "feature," aimed as a security enhancement, automatically prevents several files from being transmitted through its web services. This is in response to malicious attacks that were occurring against public-facing IIS servers across the Internet.

On internal servers that are not public-facing and protected by (usually multiple) firewalls, request filtering provides no additional security enhancements. Furthermore, it prevents a plethora of applications, such as the Microsoft Deployment Toolkit package, from being successfully transferred via HTTP, the default communication method from a DP for Nomad traffic.

Real World Note: Microsoft identified this issue with request filtering and wrote a fix into the ConfigMgr client. As such, when Nomad is deployed, if these request filtering settings are not remediated, there will be issues with content downloads from the ConfigMgr DPs that are Nomad enabled.

Therefore, IIS should be configured before Nomad is installed, removing all blocked file extensions and hidden segments from the IIS request filtering rules. A script, EnableAllExtensions.ps1, is available in the book sample files to automate the process of configuring the request filtering settings.

1. On **CM01** log on as **VIAMONSTRA\Administrator**.
2. Using **File Explorer**, create the **C:\Labfiles** folder.
3. From the downloaded sample files, copy the **Scripts** folder to **C:\Labfiles**.

4. Open **Internet Information Services (IIS) Manager**, review the **Request Filtering** settings on the default web site.

   Notice how the default values are set to Allowed=False.

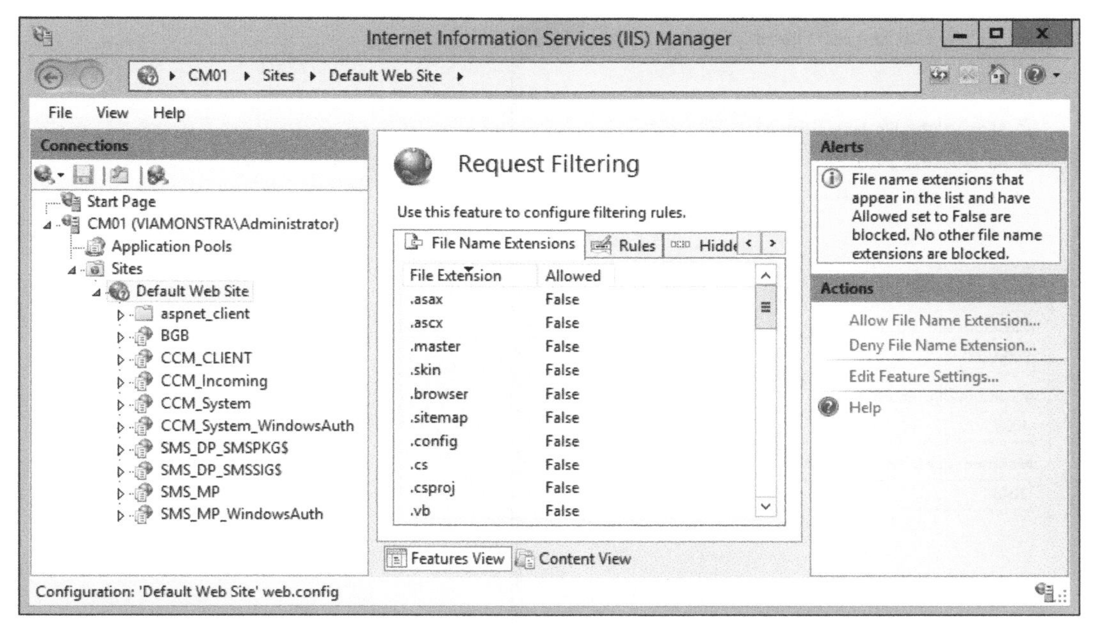

Viewing the Request Filtering configurations in IIS.

Note: These default settings will cause Nomad issues with downloading content from the virtual directories.

5. Now check the settings. On the **Request Filtering** page in **IIS Manager**, select **Edit Feature Settings** from the **Action** pane,

   Notice that Allow double escaping is not selected.

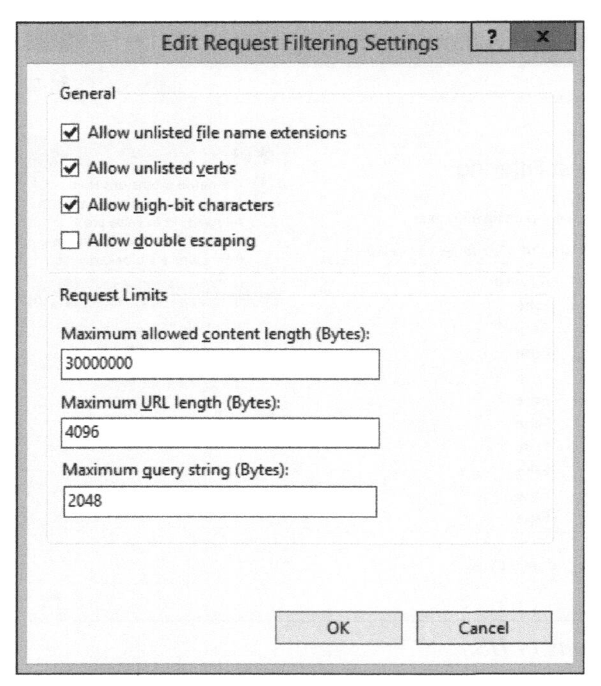

Viewing the default Request Filtering Settings in IIS.

Real World Note: Double escaping deals with special characters. In the event that your packages or applications have special characters, Nomad will have issues downloading them from the virtual directory without the Allow double escaping check box selected.

6. To enable double escaping support, select the **Allow double escaping** check box and click **OK**.
7. Open an elevated **PowerShell prompt** and type the following:

```
Set-ExecutionPolicy Unrestricted -Force
```

8. Change the directory to **C:\Labfiles\Scripts** and type the following:

```
.\EnableAllExtensions.ps1
```

9. Review the request filtering configurations from step 4, noting the new settings.

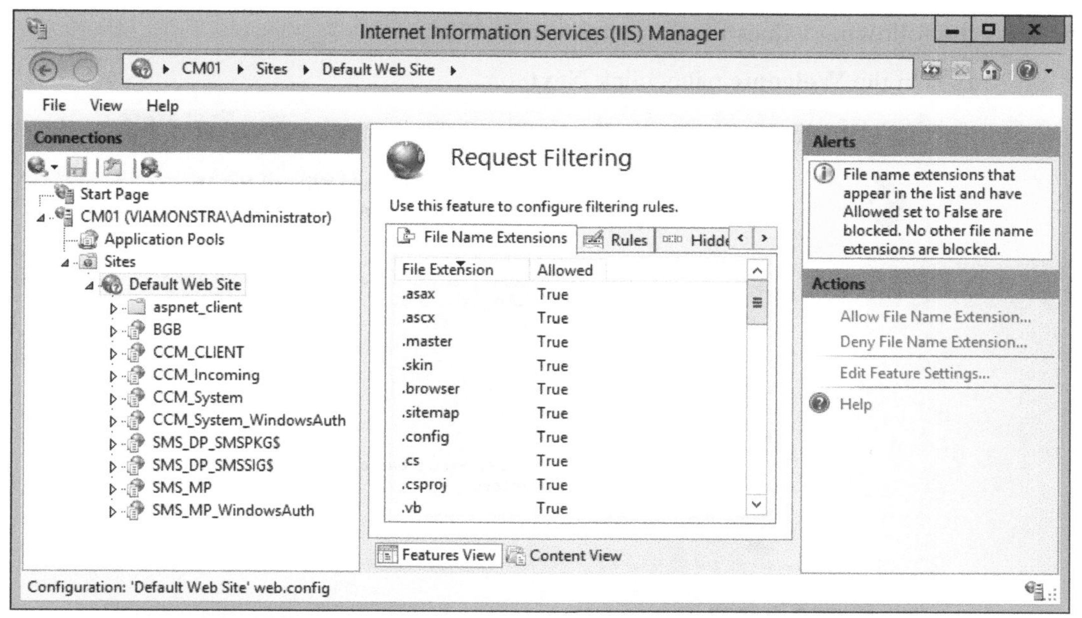

The values are now all Allowed=True.

Deploying ConfigMgr Console Extensions

In order to see the Nomad extensions in the ConfigMgr console, you must deploy NomadBranchAdminUIExt.msi to each ConfigMgr console.

If there is a central Remote Desktop Services (RDS) server or Citrix server with the ConfigMgr console as a published app, these instances must also have the preceding .msi file run. This can easily be deployed silently with ConfigMgr.

If there are local instances of the ConfigMgr console on admin or operational workstations, these must also be extended:

1. On **CM01**, from your 1E media, copy **NomadBranch v5.2.100.32** to **C:\Labfiles\Sources** (you need to create the folder).
2. Close the **ConfigMgr console**.
3. Open an elevated **Command prompt** and run the following command:

   ```
   cd \labfiles\Sources\NomadBranch v5.2.100.32\ConfigMgr2012
   ```

4. Start the installation by running the following command:

   ```
   NomadBranchAdminUIExt2012.msi
   ```

5. Use the following values for the installation:

   a. On the **Welcome** page, click **Next**.

   b. On the **License Agreement** page, accept the terms and click **Next**.

c. On the **Ready to Install the Program** page, click **Install**.

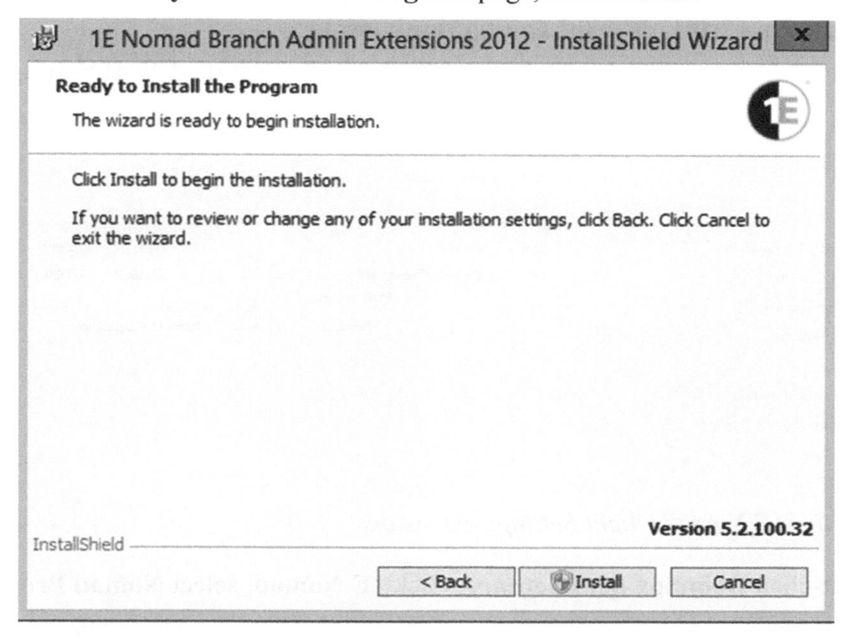

d. On the **InstallShield Wizard Completed** page, click **Finish**.

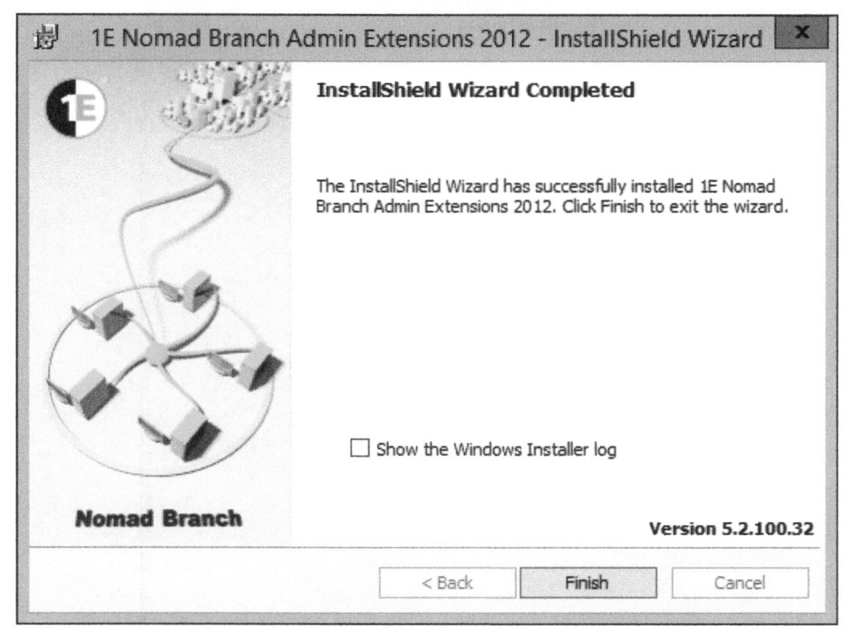

6. Validate that console extensions deployed properly:
    a. On **CM01**, open the **ConfigMgr console**.
    b. Open the **Administration** workspace and select the **Client Settings** node:

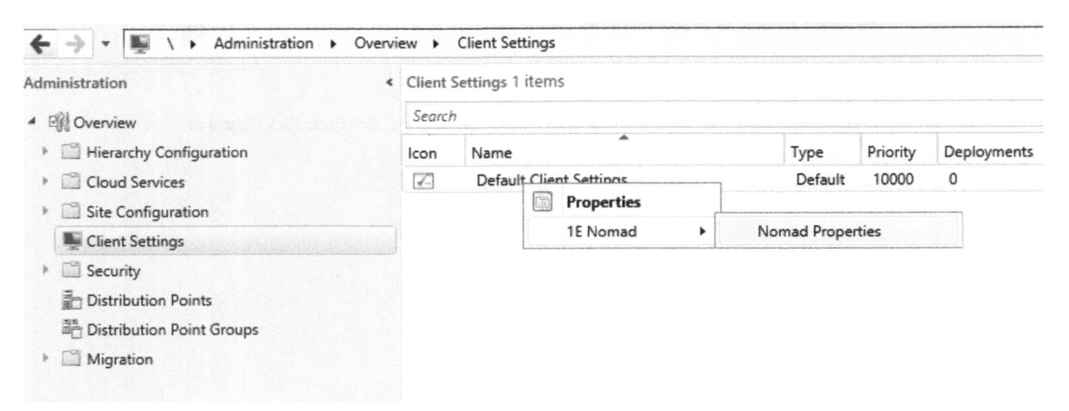

Viewing the 1E Nomad Client Settings extensions.

7. Right-click **Default Client Settings,** click **1E Nomad**, select **Nomad Properties**.
8. Select the **Enable Nomad** check box for both **Application Management** and **Software Updates**, and then click OK

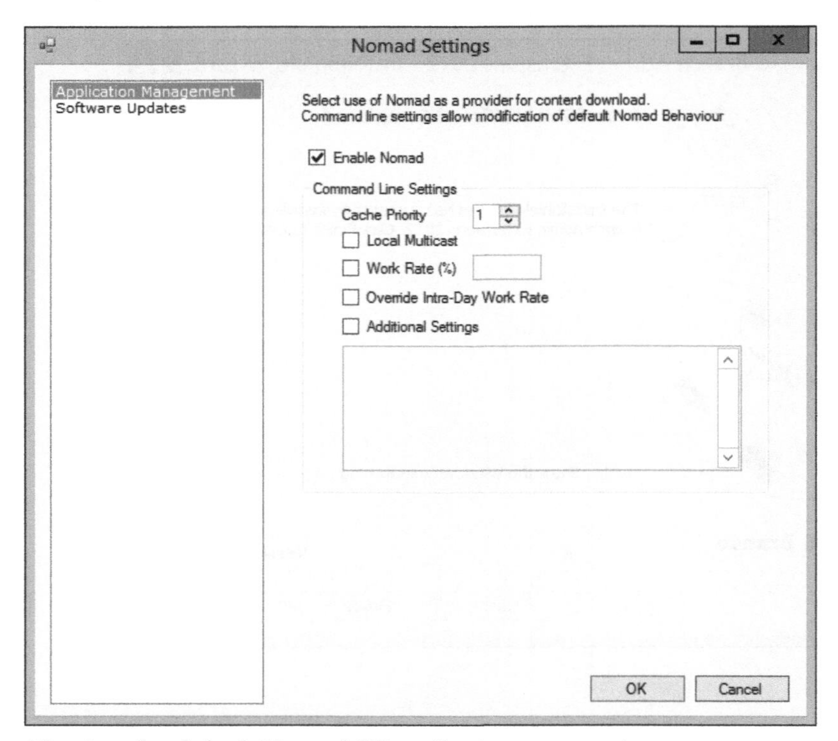

Viewing the default Nomad Client Settings properties.

Deploying Nomad on the Distribution Points

Probably the most critical part in a successful implementation is that NomadBranch must be installed on all distribution points serving branch clients and that it be properly configured.

1. On **CM01**, close the **ConfigMgr console**.
2. Open an elevated **Command prompt** and run the following command:

   ```
   cd \labfiles\Sources\NomadBranch v5.2.100.32\ConfigMgr2012
   ```

Note: In a production environment, there are installer properties that should be set via a custom install string. For this lab, you just walk through the installer and then modify the registry.

3. Start the installation by running the following command:

   ```
   NomadBranch-x64.msi
   ```

4. Use the following values for the installation:
   a. On the **Welcome** page, click **Next**.

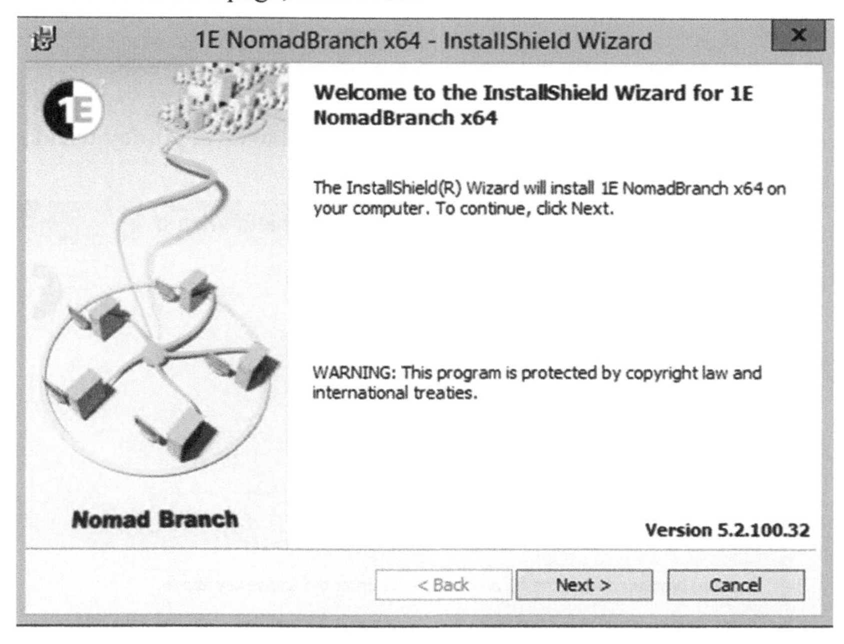

b. On the **License Agreement** page, accept the terms and click **Next**.

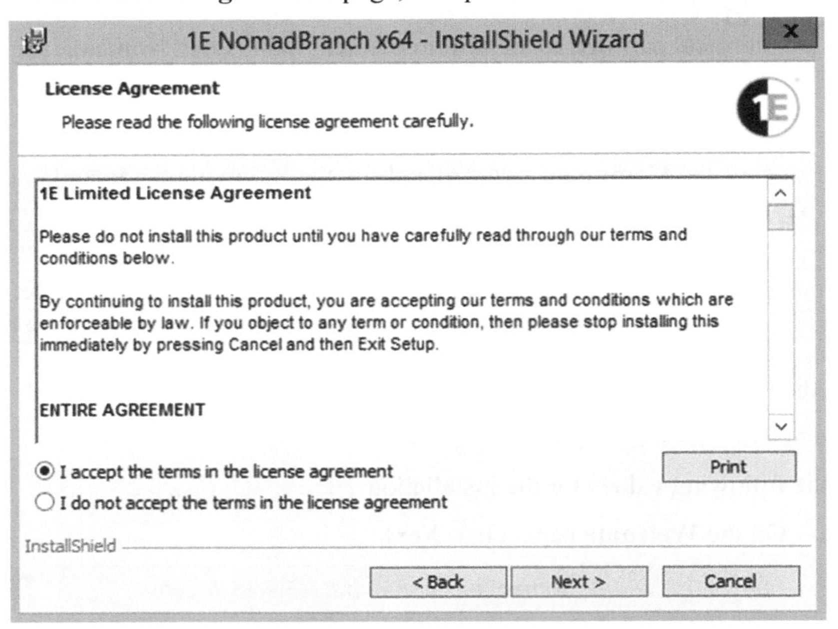

c. On the **License Key** page, leave the field blank. (A 30-day trial key will be generated.) Then click **Next**.

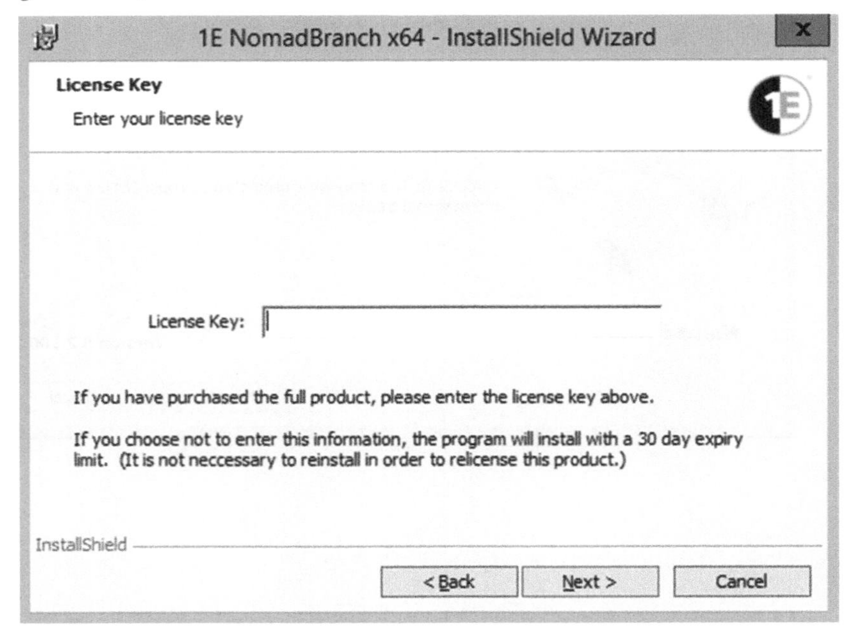

d. On the **Setup Type** page, select **Custom** and click **Next**.

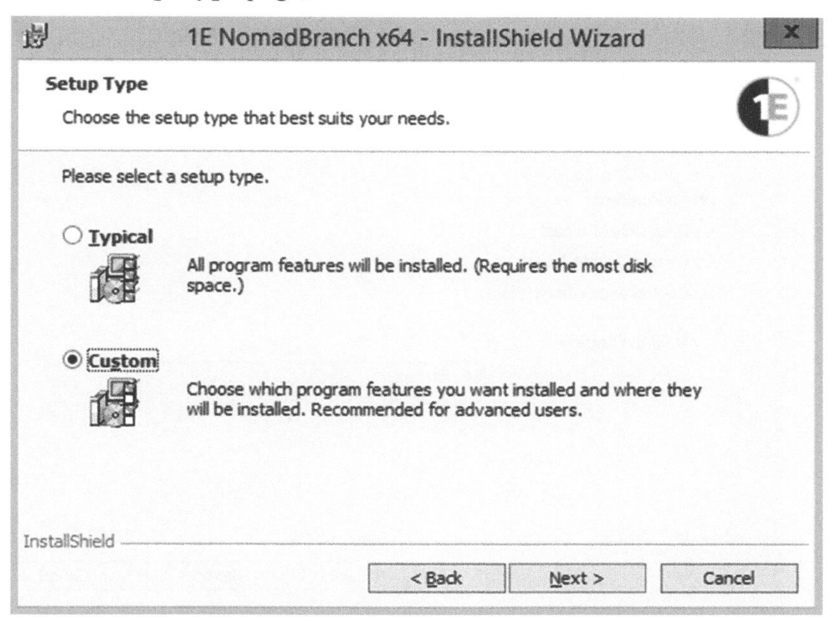

e. On the **Destination Folder** page, keep the default folder and click **Next**.

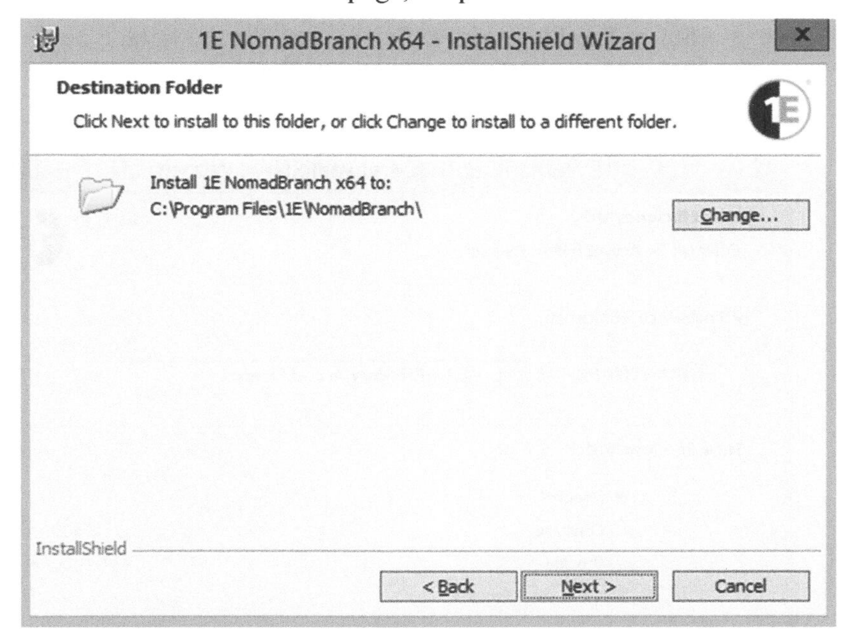

f. On the **Multicast Configuration** page, select **No Multicast** and click **Next**.

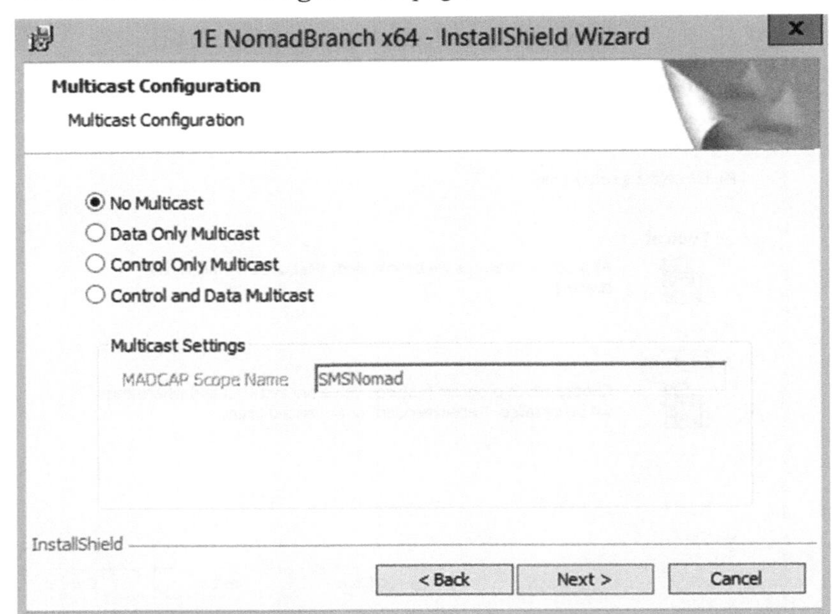

g. On the **ActiveEfficiency Url** page, use the following settings and then click **Next**:

- Select **Enable ActiveEfficiency**, and in the field, type **http://ActiveEfficiency/ActiveEfficiency**.
- Single Site Download: **Disabled**

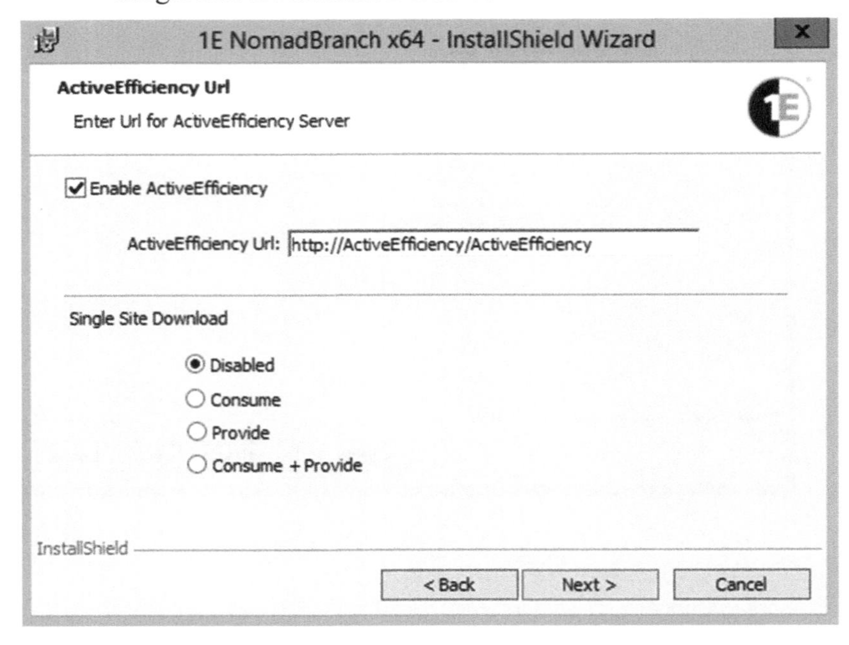

h. On the **Ready to Install the Program** page, click **Install**.

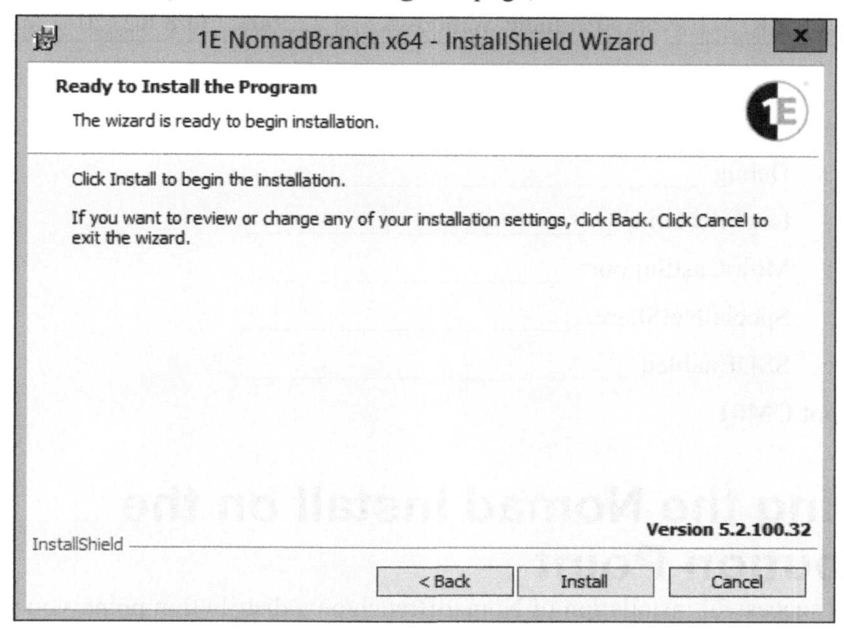

i. On the **InstallShield Wizard Completed** page, select **Show the Windows Installer log** check box, and click **Finish**.

Note: You can find the Nomad registry values for the following operating systems at HKLM\SOFTWARE\1E\NomadBranch: Windows 7, 8.1, 2008, 2008 R2, 2012, and 2012 R2.

5. Open the **HKLM\SOFTWARE\1E\NomadBranch** registry keys and write down the following values:
    - Debug ______________________________
    - LogFileName _________________________
    - MultiCastSupport ______________________
    - SpecialNetShare: _______________________
    - SSDEnabled __________________________
6. Reboot **CM01**.

Verifying the Nomad Install on the Distribution Point

To validate a successful installation of NomadBranch on a distribution point, you refer to the NomadBranch.log file. Before doing this, however, you first need to change a couple of values for the Nomad DP installation.

Real World Note: As mentioned earlier, a custom install string should be used to deploy Nomad in the field. One of the things that we missed was putting in an appropriate product key. Nomad will generate a 30-day trial key if one isn't entered. As such many real-world implementations can fail if the packagers fail to input the correct key. To relicense Nomad, you would type the following command:

```
NomadBranch.exe -relicense= ABCDEFGH-11AA-22BB-33CC-44DD
```

1. On **CM01**, open **Regedit** and browse to **HKLM\SOFTWARE\1E\NomadBranch**.
2. Change the following registry values:
    - Debug = **16 (decimal)**
    - SpecialNetShare = **4010 (hexadecimal)**

> **Real World Note:** Elevating debugging levels should be used only for troubleshooting or learning the Nomad logs. This value should be changed back to default when you are done.
>
> This is a typical value configured for the SpecialNetShare on a ConfigMgr 2012 or ConfigMgr 2012 R2 implementation. These values can be different depending on the customer's configuration. For a complete listing of values for SpecialNetShare visit:
>
> http://help.1e.com/display/NMD52/SpecialNetShare (you need to login).
>
> For your lab, you use a value of 4010 (hexadecimal) for the DP.
>
> Also, making changes to these registry values does not require a service restart.

3. Using **CMTrace** (available in D:\ConfigMgr\tools), review the **NomadBranch.log** at **C:\ProgramData\1E\NomadBranch\LogFiles**, and leave it open.
4. Restart the **1E Nomad Branch** service.
5. Review the **NomadBranch.log**. Search for **SpecialNetShare**. Do you see where the value has now changed to **4010**?

   You should see something like this:

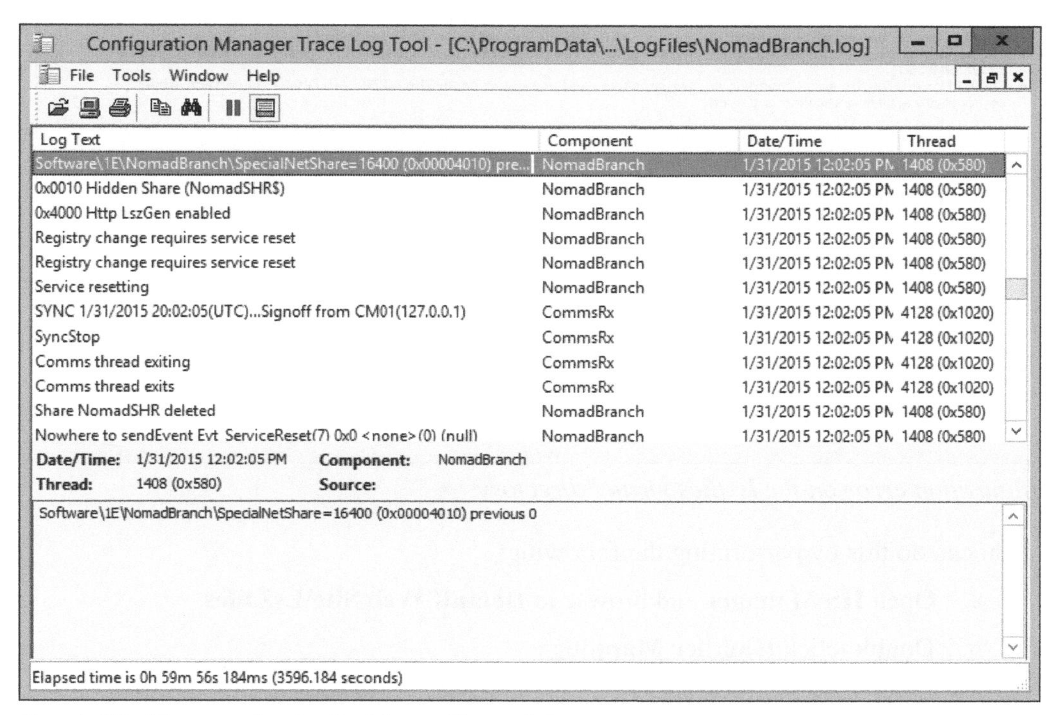

SpecialNetShare value in the NomadBranch.log.

Real World Note: You get a lot of good information from the NomadBranch.log upon service restart.

1. On **CM01**, using **Server Manager**, in the **Local Server** node, disable **IE Enhanced Security Configuration**.
2. Validate that **LsZ Web Generation** is working by going to the following URL:

   `http://cm01/lszfiles`

3. If you receive an error message **403.1 forbidden**, you likely need to configure the virtual directory for script access.

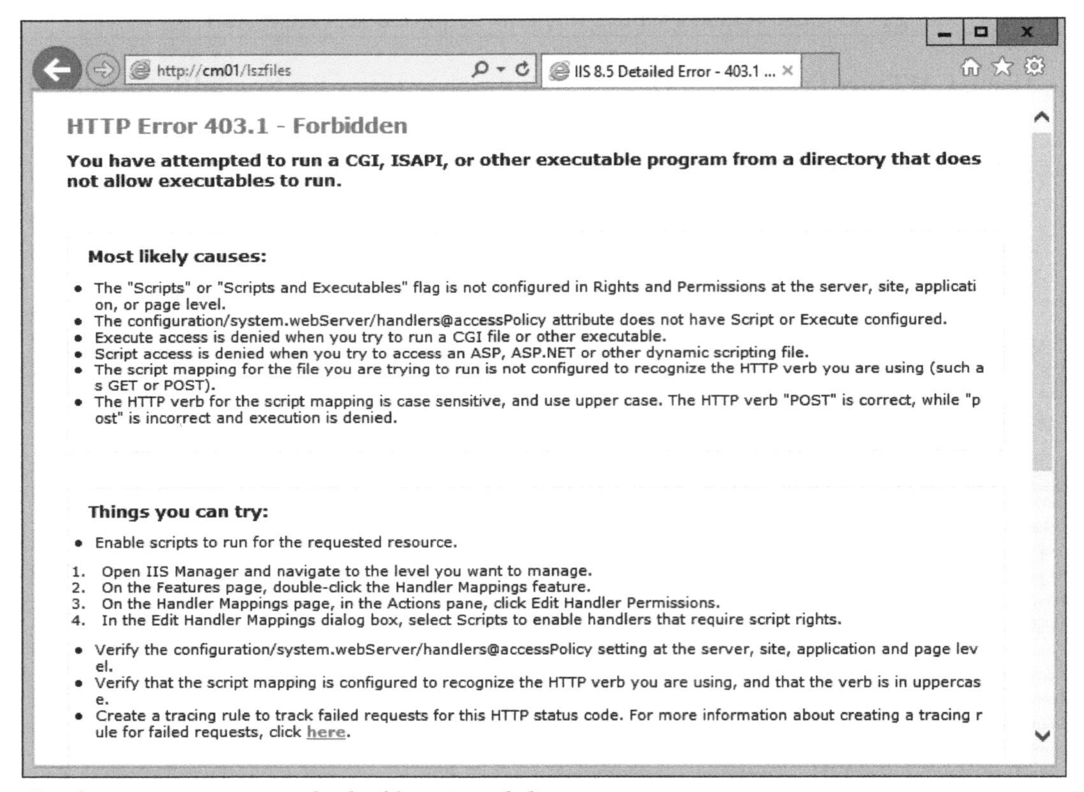

Configuration error on the lszfiles virtual directory.

You can do this by performing the following:

a. Open **IIS Manager** and browse to **Default Web Site\LsZfiles**.

b. Double-click **Handler Mappings**.

c. Click **Edit Feature Permissions**; then select **Script** and click **OK**.

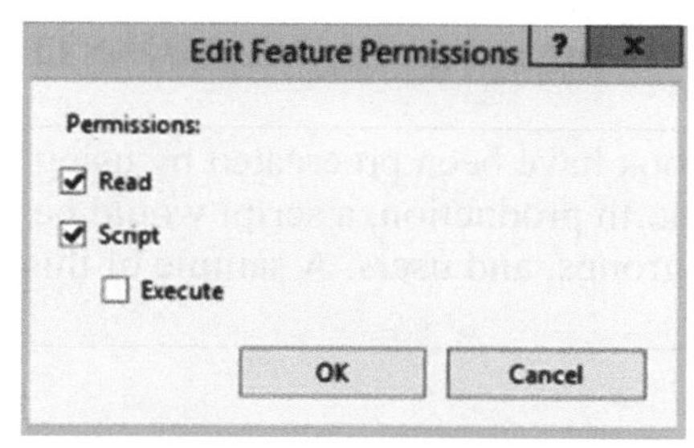

d. Try accessing **http://cm01/lszfiles** again.

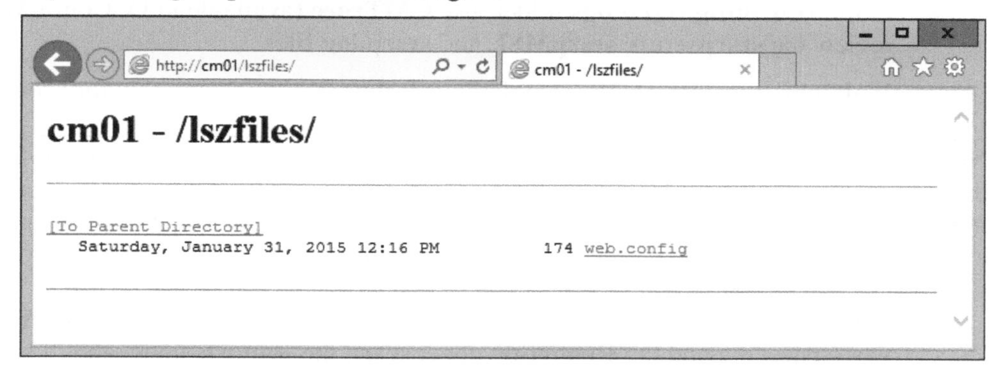

Note: You won't see anything in the virtual directory yet because no LsZ generation requests have occurred. If you check after the first 1E Nomad-enabled package is deployed, you will see content in this virtual directory.

Base Configuration of CM01

In this guide you setup ConfigMgr 2012 R2 for software distribution and monitoring (reports).

Add the Reporting Services Point

1. On **CM01**, log on as **VIAMONSTRA\Administrator** using a password of **P@ssw0rd**.
2. Using the **ConfigMgr console**, in the **Administration** workspace, expand **Site Configuration** and select **Sites**.
3. On the ribbon, select **Add Site System Roles**, and use the following settings for the **Add Site System Roles Wizard**:
    a. General: **<default>**
    b. Proxy: **<default>**
    c. System Role Selection: Select the **Reporting service point** check box.

d. Reporting Services Point: Click **Verify**, and wait for the instance to be verified.

e. User name: Select **Set / New Account** and specify **VIAMONSTRA\CM_SR**.

Note: The service accounts referenced in this book have been precreated by using the Deployment Artist hydration kit created by Johan Arwidmark. In production, a script would be used to precreate all of the necessary service accounts, groups, and users. A sample of this script can be found as part of the hydration kit.

f. Password: **P@ssw0rd**

g. Summary: **<default>**

4. In the **D:\ConfigMgr\Logs** folder, use **CMTrace** (available in D:\ConfigMgr\tools) to review the **srsrpsetup**, **srsrpMSI**, and **srsrp.log** files.

   Wait until all reports have been deployed (the srsrp.log is quiet) before continuing.

Note: It will take a short while for the srsrp.log to be created and quite a long while to create all the reports. A perfect time for a quick break. And, by the way, don't worry about all the red lines in CMTrace when deploying the reports. Lines containing the word "error" are highlighted in red, and some of the report components have that word in the path to which they are copied. ☺

5. After all reports have been deployed, in the **ConfigMgr console**, in the **Monitoring** workspace, expand the **Reporting** node, select the **Reports** node, and then review the reports available.

Configure Discovery Methods

1. On **CM01**, using the **ConfigMgr console**, in the **Administration** workspace, expand **Hierarchy Configuration / Discovery Methods**.

2. Double-click **Active Directory Forest Discovery** and enable the settings to create Active Directory site and IP address range boundaries automatically. Click **OK**, and when prompted, run the discovery.

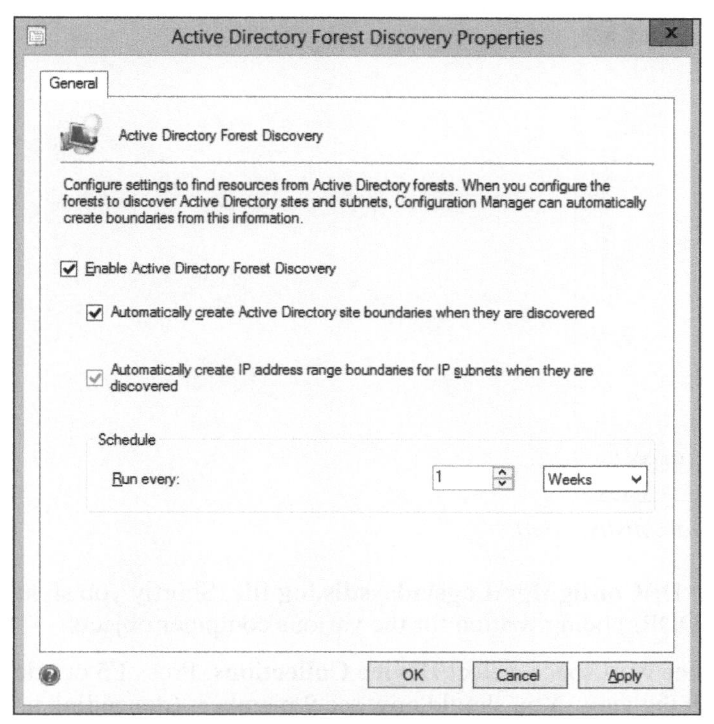

Configuring Active Directory Forest Discovery.

3. Using **CMTrace**, review the **D:\ConfigMgr\Logs\ADForestDisc.log** file.
4. Still in the **Administration** workspace, select the **Boundaries** node and review the boundaries that were created.
5. In the **Discovery Methods** node, double-click **Active Directory System Discovery**, select the **Enable Active Directory System Discovery** check box, click the **New** button (which looks like an asterisk), click **Browse**, and select the **corp** domain. Click **OK** three times, and run the discovery.

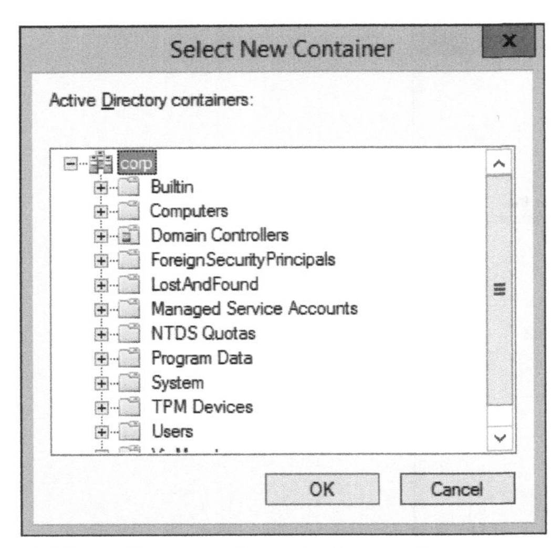

Adding the corp domain (corp.viamonstra.com).

6. Using **CMTrace**, review the **D:\ConfigMgr\Logs\adsysdis.log** file. Shortly you should see discovery data records (DDRs) being written for the various computer objects.
7. In the **Assets and Compliance** workspace, select **Device Collections**. Press **F5** or click the **Refresh** button to refresh the view. You should now see 9 members (depending how many machines you have in the domain) of the **All Systems** collection.

Note: It may take a while for the collection to refresh, but you can view progress via the Colleval.log file. If you want to speed up the process, you can manually update membership on the All Systems collection by right-clicking the collection and selecting Update Membership.

8. In the **Administration** workspace, in the **Discovery Methods** node, double-click **Active Directory User Discovery**, enable the discovery, add the **corp** domain, and run the discovery.
9. Using **CMTrace**, review the **D:\ConfigMgr\Logs\adusrdis.log** file.
10. In the **Assets and Compliance** workspace, select **User Collections**. Press **F5** or click the **Refresh** button to refresh the view. You should now see **9** members of the **All Users** collection.

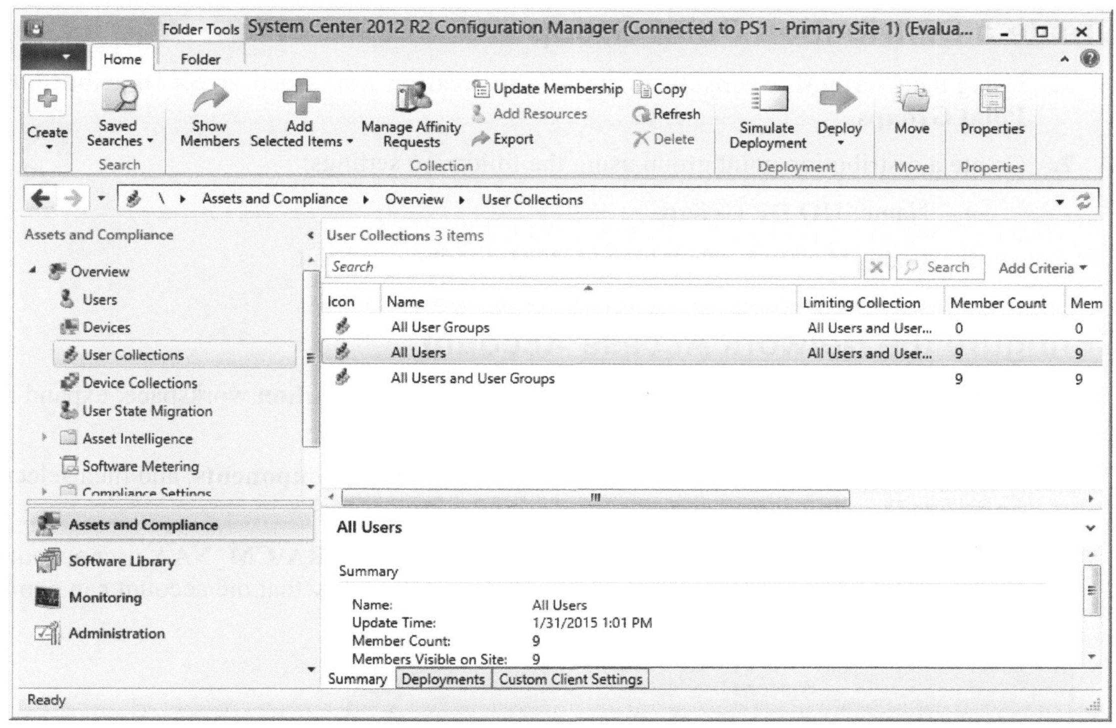

The User Collections node after Active Directory User Discovery is configured.

Create a Boundary Group

1. Using the **ConfigMgr console**, in the **Administration** workspace, select **Boundary Groups**.
2. Create a boundary group using the following settings:
   a. In the **General** tab:
      - Name: **HQ Assignment**
      - Boundaries: Add the **NewYork** and **192.168.1.1 - 192.168.1.254** boundaries.

   b. In the **Reference** tab:
      - Site assignment area: Select the **Use the boundary group for site assignment** check box.
      - Content location area: Add the **CM01** distribution point.

Create a Distribution Point Group

1. Using the **ConfigMgr console**, in the **Administration** workspace, select **Distribution Point Groups**.
2. Create a distribution point group using the following settings:
    a. Name: **HQ DP Group**.
    b. In the **Members** tab, add the **CM01** distribution point.

Configure the Network Access Account

1. On **CM01**, using the **ConfigMgr console**, in the **Administration** workspace, expand **Site Configuration** and select **Sites**.
2. Right-click **PS1 - Primary Site 1**, select **Configure Site Components**, and then select **Software Distribution**.
3. In the **Network Access Account** tab, add the **VIAMONSTRA\CM_NAA** user account as the Network Access account. Use the **Verify** option to verify that the account can connect to the **\\DC01\sysvol** network share.

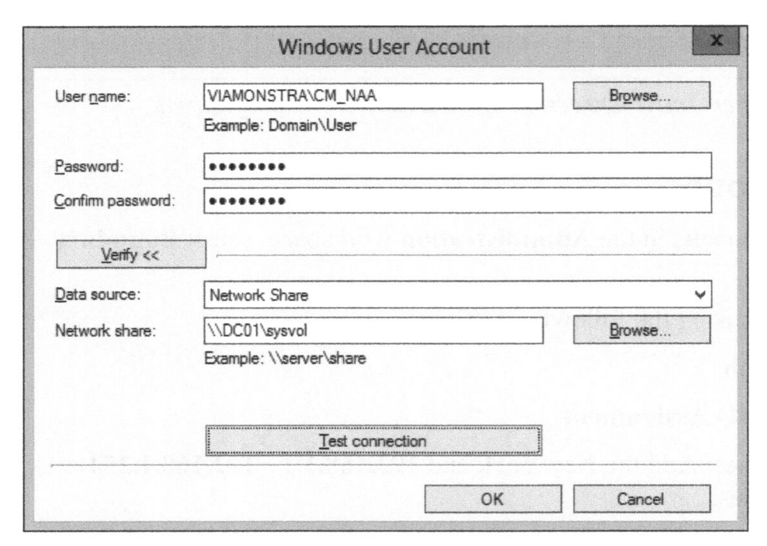

Using the Verify (Test connection) option.

Create Security Group for Local Admin Access

1. On **DC01**, log on as **VIAMONSTRA\Administrator**.
2. Using **Active Directory Users and Computers**, in the **ViaMonstra / Security Groups** OU, create a global security group named **Set Local Admins**.
3. Add the **CM_CP** user account to the **Set Local Admins** security group.

Configure Group Policy for Client Push

1. On **DC01**, using the **Group Policy Management Console**, right-click the **ViaMonstra / Workstations** OU and select **Create a GPO in this domain, and Link it here.**
2. Assign the name **ConfigMgr Client Push** to the new group policy.
3. Expand the **ViaMonstra / Workstations** OU, right-click the **ConfigMgr Client Push** policy, and select **Edit**. Configure the following policy settings:
   a. **Computer Configuration \ Policies \ Administrative Templates \ Network \ Network Connections \ Windows Firewall \ Domain Profile**
      i. Enable the **Windows Firewall: Allow inbound file and printer sharing exception** policy.
      ii. Enable the **Windows Firewall: Allow inbound remote administration exception** policy.
   b. Close the **Group Policy Management Editor**. Due to a bug in the group policy management, firewall settings are not saved when also doing other edits.
4. In the **ViaMonstra / Workstations** OU, right-click the **ConfigMgr Client Push** policy, and select **Edit**. Configure the following policy settings:

   Computer Configuration \ Policies \ Windows Settings \ Security Settings \ Restricted Groups
      i. Right-click **Restricted groups** and select **Add Group**. Browse for the **VIAMONSTRA\Set Local Admins** group and click **OK**.
      ii. In the **VIAMONSTRA\Set Local Admins Properties** page, in the **This group is a member of:** area, add and browse for the **Administrators** group. Then click **OK**.

Real World Note: This configuration of Restricted Groups only adds the VIAMONSTRA\Set Local Admins security group to the local Administrators group on each computer in the Workstations OU. The policy does not replace all existing members in the group.

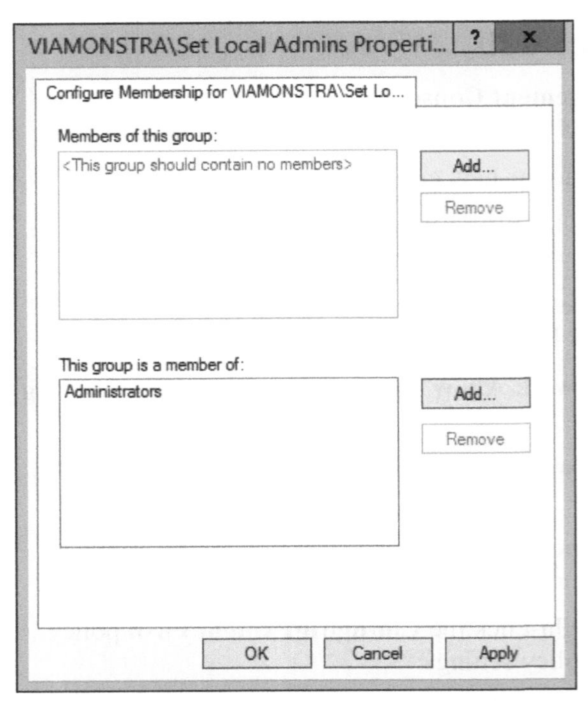

Adding the Set Local Admins group to the local Administrators group on the clients.

Configure the Client Push Account

1. On **CM01**, log on as **VIAMONSTRA\Administrator**.
2. Using the **ConfigMgr console**, in the **Administration** workspace, expand **Site Configuration** and select **Sites**.
3. Right-click the **PS1 - Primary Site 1**, select **Client Installation Settings**, and then select **Client Push Installation**.
4. In the **Accounts** tab, configure the **VIAMONSTRA\CM_CP** user account (select New Account) as the client push account.

Deploy the ConfigMgr 2012 R2 Client

1. Reboot **PC0001**, **PC0002**, **PC0003**, and **PC0004** (or run gpupdate on each machine). This refreshes the group policies created earlier.
2. Once **PC0002** is rebooted, on **CM01**, using **File Explorer**, verify that you can access the **\\PC0002\Admin$** share.
3. Using **wbemtest** (Start / Run, type in wbemtest), click **Connect**, and verify that you can connect to the **\\PC0002\root\cimv2** WMI name space on **PC0002**. Then close **wbemtest**.

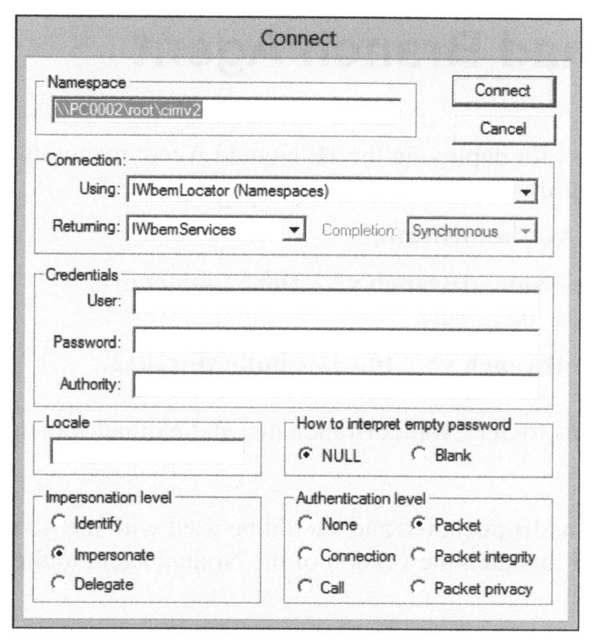

Using wbemtest to verify remote WMI access to PC0002.

4. Using the **ConfigMgr console**, in the **Assets and Compliance** workspace, select **Device Collections**, and then double-click the **All Systems** collection.

5. Right-click **PC0002** and select **Install-Client** to push the ConfigMgr 2012 R2 client to it. Use the default settings in the wizard.

6. Using **CMTrace**, review the **D:\ConfigMgr\Logs\ccm.log** file. You should see that client files (MobileClient.tcf and ccmsetup.exe) are being copied from the distribution point (CM01) to PC0002, and that the ccmsetup service is started.

7. Using **CMTrace**, also review the **\\PC0002\admin$\ccmsetup\logs\ccmsetup.log** file.

8. Wait for the **\\PC0002\admin$\ccmsetup\logs\ccmsetup.log** to create the entry **Ccmsetup is exiting with return code 0**.

9. Using **CMTrace**, review the following files in the **\\PC0002\admin$\CCM\Logs** folder:

    a. **ClientIDManagerStartup.log:** Look for **Client is registered**.

    b. **Clientlocation.log:** Look for **Current AD forest name**, **Domain joined client is Intranet**, and **Assigned MP changed from**.

    c. **LocationServices.log:** Look for **Current AD site of machine is**.

10. Using the **ConfigMgr console**, in **Assets and Compliance** workspace, select **Device Collections**, and then double-click the **All Systems** collection. **PC0002** should now display as an active client in the PS1 site.

11. Repeat steps 1–9 on **PC0001**, **PC0003**, and **PC0004**.

Deploying the 1E Nomad Branch Agent Manually

At this point, you're going to look at the process for deploying the 1E Nomad Agent manually and then build a package for deployment via ConfigMgr.

1. On **PC0002**, log on as **VIAMONSTRA\Administrator**.
2. Copy the **\\CM01\C$\Labfiles\Sources\NomadBranch v5.2.100.32** folder to **C:\Labfiles\Sources** (you need to create the folder).
3. Browse to **C:\Labfiles\Sources\NomadBranch v5.2.100.32\ConfigMgr2012**.

Note: There will be two Nomad installers in this folder: NomadBranch.msi and NomadBranch-x64.

The x86 version of the 1E Nomad agent is NomadBranch.msi and should be used with the x86 version of the ConfigMgr agent. It is important to match the version of the Nomad agent to the ConfigMgr agent.

If you try to install on the wrong platform, the installer will fail.

4. Double-click **NomadBranch-x64.msi**.
5. Install the NomadBranch agent with the following settings:
   a. On the **Welcome** page, click **Next**.

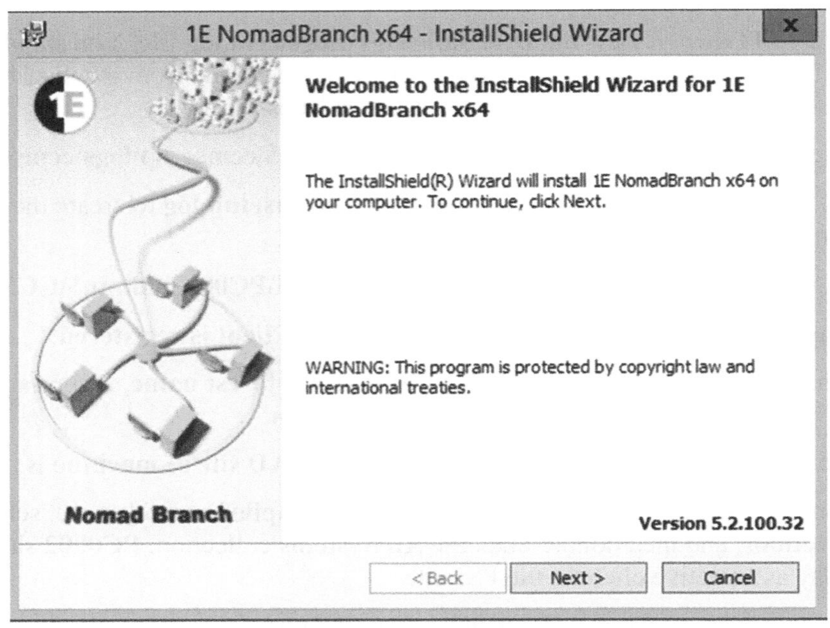

b. On the **License Agreement** page, accept the terms and click **Next**.

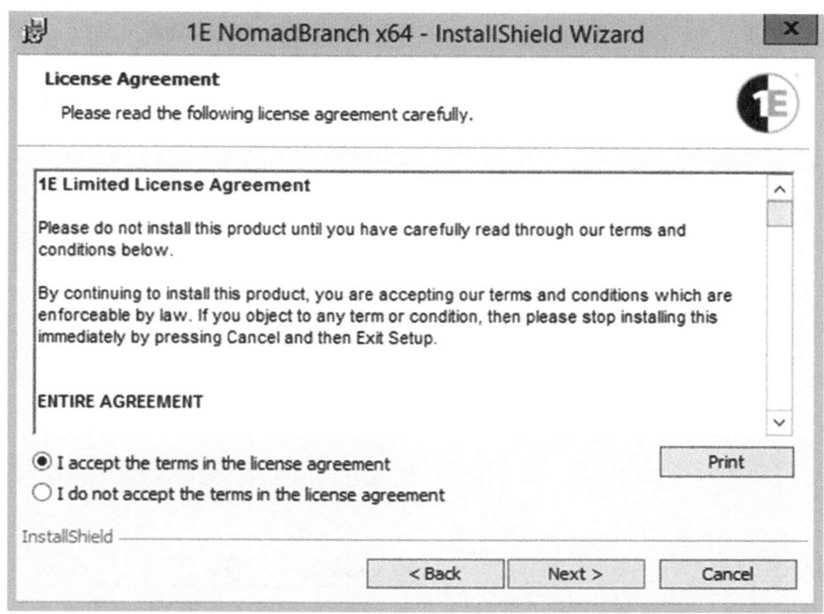

c. On the **License Key** page, leave the field blank. (If you don't enter a product key, a 30-day trial key will be generated by the installer.)

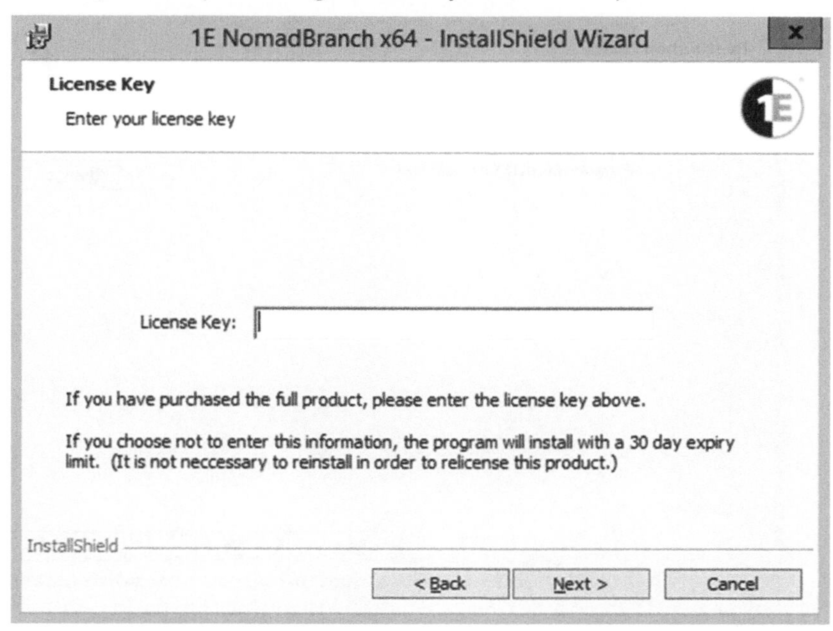

d. On the **Setup Type** page, select **Custom**.

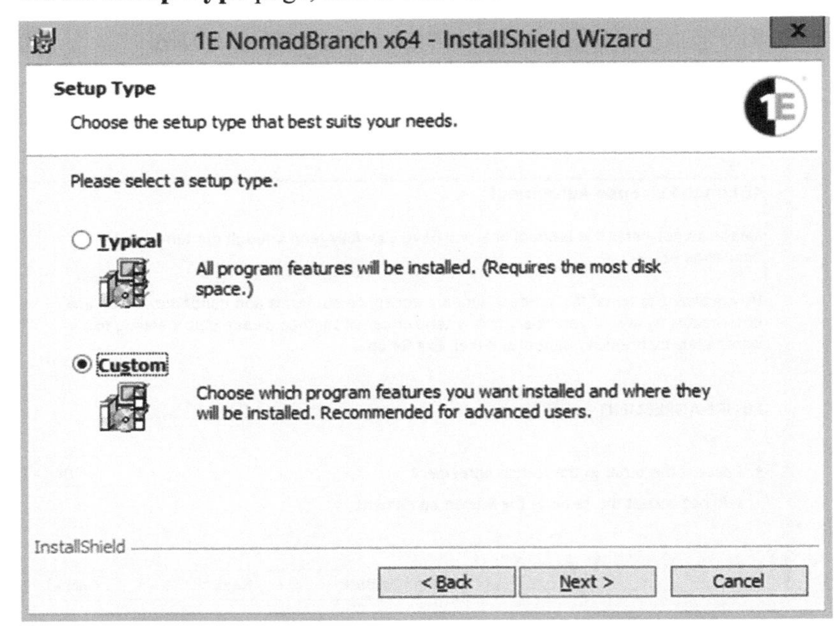

e. On the **Destination Folder** page, keep the default folder and click **Next**.

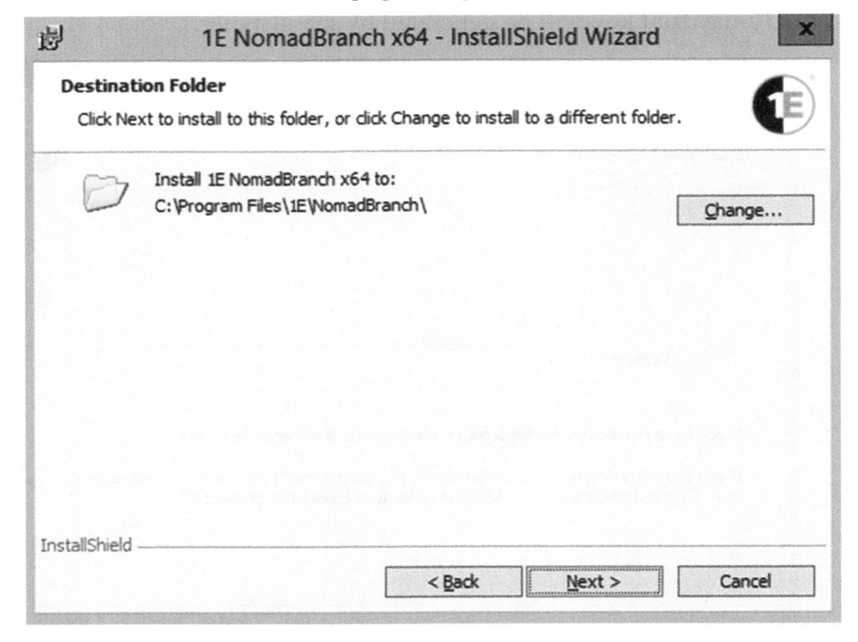

f. On the **Multicast Configuration** page, select **No Multicast** and click **Next**.

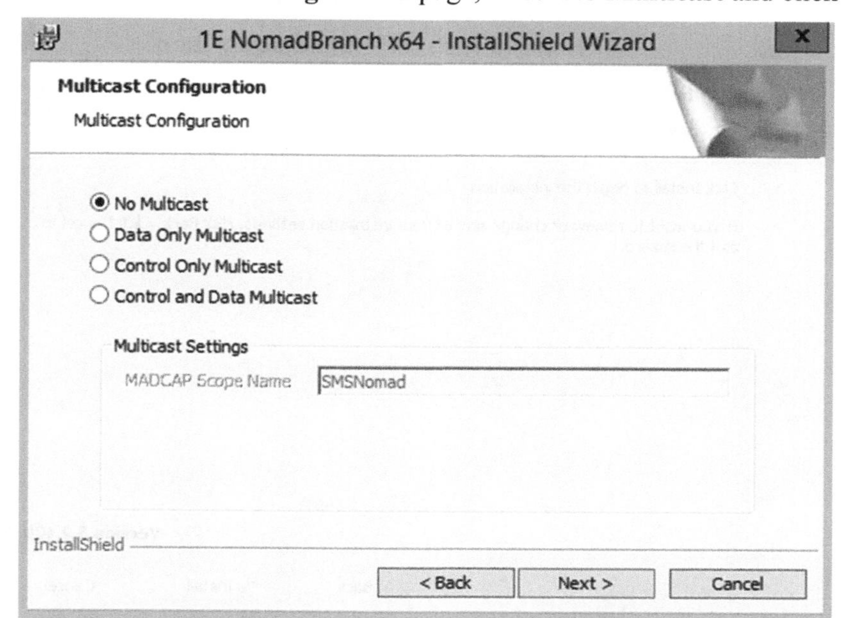

g. On the **ActiveEfficiency Url** page, use the following settings and then click **Next**:

- Select **Enable ActiveEfficiency**, and in the field, type **http://ActiveEfficiency/ActiveEfficiency**.
- Single Site Download: **Consume + Provide**

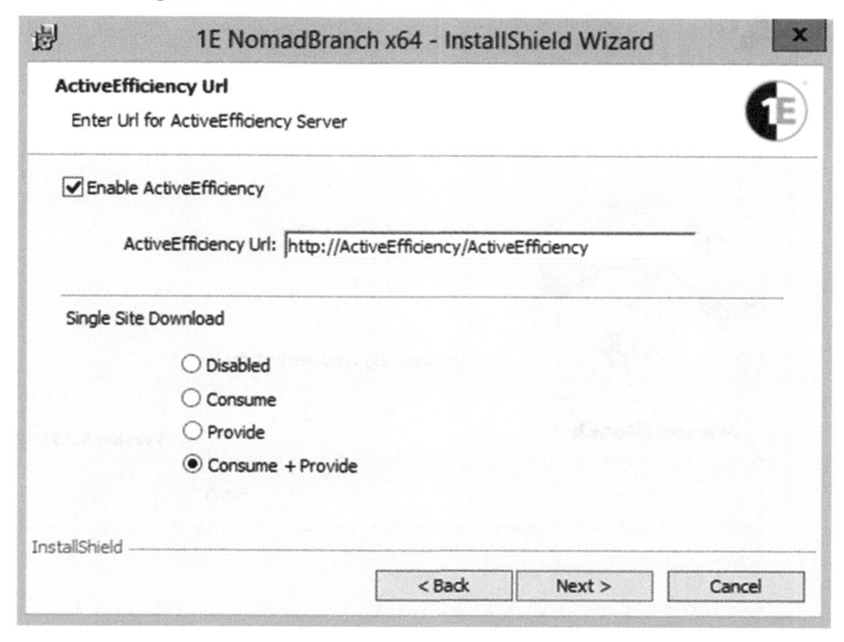

h. On the **Ready to Install the Program** page, click **Install**.

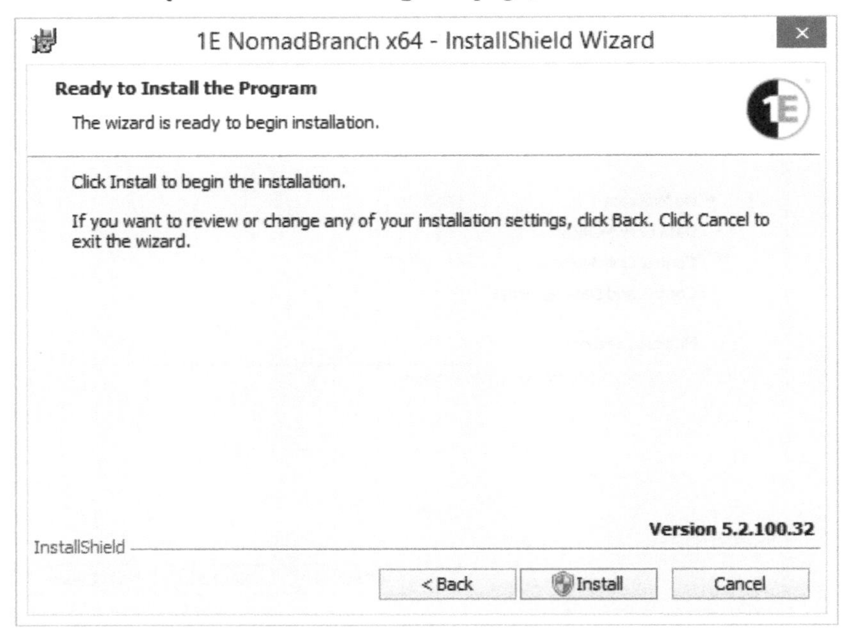

i. On the **InstallShield Wizard Completed** page, select **Show the Windows Installer log** and click **Finish**.

6. Open **Regedit** and browse to **HKLM\Software\1E\NomadBranch**.

   What is the value for **SpecialNetShare**?

   ____

Real World Note: During a production rollout, it is important to get the agent install strings correct. Currently, you have selected a 30-day trial product key that will require a relicense of the Nomad agents. In a large environment, this can be a big issue.

Also, there are no options in the GUI installer to set the value for the SpecialNetShare. A sample install string follows:

```
msiexec.exe /qn /I "NomadBranch-x64.msi" PIDKEY=<YOUR PIDKEYHERE>
SPECIALNETSHARE=8272 MULTICASTSUPPORT=0
PLATFORMURL=http://activeefficiency/activeefficiency SSDENABLED=3
```

During a scripted install, the value for SPECIALNETSHARE is the decimal value. In the preceding example, this would be 2050 hexadecimal:

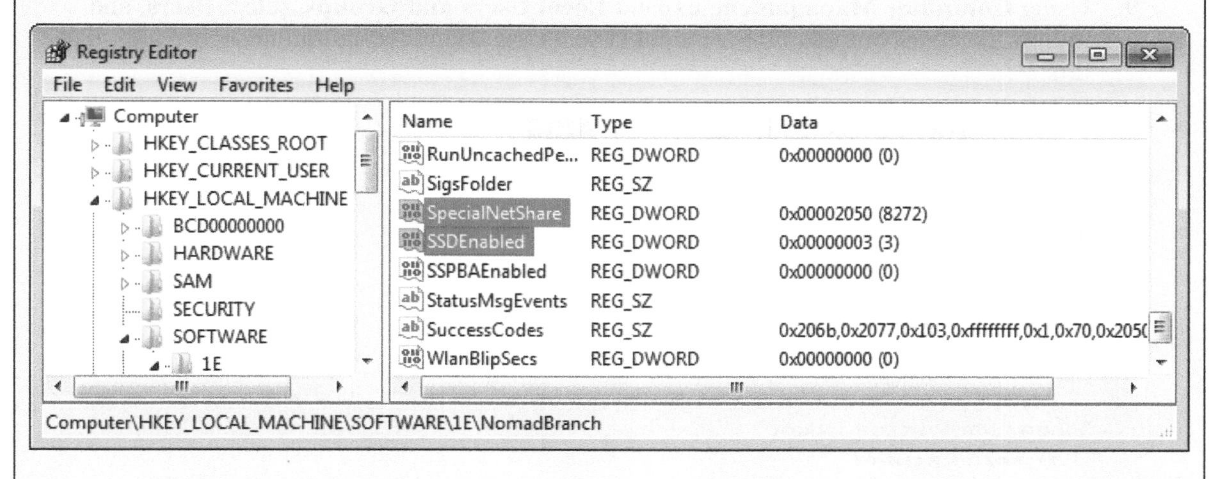

A common mistake is incorrectly setting these values and mixing up the hexadecimal and decimal values.

7. Review the Nomad share (**NomadSHR**) configuration. From a **Command prompt**, run the following command:

```
net share
```

8. The share has been configured as non-hidden and can be accessed by going to **\\PC0002** and then double-click the **NomadSHR**.

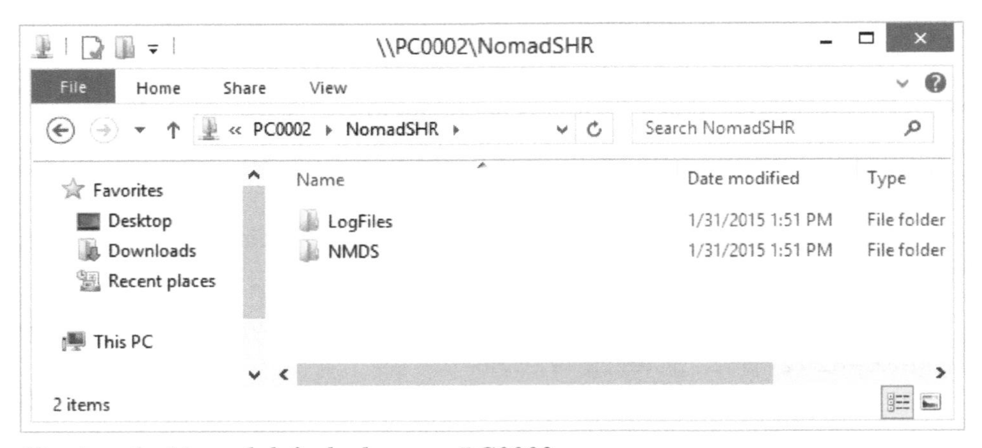

Viewing the Nomad default share on PC0002.

9. Using **Computer Management**, expand **Local Users and Groups**, select **Users**, and review the **SMSNomadP2P&** account. The user account configuration should look like this:

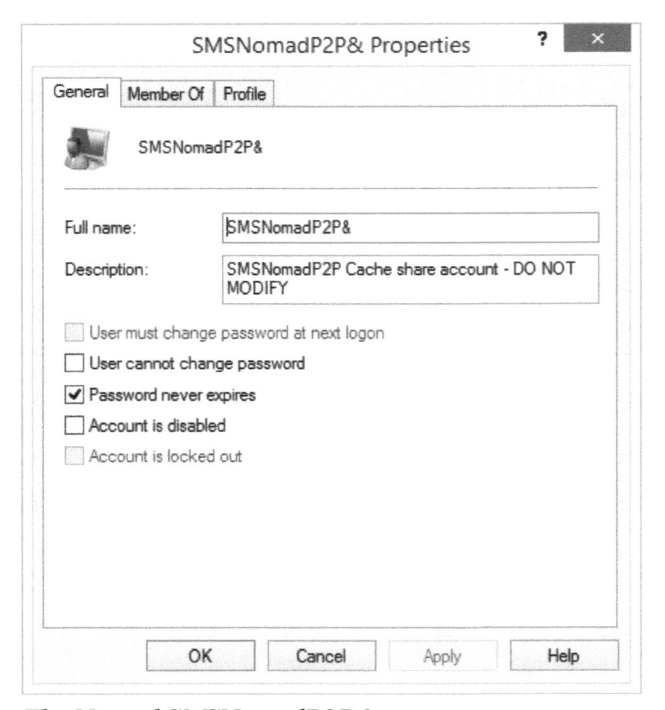

The Nomad SMSNomadP2P& account.

10. Copy **cmtrace.exe** from **\\CM01\SMS_PS1\tools** to **C:\Tools** (you need to create the folder).

11. In the **C:\tools** folder, open **CMTrace**, click **Yes** to make it the default viewer for LOG files, and then open **C:\ProgramData\1E\NomadBranch\logfiles\NomadBranch.log**.

12. In **CMTrace**, search for **SpecialNetShare**. You should find something like this:

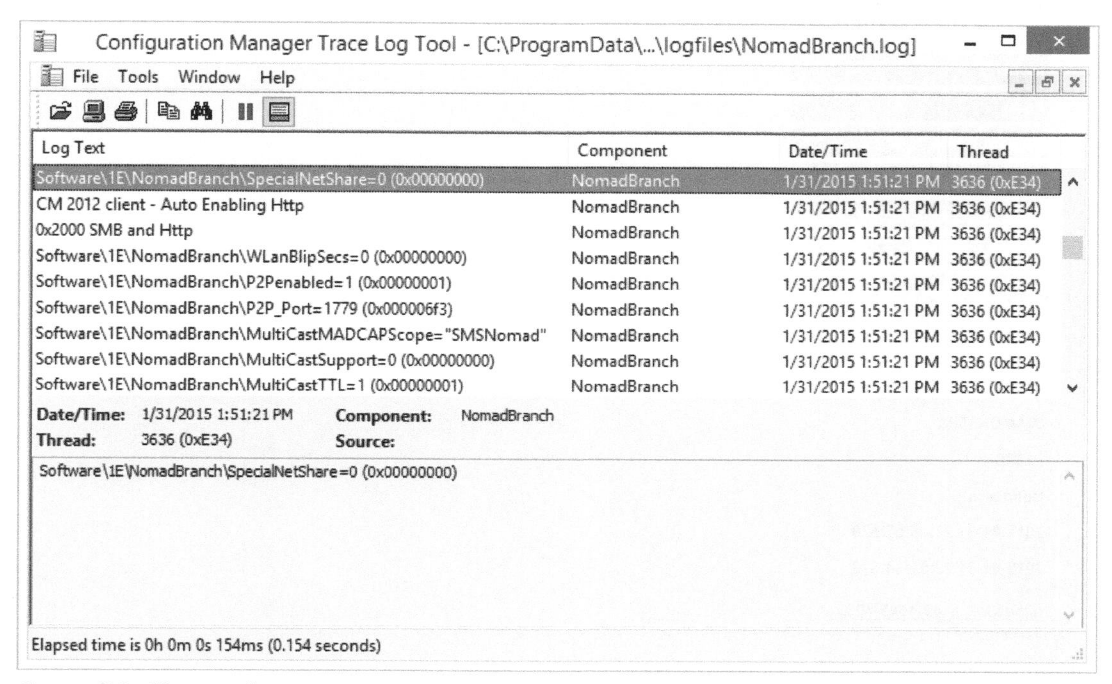

SpecialNetShare values.

Note: When the ConfigMgr 2012 client or ConfigMgr DP role is detected, there are several settings that are added "on the fly." One of them is the value for SpecialNetShare. It defaults to 0, and when either of these roles is detected, it changes to a value of 0x2000 hexadecimal, which enables Nomad for SMB and HTTP transfers. This behavior is not the same for a ConfigMgr 2007 environment.

13. Leave the **NomadBranch.log** open in CMTrace.

14. Using the **Registry Editor**, in the **HKLM\SOFTWARE\1E\NomadBranch** key, configure the **SpecialNetShare** value with **2050 (hexadecimal)**

15. Review the log file. Look for **SpecialNetShare Option = 0x10 (hidden Share)**.

16. Validate that the **NomadSHR$** share is working by browsing to **\\PC0002\ NomadSHR$**.

17. Now, see whether ActiveEfficiency is working properly by searching for **ActiveEfficiency** in the **NomadBranch.log.** You should see **httpstatus 200 from server 'activeefficiency' port 80**.

18. Open **Internet Explorer** and browse to **http://ActiveEfficiency/ActiveEfficiency/devices**.

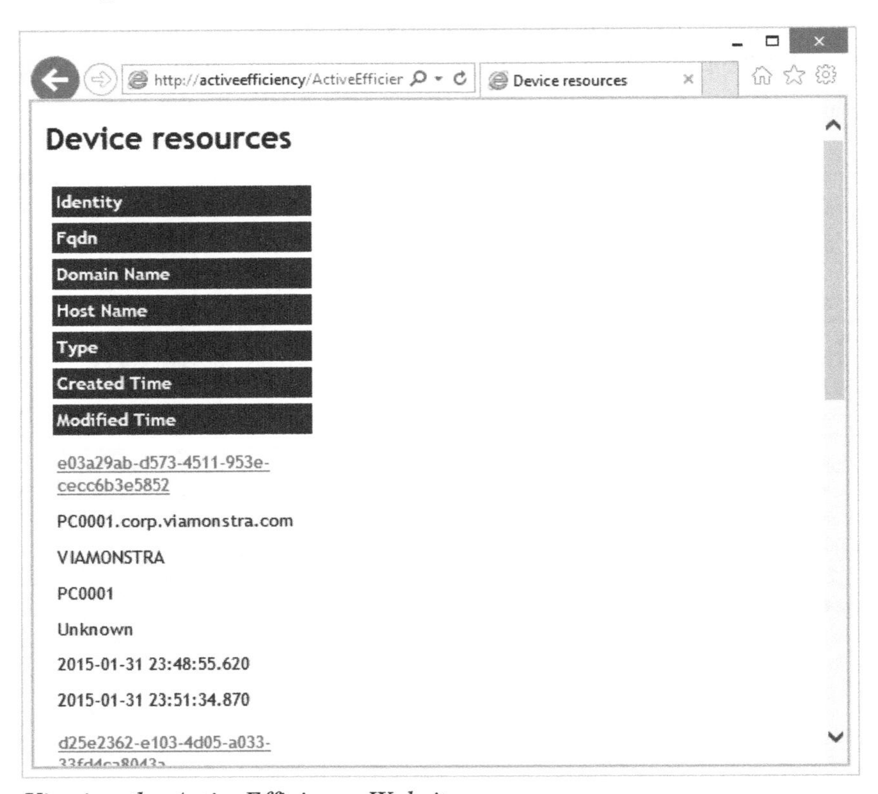

Viewing the ActiveEfficiency Website.

Creating the SCCM_Sources Folder Structure

1. Log on to **CM01** as **VIAMONSTRA\Administrator**.
2. Create a folder structure by running the following script in an elevated **PowerShell** prompt:

   ```
   C:\Labfiles\Scripts\Create-ConfigMgrFolders.ps1
   ```

3. The **Create-ConfigMgrFolders.ps1** script creates the following folder structure and also shares the **D:\Logs** as **Logs$** and **D:\SCCM_Sources** folder as **SCCM_Sources$**. The script also assigns the correct permissions.

   D:\MigData

   D:\Logs

   D:\SCCM_Sources

   D:\SCCM_Sources\OSD

D:\SCCM_Sources\OSD\Boot

D:\SCCM_Sources\OSD\DriverPackages

D:\SCCM_Sources\OSD\DriverSources

D:\SCCM_Sources\OSD\MDT

D:\SCCM_Sources\OSD\OS

D:\SCCM_Sources\OSD\Settings

D:\SCCM_Sources\Software

D:\SCCM_Sources\Software\Adobe

D:\SCCM_Sources\Software\Microsoft

Creating a Nomad Branch Package and Deployment

1. Log on to **CM01** as **VIAMONSTRA\Administrator**.
2. Browse to **C:\Labfiles\Sources\NomadBranch v5.2.100.32\ConfigMgr2012**.
3. Copy **NomadBranch.msi** and **NomadBranch-x64.msi** to **D:\SCCM_Sources\Software\NomadBranch** (you need to create the folder).
4. Open the **ConfigMgr console** and in the **Software Library** workspace, expand **Application Management / Packages**.
5. Create a **New Package from Definition** with the following settings:
    - Package Definition: For the **Publisher**, browse to **D:\SCCM_Sources\Software\NomadBranch\NomadBranch-x64.msi**.
    - Source Files: **Always obtain source files from a source folder**.
    - Source Folder: **\\CM01\SCCM_Sources$\Software\NomadBranch**
    - Nomad Settings: **<Default>**
    - Summary: **<Default>**
6. Select the **1E NomadBranch x64** package, select the **Programs** tab, and replace the **Per-system unattended** program's command line with:

```
msiexec.exe /qn /I NomadBranch-x64.msi SPECIALNETSHARE=8272
MULTICASTSUPPORT=0
PLATFORMURL=http://activeefficiency/activeefficiency
SSDENABLED=3
```

7. Create a New Package from Definition for the x86 installer with the following settings:
   - Package Definition: For the **Publisher**, browse to **D:\SCCM_Sources\Software\NomadBranch\NomadBranch.msi**.
   - Source Files: Always obtain source files from a source folder.
   - Source Folder: **\\CM01\SCCM_Sources$\Software\NomadBranch**
   - Nomad Settings: **<Default>**
   - Summary: **<Default>**
8. Select the **1E NomadBranch** package, select the **Programs** tab, and replace the Per-system unattended Program's command line with:

```
msiexec.exe /qn /I NomadBranch.msi SPECIALNETSHARE=8272
MULTICASTSUPPORT=0
PLATFORMURL=http://activeefficiency/activeefficiency
SSDENABLED=3
```

9. Distribute the content of the two Nomad packages to the **CM01** distribution point.
10. In the **Assets and Compliance** workspace, create a collection called **Deploy Nomad Branch**, limit it to **All Systems**, and add **PC0001**, **PC0003**, and **PC0004** as direct members.
11. Deploy the **1E NomadBranch x64** package to the **Deploy Nomad Branch** collection:
    - Software: **Per-system unattended**
    - Collection: **Deploy Nomad Branch**
    - Content: **<Default>**
    - Deployment Settings: **Required**
    - Scheduling: **As Soon as possible**
    - User Experience: **Allow users to run the program independently of assignments**.
    - Distribution Points: **<Default>**
12. Right-click the **Deploy Nomad Branch** collection, and select **Client Notification / Download Computer Policy**.
13. Log on to **PC0001** and open the **Software Center**. (The installation should start shortly.)
14. Validate that the deployment completes successfully on **PC0001**, **PC00003**, and **PC0004**.

Advanced Windows Deployment Lab Hydration

To facilitate the material covered in this book, a group of packages, programs, deployments, and collections must be built. In the interest of maintaining focus on the subject at hand, we have taken the liberty of creating a PowerShell script, HydrationCMConfiguration.ps1, that automate the entire process for you. When the script completes, you will have a sample environment that includes the following:

- Collections: AWD deployment collections
- Collection membership: PC000x's added as direct collection membership
- Packages: AWD sample packages
- Programs: AWD deployment programs for Nomad software and task sequences
- Deployments: AWD sample deployments
- Alternate content provider settings: Enabled on all AWD packages

Note: The script is using functions from the CM12 Function Library written by Kaido Järvemets, which Kaido graciously allowed us to include the library in the book sample files. Also, if you ever wondered, AWD is just an acronym for Advanced Windows Deployment ☺

The advanced hydration script is part of the book sample files, and in addition you need to request and download a somewhat long list of software. Once completed you will have two folders, one named AWD_Software, and one named Sources.

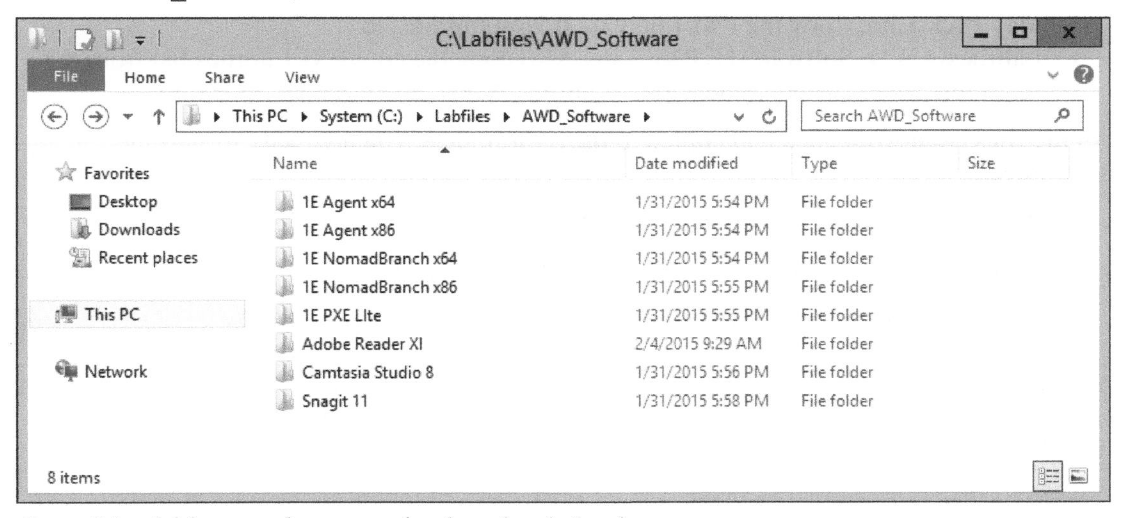

One of the folders used to store the downloaded software.

The following list includes the software needed and the folders to which to copy it:

- **1E Agent x64.** Copy 1EAgent-x64.msi to C:\Labfiles\AWD_Software\1E Agent x64.
- **1E Agent x86.** Copy 1EAgent.msi to C:\Labfiles\AWD_Software\1E Agent x86.
- **TechSmith Snagit 11.** Copy snagit.msi to C:\Labfiles\AWD_Software\Snagit 11.
- **TechSmith Camtasia Studio 8.** Copy camtasia.msi to C:\Labfiles\AWD_Software\Camtasia Studio 8.

Note: You can get the MSI packages of the TechSmith products from their FTP site: ftp://ftp.techsmith.com/Pub/products.

- **Adobe Reader XI.** Copy AdbeRdr11000_en_US.msi to C:\Labfiles\AWD_Software\Adobe Reader XI.

Note: The MSI package for Adobe Reader can be downloaded from ftp://ftp.adobe.com/pub/adobe/reader/win/11.x/11.0.00/en_US.

- **Nomad Branch X64.** Copy NomadBranch-x64.msi to C:\Labfiles\AWD_Software\1E NomadBranch x64.
- **Nomad Branch X86.** Copy NomadBranch.msi to C:\Labfiles\AWD_Software\1E NomadBranch x86.
- **Nomad Download Monitor.** Copy the NomadBranch v5.2.100.32 setup files (including NomadBranchGUI.msi) to C:\Labfiles\Sources\NomadBranch v5.2.100.32.
- **Deploy PXE Lite.** Copy the PXELite v2.2.0.26 setup files to C:\Labfiles\AWD_Software\1E PXE Lite. Also copy the copyPXELitefiles.bat from the book sample files (Scripts folder) to C:\Labfiles\AWD_Software\1E PXE Lite.

After all the files are downloaded and copied to the right folders, you are ready to start the hydration process.

1. On **CM01**, log on as **VIAMONSTRA\Administrator**.
2. Open the **PowerShell (x86) ISE** elevated as **Administrator**.
3. Open **C:\Labfiles\Scripts\HydrationCMConfiguration.PS1**.

Real World Note: You can view the progress of the script by opening the SMSProvider log file at D:\ConfigMgr\Logs\SMSProv.log. This log gives a lot of insight and helps in troubleshooting when developing scripts for ConfigMgr.

4. Run the script.
5. When prompted, click **Run Once**.
6. When the script completes, review the output and ensure that no errors have occurred.

7. Open the **ConfigMgr console** and review the collections and the members in the AWD folder.

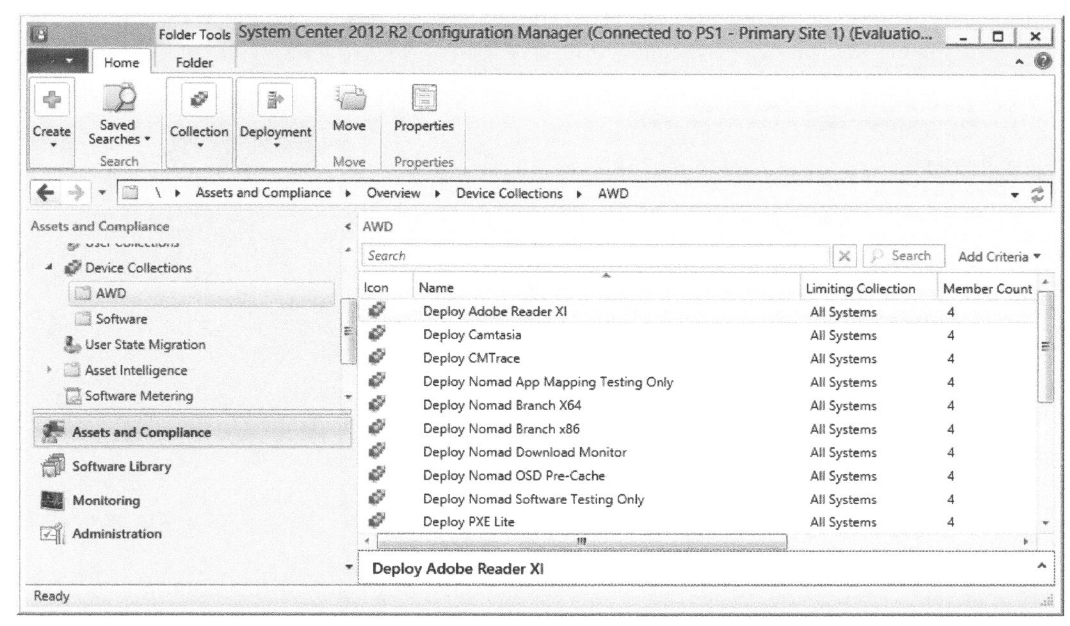

Viewing the device collections created post-ConfigMgr hydration.

8. Browse to the **Software Library** and review the new packages and programs created.

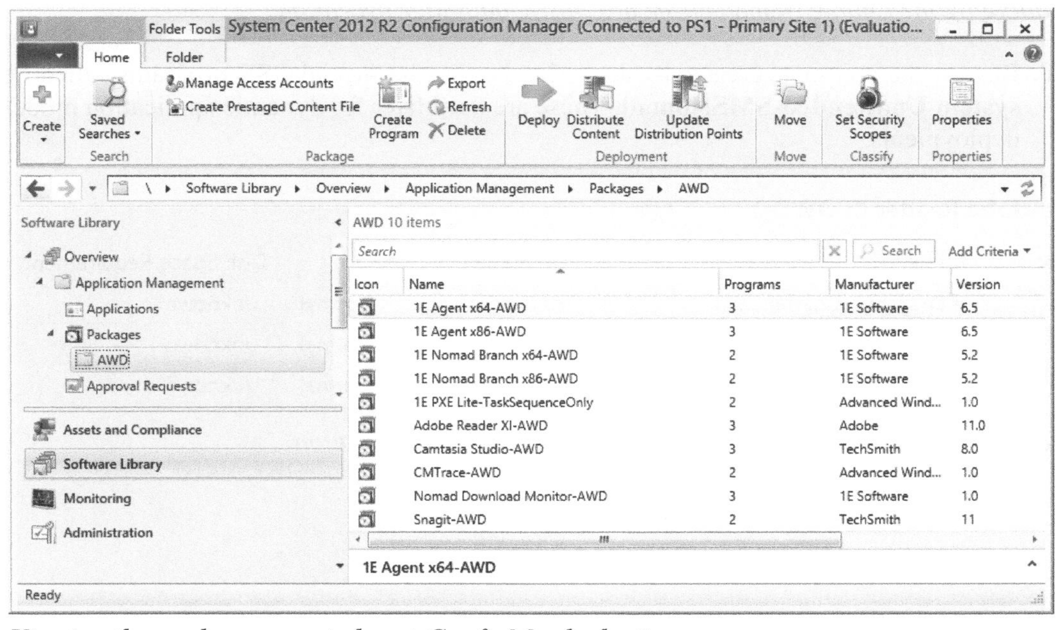

Viewing the packages created post-ConfigMgr hydration.

9. Right-click a package and review the **Nomad** tab. The AWD script selected the **Enable Nomad** check box on these new packages.

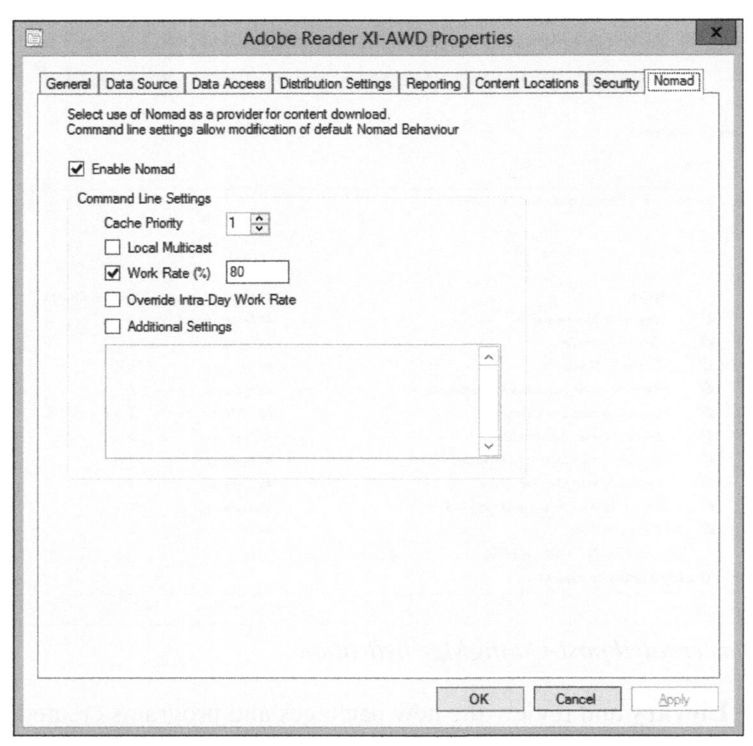

Validating the Enable Nomad check box post-ConfigMgr hydration.

10. Review the programs created by the script. Notice the special OSD programs called **Per-system Unattended-SMSNomad**. These are used later for dynamic application model deployments.

Adobe Reader XI-AWD

Icon	Name	Command Line	Run	Disk Space Requirement	User Des
	Per-system Unattended	msiexec.exe /q...	Normal	Unknown	
	Per-system Unattended-SMSNomad	smsnomad.exe...	Normal	Unknown	
	Per-system uninstall	msiexec.exe /q...	Normal	Unknown	

Validating programs that were created post-ConfigMgr hydration.

11. The AWD script also distributes the packages and creates available deployments to the collections so that the software can be installed.

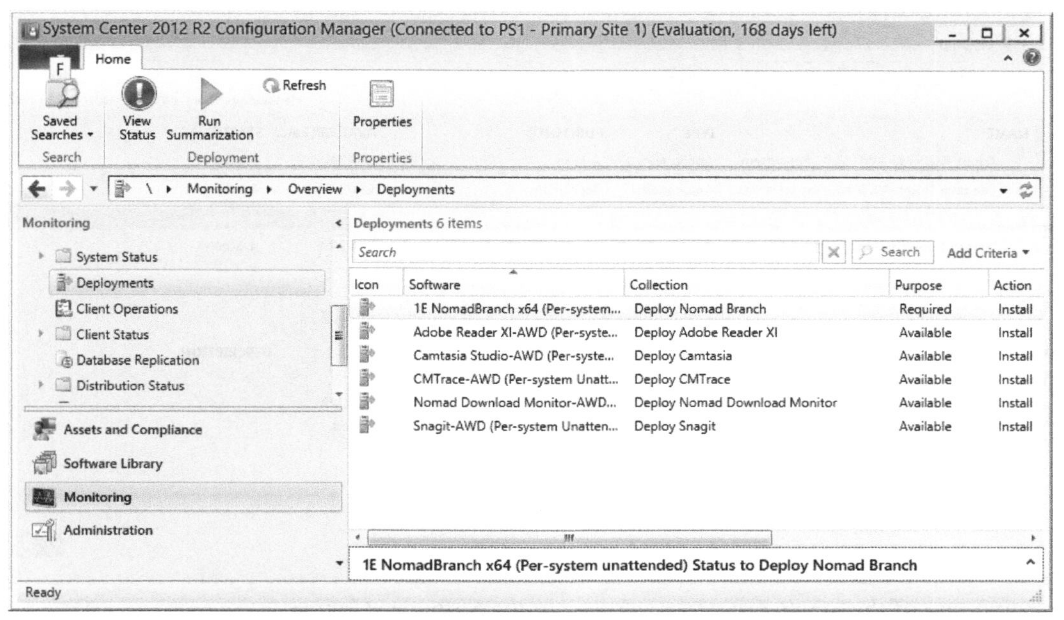

Validating deployments post-ConfigMgr hydration.

Deploying a Nomad-Enabled Package

With Nomad now installed on your client, you can deploy some software to it and see how the content transfer process differs with a Nomad-enabled package.

1. Log on to **PC0003** as **VIAMONSTRA\Administrator**.
2. Run a ConfigMgr machine policy refresh to get the current policy that includes the new deployments.
3. Open **Software Center** and install **CMTrace-AWD 1.0 - Per-system Unattended**.

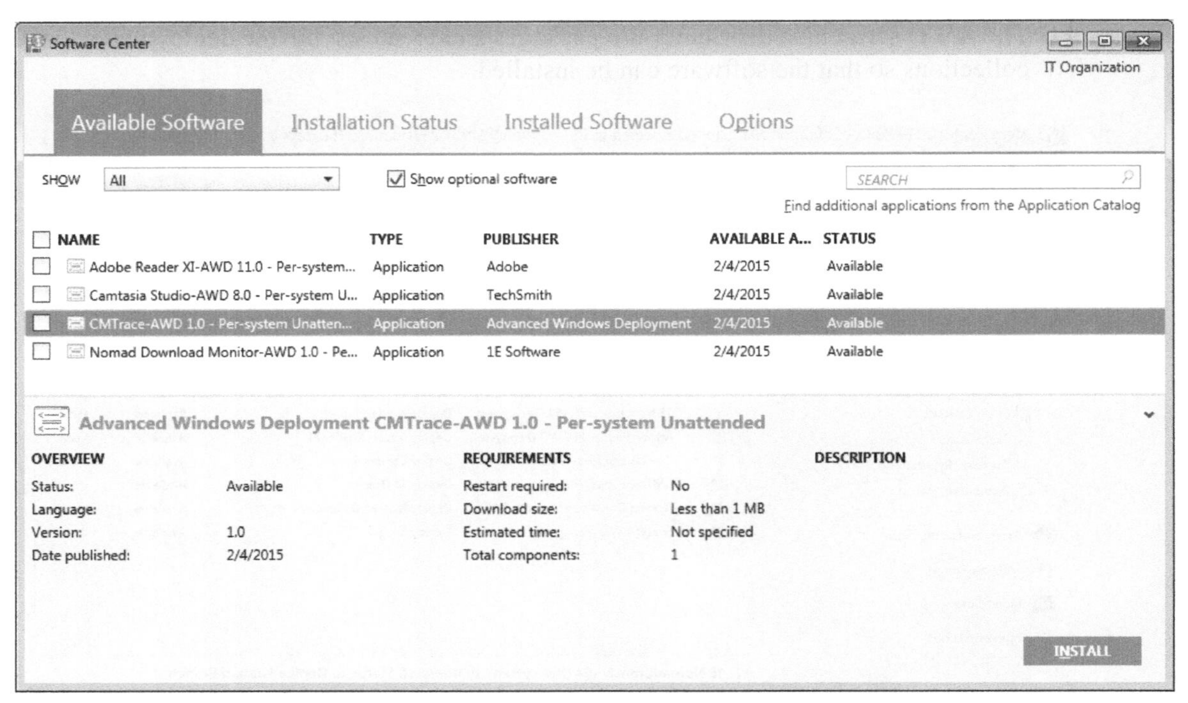

Viewing one of the newly created packages in the Software Center.

4. Open **CMTrace** from **C:\Windows\cmtrace.exe**.
5. With **CMTrace**, open the **NomadBranch.log** file from **C:\ProgramData\1E\NomadBranch\LogFiles**.
6. Review the transfer as seen in the following figures and descriptions:
    a. **ICcmAlternateDownloadProvider.DownloadContent:** The resulting log entry from where you clicked the INSTALL button within Software Center.
    b. **ContentID:** The corresponding ConfigMgr PackageID
    c. **Content Version:** The source version of the respective ConfigMgr package
    d. **Source:** The HTTP path to the package in the distribution point's content library
    e. **Destination:** The ConfigMgr client cache location (hard-linked to C:\ProgramData\1E\NomadBranch)

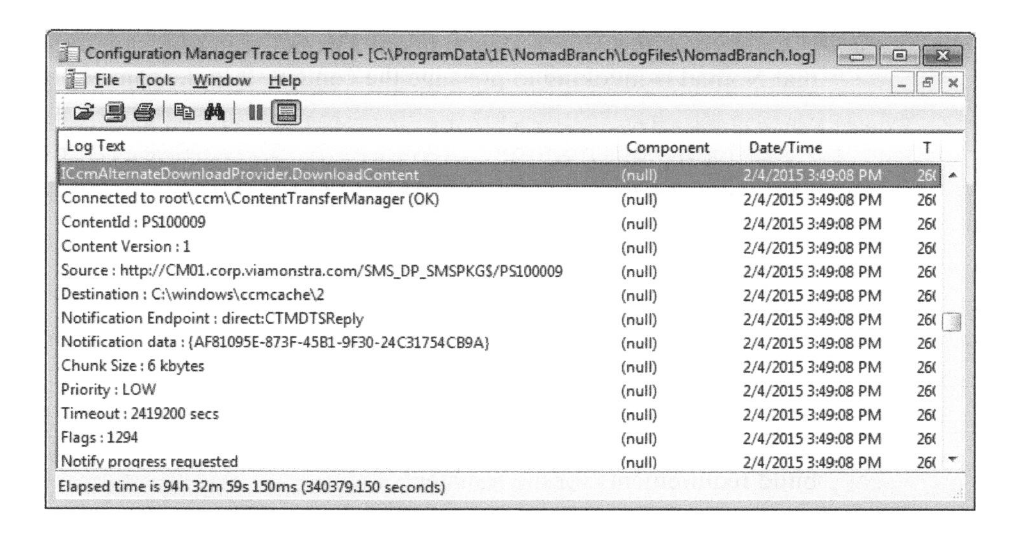

f. A little down the log, there are two more important lines:

- **Package data:** The alternate content provider settings. (You can view these on a package by using Get-CMPackage.)
- You also can see the path you are connecting to on the DP by looking at **Order 0 URL….**

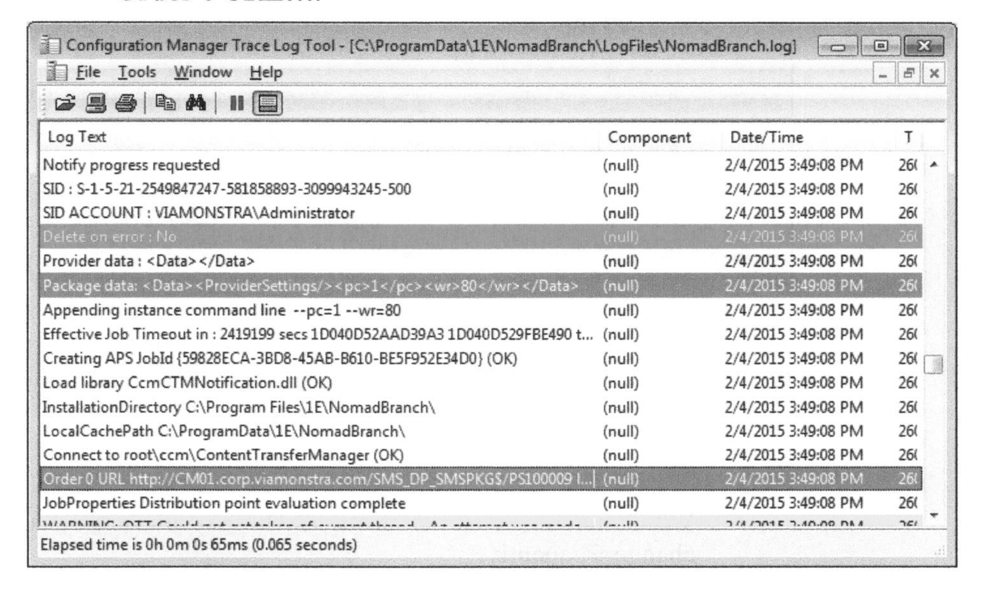

g. If you look at the source of **StartCopyThread**, you can actually see the command that Nomad is invoking to prestage the content. It looks something like this:

```
StartCopyThread:- --pp="http://CM01.corp.viamonstra.com/
SMS_DP_SMSPKG$/PS100009" --prestage --contentid=PS100009
--timeout=2419200 --ver=1 --pc=1 --wr=80 [*no curr dir*]
```

- The value **pc** = cache priority
- The value **wr** = work rate

You can view these settings on a package-by-package basis by viewing the Nomad tab.

It is also important to note what Nomad is doing by checking the **Component** column in the log. Right now you are gathering information for the copy thread to build requirements for the transfer.

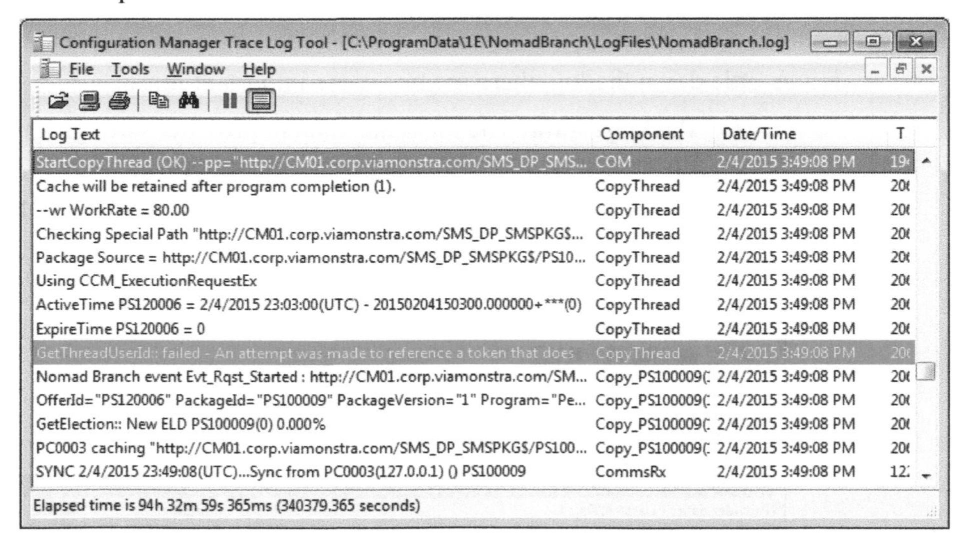

h. Now before you can start the copy, Nomad must perform an election to determine the transfer master. This section of the log is extremely important.

- What is the value for **P2PMASTER** in your log file?

  ____

- Which machine won the election? These results are dynamic and can change frequently.
- Will the next machine that starts the transfer be elected as the master?

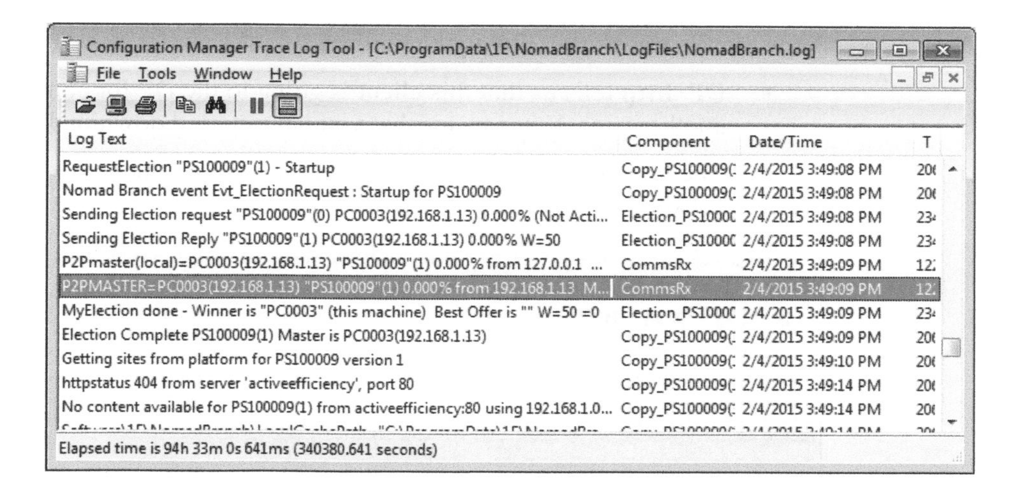

i. The next few important lines appear only when local content is not available. They show the connection and validation process with a distribution point.

- **Connection::SetDownloadSource = DP** means that there are no local copies of this content on this subnet. This means that Nomad will go back to the DP as the master for this subnet.
- **Requesting ".LsZ" Generation…** is what creates the .LsZ file on the DP.

  You should be able to browse to **http://cm01/lszfiles** and view the .LsZ file for PS100009.

Note: Your Package ID may be different from these screen shots.

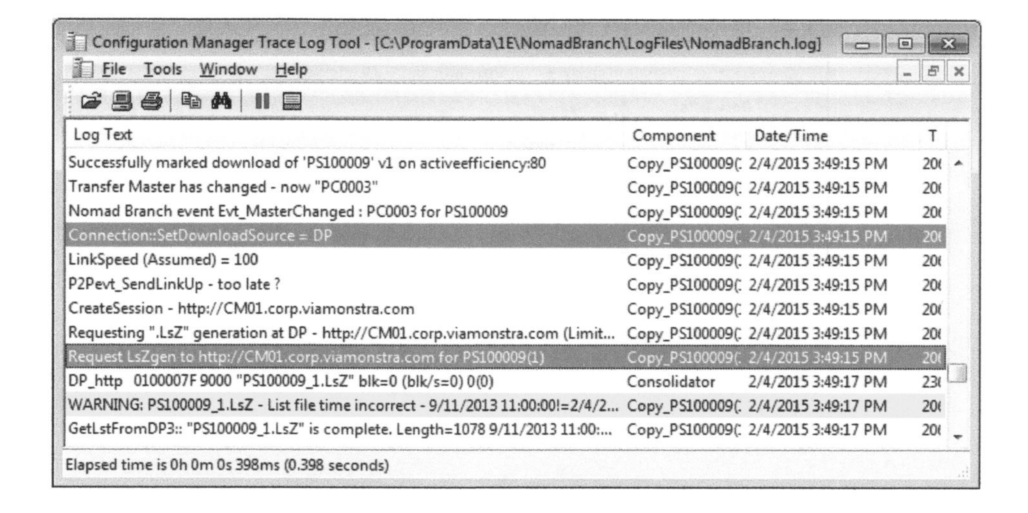

j. Now the file transfer is actually beginning.

- **DP_http** tells us that this client is going to the DP for content and not to another peer. You can see that you have started downloading cmtrace.exe.
- The next line, **PkgCacheStatusSet…**, gives us the percentage of the package downloaded.

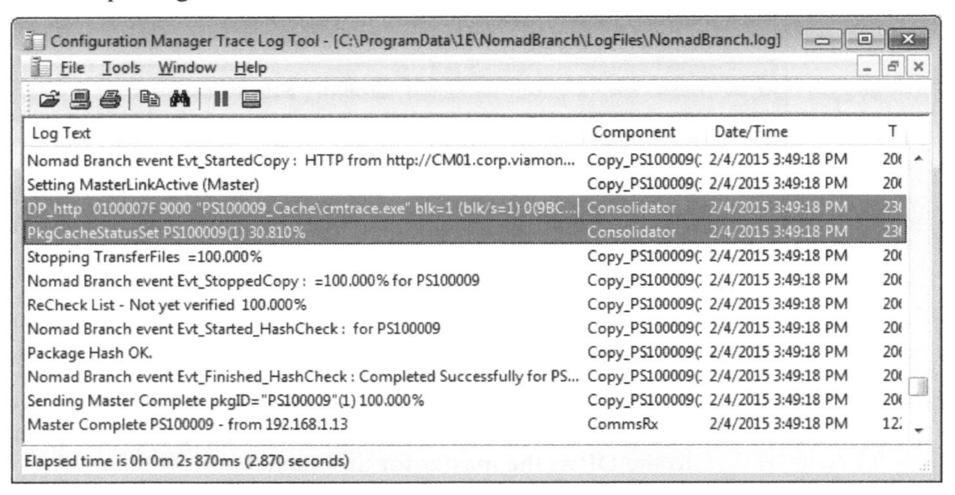

k. Notice that the cache files are in both locations. Remember this is because Nomad hard-links the content automatically into the ConfigMgr client cache (without duplicating the hard disk space requirements).

Review the contents of the cache files.

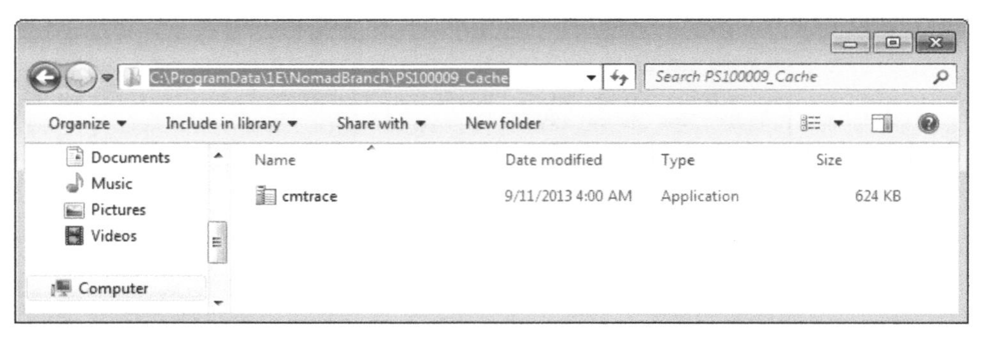

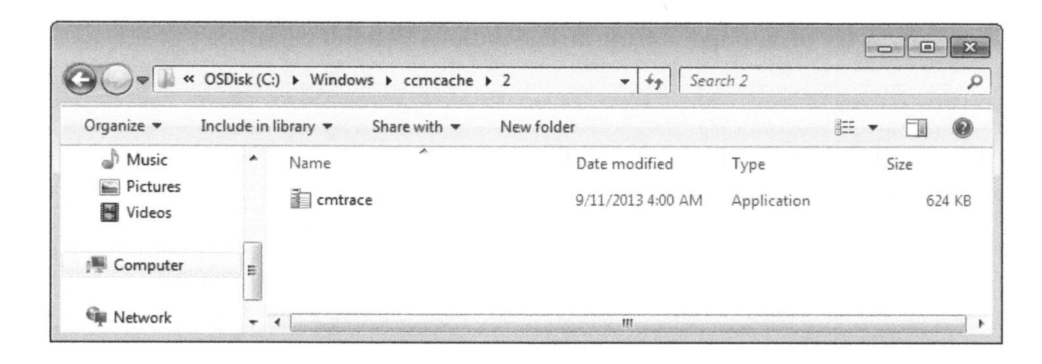

1. Now, from the **C:\ProgramData\1E\NomadBranch** folder, open the **.LsZ** file with **Notepad** and check the contents.

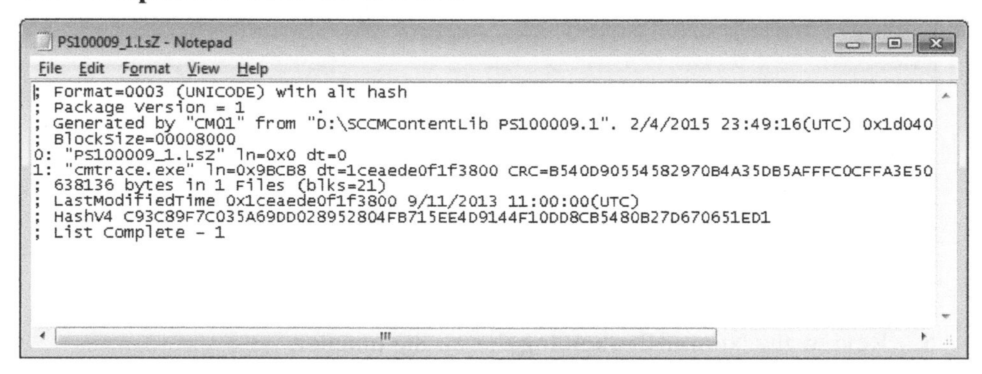

Note: The .LsZ file indicates that there are 21 blocks. If you multiply 32767 × 21, you get approximately the number of bytes total in the package. There are two items in the .LsZ file in the preceding image: Item 0, which is the .LsZ file itself, and item 1, which is the cmtrace.exe file (the content of the package).

7. Now try installing the **Camtasia Studio-AWD 8.0** package.

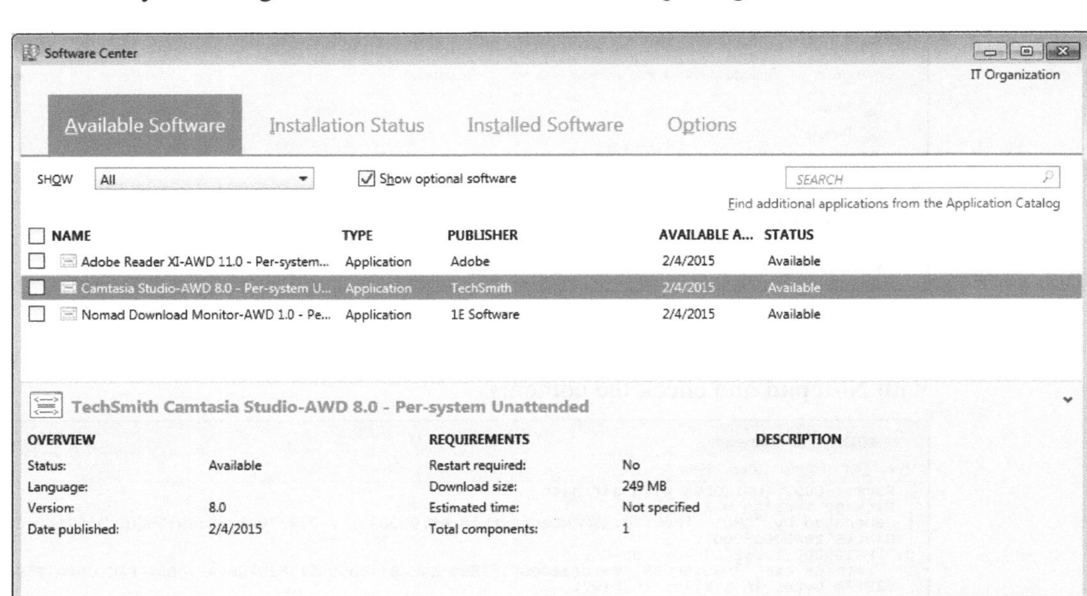

Viewing the Camtasia Studio package in the Software Center.

8. Review the **NomadBranch.log** during the transfer.
9. Check the **.LsZ** file created in **C:\ProgramData\1E\NomadBranch**.
10. Check the **Nomad cache** in **C:\ProgramData\1E\NomadBranch**.
11. On **PC0002**, log on as **VIAMONSTRA\Administrator**.
12. Using **Software Center**, install **CMTrace** and **Camtasia Studio**.
13. Review the **C:\ProgramData\1E\NomadBranch\logfiles\NomadBranch.log**.
14. What is different in this log from the first transfer?

    ____

    ____

15. Which machine was selected as the master?

    ____

16. You should see something like this in your logs on **PC0002**.

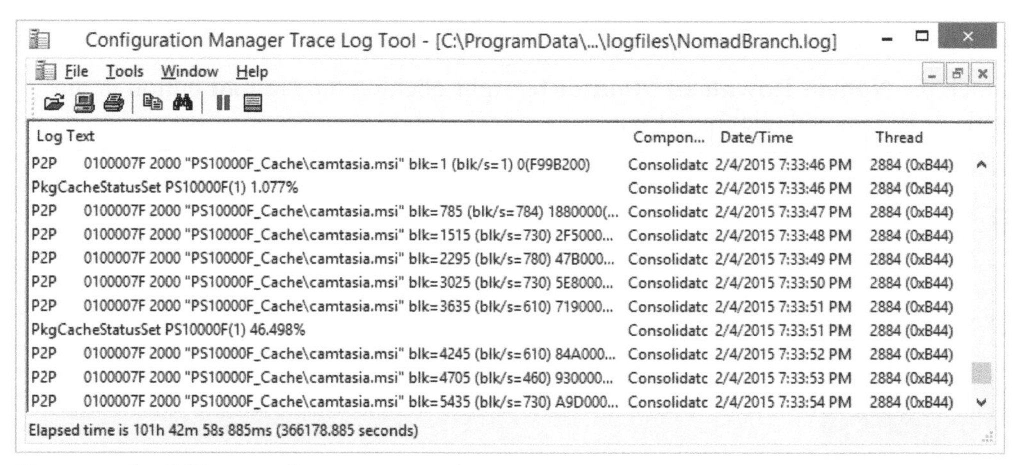

Viewing the P2P transfer process with Nomad.

Real World Note: P2P in the NomadBranch.log file is a clear indication that the content is transferring from a peer. DP_HTTP tells us that this machine went back to the distribution point. Clients often wonder if a client is actually going back to a DP or peering from another machine. This is a quick way to determine where the traffic is going.

17. On **PC0002**, install the **Nomad Download Monitor** package from the **Software Center**.

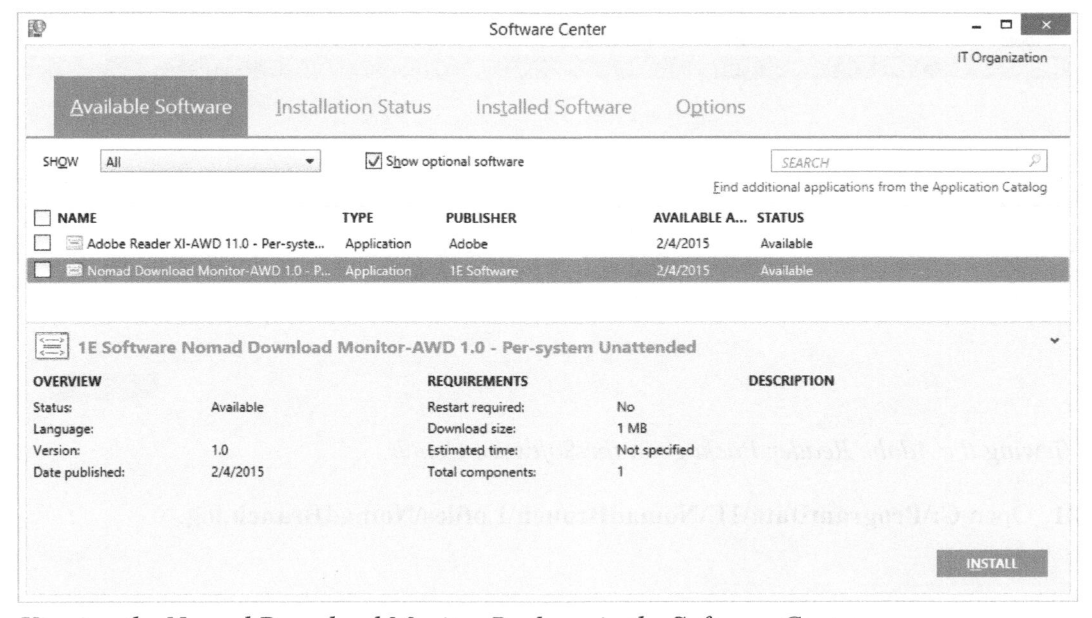

Viewing the Nomad Download Monitor Package in the Software Center.

18. On the **Start screen**, type in **NomadBranchGUI**, and select it.
19. Launch the **Nomad Download Monitor** by right-clicking the **Nomad** button in the notification area and clicking **Open**.

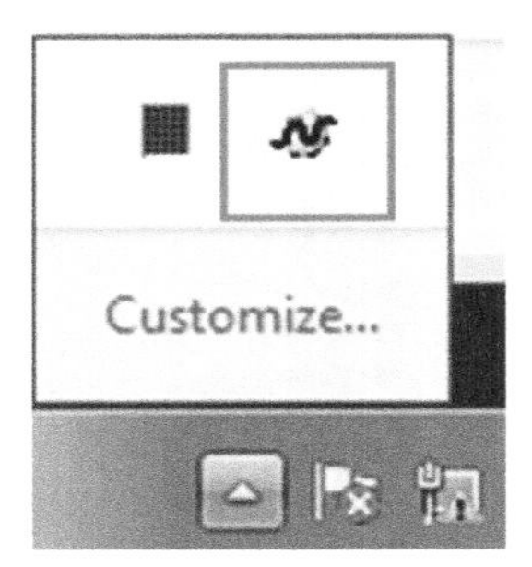

The Nomad Branch GUI in the system tray.

20. Now install **Adobe Reader XI-AWD 11.0** from the **Software Center**.

Viewing the Adobe Reader Package in the Software Center.

21. Open **C:\ProgramData\1E\NomadBranch\Lofiles\NomadBranch.log**.

22. Leave both the **Nomad Branch** log file and the **Nomad Download Monitor** open in side-by-side windows.

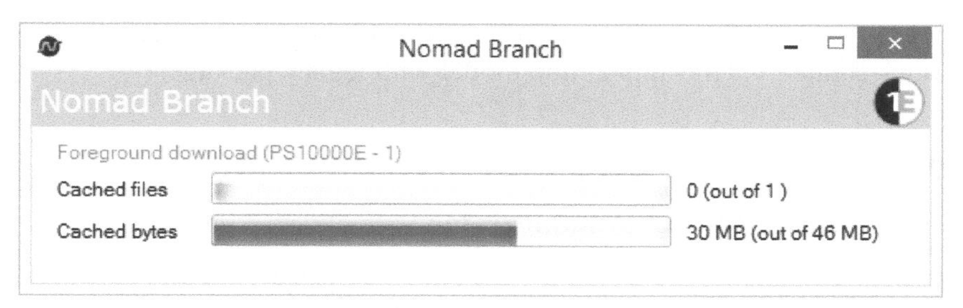

An example of the Nomad Branch GUI in action.

Real World Note: You can also install Nomad Branch GUI (Download Monitor) in advanced mode by adding UI=1 to the setup install string: msiexec.exe /i NomadBranchGUI.msi UI=1 /qn

Another option to start Nomad Branch GUI in advanced mode is to change the UI value in HKLM\SOFTWARE\Wow6432Node\1E\NomadBranch\is from 0 to 1.

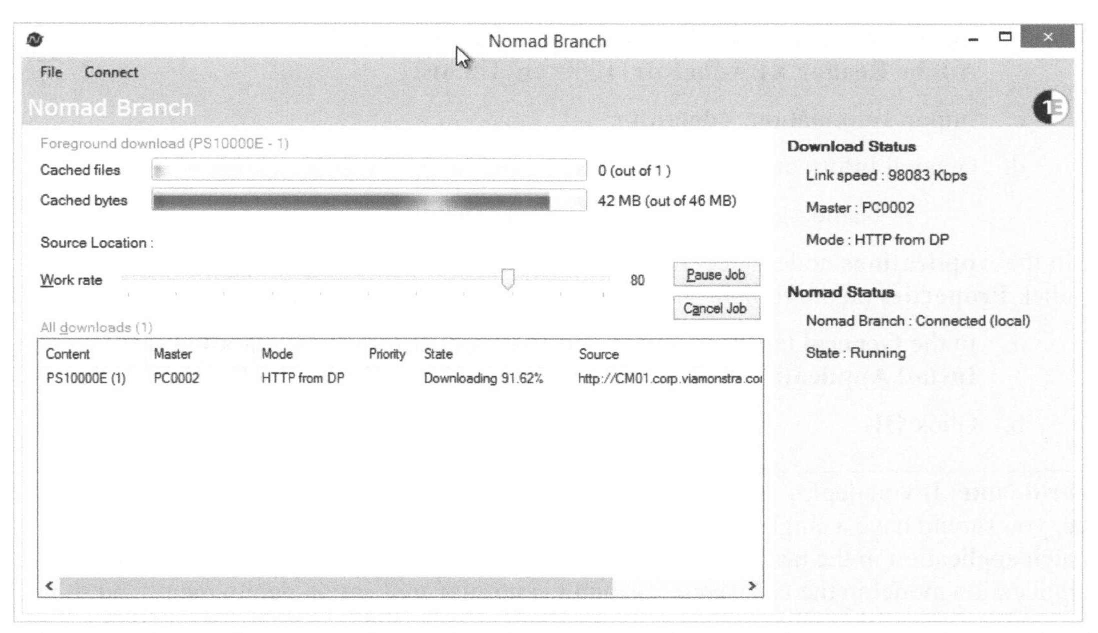

The Nomad Branch GUI in advanced mode, showing additional details about the download.

Deploying Applications Using Nomad

In this guide, you create an application for the application model in ConfigMgr. This application will be used later, in Chapter 8, for OSD. But for now you deploy this application to compare how Nomad handles applications created via the application model with legacy packages.

Create the Adobe Reader XI – OSD Install application

1. On **CM01**, log on as **VIAMONSTRA\Administrator**.
2. Using the **ConfigMgr console**, in the **Software Library** workspace, expand **Application Management**, right-click **Applications**, and select **Create Application**.
3. Use the following settings for the **Create Application Wizard**:
   a. General
      i. **Automatically detect information about this application from installation files**
      ii. Type: **Windows Installer (*.msi file)**
   b. Location: **CM01\SCCM_Sources$\AWD_Software\Adobe Reader XI\AdbeRdr11000_en_US.msi**
   c. Import Information: **<default>**
   d. General Information
      Name: **Adobe Reader XI - OSD Install**
4. In the **Applications** node, select the **Adobe Reader XI - OSD Install** application, and click **Properties** on the ribbon. Then complete the following:
   a. In the **General** tab, select the **Allow this application to be installed from the Install Application task sequence action without being deployed** check box.
   b. Click **OK**.

Real World Note: If you deploy an application created via the application model in a task sequence, you should have a single deployment type. There is no way to reference a deployment type of such application in the task sequence. This means if you are deploying applications created via the application model in the task sequence, and via normal application deployment, you should have two applications of the same software. We recommend you add something like "OSD Install" as a suffix. When done, applications that are designed for a task sequence can be easily identified and used.

It is still best practice to use legacy packages inside any task sequence. This is because the applications created via the application model are designed to be deployed in multiple scenarios, which introduces additional logic into the software installation process. This can become difficult to troubleshoot, and as a result only legacy packages should be used whenever possible.

Deploy Adobe Acrobat Reader Application Using Nomad

1. On **CM01**, create a new deployment for **Adobe Reader XI - OSD Install** application.
2. Configure the deployment to use the **Deploy Adobe Reader XI** collection, specify **CM01** as the distribution point, and make the deployment **Available**.
3. On **PC0004**, log on as **VIAMONSTRA\Administrator** and using **Software Center**, install both the **CMTrace**, and the **Adobe Reader XI - OSD Install** application (you may have to refresh the machine policy to see the new deployment).
4. Using **CMTrace**, review the **NomadBranch.log** file.
5. Review the **Nomad cache**.
6. What was different in an application deployment vs. a package deployment?

   ____

   ____

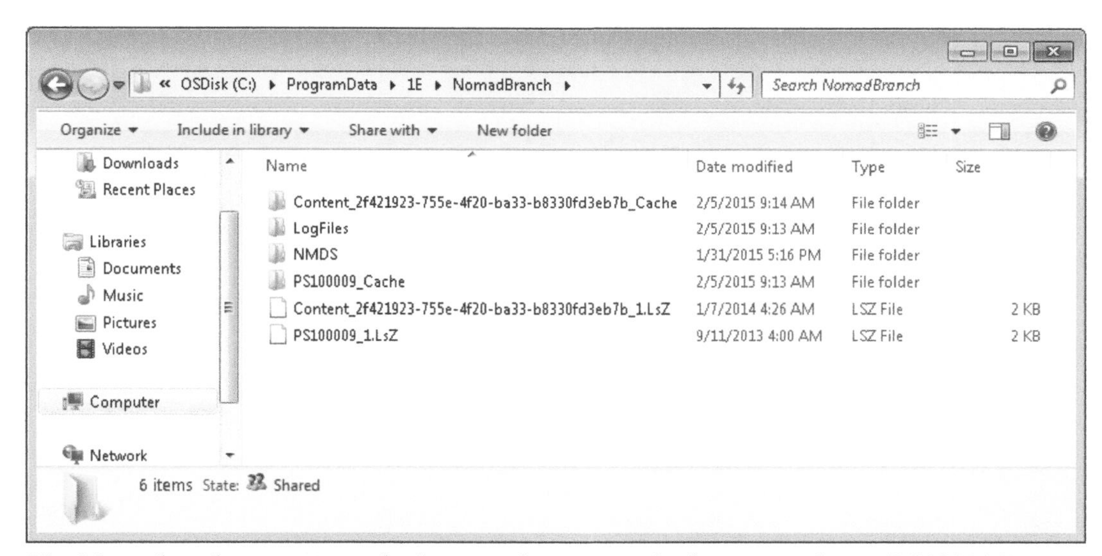

The Nomad cache containing both an application and a legacy package (PS100009).

Chapter 6

Nomad for Software Updates

In this chapter, you learn how Nomad can be integrated into your software update solution and about the benefits achieved with using this delivery mechanism for workstation and server patching.

Nomad-Enabled Software Updates

Enabling Nomad for software update management in ConfigMgr is performed with a single option that is available from Client Settings. It uses its technology to ensure that updates are quickly distributed across the enterprise with no impact to network traffic.

The burden of patching servers and workstations has been a heavily involved process for years due to the complexities and sheer size of software updates in an enterprise. Now, by combining the automation capabilities of Automatic Deployment Rules in ConfigMgr with that of 1E Nomad Enterprise, patching becomes a fire-and-forget process.

Nomad for Software Updates Key Concepts

By not having to be concerned with delivery traffic, your software update processes become much more streamlined:

- Definition updates are now managed by a single ADR and a completely automated process.
- The process ensures your software is updated up to three times a day.
- The requirement to prestage updates across the enterprise has been eliminated.
- Remediation solutions for zero-day threats can now be deployed quickly and without concerns related to increased network utilization.
- A greater number of patches can be deployed simultaneously.

Nomad Cache

Similar to packages and applications created via the application model that are deployed to a client, software updates downloaded from ConfigMgr into the Nomad cache to be offered to peer clients upon request. This can be both a blessing and a curse, as using a staged deployment method for your Automatic Deployment Rules allows you to target, say, one machine at each branch for not only pilot testing of a monthly patch cycle, but also to pre-cache for the production rollout, reducing the actual required deployment window. However, there is no automated method to download patches to a client that it has evaluated as not required, creating a potential delta across site workstations for disparate hardware/software combinations.

There are only two ways to address this:

1. Bundle the updates as a standard SCCM package, and have a package execution script that extracts the cached folders and corresponding LsZ files and then performs a NomadBranch activation.
2. Analyze reports to ascertain patches that will not be included in both sets and create a deployment with advanced availability to permit clients to download required packages well in advance.

Nomad for Software Updates Log files

When monitoring the software update process on a Nomad-enabled client, the process is very similar to a native ConfigMgr client software update process without Nomad. The only real difference is that you view the NomadBranch.log instead of the CAS.log to view actual software update downloads.

Log Name	Description
NomadBranch.log	Records all information pertaining to the Nomad client. Package requests for software updates are logged here, as well as information regarding download details and content location. Located in C:\ProgramData\1E\NomadBranch\LogFiles
WindowsUpdate.log	A Windows log that provides information about when the Windows Update Agent connects to the WSUS server and retrieves the software updates for compliance assessment and whether there are updates to the agent components Located in C:\Windows
ScanAgent.log	Provides information about the scan requests for software updates, what tool is requested for the scan, the WSUS location, and so forth Located in C:\Windows\CCM\Logs
UpdatesDeployment.log	Records details about deployments on the client, including software update activation, evaluation, and enforcement. Verbose logging shows additional information about the interaction with the client user interface. Located in C:\Windows\CCM\Logs
UpdatesHandler.log	Records details about software update compliance scanning and about the download and installation of software updates on the client Located in C:\Windows\CCM\Logs

Log Name	Description
UpdatesStore.log	Provides information about the compliance status for the software updates that were assessed during the compliance scan cycle Located in C:\Windows\CCM\Logs
WUAHandler.log	Records details about the Windows Update Agent on the client when it searches for software updates Located in C:\Windows\CCM\Logs

Nomad for Software Updates Design Notes (ViaMonstra)

As we've already discussed, configuring Software Updates to use Nomad is performed by a single check box. As a result, there's no actual conceptual design for using Nomad with Software Updates. However, it's worth mentioning the operational differences that are introduced when you incorporate Nomad.

With ConfigMgr 2012, Automatic Deployment Rules provide administrators with increased automation capabilities for deploying software updates. When configuring these rules, they are deployed in such a fashion that delays occur during the update process across the enterprise, to ensure time for adequate quality assurance processes and to ensure that small groups of machines are targeted at a time to reduce network impact. Though this type of implementation requires administrators to revisit the software update configuration only when patches need to be removed from production, it often takes weeks, or even months, to completely patch an enterprise.

By introducing Nomad into the software update solution, deployments no longer need to be staggered to prevent network overutilization. All production workstations can be safely patched after QA processes are complete. This allows for many fewer ADR deployments to manage, as well as a drastic reduction in the amount of time required to fully patch an operating environment.

Validating Nomad and Software Updates

In order to use Nomad to deliver software updates through ConfigMgr, three things need to be in place: 1) Nomad is required to be installed and configured on a client's distribution point; 2) Nomad is required to be installed and configured on the client; and 3) Nomad must be enabled to use software updates in ConfigMgr Client Settings. Providing these three items have been implemented correctly, clients utilize Nomad software distribution for the delivery of software updates.

To ensure that clients are actually using Nomad to download these updates, simply check log files for ultimate confirmation. Because all software distribution in ConfigMgr is handled the same way, the process to validate the content source is the same. Open the NomadBranch.log and look for details pertaining to packages being downloaded that are named with a GUID rather than a PackageID.

Nomad Cache and Updates

As a client downloads software updates from ConfigMgr via Nomad, they are cached locally and shared via the NomadSHR$ share. They are stored in the same fashion as regular software packages, but are stored as GUID names rather than PackageIDs, aligning with other views of the software updates.

Chapter 7

Building the Perfect Reference Image Using MDT 2013

In order to deploy operating systems using ConfigMgr, it is a best practice to first create a reference image to deploy rather than simply using the install.wim file that is included on the Windows 8.1 ISO file. This allows you to perform customizations to the reference image that are applicable to all enterprise clients, effectively reducing the time it takes to perform an operating system deployment. For the purposes of this book, you need to get to a point where you have a stable image that you can deploy and optimize with Nomad.

The goal of this chapter is to focus only on the build of a reference image and captured WIM that will be used in later chapters.

MDT 2013 Key Concepts

Although functionality exists within ConfigMgr to build and create a reference image, it isn't the desirable method. This is mainly for two reasons: 1) The build and capture process in ConfigMgr does not provide a customizable interface during the build process, preventing you from performing manual modifications to the image; and, 2) as part of the installation process, ConfigMgr automatically installs the ConfigMgr client, effectively eliminating the possibility of deploying this image in other environments or using tools outside of ConfigMgr.

The beauty of using the Microsoft Deployment Toolkit is that it was created by the same team who developed operating system deployment in ConfigMgr, and as a result the process of using task sequences is almost exactly the same. This drastically reduces the learning curve for ConfigMgr administrators to learn MDT and vice versa.

MDT 2013 has the following key components:

- ADK 8.1 is required for the installation of MDT 2013.
- All work activities related to MDT can be performed in the Deployment Workbench or PowerShell.
- Application installations can be scripted as part of the reference image build process.
- Role and feature installations can be automated.
- MDT-style deployments are referred to as Lite Touch.

- Advanced customizations can be performed by using settings files and the MDT database.
- Monitoring should be enabled to track in-flight deployments.
- Driver injection can be automated for WinPE and Windows deployments.
- Lite Touch installations can be performed via deployment share, boot media, or PXE.
- Linked deployment shares can be created for larger deployments.
- An *image factory* can be created using community scripts.

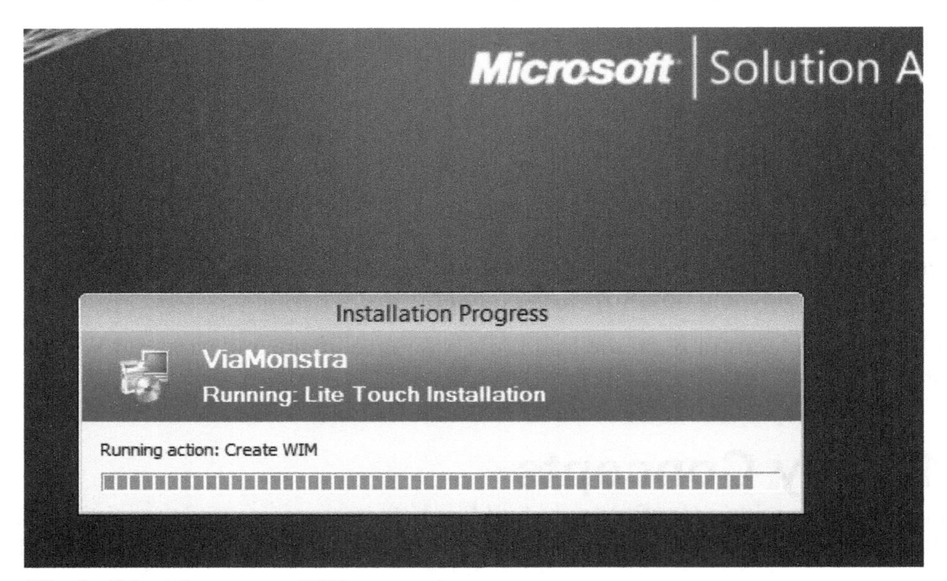

The build and capture OSD process.

Reference Image Version Management

One of the major issues with reference "Gold" images is configuration drift. It is imperative that a proper set of processes be implemented for the management of these images. We have come across customers who are unaware as to how their Gold images were created. When it comes time to make changes to that image, they normally crack the WIM and inject files or have some other antiquated way of managing it.

There is a better solution. Mikael Nystrom, a Microsoft MVP, has created a great solution for building a *reference image factory*. You see how to do this later in the chapter.

MDT 2013 Key Log Files and Paths

When monitoring the deployment using MDT 2013, there are several log files that can be used for troubleshooting. The following list represents the most common log files that can be found in the field. The log files used in MDT for deploying sequences are very similar to those used for operating system deployment in ConfigMgr. This is logical because both products were developed by the same team. There is one major difference: in ConfigMgr, you can see the actual task sequence execution process detailed in the Execmgr.log. In MDT, however, this file does not exist. Instead, a log file from legacy days rears its head, the BDD.log. Here are a few of the logs that we consistently view when performing deployments using MDT:

- **BDD.log.** Short for Business Desktop Deployment log, the BDD.log has been around since this was the product name for Microsoft Deployment Toolkit. It contains all the information normally available in the Execmgr.log, as well as a high-level rollup for the other active deployment log files.
- **LiteTouch.log.** Created during Lite Touch Installation (LTI) deployments, this log resides in the %WinDir%\System32\ccm\logs directory.
- **Setupact.log.** This is the primary log file for most errors that occur during the Windows installation process.
- **SMSTS.log.** This file is created when the task sequence first starts and logs all actions performed during the task sequence execution process. It will move around during the process of imaging a workstation, and depending on the stage of the installation, it may reside in one of the following: %Temp%, %WinDir%\System32\CCM\Logs, C:_SMSTaskSequence, or C:\SMSTSLog.
- **WPEinit.log.** When a client is rebooted into WinPE as a result of a task sequence restart step, this file is created to log the initialization process.

MDT 2013 Reference Image Factory Conceptual Design (ViaMonstra)

The conceptual design for ViaMonstra's reference image factory is show in the following image. The goal of this design was complete automation and management of the Gold reference image creation process. This is accomplished by using a series of scripts developed by Microsoft MVP Mikael Nystrom called Image Factory V2.

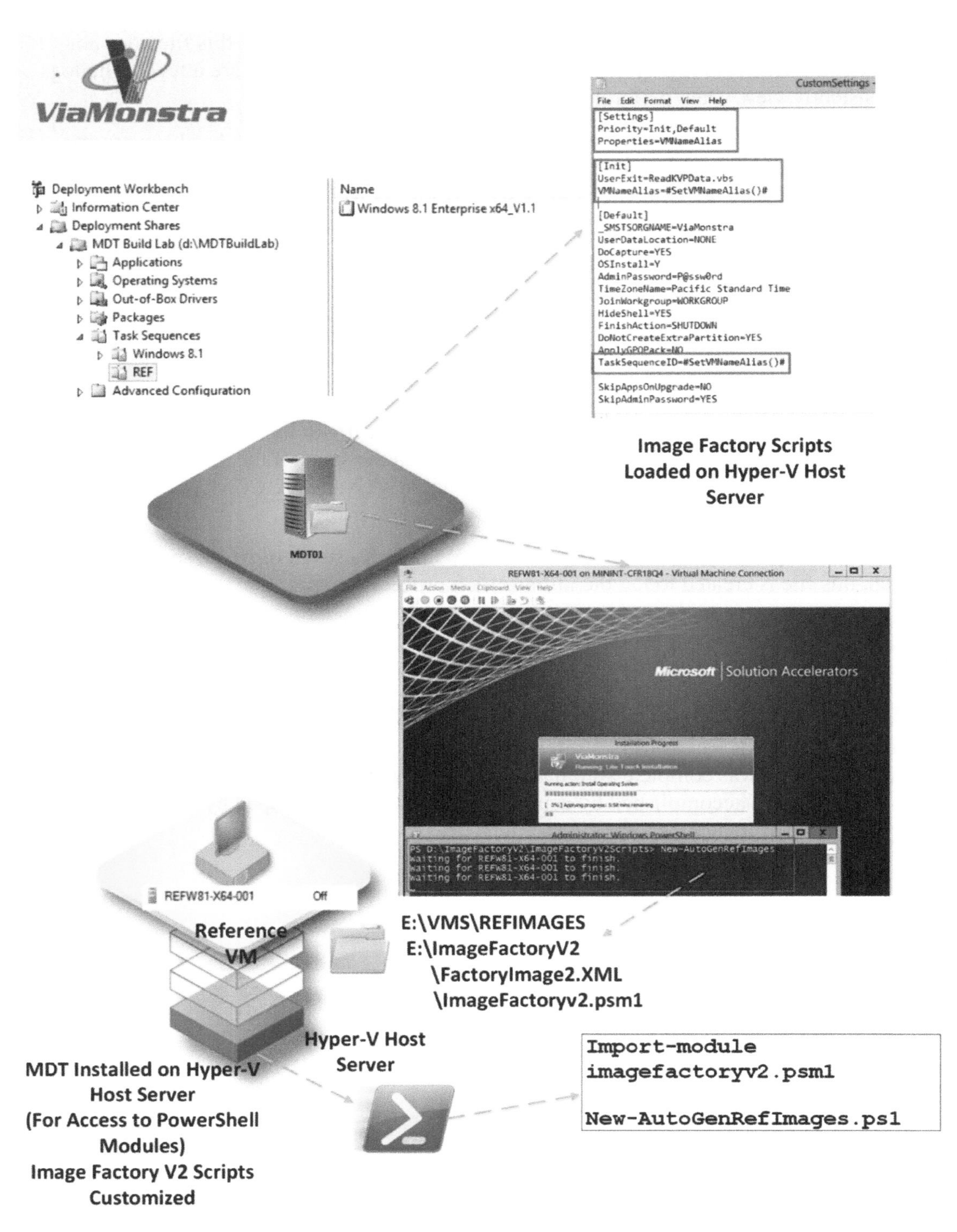

The ViaMonstra MDT reference image conceptual design.

Creating the Server Structure

Review the Service Account

1. On **DC01**, log on as **VIAMONSTRA\Administrator**.
2. Using **Active Directory Users and Computers**, in the **ViaMonstra \ Service Accounts** OU, review the service accounts that are created. For the MDT 2013 build and capture process, the **MDT_BA (MDT 2013 Build Account)** is used.

Install MDT 2013

1. On **MDT01**, log on as **VIAMONSTRA\Administrator**.
2. Download **MDT 2013** to the **C:\Labfiles\Sources\MDT 2013** folder.
3. Install **MDT 2013** by running the following command in an elevated **PowerShell** prompt:

```
& msiexec.exe /i 'C:\Labfiles\Sources\MDT 2013\
MicrosoftDeploymentToolkit2013_x64.msi' /qb /l*v
C:\Windows\Temp\MDTInstall.log
```

Create and Share the Logs Folder

1. Using **File Explorer**, create the **D:\Logs** folder and share it as **Logs$**. (Use the Advanced Sharing dialog box and not the Share dialog box.)
2. Allow the **Everyone** group **Change** permissions (Sharing Permissions).
3. Allow the **MDT_BA** account **Modify** permissions (NTFS Permissions).

Copy Sample Files

1. Using **File Explorer**, navigate to the folder where you download the sample files for this book.
2. Copy the **LTI Support Files** folder to **C:\Labfiles**.

Create the MDT Build Lab Deployment Share

1. Using the **Deployment Workbench** (via the Start screen), right-click **Deployment Shares** and select **New Deployment Share**. Use the following settings for the **New Deployment Share Wizard**:
    - Deployment share path: **D:\MDTBuildLab**
    - Share name: **MDTBuildLab$**
    - Deployment share description: **MDT Build Lab**
    - Options: **<default settings>**

> **Real World Note:** There is no real point of configuring the remaining options because they will be updated anyway when you edit the rules in the Deployment share later.

2. Verify that you can access the **MDT01\MDTBuildLab$** share.

Configure Permissions for the Deployment Share

Using **File Explorer**, allow the **MDT_BA** account **Modify** permissions (NTFS Permissions) to the **D:\MDTBuildLab\Captures** folder.

Adding Windows 8.1 Installation Files

Import the Windows 8.1 Operating System

1. On **MDT01**, mount the **Windows 8.1 Enterprise x64.iso** media.

> **Real World Note:** You can easily grab the latest download from Microsoft to ensure that the service packs and updates are up to date. You also can use offline servicing to update the WIM file before using it as the base.

2. Using the **Deployment Workbench**, expand the **Deployment Shares** node, expand **MDT Build Lab**, select the **Operating Systems** node, and create a folder named **Windows 8.1**.
3. Right-click the **Windows 8.1** node and select **Import Operating System**. Use the following settings for the **Import Operating System Wizard**:
    - **Full set of source files**
    - Source directory: **E:**
    - Destination directory name: **W81X64**
4. After adding the operating system, using the **Deployment Workbench**, in the **Windows 8.1** node, change the operating system name to **Windows 8.1 Enterprise x64**.

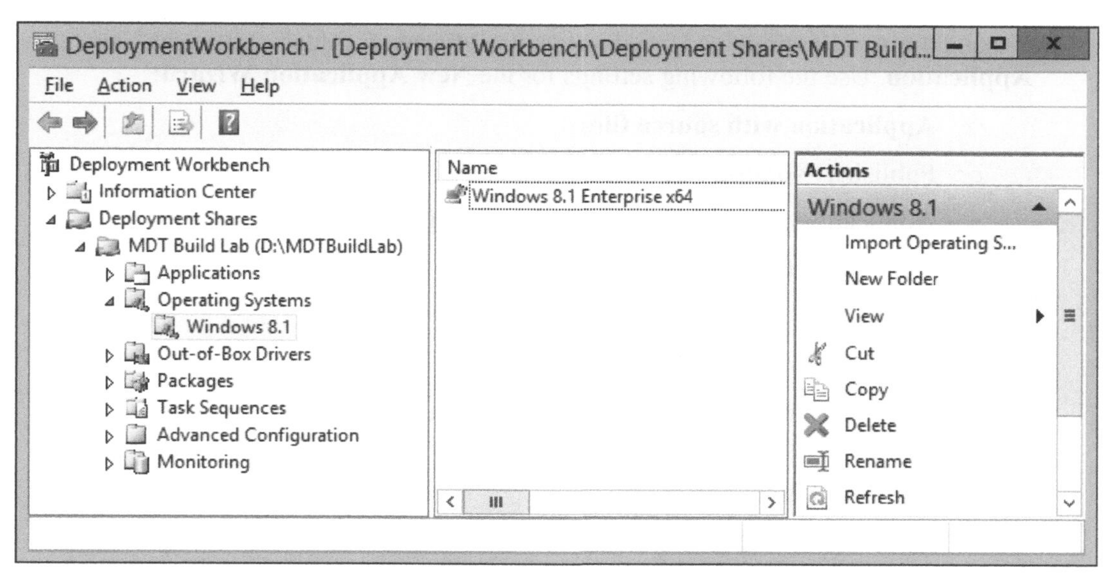

The Windows 8.1 node after renaming the imported operating system.

Adding Applications

In this section's step-by-step guides, you create the following applications:

- Install - Microsoft Office 2013 Pro Plus - x86
- Install - Microsoft Visual C++ 2005 SP1 - x86-x64
- Install - Microsoft Visual C++ 2008 SP1 - x86-x64
- Install - Microsoft Visual C++ 2010 SP1 - x86-x64
- Install - Microsoft Visual C++ 2012 - x86-x64

In these examples, we assume that you downloaded the software in this list to D:\Setup and that you have copied the book's sample files to C:\Labfiles on MDT01.

Note: All the Microsoft Visual C++ downloads can be found on the following page: http://support.microsoft.com/kb/2019667.

Add Office 2013

1. On **MDT01**, mount the **Office 2013 Pro Plus x86 VL.iso** media. (You can grab your own copy of the media and mount it into Hyper-V.)
2. Using the **Deployment Workbench**, expand the **Deployment Shares** node, expand **MDT Build Lab**, select the **Applications** node, and create a folder named **Microsoft**.

3. Expand the **Applications** node, right-click the **Microsoft** folder, and select **New Application**. Use the following settings for the **New Application Wizard**:
   - **Application with source files**
   - Publisher: **<blank>**
   - Application Name: **Install - Microsoft Office 2013 Pro Plus - x86**
   - Version: **<blank>**
   - Language: **<blank>**
   - Source Directory: **E:**
   - Specify the name of the directory that should be created: **Install - Microsoft Office 2013 Pro Plus - x86**
   - Command Line: **Setup.exe**
   - Working Directory: **<default>**

Automate the Office 2013 Setup

1. Using **Deployment Workbench**, in the **Applications / Microsoft** node, double-click the **Install - Microsoft Office 2013 Pro Plus - x86** application.
2. In the **Office Products** tab, click **Office Customization Tool**, and click **OK** in the **Information** dialog box.

Note: It may take a little while for the Office Customization Tool to start.

3. In the **Office Customization Tool** dialog box (which may take a while to load), select the **Create a new Setup customization file for the following product** option button and click **OK**. Use the following settings to configure the Office 2013 installation to be fully unattended:
   - Install Location and Organization Name

     Organization Name: **ViaMonstra**
   - Licensing and User Interface
     - **Use KMS client key**
     - **I accept the terms in the License Agreement**
   - Display Level: **None**
   - Modify Setup Properties

     Add the **SETUP_REBOOT** property and set the value to **Never**.
   - Modify User Settings

Expand **Microsoft Office 2013**, expand **Privacy**, select **Trust Center**, and enable the **Disable Opt-in Wizard on first run** setting.

4. In the **File** menu, select **Save**. Save the configuration as **0_ViaMonstraOffice2013ProPlus_x86.msp** in the **D:\MDTBuildLab\Applications\Install - Microsoft Office 2013 Pro Plus x86 \Updates** folder.

Real World Note: The reason for using a named beginning with zero (0) is that the Office 2013 setup applies updates in alphabetical order, and you want the setup to be the very first action.

5. Close the **Microsoft Office Customization Tool**, and click **Yes** in the dialog box.
6. In the **Install - Microsoft Office 2013 Pro Plus - x86** window, click **OK**.

Add Additional Applications via PowerShell

In this section, you use PowerShell to add more applications to MDT. In this guide, we assume you have done the following:

- Copied the Microsoft Visual C++ 2005 SP1 x86 and Microsoft Visual C++ 2005 SP1 x64 installation files (vcredist_x86.exe and vcredist_x64.exe) to the C:\Labfiles\LTI Support Files\MDT Build Lab\Applications\Install - Microsoft Visual C++ 2005 SP1 - x86-x64\Source folder.
- Copied the Microsoft Visual C++ 2008 SP1 x86 and Microsoft Visual C++ 2008 SP1 x64 installation files (vcredist_x86.exe and vcredist_x64.exe) to the C:\Labfiles\LTI Support Files\MDT Build Lab\Applications\Install - Microsoft Visual C++ 2008 SP1 - x86-x64\Source folder.
- Copied the Microsoft Visual C++ 2010 SP1 x86 and Microsoft Visual C++ 2010 SP1 x64 installation files (vcredist_x86.exe and vcredist_x64.exe) to the C:\Labfiles\LTI Support Files\MDT Build Lab\Applications\Install - Microsoft Visual C++ 2010 SP1 - x86-x64\Source folder.
- Copied the Microsoft Visual C++ 2012 x86 and Microsoft Visual C++ 2012 x64 installation files (vcredist_x86.exe and vcredist_x64.exe) to the C:\Labfiles\LTI Support Files\MDT Build Lab\Applications\Install - Microsoft Visual C++ 2012 - x86-x64\Source folder.

Note: The PowerShell script validates that the content is available before importing the applications into MDT 2013.

1. On **MDT01**, in an elevated **PowerShell** prompt (run as Administrator), run the following command:

   ```
   C:\Setup\Scripts\ImportMDTApplications.ps1
   ```

2. Using **Deployment Workbench**, select the **Applications / Microsoft** node, press **F5** to refresh the node, and then review the list of imported applications.

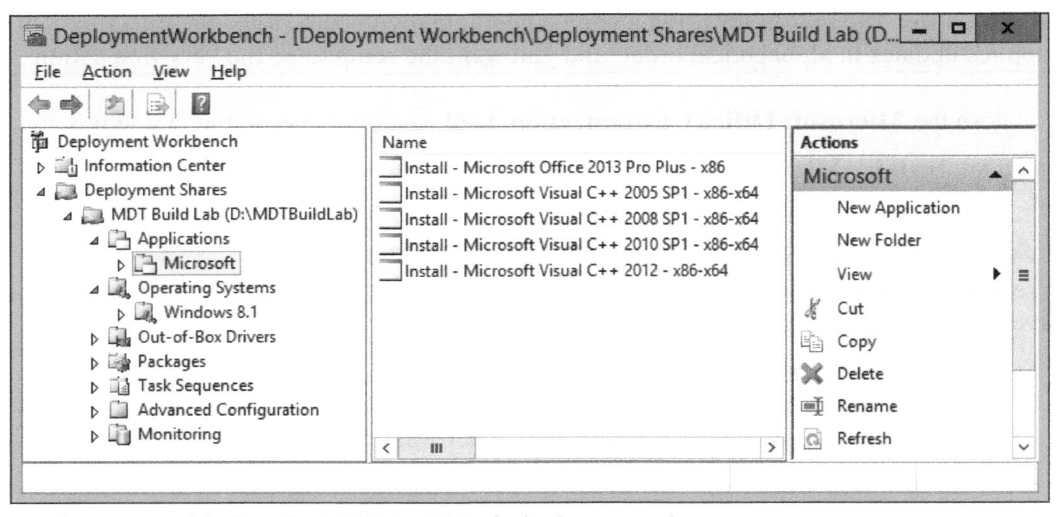

Applications added to the MDT Build Lab deployment share.

Creating the MDT Task Sequence

Create and Configure a Task Sequence

1. On **MDT01**, using the **Deployment Workbench**, in the **MDT Build Lab** deployment share, select the **Task Sequences** node, and create a folder named **Windows 8.1**.

2. Expand the **Task Sequences** node, right-click the **Windows 8.1** node, and select **New Task Sequence**. Use the following settings for the **New Task Sequence Wizard**:

   - Task Sequence ID: **REFW81-X64-001**
   - Task Sequence Name: **Windows 8.1 Enterprise x64**
   - Task Sequence Comments: **Reference Build**
   - Template**: Standard Client Task Sequence**
   - Select OS: **Windows 8.1 Enterprise x64**
   - Specify Product Key: **Do not specify a product key at this time**
   - Full Name: **ViaMonstra**

- Organization: **ViaMonstra**
- Internet Explorer Home Page: **about:blank**
- **Do not specify an Administrator password at this time**

Edit the Task Sequence

1. In the **Task Sequences / Windows 8.1** node, right-click the **Windows 8.1 Enterprise x64 Default Image** and select **Properties**.
2. In the **Task Sequence** tab, configure the **Windows 8.1 Enterprise x64** task sequence with the following settings:
   a. State Restore. After the Tattoo action, add a New Group action with the following setting:

      Name: **Windows 8.1 Applications**

   b. State Restore / Windows 8.1 Applications. Add a new Install Roles and Features action with the following settings:
      - Name: **Install - Microsoft NET Framework 3.5.1**
      - Select the operating system for which roles are to be installed: **Windows 8.1**
      - Select the roles and features that should be installed: **.NET Framework 3.5 (includes .NET 2.0 and 3.0)**

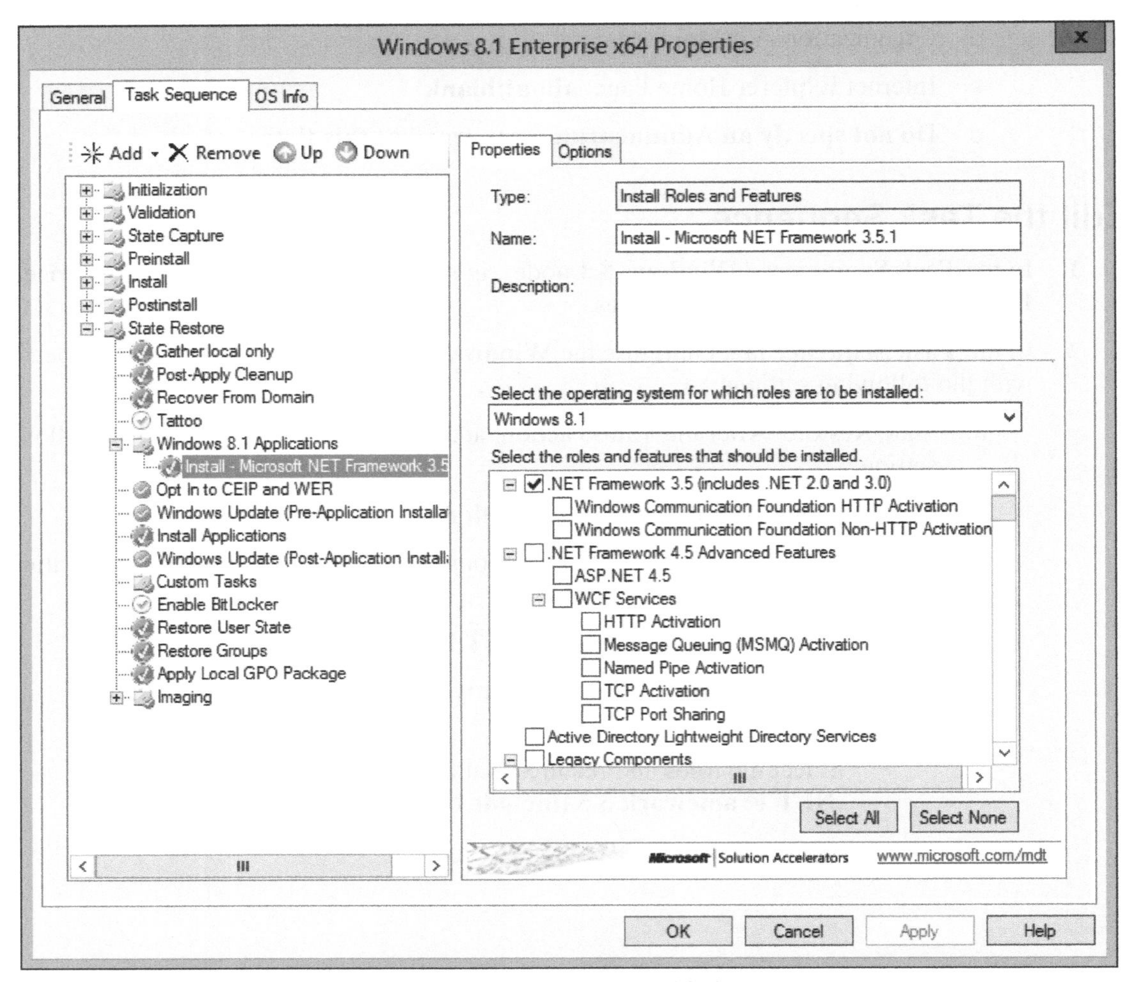

The Install - Microsoft NET Framework 3.5.1 action added.

c. **State Restore - Windows 8.1 Applications.** After the **Install - Microsoft NET Framework 3.5.1** action, add a new **Install Application** action with the following settings:

- Name: **Install - Microsoft Visual C++ 2005 SP1 - x86-x64**
- Install a Single Application: **Install - Microsoft Visual C++ 2005 SP1 - x86-x64**

d. Repeat the preceding step (add a new **Install Application**) to add the following applications:

- **Install - Microsoft Visual C++ 2008 SP1 - x86-x64**
- **Install - Microsoft Visual C++ 2010 SP1 - x86-x64**
- **Install - Microsoft Visual C++ 2012 - x86-x64**
- **Install - Microsoft Office 2013 Pro Plus - x86**

e. After **the Install - Microsoft Office 2013 Pro Plus - x86** action, add a new **Restart computer** action.

3. Click **OK**.

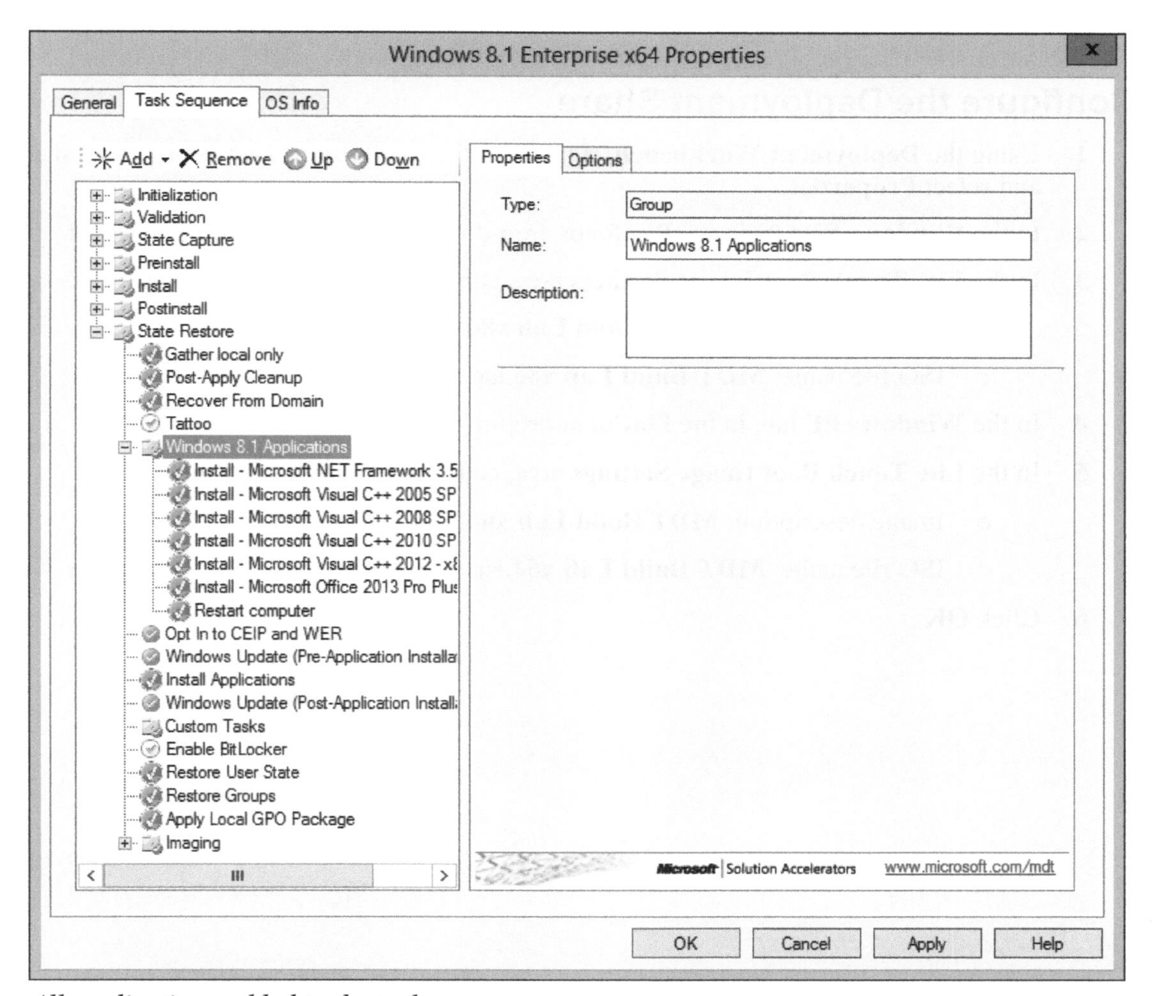

All applications added to the task sequence.

Configuring the Deployment Share

Prepare the Deployment Share Rules

1. On **MDT01**, using **File Explorer**, navigate to the **C:\Labfiles\LTI Support Files\MDT Build Lab\Control** folder.
2. Copy the following files to **D:\MDTBuildLab\Control**, replace the existing files.
    - **Bootstrap.ini**
    - **CustomSettings.ini**
3. Review the **D:\MDTBuildLab\Control\Bootstrap.ini** file, noting the **DeployRoot** value.

Configure the Deployment Share

1. Using the **Deployment Workbench**, right-click the **MDT Build Lab** deployment share and select **Properties**.
2. In the **Windows PE** tab, in the **Platform** drop-down list, make sure **x86** is selected.
3. In the **Lite Touch Boot Image Settings** area, configure the following settings:
    - Image description: **MDT Build Lab x86**
    - ISO file name: **MDT Build Lab x86.iso**
4. In the **Windows PE** tab, in the **Platform** drop-down list, select **x64.**
5. In the **Lite Touch Boot Image Settings** area, configure the following settings:
    - Image description: **MDT Build Lab x64**
    - ISO file name: **MDT Build Lab x64.iso**
6. Click **OK**.

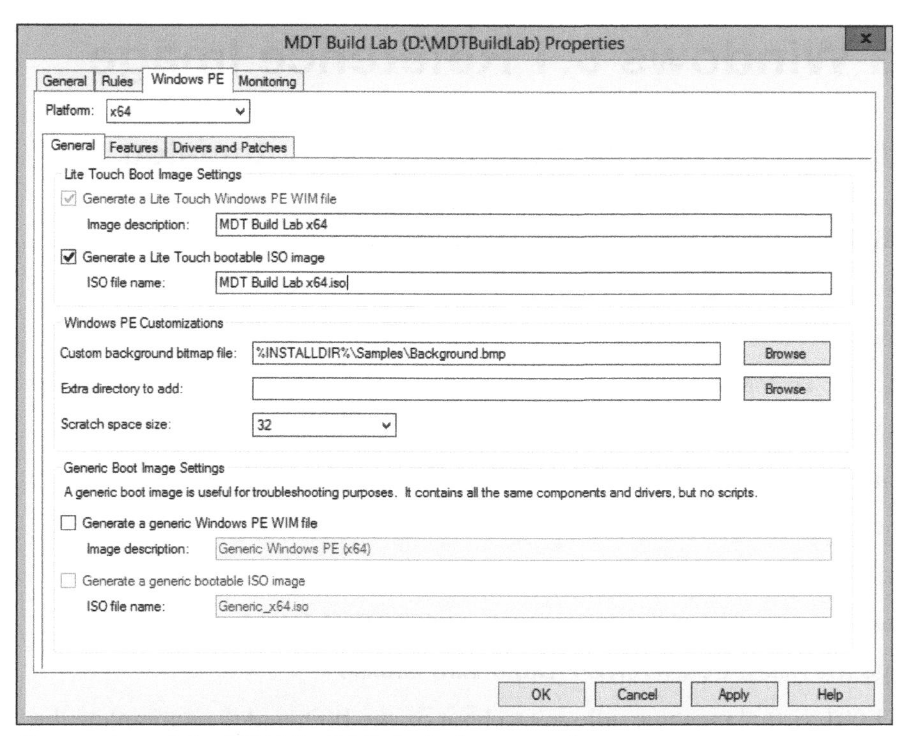

Properties of the MDT Build Lab deployment share.

Real World Note: In MDT 2013, one of the new features is that the x86 boot image can deploy both x86 and x64 operating systems (except deployments to UEFI-enabled hardware).

However, if you also use MDT 2013 for production deployments (with a separate deployment share), you may still need to have both architectures available since the x64 boot image is still being used during computer refresh and other scenarios that is staging WinPE on to the hard drive.

Update the Deployment Share

1. Right-click the **MDT Build Lab** deployment share and select **Update Deployment Share**.
2. Use the default options for the **Update Deployment Share** wizard.

Note: The update process will take 5–10 minutes.

Creating a Windows 8.1 Reference Image

Create a Windows 8.1 Reference Image, Fully Automated

1. On the **Host PC**, copy the **MDT Build Lab x86.iso** file from **\\MDT01\MDTBuildLab$\Boot** to **C:\ISO** on the **Host PC**.
2. Create a Generation 1 Hyper-V virtual machine with the following settings:
   - Name: **REF001**
   - Location: **D:\VMs**
   - Generation: **Generation 1**
   - Memory: **1024 MB**
   - Network: **AWD_Internal**
   - Hard disk: **<default>**
   - **Install an operating system from a boot CD/DVD-ROM**
   - Image file (.iso): **C:\ISO\MDT Build Lab x86.iso**
3. Start the **REF001** virtual machine, allow it to boot on the ISO, and then complete the **Deployment Wizard** using the below settings:
   a. Select a task sequence to execute on this computer: **Windows 8.1 Enterprise x64**
   b. Specify whether to capture an image: **Capture an image of this reference computer**
      - Location: **\\MDT01\MDTBuildLab$\Captures**
      - File name: **REFW81-X64-001.wim**
4. At the end of this task sequence, you have the following:
   - Install the Windows 8.1 operating system
   - Install the Visual C++ runtimes
   - Install Office 2013 Pro
   - Stage WinPE on the local disk
   - Run Sysprep and reboot into WinPE
   - Capture the installation to a WIM file on the server

Building a Reference Image Factory

As you learned earlier in this chapter, the goal for ViaMonstra is complete automation and management of the Gold reference image creation process. In this section, you set up and configure the image factory solution.

Using PowerShell to Fully Automate the Reference Image Factory

Managing reference images in a production environment can be a nightmare. To address this, there has been some incredible work done in the deployment community, including that of Mikael Nystrom. He has created a reference image factory kit that can be downloaded from www.deploymentbunny.com. Mikael also graciously allowed us to include the solution in the book sample files.

This kit saves countless hours in a production environment and automates a lot of manual processes.

To create the reference image factory, you must complete the following steps:

1. Set up and configure MDT 2013. **Already Done!**
2. Import operating systems and applications, and create task sequences. **Already Done!**
3. Have a Windows Server 2012 R2 Hyper-V server as a host. **Already Done!**
4. Copy **ImageFactoryV2** from the book samples files to **C:** on your Hyper-V host.
5. Use the scripts listed in the following sections.

Additional details on how to use the scripts can be found on the deploymentbunny.com site. We will focus on the output that comes from using this in your environment.

Modify CustomSettings.ini

1. Log on to **MDT01** as **VIAMONSTRA\Administrator**.
2. Open **D:\MDTBuildLab\Control\CustomSettings.ini**.
3. Add the following lines:

```
[Settings]
Priority=Init,Default
Properties=VMNameAlias

[Init]
UserExit=ReadKVPData.vbs
VMNameAlias=#SetVMNameAlias()#

[Default]
TaskSequenceID=%VMNameAlias%
```

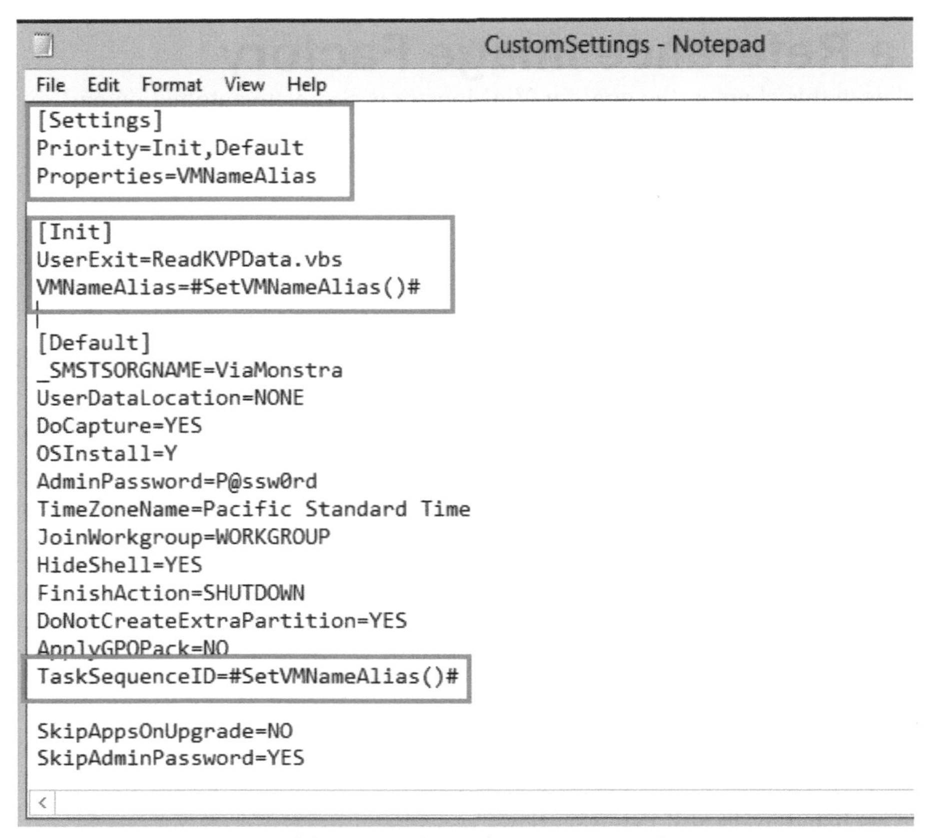

CustomSettings.ini modifications for reference image factory.

Modify Bootstrap.ini

1. Open **D:\MDTBuildLab\Control\Bootstrap.ini**.
2. Add the following lines:

```
[Default]
SubSection=ISVM-%IsVM%

[ISVM-True]
UserExit=LoadKVPInWinPE.vbs
```

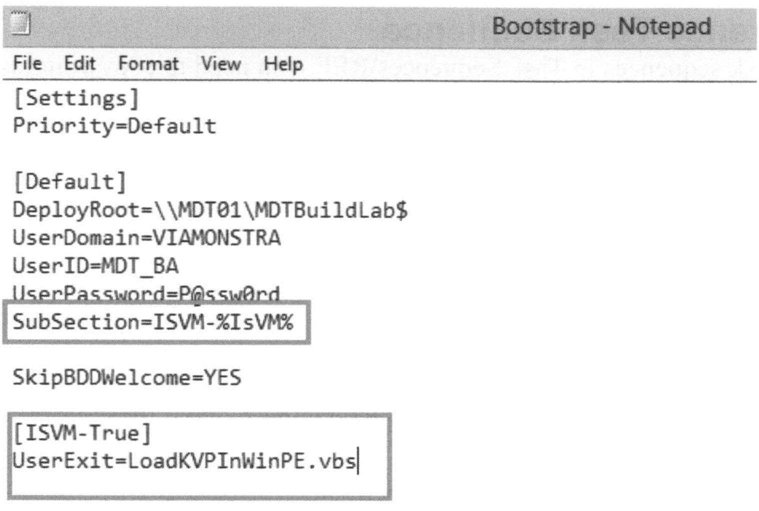

Bootstrap.ini modifications for reference image factory.

Modify FactoryImage2.xml

Factoryimage2.xml in C:\ImageFactoryV2\ImageFactoryV2Scripts is the key control file that is used for this process. In the book sample we have modified the file with the following settings:

```
<Settings>

 <DeploymentShare>\\MDT01\MDTBuildLab$</DeploymentShare>
 <HyperVHost>Localhost</HyperVHost>
 <HyperVHostNetwork>AWD_Internal</HyperVHostNetwork>
 <HyperVStorage>D:\VMs</HyperVStorage>
 <HyperVISOFolder>D:\ISO</HyperVISOFolder>
 <HardwareProfile>MDT 2010 Profile</HardwareProfile>
 <TaskSequenceFolder>MDT:\Task Sequences\REF</TaskSequenceFolder>
 <StartUpRAM>2</StartUpRAM>
 <VLANID>0</VLANID>
 <VHDSize>60</VHDSize>

 </Settings>
```

Copy the Base Reference Task Sequence

Because the script parses all task sequences in Task Sequences\REF, you need to copy your task sequence that was created here:

1. On **MDT01**, open the **Deployment Workbench**.
2. Expand **Deployment Shares / MDT Build Lab / Task Sequences**.
3. Create a new folder called **REF**.
4. Copy the **Windows 8.1 Enterprise x64** task sequence to the **REF** folder.

Modify the Boot Image

This section assume you have copied the ImageFactoryV2 from the book sample files to C:\ on your Hyper-V host.

1. On your **Hyper-V** host, using **File Explorer**, navigate to the **C:\ImageFactoryV2\DeploymentShareFolder** folder.
2. Copy the **Extra** folder to **D:\MDTBuildLab** on **MDT01**.

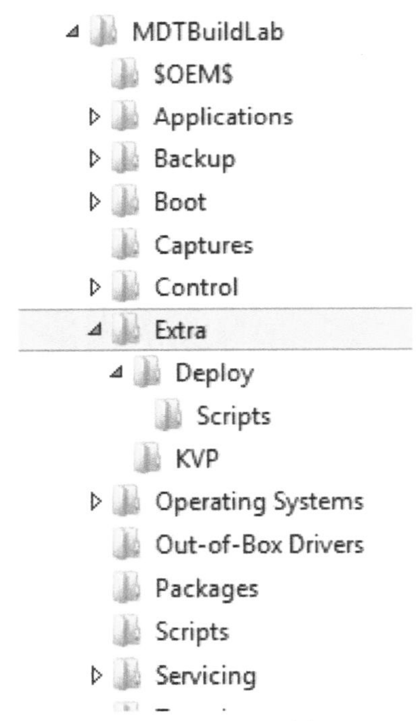

The MDTBuildLab folder structure.

Populate the KVP Folder

To populate the KVP folder with the required files, you need to devcon.exe from http://support.microsoft.com/kb/311272/en-us. For KVP to work, it requires Hyper-V drivers from the Integrated Services ISO (vmguest.iso). After you mount the vmguest.iso, you need to copy them to the Extra subfolders copied in the preceding section. In essence, you load the Hyper-V Integration Services into WinPE.

1. On **MDT01**, download **devcon.exe** from http://support.microsoft.com/kb/311272 and extract it to a temporary folder.
2. From the temporary folder, navigate to the **i386** folder, and copy **devcon.exe** to **D:\MDTBuildLab\Extra\KVP**.
3. Mount **C:\Windows\System32\vmguest.iso**, and browse to **E:\support\x86**.
4. Using **File Explorer**, open **Windows6.x-HyperVIntegrationServices-x86.cab**.
5. Copy the following files to **D:\MDTBuildLab\Extra\KVP**:
   - **iccoinstall2.dll**
   - **icsvc.dll**
   - **vmapplicationhealthmonitorproxy.dll**
   - **vmicres.dll**
   - **vmictimeprovider.dll**
   - **vmrdvcore.dll**
   - **wvmic.inf**

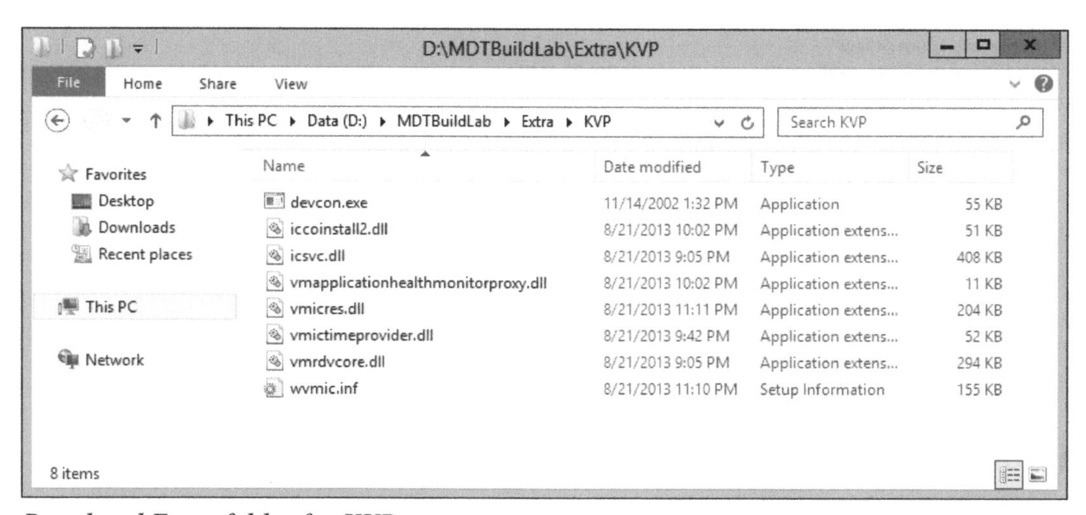

Populated Extra folder for KVP.

6. On your **Hyper-V** host, using **File Explorer**, navigate to the **C:\ImageFactoryV2\DeploymentShareFolder\Scripts** folder.

7. Copy the **ReadKVPData.vbs** file to the **D:\MDTBuildLab\Scripts** folder on **MDT01**.

Update the Boot Image

1. On **MDT01**, open the **Deployment Workbench**.
2. Expand **Deployment Shares / MDT Build Lab**.
3. Right-click **MDT Build Lab** and click **Properties**.
4. In the **WindowsPE** tab, for **Extra directory to add**, browse and select **D:\MDTBuildLab\Extra**. Then click **OK**.

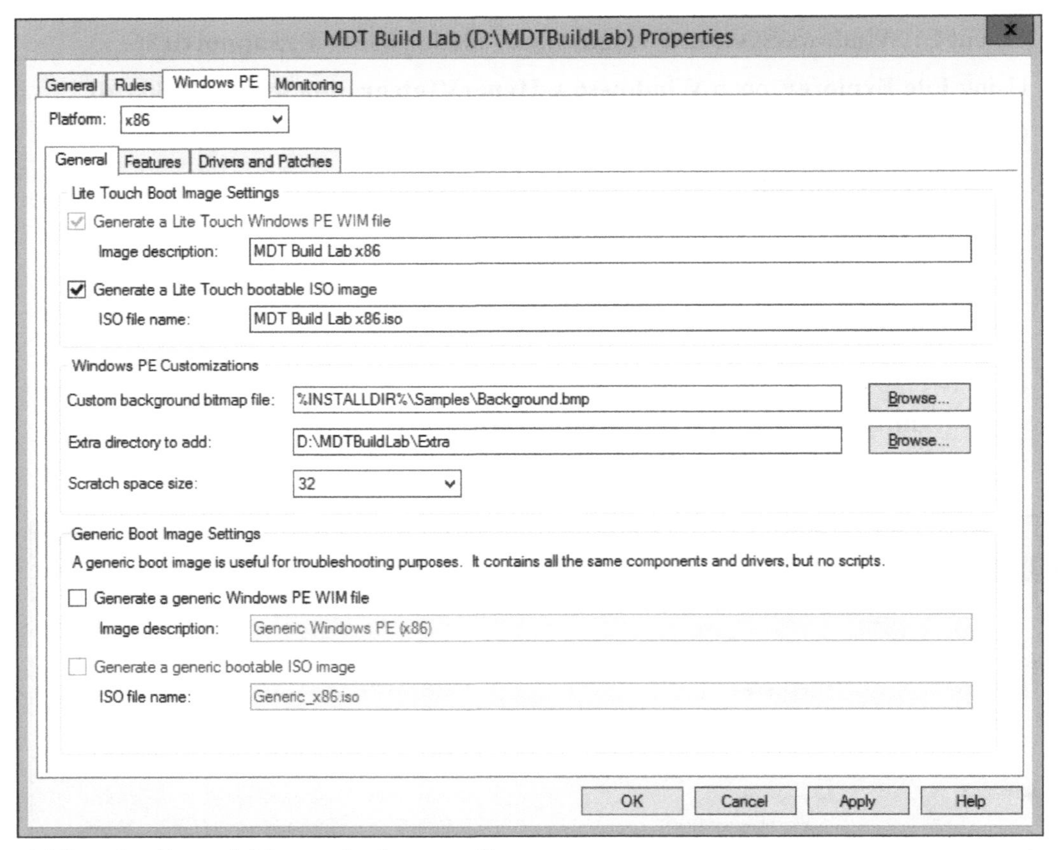

Adding the Extra folder to the boot media.

Update the Deployment Share

1. Using the **Deployment Workbench**, right-click **MDT Build Lab** and click **Update Deployment Share**.
2. Accept all the defaults.

New-AutoGenRefImages

The New-AutoGenRefImages cmdlet, available once the ImageFactoryV2.psm1 is imported, performs the following functions:

- Connects to the MDT server
- Grabs the boot ISO
- Reads all task sequences from the Task Sequences\REF folder
- Builds a VM with the same name as the reference task sequence
- Powers on the VM
- Runs the corresponding task sequence
- Builds the VM and reference image

The magic behind the scenes on this script comes from the use of Hyper-V Data Exchange and not from a custom MDT database, GUID, or anything like that. It simply does the job and saves a ton of time. In order to automate the reference image factory process, MDT 2013 must be installed on the host server, as the process cannot be run from within a VM.

1. On your **Hyper-V** host, open an elevated **PowerShell** prompt.
2. Change the directory to **C:\ImageFactoryV2\ImageFactoryV2Scripts**.
3. Run the following command:

```
Set-ExecutionPolicy Unrestricted -Force
Import-module .\ImageFactoryV2.psm1
New-AutoGenRefImages
```

3. Open **Hyper-V Manager** and look for the newly created **REFW81-X64-001** virtual machine.

Virtual Machines

Name	State	CPU Usage	Assigned M...	Uptime	Status
REFW81-X64-001	Running	0 %	2048 MB	00:00:58	
MDT01	Running	0 %	4096 MB	7.21:25:19	
CM01	Running	1 %	16384 MB	8.01:24:39	
DC01	Running	0 %	1024 MB	18.01:10:24	
KMS01	Running	0 %	1024 MB	16.21:59:49	
PC0001	Running	0 %	1024 MB	7.22:12:36	
PC0002	Running	0 %	1024 MB	7.23:10:26	
PC0003	Running	0 %	1024 MB	7.23:10:19	
PC0004	Running	0 %	1024 MB	7.23:10:12	

Using the Image Factory to generate a reference image.

4. Using **Hyper-V Manager** right-click **REFW81-X64-001** virtual machine and select **Settings**. In the **IDE Controller 0** node, select the **DVD Drive** and note the settings.

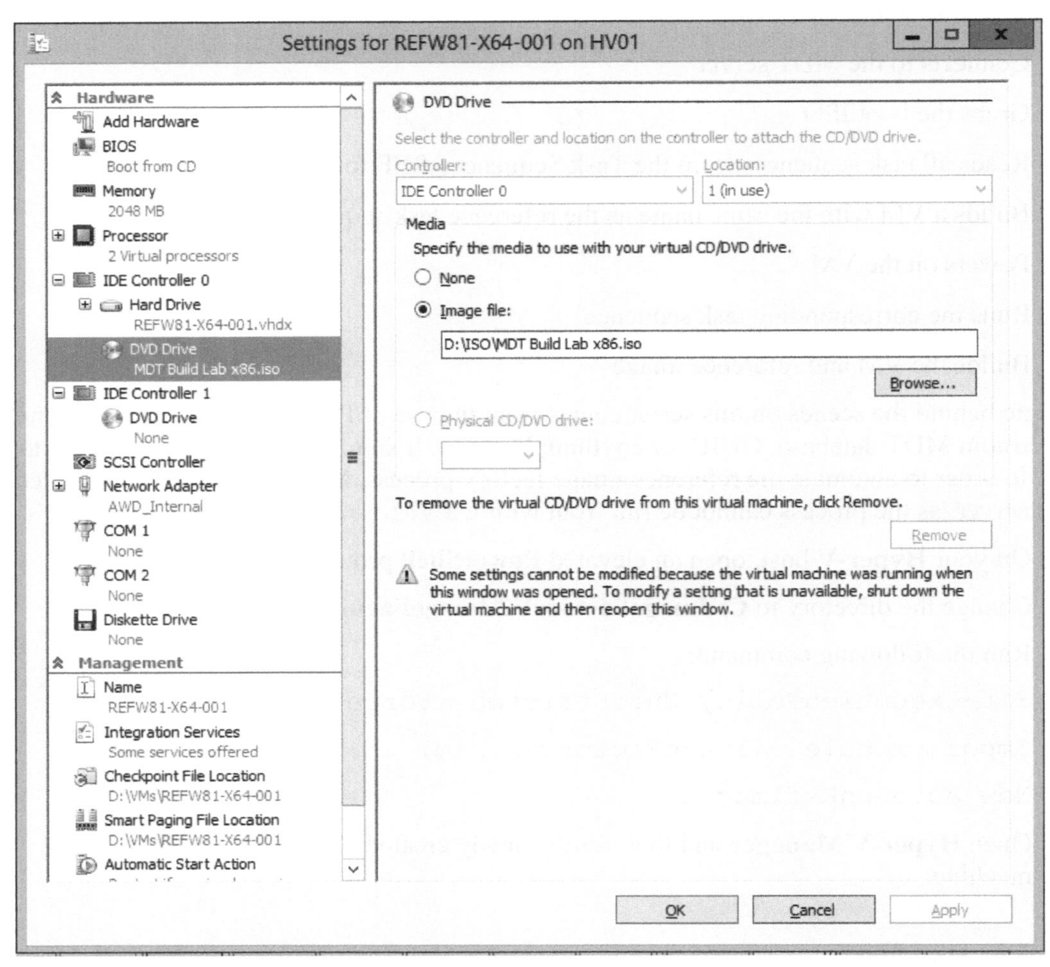

The configured boot media in Hyper-V.

5. Open the **Hyper-V** console for **REFW81-X64-001** and ensure that the task sequence engine starts and automatically selects the correct task sequence. Click **Next**.

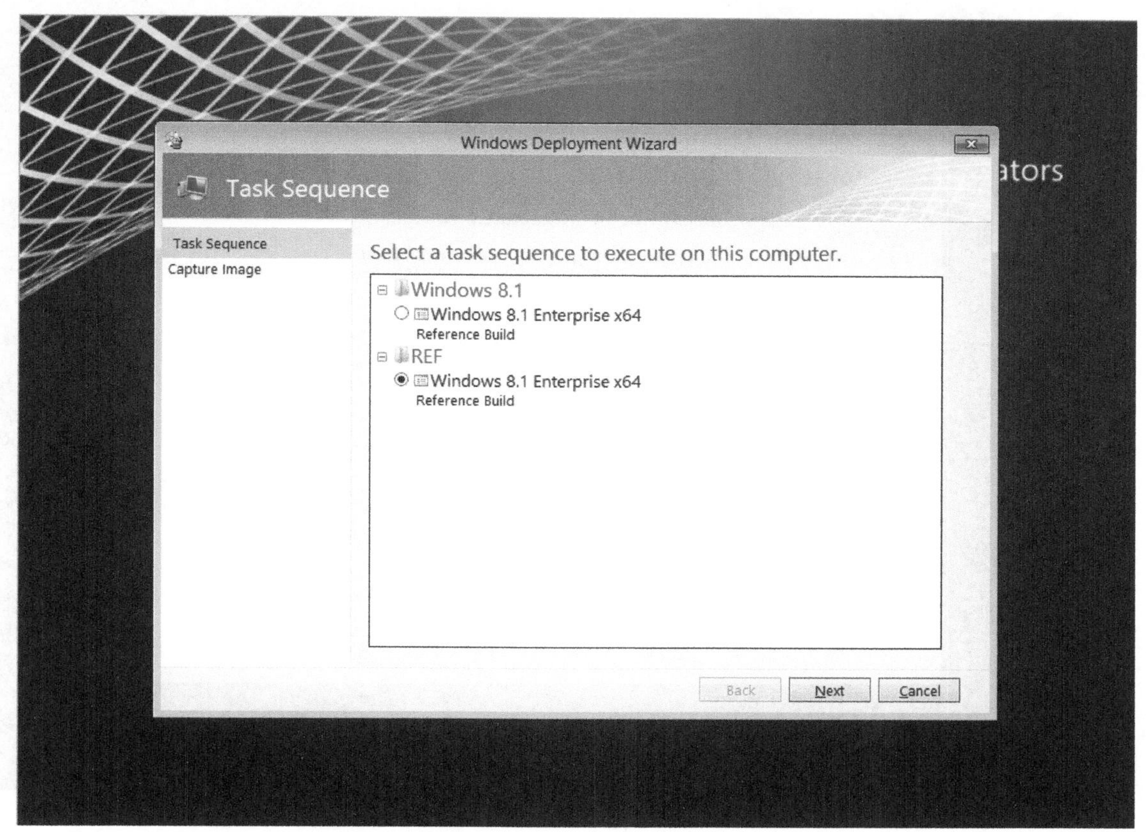

The reference image capture is automatically selected.

6. On the **Specify whether to capture an image** page, click **Next**.

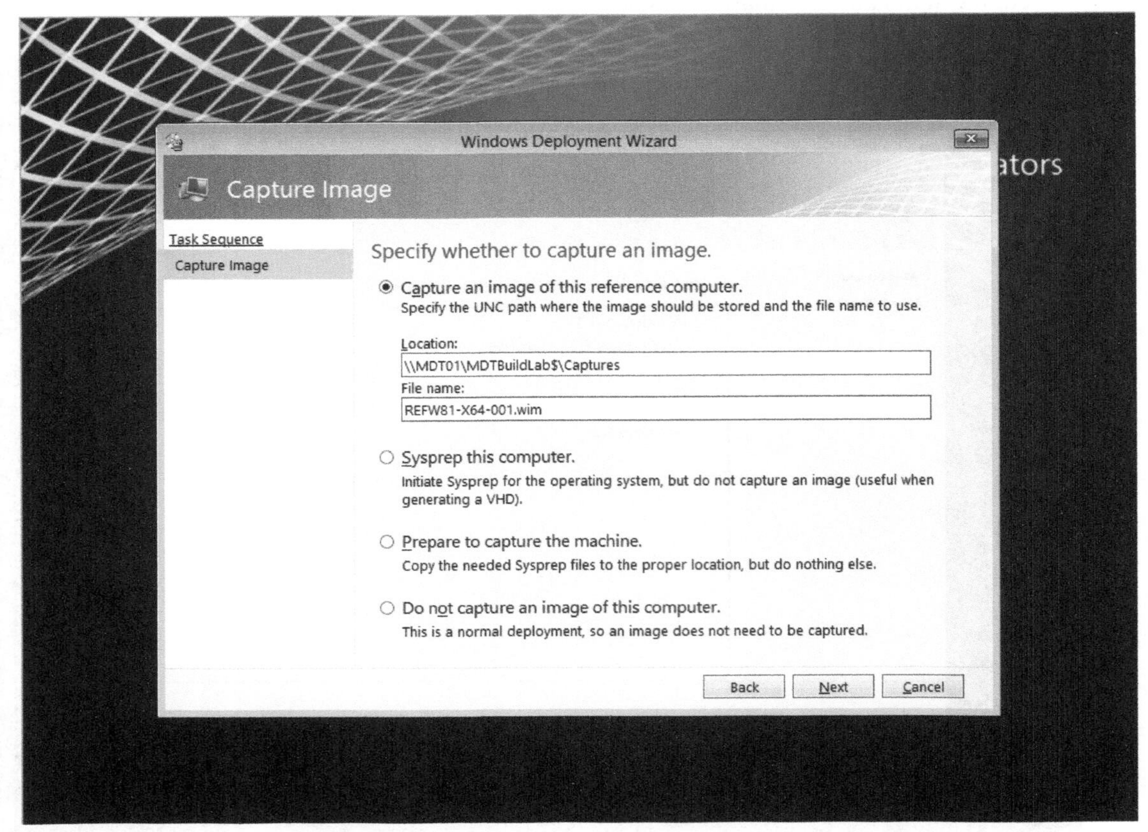

Selecting the path for the Capture Image.

As the factory reference image builds, the script waits in a loop until it completes looking for the next task sequence.

Real World Note: If you want to fully automate the process you simply change the values of the SkipTaskSequence and SkipCapture variables from NO to YES.

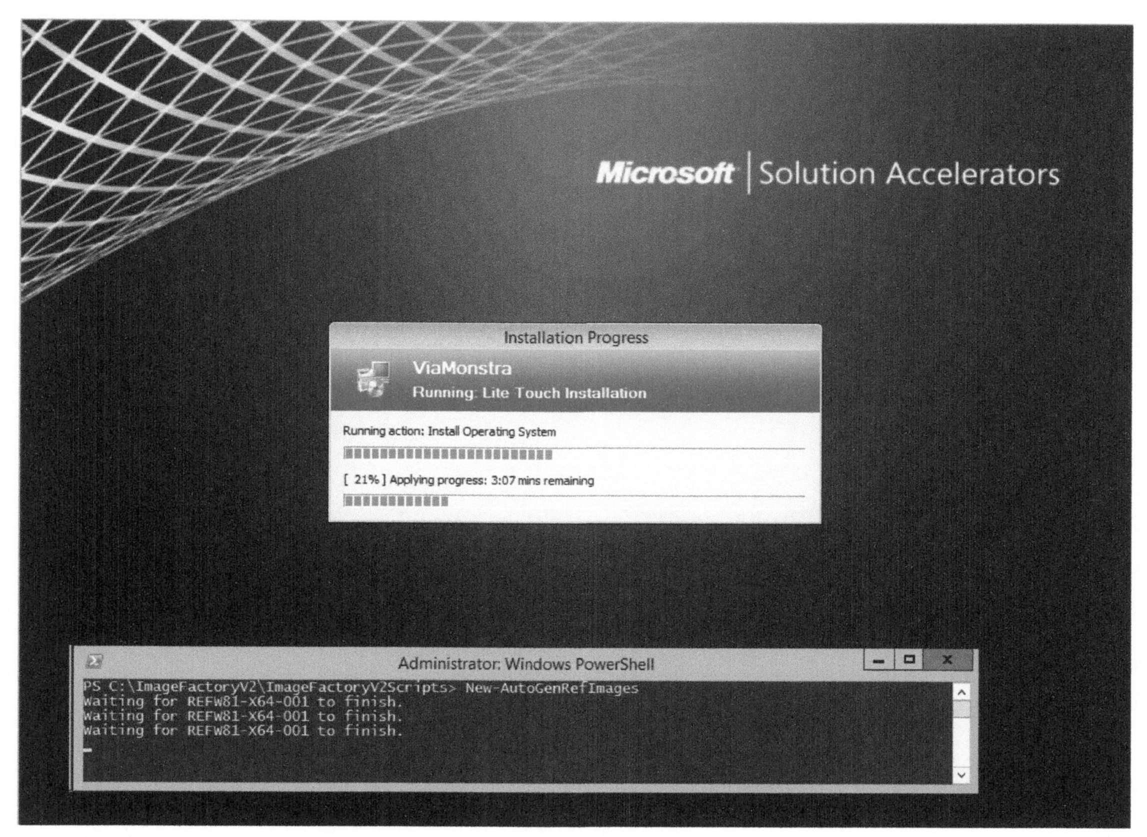

The finished product of the reference image factory.

Chapter 8

Deploying Windows 8.1 Using ConfigMgr 2012 R2 (Native ConfigMgr)

To have an OSD task sequence that utilizes the efficiencies introduced to ViaMonstra by the implementation of 1E Nomad, you need to have a functional task sequence. To ensure that this sequence is not only functional, but also optimized, you will follow instructions laid out by Johan Arwidmark in his *Stealing with Pride - Volume 1: Advanced OSD Customizations for MDT 2013 and ConfigMgr 2012 R2* book.

ConfigMgr OSD Key Concepts

The Microsoft Deployment Toolkit (Lite Touch) is a powerful solution for creating and deploying images; however, it is not scalable for large enterprises and provides no functionality for deploying operating systems using Zero Touch methodologies.

However, when the OSD process using task sequences is combined with the centralized management capabilities of ConfigMgr, an enterprise class deployment solution is born.

Delegation Is Key! Don't Wipe Your Infrastructure in One Click

We often refer to ConfigMgr OSD as a gun. If you point it and pull the trigger, things happen. It is imperative that any organization implement controls over who can deploy task sequences and to what types of devices. Role-based access control, introduced in ConfigMgr 2012, provides the capability to strictly define actions that an operator can perform within a ConfigMgr hierarchy. Though not expressly covered in this book, it has to be mentioned: limit the ability to deploy task sequences to *only* those who require it as part of their job.

Key ConfigMgr OSD Log Files

Arguably the most important part of troubleshooting operating system deployments is a thorough understanding of the log files that are active during task sequence execution and where to go to access these files. When dealing with complex task sequences in excess of 400 steps, knowing where the files are located is only a part of the battle. Being able to follow the execution steps in multiple logs is also vitally important. The key to establishing an accurate timeline is actually quite simple: Open two CMTrace windows, one for the SMSTS.log and one for a subsidiary log you want to view. The SMSTS.log becomes your timeline, and using its timestamps, you can view other actions that occurred at specific times.

Given a specific issue, you can sometimes look at up to 30 log files to determine the root cause of a failure. We're not going to go into each and every log file; however, here are the most important ones:

Log Name	Description
Execmgr.log	Stores details about package and task sequence execution Location: C:\Windows\CCM\Logs
CAS.log	Records details when distribution points are found for referenced content Location: C:\Windows\CCM\Logs
CreateTSMedia.log	Logs the process for creating task sequence media on machines that have the ConfigMgr client installed Location: <ConfigMgrInstallPath>\AdminUILog\AdminUILog
DISM.log	Stores driver installation actions or update apply actions for offline servicing Location: %Temp%\SMSTSLog\Dism.log
Distmgr.log	Records details about distribution point operations, including the configuration of enabling a distribution point for PXE Location: <ConfigMgrInstallPath>\Logs
SMSTS.log	Records all actions that are executed by the task sequence on a client. During OSD this log will move around to multiple locations depending on the stage of deployment Location: C:\Windows\CCM\Logs
SMSPXE.log	Stores details about the responses to clients that PXE boot and details about the expansion of boot images and boot files Location: <ConfigMgrInstallPath>\SMS_CCM\Logs
NomadBranch.log	Records all information pertaining to the Nomad client. Package requests for software updates are logged here, as well as information regarding download details and content location. Location: C:\ProgramData\1E\NomadBranch\Logfiles
WindowsUpdate.log	A Windows log that provides information about when the Windows Update Agent connects to the WSUS server and retrieves the software updates for compliance assessment and whether there are updates to the agent components Location: C:\Windows
WPEinit.log	Records initialization steps when a client boots into WinPE Location: C:\Windows\System32\WPEinit.log

Log Name	Description
CCMSetup.log	Records the CCM client installation process Location: C:\Windows\CCMSetup\Logs\CCMSetup.log
UpdatesDeployment.log	Records details about deployments on the client, including software update activation, evaluation, and enforcement. Verbose logging shows additional information about the interaction with the client user interface. Location: C:\Windows\CCM\Logs

ConfigMgr OSD Conceptual Design (ViaMonstra)

This conceptual design is based on common large-scale ConfigMgr deployments. This design is required as a foundational design. You will built upon it after existing task sequences are extended using 1E Nomad.

Real World Note: In production, it is very common for 1E to show business value by the removal of unnecessary ConfigMgr distribution points. We often see in real-world deployments a 90–95 percent or higher reduction in field distribution points. In the case of the ViaMonstra design, this equates to a reduction of approximately 1250 distribution points.

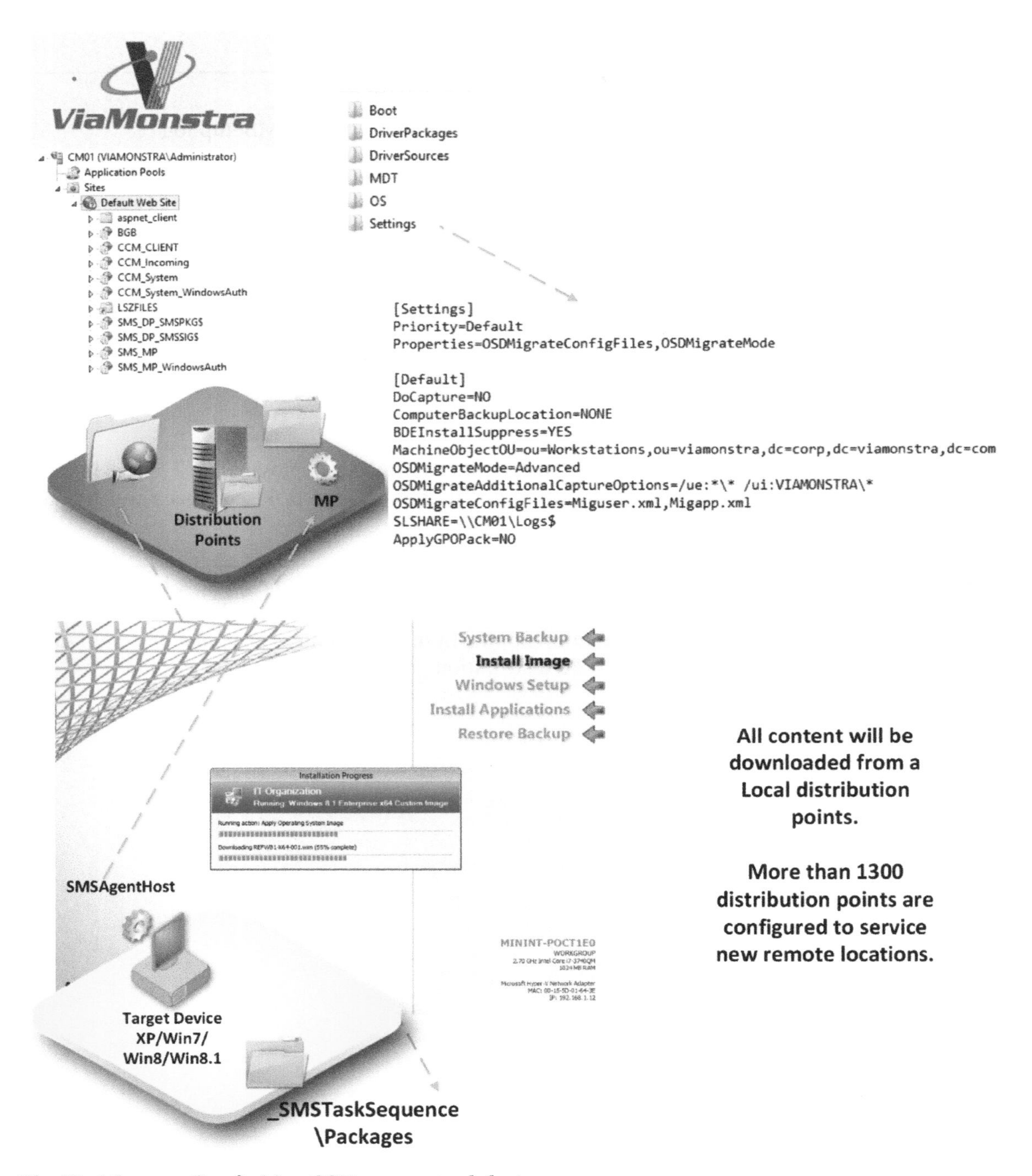

The ViaMonstra ConfigMgr OSD conceptual design.

Installing MDT 2013 Zero Touch on CM01

The following step-by-step instructions help you build your very own native ConfigMgr 2012 R2 Zero Touch environment. This process has been broken down into the following elements:

- Configure the required Active Directory permissions
- Install the needed hotfixes on CM01
- Install MDT 2013 on CM01
- Set up ConfigMgr 2012 integration
- Create the ConfigMgr source folder structure
- Create an updated ConfigMgr client package
- Enable PXE on the CM01 distribution point
- Create boot images
- Add operating system images
- Add drives
- Create task sequences
- Deploy Windows 8.1 using boot media

Although there are many steps to follow, if executed properly, this process builds a foundational environment that you use in later advanced deployment chapters. Enjoy the ride and learn as much as you can.

Configure Active Directory Permissions

In this guide we assume you have downloaded the book sample files and copied them to C:\Labfiles on DC01.

1. On **DC01**, in an elevated (run as Administrator) **PowerShell** command prompt, configure **Execution Policy** in PowerShell by running the following command:

```
Set-ExecutionPolicy -ExecutionPolicy RemoteSigned -Force
```

Real World Note: In Windows Server 2012 R2 the default execution policy is already set to RemoteSigned, but the hydration process hardens that policy, so it needs to be configured.

2. Grant permissions for the **CM_JD** account to the **ViaMonstra / Workstations** OU by running the following command:

```
C:\Labfiles\Scripts\Set-OUPermissions.ps1 -Account CM_JD
-TargetOU "OU=Workstations,OU=ViaMonstra"
```

The Set-OUPermissions.ps1 script grants the minimum permissions needed to create and update computer objects in the OU that is specified. The permissions granted by the script are:

- **This object and all descendant objects.** Create Computer objects, and Delete Computer objects.
- **Descendant Computer objects.** Read All Properties, Write All Properties, Read Permissions, Modify Permissions, Change Password, Reset Password, Validated write to DNS host name, and Validated write to service principal name.

Install Needed Updates (ConfigMgr 2012 R2 CU3) on CM01

1. Request, download and extract **KB2994331 (ConfigMgr 2012 R2 CU3)** from https://support.microsoft.com/kb/2994331 to your Hyper-V host.
2. Copy **CM12-R2CU3-KB2994331-X64-ENU.exe** to **\\CM01\C$\Labfiles\Sources\ConfigMgr 2012 R2 CU3**.
3. On **CM01**, log on as **VIAMONSTRA\Administrator**.
4. Make sure the **ConfigMgr console** is closed before continuing.
5. Install **KB2994331** (C:\Labfiles\Sources\ConfigMgr 2012 R2 CU3\CM12-R2CU3-KB2994331-X64-ENU.exe) with the default settings.

Note: If the setup warns you about an earlier software installation that still has outstanding file rename operations pending, cancel the setup, restart the server, and then start the CU3 setup again.

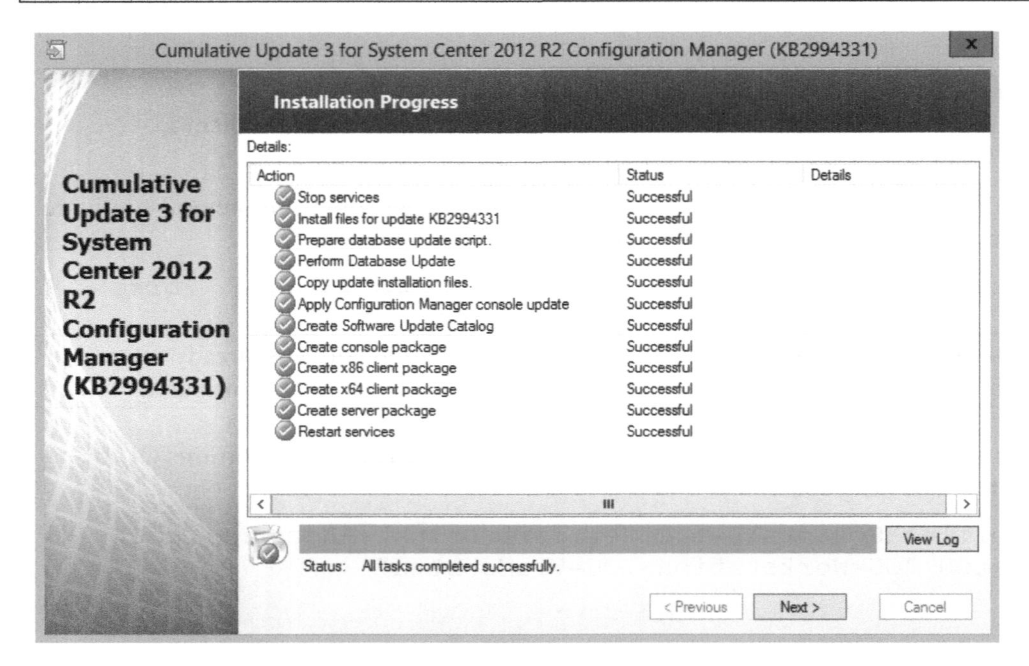

Installing ConfigMgr 2012 R2 CU3 on CM01.

Install MDT 2013 on CM01

In this guide we assume you have downloaded MDT 2013 to C:\Labfiles\Sources\MDT 2013 on CM01.

1. On **CM01**, log on as **VIAMONSTRA\Administrator**.
2. Install **MDT 2013** by running the following command in an elevated **PowerShell** prompt:

```
& msiexec.exe /i 'C:\Labfiles\Sources\MDT 2013\
MicrosoftDeploymentToolkit2013_x64.msi' /qb /l*v
C:\Windows\Temp\MDTInstall.log
```

Set Up ConfigMgr 2012 Integration

1. On **CM01**, close the **ConfigMgr console** if it is open.
2. From the **Start screen**, run the **Configure ConfigMgr Integration** wizard with the following settings:
   - Site Server Name: **CM01.corp.viamonstra.com**
   - Site code: **PS1**

Note: It may take a while for the integration wizard to display.

Create a New ConfigMgr Client Package

1. On **CM01**, in the **D:\SCCM_Sources** folder, create a subfolder named **ConfigMgr Client with Hotfixes**.
2. Using **File Explorer**, navigate to the **D:\ConfigMgr\Client** folder.

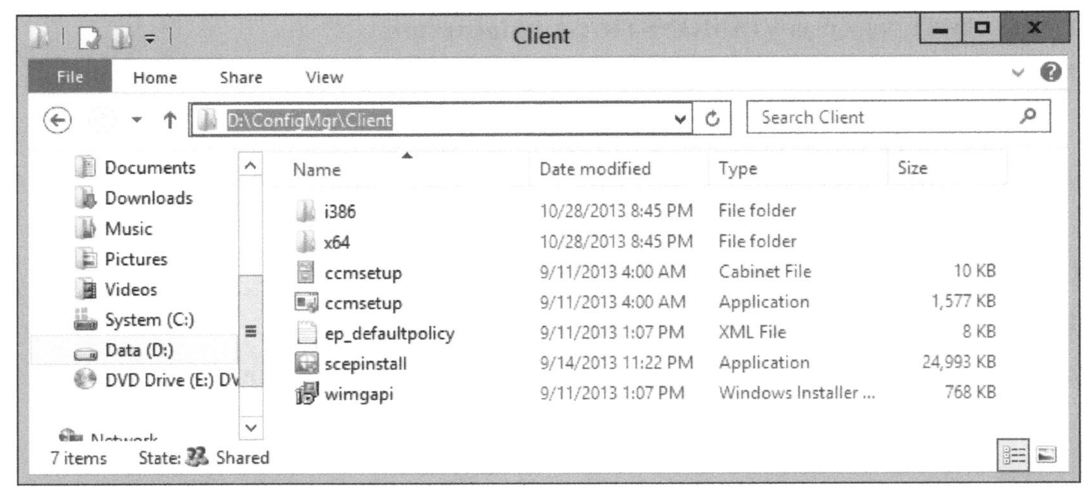

The content of the D:\ConfigMgr\Client folder.

3. Copy the contents of **D:\ConfigMgr\Client** to the newly created folder, **D:\SCCM_Sources\ConfigMgr Client with Hotfixes**.
4. In **D:\SCCM_Sources\ConfigMgr Client with Hotfixes**, create a folder named **Hotfix**.
5. Using **File Explorer**, navigate to the **D:\ConfigMgr\hotfix\KB2994331\Client** folder.

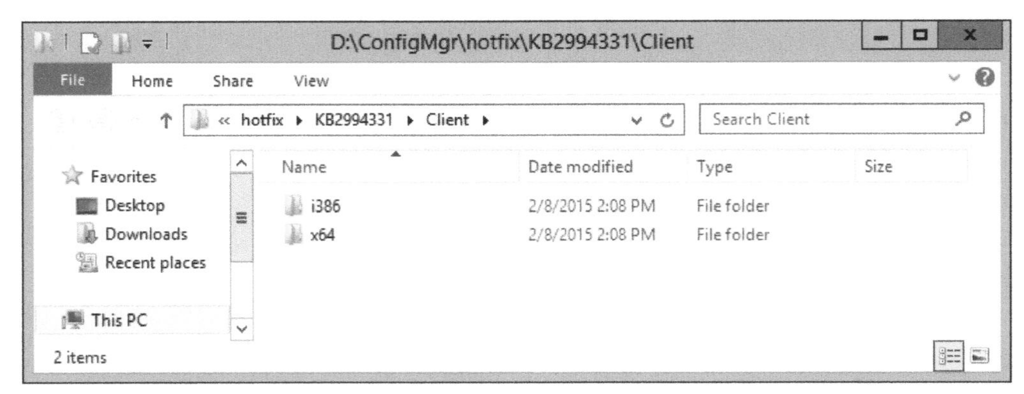

The content of the D:\ConfigMgr\hotfix\KB2994331\Client folder.

6. Copy the two subfolders (**i386** and **x64**) to **D:\SCCM_Sources\ConfigMgr Client with Hotfixes\Hotfix**.

7. Using the **ConfigMgr console**, in the **Software Library** workspace, create a new package with the following settings:
   - Name: **Configuration Manager Client with Hotfixes**
   - Source folder: **CM01\SCCM_Sources$\ConfigMgr Client with Hotfixes**
   - Select **Do not create a program**.
   - Enable Nomad by selecting the check box.
8. Make a note of the new Package ID. In this example, it was **PS100018.**
9. Distribute the new **ConfigMgr Client with Hotfixes** package to the **CM01** distribution point by selecting the **Packages** node, right-clicking the **ConfigMgr Client with Hotfixes** package, and selecting **Distribute Content**.
10. Use the following setting for the **Distribute Content Wizard**:

    Content Destination: Add the **CM01** distribution point.

Note: This newly created ConfigMgr Client Package with the CU3 Update will be used later when the OSD Task Sequence is created.

Enable PXE on the CM01 Distribution Point

STOP: Due to a major bug in the PXE implementation in ConfigMgr 2012 R2, make sure you installed the KB2994331 update as described previously, or the setup of PXE will fail.

1. Using the **ConfigMgr console**, in the **Administration** workspace, select **Distribution Points**.
2. Right-click the **CM01.CORP.VIAMONSTRA.COM** distribution point and select **Properties**.
3. In the **PXE** tab, enable the following settings:
   - Enable PXE support for clients
   - Allow this distribution point to respond to incoming PXE requests
   - Enable unknown computer support
   - Require a password when computers use PXE
   - Password and Confirm password: **P@ssw0rd**
4. Using **CMTrace**, review the **D:\ConfigMgr\Logs\distmgr.log** file. Look for the **ConfigurePXE** and **CcmInstallPXE** lines.
5. Verify that you have 7 files in **D:\RemoteInstall\SMSBoot\x86** and **D:\RemoteInstall\SMSBoot\x64** folders.

Note: If the files are not there, or if you don't have a **D:\RemoteInstall\SMSBoot** folder, make sure that the **Windows Deployment Services Server** service is started.

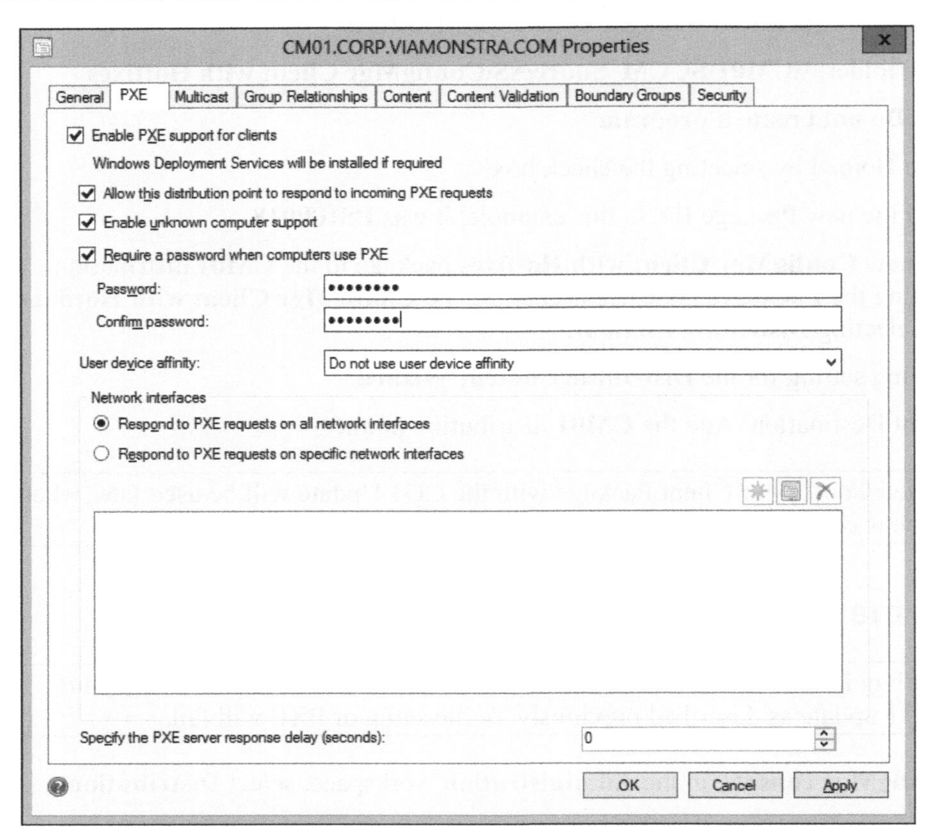

Configuring CM01 for PXE.

Creating the Boot Image

1. On **CM01**, using the **ConfigMgr console**, in the **Software Library** workspace, expand **Operating Systems**, right-click **Boot Images**, select **Create Boot Image using MDT**, and create a new boot image package using the following settings
   - Package source folder to be created (UNC Path): **\\CM01\SCCM_Sources$\OSD\Boot\Zero Touch WinPE 5.0 x64**

Note: The Zero Touch WinPE 5.0 x64 folder does not yet exist, you need to type the name, and the folder will be created later by the wizard.

   - Name: **Zero Touch WinPE 5.0 x64**
   - Platform: **x64**

- Scratch Space: **<default>**
- Components: **<default>**
- **Enable command support (F8)**

> **Note:** It will take a few minutes to generate the boot image. The wizard progress bar may even appear to stop, but no worries, if you just give it some more time it will continue.

2. Distribute the boot image to the **CM01** distribution point by selecting the **Boot images** node, right-click the **Zero Touch WinPE 5.0 x64** boot image, and select **Distribute Content**. Use the following settings for the **Distribute Content Wizard**:

   Content Destination: Add the **CM01** distribution point.

3. Using **CMTrace**, review the **D:\ConfigMgr\Logs\distmgr.log** file. Do not continue until you can see the boot image is distributed. Look for the line saying **STATMSG: ID=2301...**.You can also view Content Status in the ConfigMgr console by selecting the **Zero Touch WinPE 5.0 x64** boot image.
4. Using **ConfigMgr console**, right-click the **Zero Touch WinPE 5.0 x64** boot image and select **Properties.**
5. In the **Data Source** tab, select the **Deploy this boot image from the PXE-enabled distribution point** check box, and click **OK**.
6. Using **CMTrace**, review the **D:\ConfigMgr\Logs\distmgr.log** file.
7. Review the **D:\RemoteInstall\SMSImages** folder, you should see three folders containing boot images, two are from the default boot images.

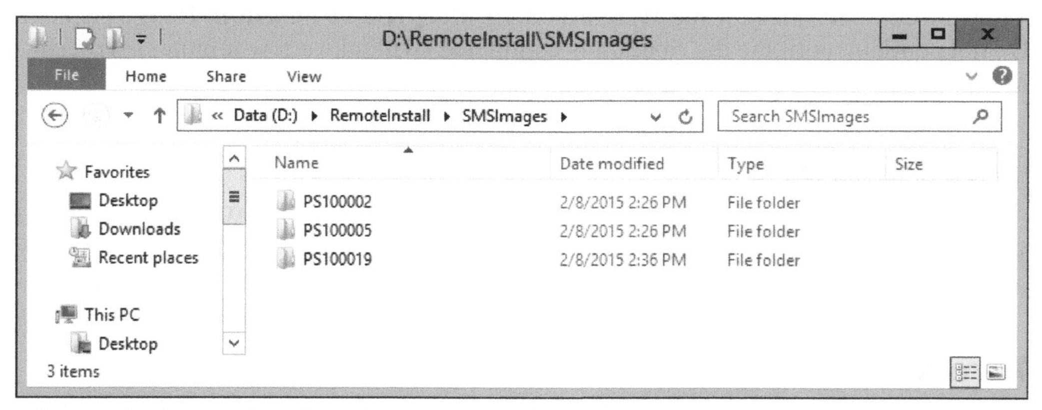

The new boot image in the D:\RemoteInstall\SMSImages folder.

Adding Operating System Images

Add a Windows 8.1 Operating System Image

1. On **CM01**, using **File Explorer**, create the **D:\SCCM_Sources\OSD\OS\Windows 8.1 Enterprise x64 Custom Image** folder.
2. Browse to the **\\MDT01\MDTBuildLab$\Captures** folder.
3. Copy the **REFW81-X64-001.wim file** to the **D:\ SCCM_Sources\OSD\OS\ Windows 8.1 Enterprise x64 Custom Image** folder.
4. Using **ConfigMgr console**, add an **Operating System Image** with the following settings. Use default settings for all other options.
   - Path: **\\CM01\SCCM_Sources$\OSD\OS\ Windows 8.1 Enterprise x64 Custom Image\REFW81-X64-001.wim**
   - Name: **Windows 8.1 Enterprise x64 Custom Image**
   - Enable Nomad by selecting the checkbox on the Nomad Settings tab
5. Distribute the operating system image to the **HQ DP Group** distribution point group by right-clicking the **Windows 8.1 Enterprise x64 Custom Image** operating system image, and select **Distribute Content**. Use the following settings for the **Distribute Content Wizard**:

   Content Destination: Add the **HQ DP Group** distribution point group.
6. View the content status for the **Windows 8.1 Enterprise x64 Custom Image** package. Do not continue until the distribution is completed (will take a few minutes). You can also review the **D:\ConfigMgr\Logs\distmgr.log** file.

Adding Drivers

In this section, you add drivers to the WinPE 5.0 boot image as well as the Windows 8.1 operating system. WinPE 5.0 and Windows 8.1 are using the same drivers, but you add only a limited set of drivers for the boot image (most often network and storage).

Add Drivers for WinPE 5.0

In this section, we assume you have downloaded drivers that you want to add to your x64 boot image.

1. On **CM01**, using **File Explorer**, in the **D:\SCCM_Sources\OSD\DriverSources** folder, create a new folder named **WinPE x64**.
2. Copy the **WinPE 5.0** drivers you want to add to the new folder.

3. Using the **ConfigMgr console**, in the **Software Library** workspace, right-click the **Drivers** folder and select **Import Driver**, and then use the following settings for the **Import New Driver Wizard**:

   a. Locate Driver

      - Source folder: **\\CM01\SCCM_Sources$\OSD\DriverSources\WinPE x64**
      - Specify the option for duplicate drivers: **Import the driver and append a new category to the existing categories**

   b. Driver Details

      Click **Categories**, and create a category named **WinPE x64**

   c. Add Driver to Packages

      <default>

   d. Add Driver to Boot Images

      - Select the **Zero Touch WinPE 5.0 x64** boot image
      - Select the **Update distribution points when finished** check box.

> **Real World Note:** The Updating Boot Image part of the wizard will appear to hang when displaying "Done", but no worries after (quite) a while it will complete.

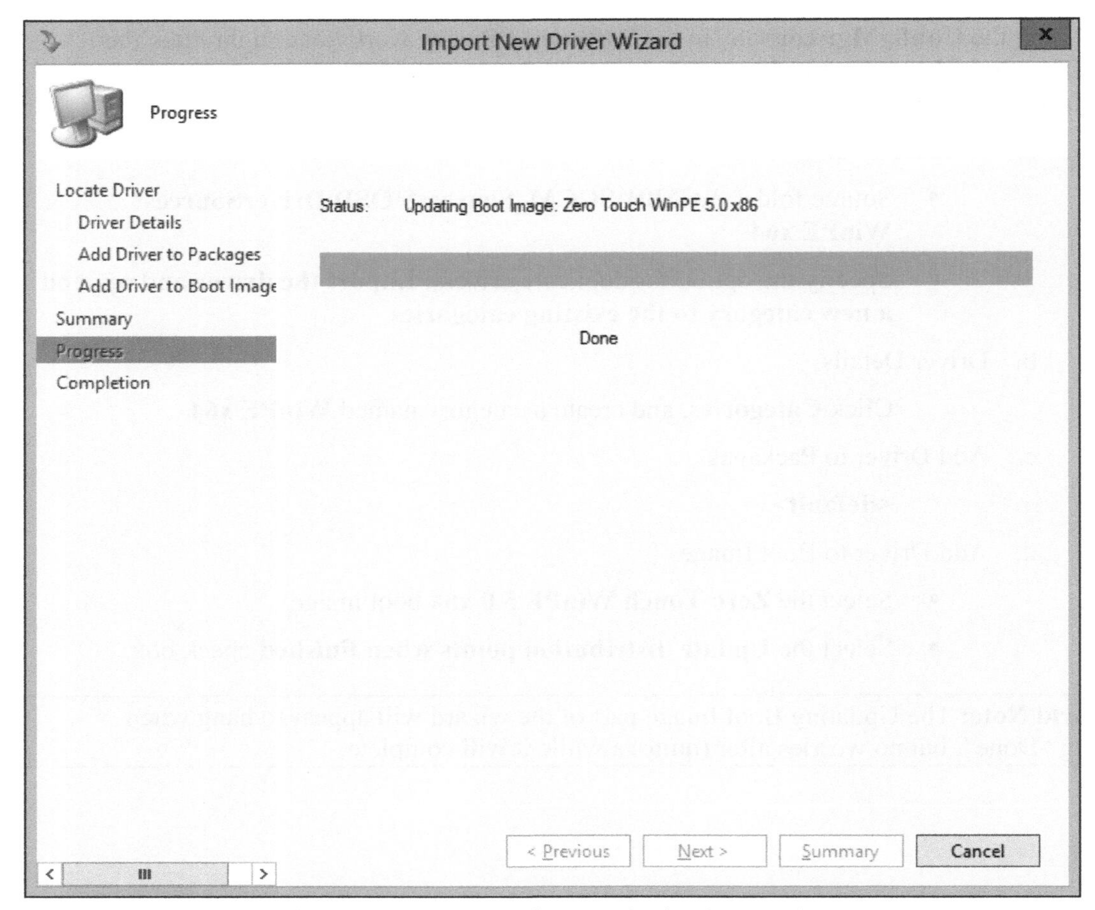

ConfigMgr 2012 R2 taking a nap (still working in the background).

Add Drivers for HP EliteBook 8560w

In this guide we assume you have downloaded the Windows 8.1 drivers for HP EliteBook 8560w.

1. On **CM01**, using **File Explorer**, in the **D:\SCCM_Sources\OSD\DriverSources** folder, create a new folder named **Windows 8.1 x64**, and then, in that a folder, create a new folder named **HP EliteBook 8560w**.
2. Copy the downloaded **HP EliteBook 8560w** drivers to the new folder.
3. Using the **ConfigMgr console**, right-click the **Drivers** folder and select **Import Driver**, use the following settings for the **Import New Driver Wizard**.
    a. Locate Driver

        Source folder: **\\CM01\SCCM_Sources$\OSD\DriverSources\Windows 8.1 x64\HP EliteBook 8560w**

b. Driver Details

   Click **Categories**, and create a category named **Windows 8.1 x64 - HP EliteBook 8560w**

c. Add Driver to Packages

   - New Package
   - Name: **Windows 8.1 x64 - HP EliteBook 8560w**
   - Path: **\\CM01\SCCM_Sources$\OSD\DriverPackages\Windows 8.1 x64\HP EliteBook 8560w**

d. Add Driver to Boot Images

   <default>

Creating Task Sequences

Create a Deployment Image Task Sequence

Using **ConfigMgr console**, in the **Software Library** workspace, expand **Operating Systems**, right-click **Task Sequences**, select **Create MDT Task Sequence**, and create a new task sequence using the following settings

a. Choose Template

   Template: **Client Task Sequence**

b. General

   - Task sequence name: **Windows 8.1 Enterprise x64 Custom Image**
   - Task sequence comments: **Production image with Office 2013**

c. Details

   - Join a Domain
     - Domain: **corp.viamonstra.com**
     - Account: **VIAMONSTRA\CM_JD**
     - Password: **P@ssw0rd**
   - Windows Settings
     - User name: **ViaMonstra**
     - Organization name: **ViaMonstra**
     - Product key: **<blank>**

d. Capture Settings

   This task sequence will never be used to capture an image.

e. Boot Image

Specify a boot image package to use

Select the **Zero Touch WinPE 5.0 x64** boot image package

f. MDT Package

Create a new Microsoft Deployment Toolkit Files package

Package source folder to be created (UNC Path):
\\CM01\SCCM_Sources$\OSD\MDT\MDT 2013

g. MDT Details

Name: **MDT 2013**

h. OS Image

Specify an existing OS image

Select the **Windows 8.1 Enterprise x64 Custom Image** package

i. Deployment Method

Perform a "Zero Touch Installation" OS Deployment, with no user interaction

j. Client Package

Specify an existing ConfigMgr client package

Select the **Configuration Manager Client with Hotfixes** package.

k. USMT Package

Specify an existing USMT package

Select the **Microsoft Corporation User State Migration Tool for Windows 8 6.3.9600.16384** package

l. Settings Package

Create a new settings package

Package source folder to be created (UNC Path):
\\CM01\SCCM_Sources$\OSD\Settings\Windows 8.1 x64 Settings

m. Settings Details

Name: **Windows 8.1 x64 Settings**

n. Sysprep Package

No Sysprep Package is required

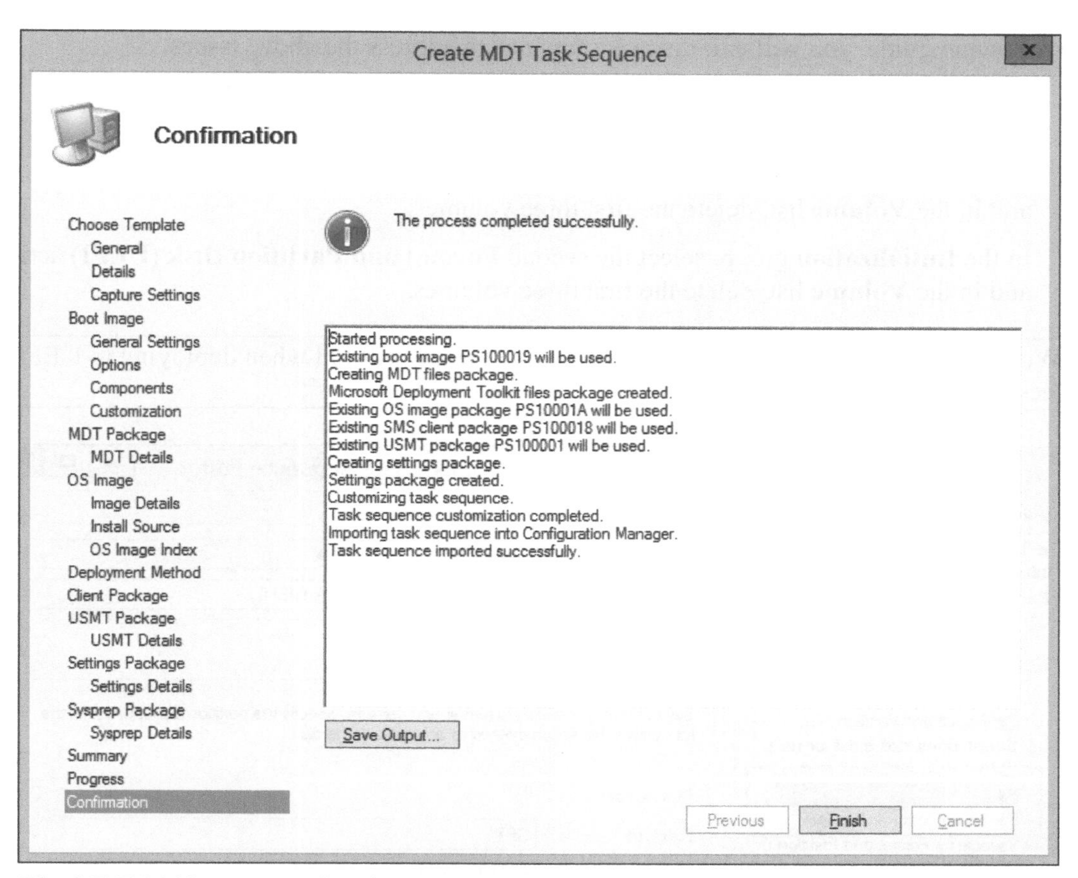

The MDT 2013 integrated task sequence created.

Edit the Task Sequence

The MDT standard client task sequences unfortunately have the following known issues that need to be addressed before it can be used.

- Issue #1. UEFI deployments does not work (at all).
- Issue #2. The local Administrator account is set to blank
- Issue #3. The image is install to the E: drive instead of C: drive
- Issue #4. The backup is never restored in replace scenarios
- Issue #5. Dynamically changing OU doesn't work
- Issue #6. Deployment is four times (at least) slower than in ConfigMgr 2012 SP1

In the following guide, you will edit the task sequence to address the above issues.

1. Using the **ConfigMgr console**, select **Task Sequences**, right-click **Windows 8.1 Enterprise x64 Custom image** task sequence and select **Edit**.
2. In the **Initialization** group, select the first **Format and Partition Disk (UEFI)** action, and in the **Volume** list, delete the first three volumes.
3. In the **Initialization** group, select the second **Format and Partition Disk (UEFI)** action, and in the **Volume** list, delete the first three volumes.

Real World Note: Without these changes, the task sequence will fail when deploying to UEFI machines.

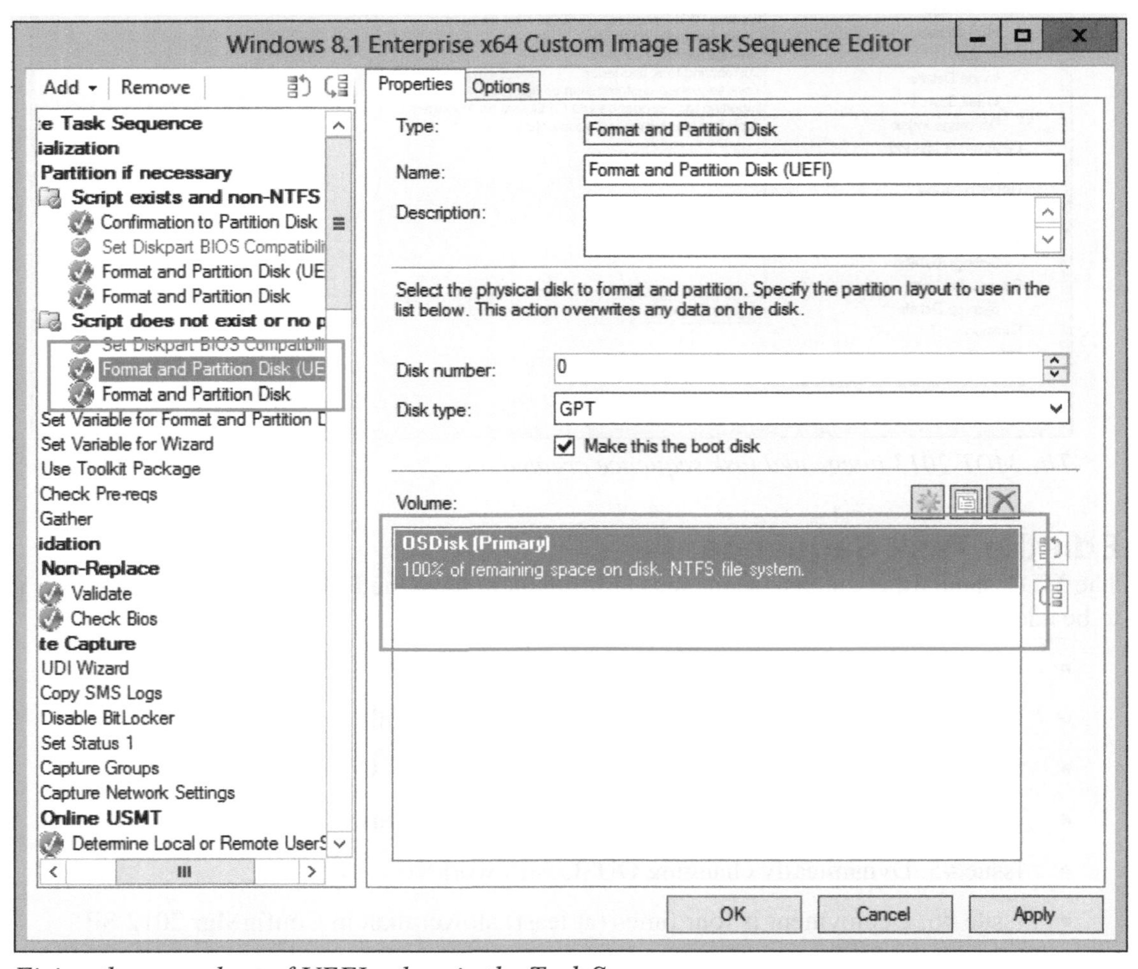

Fixing the second set of UEFI values in the Task Sequence.

4. In the **Install** group, select **Set Variable for Drive Letter** and configure the following:

   OSDPreserveDriveLetter: **True**

Real World Note: If this value is not changed, your Windows installation will end up in E:\Windows. This behavior was introduced in ConfigMgr 2012 SP1.

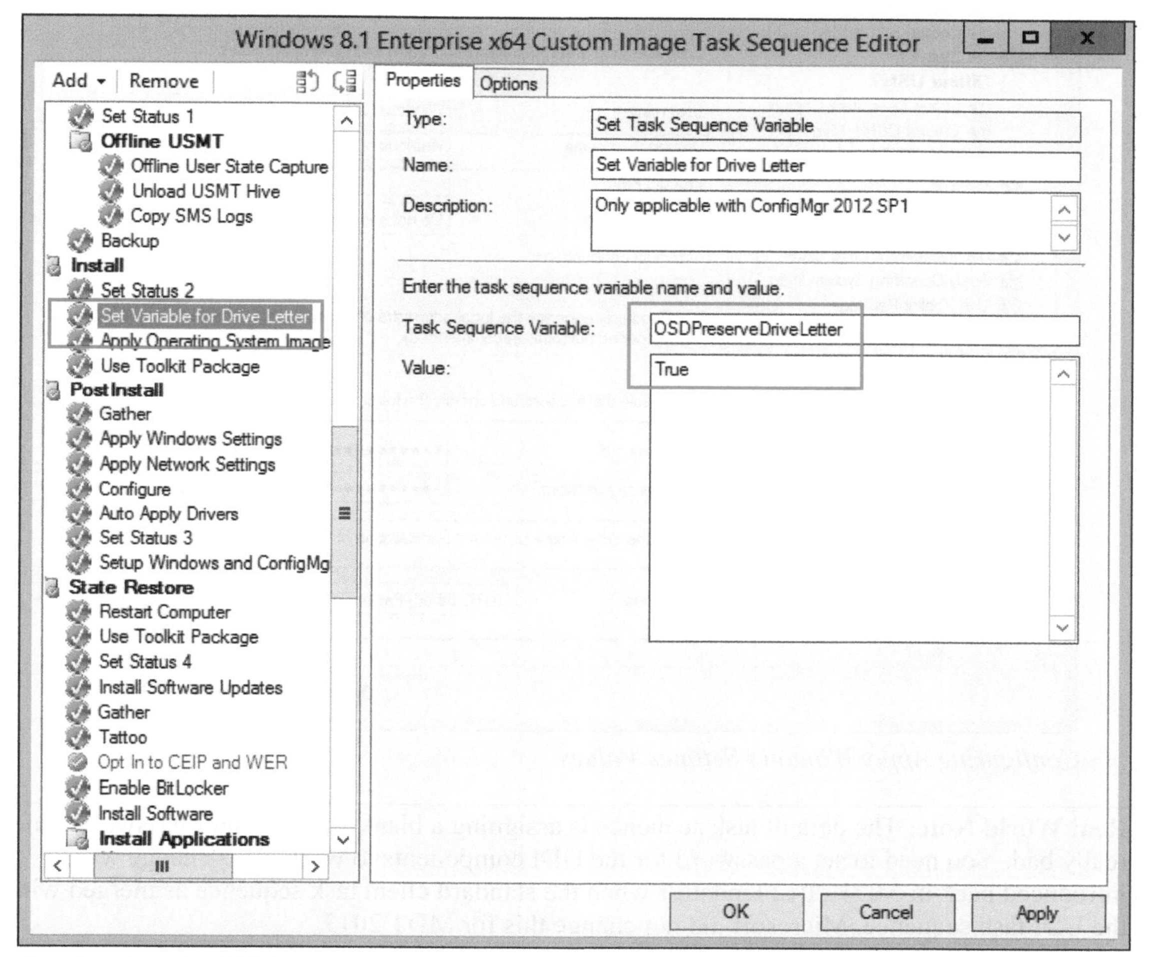

Configuring the OSDPreserveDriveLetter variable.

5. In the **Post Install** group, select **Apply Windows Settings** and configure the following:

   a. Select the **Enable the account and specify the local administrator** option, and assign a password of **P@ssw0rd**.

   b. Time zone: select the same time zone as the **CM01** server is using.

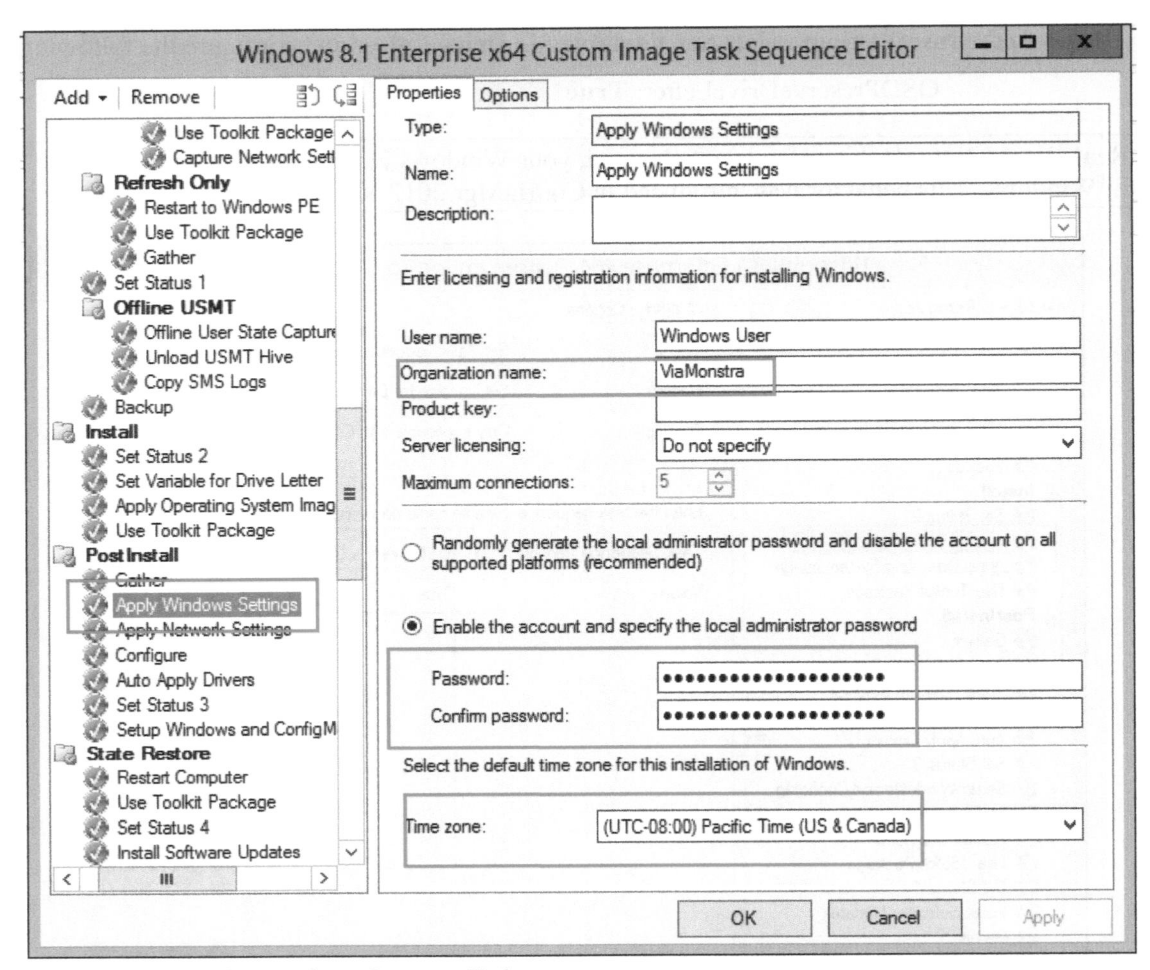

Configuring Apply Windows Settings Values

Real World Note: The default task sequence is assigning a blank administrator password which is really bad. You need to set a password for the UDI components to work. This change was introduced back in MDT 2012 Update 1 when the standard client task sequence as merged with the UDI task sequence. Microsoft did not change this for MDT 2013.

6. In the **Post Install** group, select **Apply Network Settings**, and configure the **Domain OU** value to use the **ViaMonstra / Workstations** OU (browse for values).

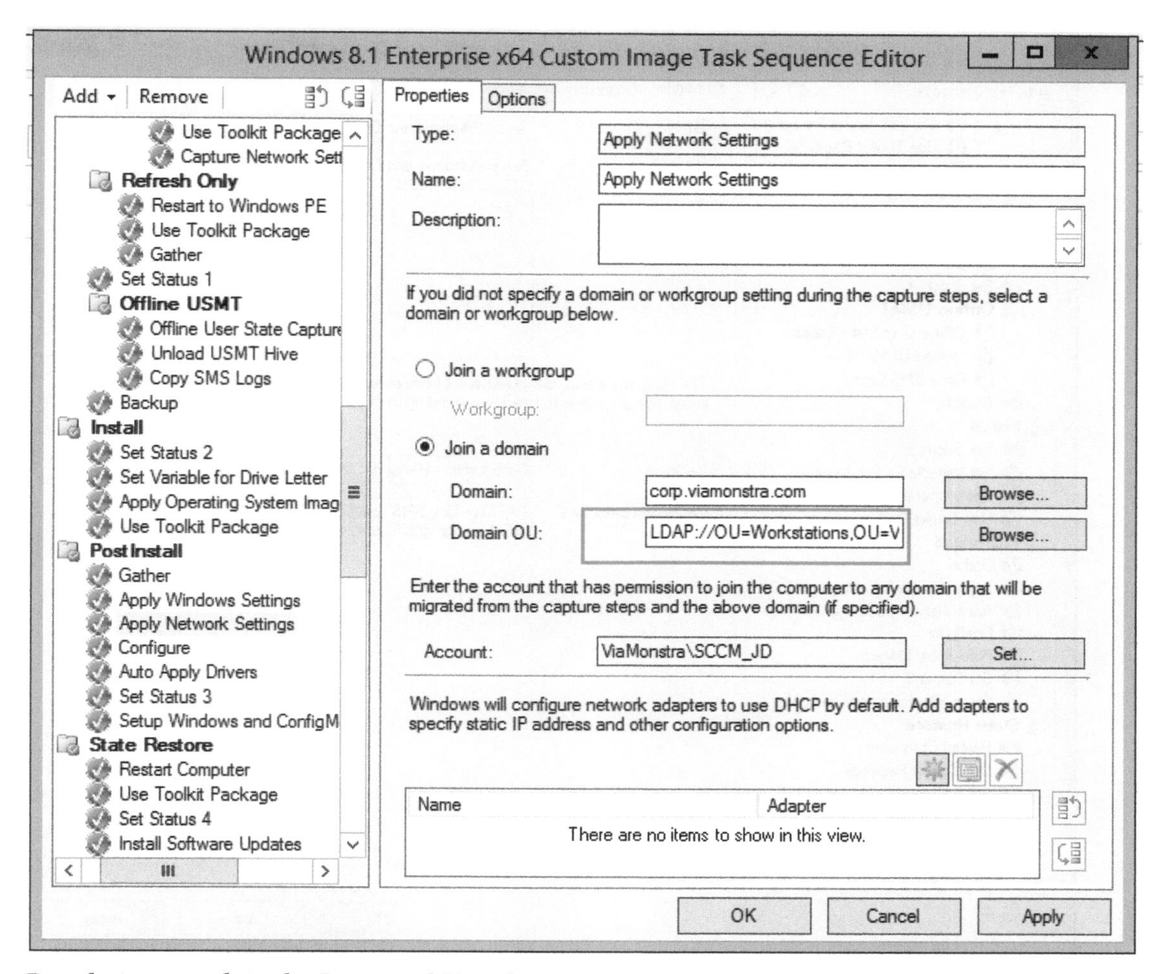

Populating a path in the Domain OU and Domain

Real World Note: The Domain OU value must be set to a non-blank value.

7. In the **Post Install** group, select **Setup Windows and ConfigMgr**, and in the **Installation properties** type in the following (remember: the Package ID for the ConfigMgr Client with Hotfixes was PS100018 in our example).

   PATCH="C:_SMSTaskSequence\OSD\PS100018\Hotfix\x64\configmgr2012ac-r2-kb2994331-x64.msp"

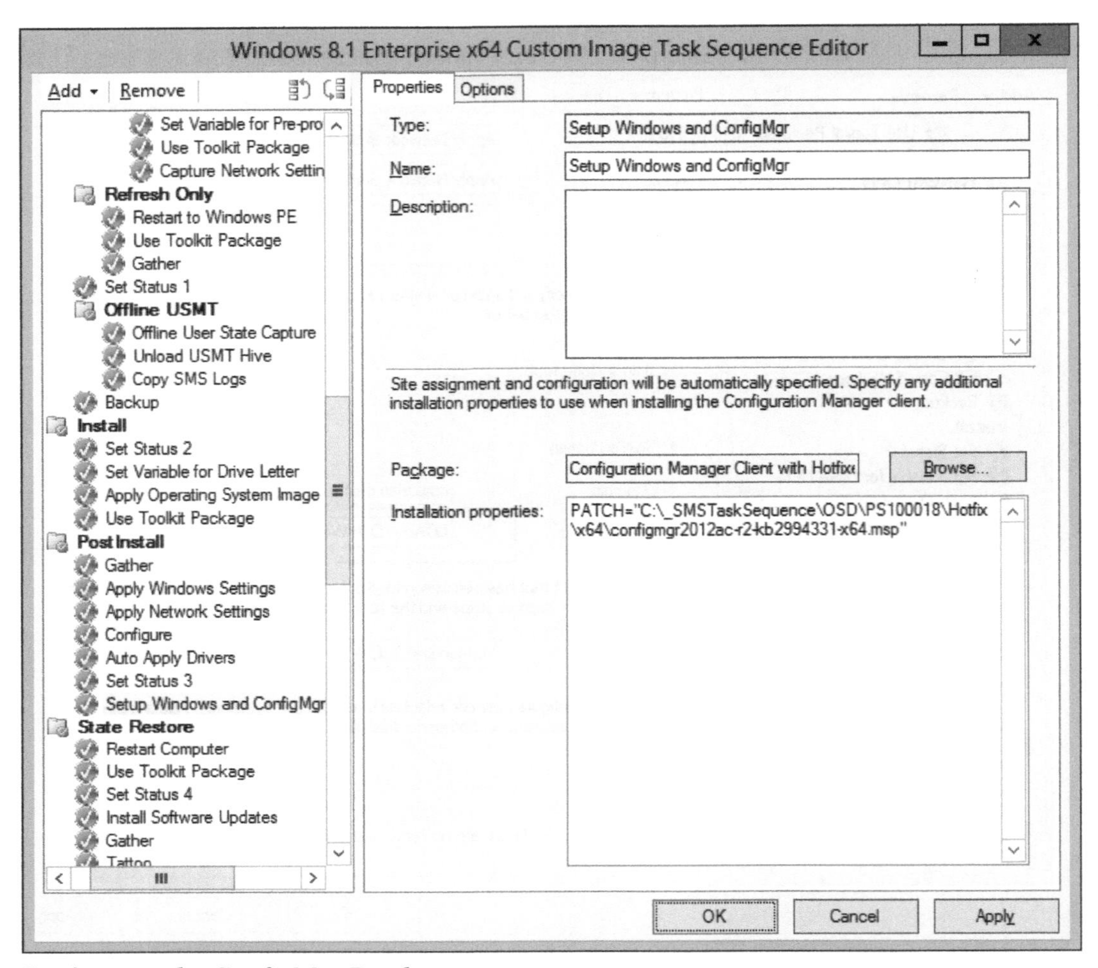

Configuring the ConfigMgr Patch property.

Real World Note: If you also create task sequence for x86 editions of Windows 8.1, you need to change the PATCH property to use the x86 update (configmgr2012ac-r2-kb2994331-i386.msp)

8. In the **PostInstall** group, disable the **Auto Apply Drivers** action. (Disabling is done by selecting the action and, in the Options tab, select the **Disable this step** check box.)

9. After the disabled **PostInstall / Auto Apply Drivers** action, add a new group name **Drivers**.

10. Within the **PostInstall / Drivers** group, add an **Apply Driver Package** action with the following settings:

a. Name: **HP EliteBook 8560w**

b. Driver Package: **Windows 8.1 x64 - HP EliteBook 8560w**

c. **Options**, add a **Query WMI condition** with the following query

SELECT * FROM Win32_ComputerSystem WHERE Model LIKE '%HP EliteBook 8560w%'

d. Click **Test query** to verify the syntax, it should return "contains valid syntax".

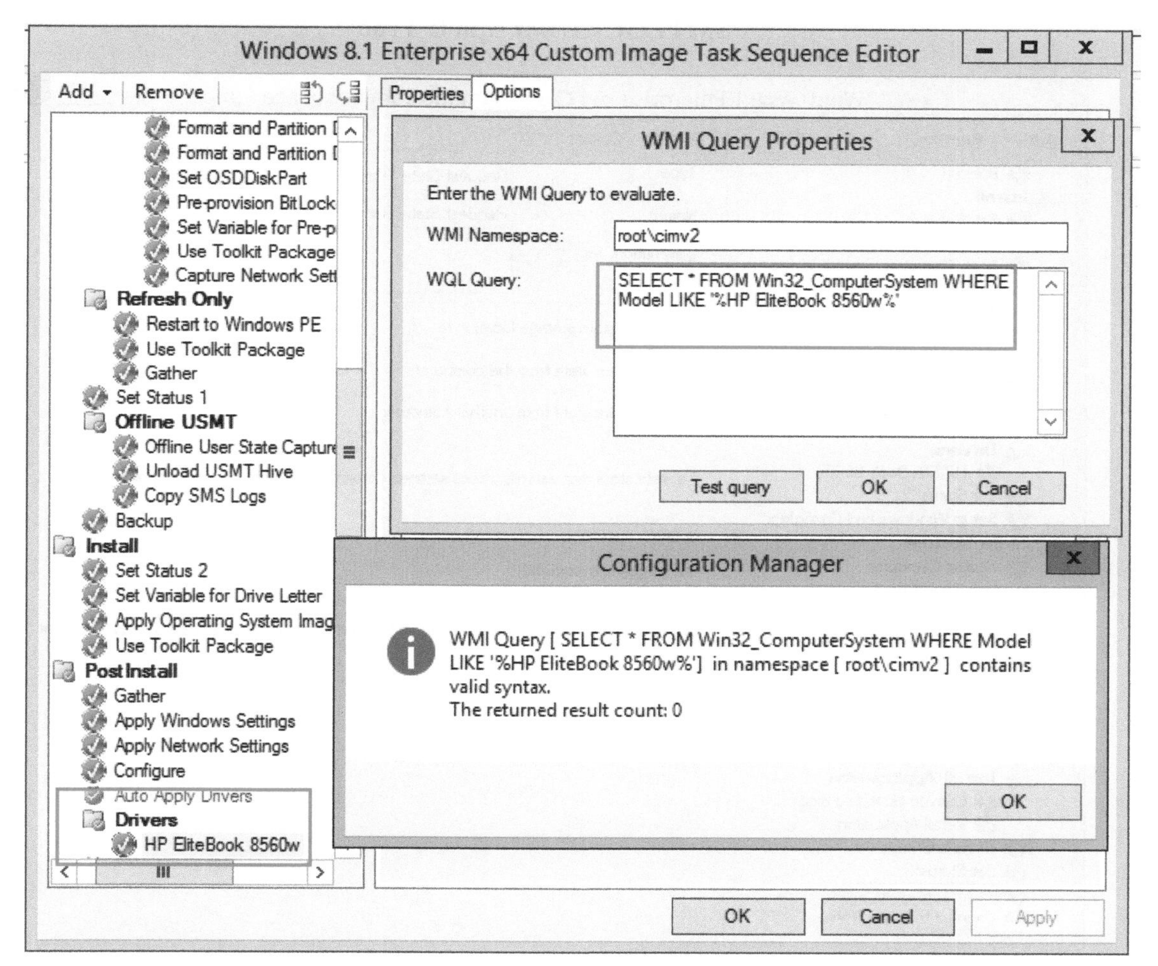

Adding Drivers.

11. In the **State Restore** group, after the **Set Status 5** action, add a **User State / Request State Store** action with the following settings:
    a. **Restore state from another computer**
    b. **If computer account fails to connect to state store, use the Network Access account**
    c. Options: **Continue on error**
    d. Options / Condition:

        Task Sequence Variable

        USMTLOCAL not equals True

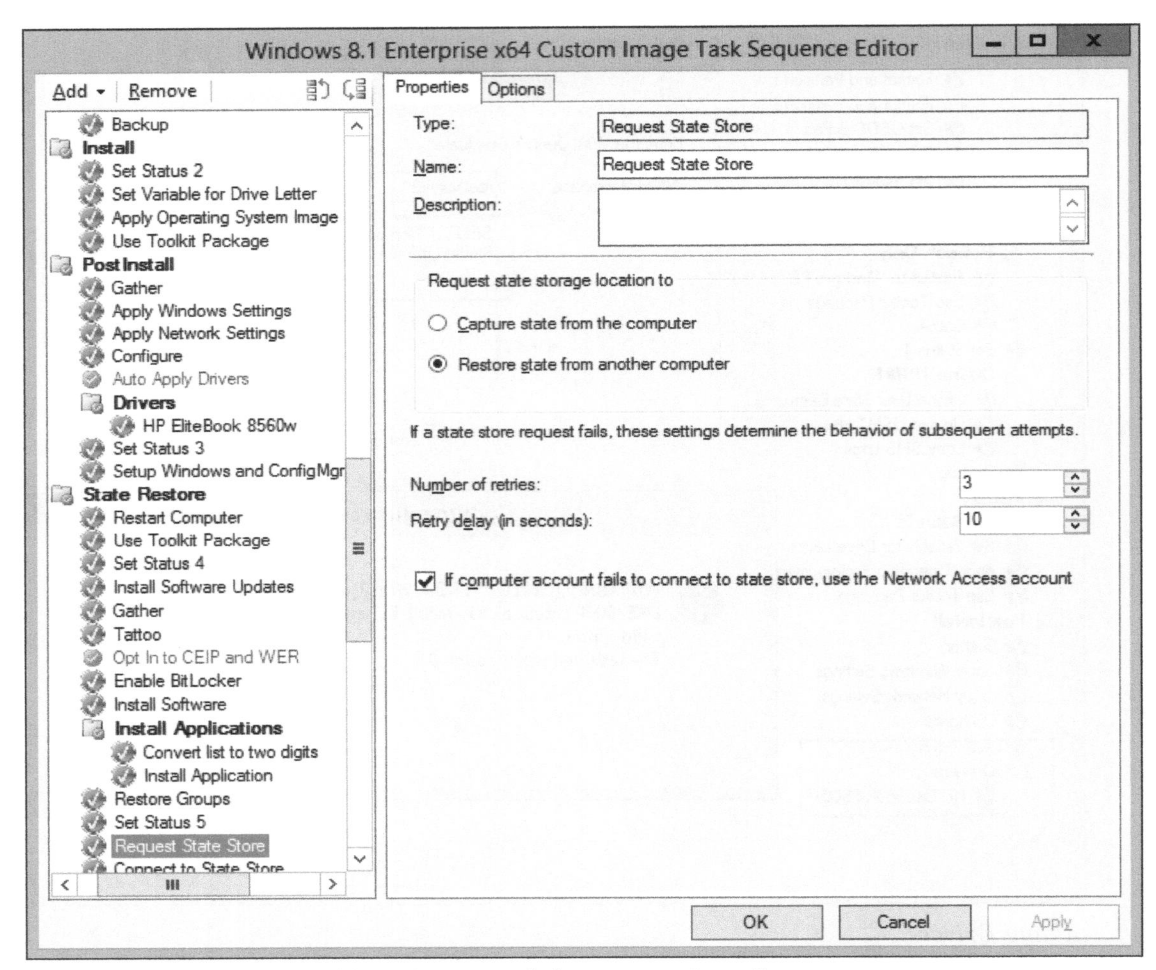

The task sequence after adding drivers and the Request State Store action.

12. In the **State Restore** group, after the **Restore User State** action, add a **Release State Store** action with the following settings:

    a. Options: **Continue on error**

    b. Options / Condition:

        Task Sequence Variable

        USMTLOCAL not equals True

13. In the **State Restore / Install Applications** group, select the **Install Application** action.

    Select the **Install the following applications** option, and add the **Adobe Reader X - OSD Install** application to the list.

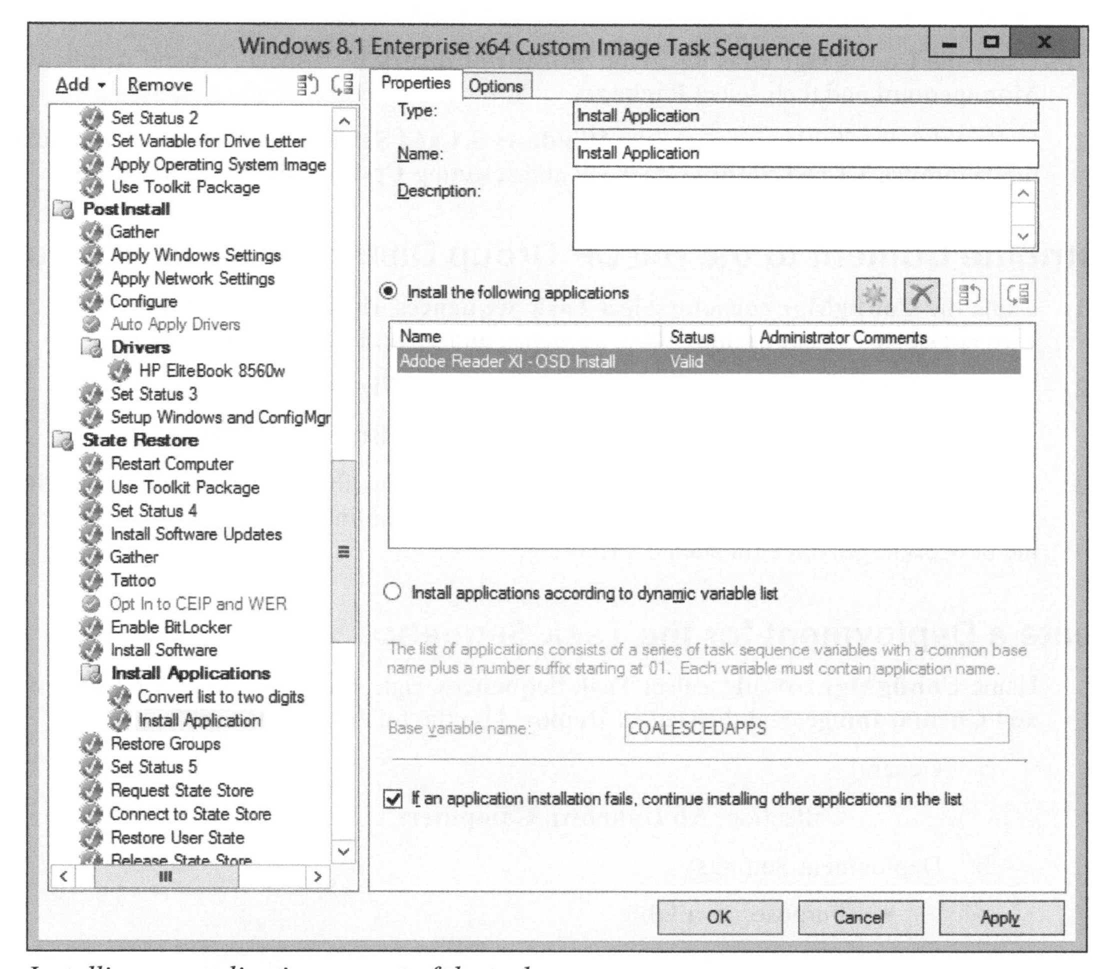

Installing an application as part of the task sequence

14. Click **OK**.

Configuring the Rules, Distributing Content, and Deploying Task Sequences

Configure the Rules (Windows 8.1 x64 Settings Package)

Using **File Explorer**, copy the **C:\Labfiles\ZTI Support Files\Windows 8.1 Deploy Settings\Customsettings.ini** file to the following folder (replacing the existing file):

D:\SCCM_Sources\OSD\Settings\Windows 8.1 x64 Settings

Update the Windows 8.1 x64 Settings Package

1. Using the **ConfigMgr console**, in the **Software Library** workspace, expand **Application Management** and then select **Packages**.
2. Update the distribution point for the **Windows 8.1 x64 Settings** package by right-clicking the **Windows 8.1 x64 Settings** package and selecting **Update Distribution Points**.

Distribute Content to the HQ DP Group Distribution Point Group

1. Using the **ConfigMgr console**, select **Task Sequences**, right-click the **Windows 8.1 Enterprise x64 Custom image** task sequence and select **Distribute Content**.
2. Use the following setting for the **Distribute Content Wizard**:

   Content Destination: Add the **HQ DP Group** distribution point group.
3. Using **CMTrace**, verify the distribution to the **CM01** distribution point (part of the HQ DP Group) by reviewing the **distmgr.log** file. Do not continue until you confirm that all the new packages have finished distributing.

Create a Deployment for the Task Sequence

Using **ConfigMgr console**, select **Task Sequences**, right-click **Windows 8.1 Enterprise x64 Custom Image**, and then select **Deploy**. Use the following settings:

a. General

   Collection: **All Unknown Computers**

b. Deployment Settings

   - Purpose: **Available**
   - Make available to the following: **Only media and PXE**

c. Scheduling

   <default>

d. User Experience

<default>

e. Alerts

<default>

f. Distribution Points

<default>

Deploying Windows 8.1 Using Boot Media

At this point, you should have a functioning task sequence for bare metal, refresh, and replace scenarios. It is imperative that the sequence be validated before continuing, as any initial issues with the task sequence will take significantly longer to troubleshoot after additional task sequence injections have taken place.

Create a ConfigMgr 2012 R2 Boot Image

1. On **CM01**, using **File Explorer**, create the **D:\Media** folder.
2. Using the **ConfigMgr console**, in the **Software Library** workspace, right-click **Task Sequences** and select **Create Task Sequence Media**.
3. Use the following settings for the **Create Task Sequence Media Wizard**:

    a. Select Media Type

    Bootable media

    b. Media Management

    Site-based media

    c. Media Type

    - **CD/DVD set**
    - Media file: **D:\Media\ZTI Install CD.iso**

    d. Security

    - Enable unknown computer support.
    - Protect media with a password.
    - Password and Confirm password: **P@ssw0rd**

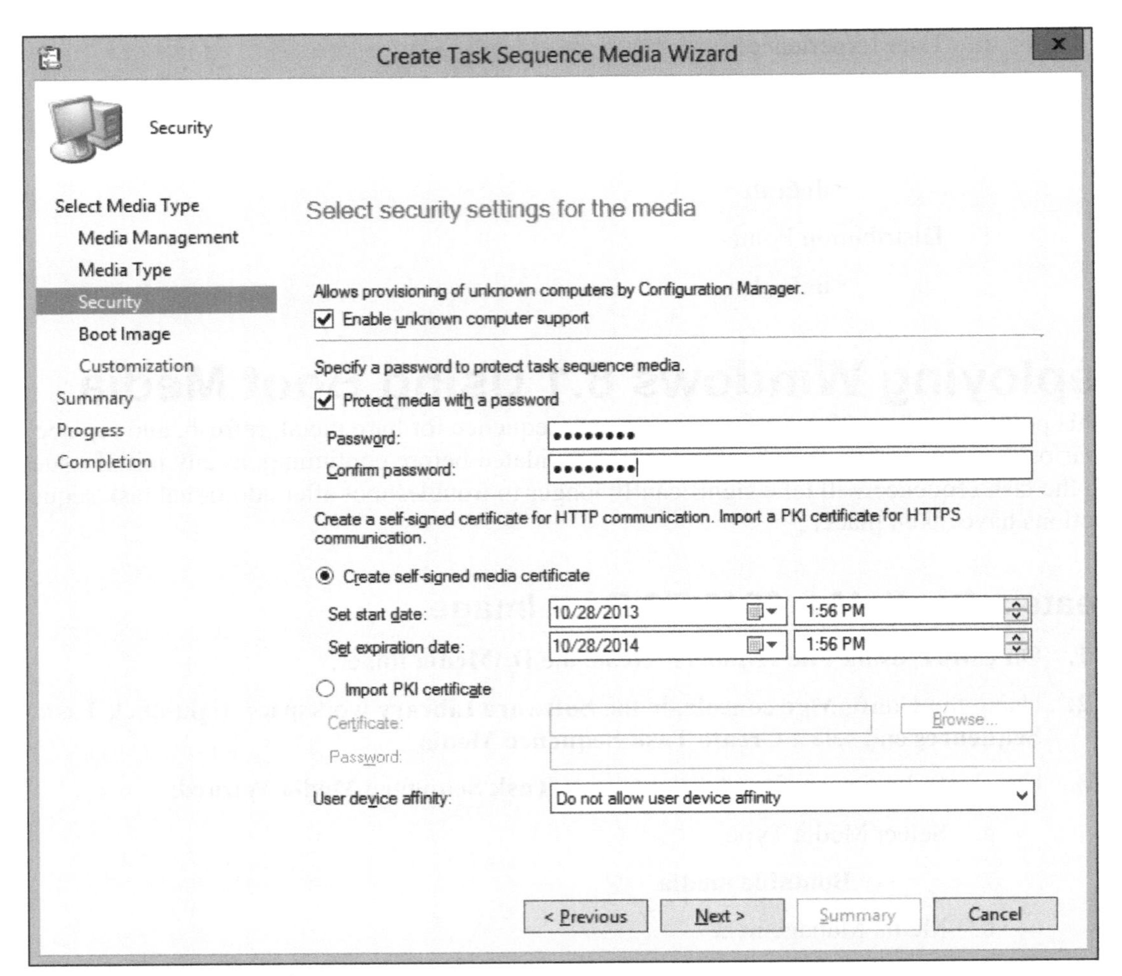

Creating the boot media.

e. Boot Image:

- Boot image: **Zero Touch WinPE 5.0 x64**
- Distribution point: **CM01.CORP.VIAMONSTRA.COM**
- Management point: **CM01.corp.viamonstra.com**

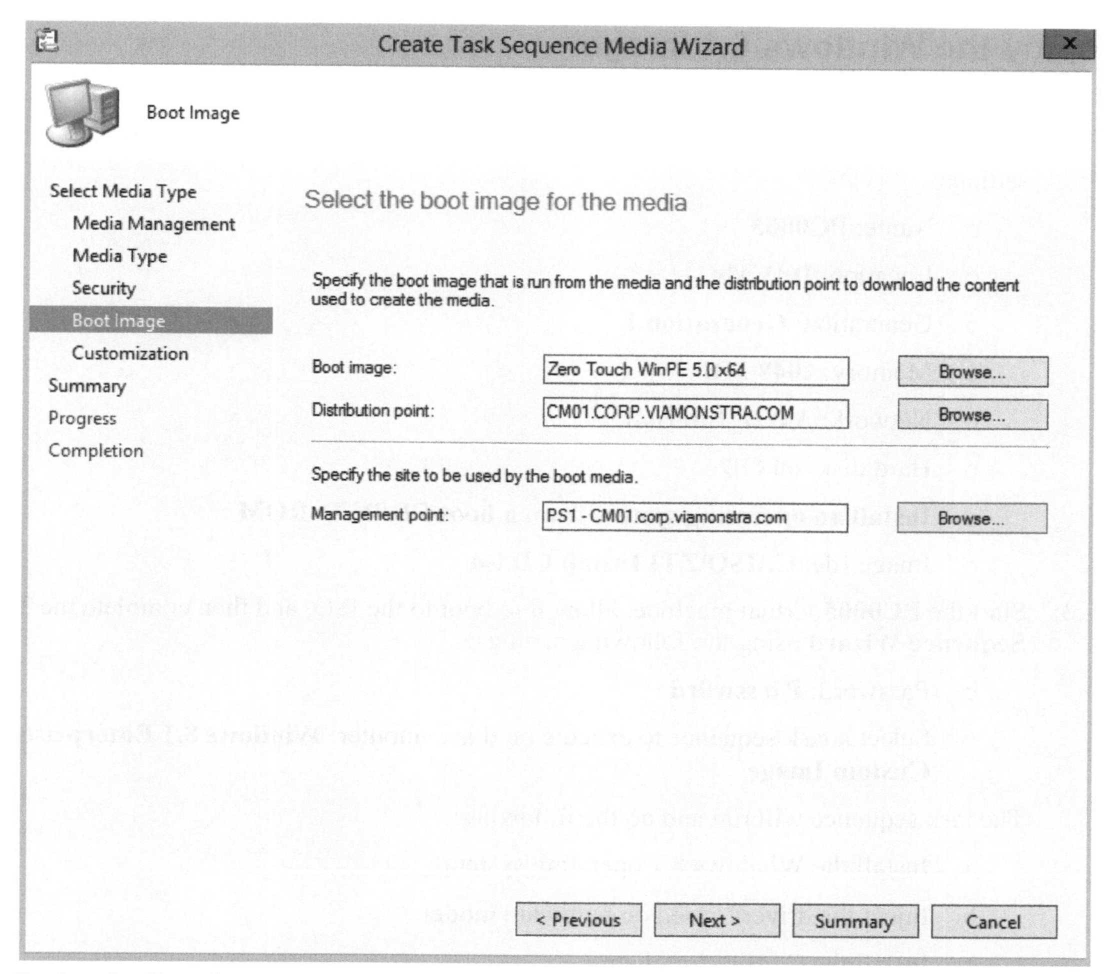

Setting the Boot Image options.

f. Customization

<default>

g. Summary

<default>

Deploy the Windows 8.1 Image

1. On the host PC, copy the **ZTI Install CD.iso** file from **\\CM01\D$\Media** to **C:\ISO**.
2. On the host PC, create a **Generation 1** Hyper-V virtual machine with the following settings:
    - Name: **PC0005**
    - Location: **D:\VMs**
    - Generation: **Generation 1**
    - Memory: **2048 MB**
    - Network: **AWD_Internal**
    - Hard disk: **60 GB**
    - **Install an operating system from a boot CD/DVD-ROM**
    - Image file: **C:\ISO\ZTI Install CD.iso**
3. Start the **PC0005** virtual machine, allow it to boot to the ISO, and then complete the **Task Sequence Wizard** using the following settings:
    - Password: **P@ssw0rd**
    - Select a task sequence to execute on this computer: **Windows 8.1 Enterprise x64 Custom Image**

    The task sequence will run and do the following:

    a. Install the Windows 8.1 operating system
    b. Inject the drivers based on hardware model
    c. Install the ConfigMgr client
    d. Join it to the domain
    e. Install the selected application

Backup Existing Task Sequence

Now that you've validated that your native ConfigMgr/MDT sequence completes successfully without error, you now make a copy of it to archive. It's not a bad idea to actually take an export of the task sequence as well and store in another location, just to be sure.

Make a backup copy of the working deployment task sequence:

1. Log on to **CM01** and start the **ConfigMgr console**.
2. In the **Software Library** workspace, expand **Operating Systems**, and select **Task Sequences**.
3. Right-click **Windows 8.1 Enterprise x64 Custom Image** and select **Copy**.

> **Note:** Ensure that you have a working task sequence. If you do not have a working "Gold" task sequence, do not proceed as the rest of the chapters rely on this working.

4. Right-click the new copied task sequence and click **Properties**. Rename the task sequence as follows:

   Name: **Windows 8.1 Enterprise x64 Custom Image-AWD**

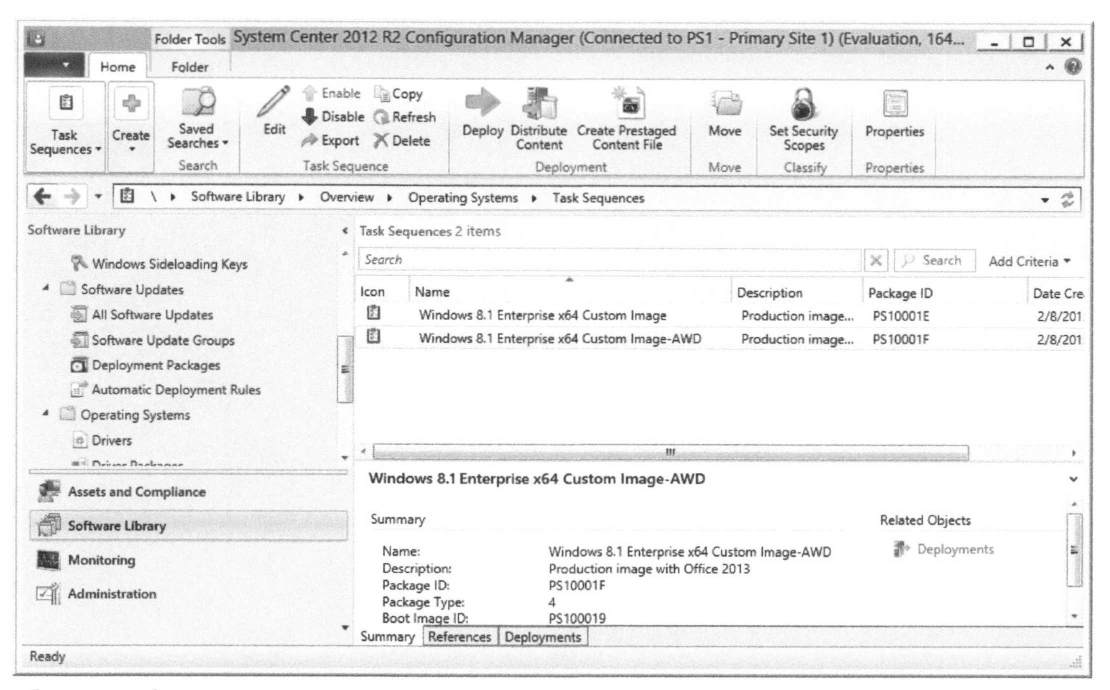

The two task sequences.

Chapter 9

Nomad for an OSD Refresh Scenario

Arguably the most popular reason why organizations choose Nomad to augment their ConfigMgr hierarchy is the ability to deliver Windows OSD at remote locations with limited bandwidth. Performing this without local servers or on-site personnel has been a saving grace for many companies. It has empowered organizations to treat all remote locations exactly like the HQ and therefore guarantee the delivery of operating systems and Windows migrations to poorly connected clients. By eliminating that last major hurdle in local server requirements, 1E customers have taken this opportunity to centralize other services, completely removing the server footprint from branch environments.

Nomad for OSD Key Concepts

To facilitate a full-featured OSD solution that doesn't require local server resources, there are many pieces that must be configured for each environment. Boot images must be altered so they do not rely on DP resources for site assignment, extensions need to be added into the actual task sequence to perform Nomad caching actions, and Peer Backup Assistant (PBA) must be configured to provide user state migration.

Modifying the Boot Image

To use Nomad for OSD, you must install NomadBranchTools.msi on the primary site server. The installer provides several tools that enable Nomad within the WinPE boot images. This extends the boot WIMs with the required Nomad components for OSD.

Nomad Task Sequence Extensions

A task sequence in ConfigMgr is comprised of two components: packages and policy. *Packages* are the actual applications and files that are used during the imaging process, whereas *Policy* defines the steps that the sequence will take and a list of the packages that are required.

Nomad, acting as an alternate content provider, receives package and application content requests from ConfigMgr and downloads the required content (either locally if it is available or from a remote distribution point). If a deployment is configured to download all packages before running the task sequence, the Package IDs are sent down with the initial policy; the Content Transfer Manager recognizes that the Nomad agent is installed and hands the content retrieval process over to it. However, typically OS deployments are configured to download packages as required in the task sequence; with this configuration, Nomad never sees the policy request for a package download and therefore does not control the content download.

By adding some custom task sequence steps, you will use an application called NomadPackageLocator.exe to instruct Nomad to prestage the required packages. The actual placement of these steps is determined by how and when a package is referenced in a sequence.

The available custom task sequence actions are:

Nomad Task Sequence Extension	Description
Install and Configure Nomad in Windows PE	Used to install and configure Nomad in WinPE. It is a "Lite" version of Nomad that does not depend on a functioning ConfigMgr client.
Pre-stage Content Using Nomad	Used to prestage content in Windows or WinPE using Nomad. It references the NomadPackageLocator tool to locate any locally available copies of the requested specified content. If no copies are available, it downloads from the assigned distribution point.
Create Nomad Application Policy	Creates a Nomad application policy and is used in an operating system deployment task sequence during the provisioning phase prior to any applications being installed. It uses the NomadPackageLocator tool to enable Nomad for use as an alternative content provider during provisioning.
Delete Nomad Application Policy	Removes the application policy that is created with the preceding step
Save Nomad Cache	Saves the Nomad cache to the protected task sequence directory
Restore Nomad Cache	Used to restore the Nomad cache in the new operating system during provisioning after Nomad has been installed
Enable Run from Distribution Point	Enables the content to be run from the local Nomad cache
Disable Run from Distribution Point	Reverts changes made in the Enable Run from Distribution Point step
Peer Backup Assistant: Provision Nomad PBA Data Store	Initiates an election to determine potential PBA hosts at a client site
Peer Backup Assistant: Close Nomad PBA Data Store	Disconnects a session between a PBA client and host

Nomad Task Sequence Extension	Description
Peer Backup Assistant: Locate Existing Nomad PBA Data Store	Performs an election to request a specific migration file
Peer Backup Assistant: Release Nomad PBA Data Store	Finalizes the state restore process and instructs the PBA host to delete the stored .mig file if retention periods are not specified
Peer Backup Assistant: Nomad PBA Data Store High Availability	Instructs a PBA host to copy a received migration file to one or more Nomad clients to ensure high availability

SMSNomad.exe

SMSNomad.exe is a core process for everything that is Nomad and can be run in Standalone mode to pull down content from a remote location. Please see help.1e.com for more information.

Key Nomad OSD Log Files

Arguably the most important part of troubleshooting operating system deployments is a thorough understanding of the log files that are active during task sequence execution, and where to go to access these files. When dealing with complex task sequences in excess of 400 steps, knowing where the files are located is only a part of the battle. Being able to follow the execution steps in multiple logs is also vitally important. The key to establishing an accurate timeline is actually quite simple: Open two CMTrace windows, one for the SMSTS.log and one for the other log you want to view. The SMSTS.log becomes your timeline, and using its timestamps you can view other actions that occurred at specific times.

Given a specific issue, you can sometimes look at up to 30 log files to determine the root cause of a failure. We're not going to go into each and every log file; however, here are the most important ones:

Log Name	Description
SMSTS.log	This is the main ConfigMgr 2012 task sequence execution log. Nomad-specific task sequence information is published to this log during task sequence execution. Default location: Changes depending on the stage of task sequence execution
NomadPackageLocator.log	Used in WinPE when there is no functioning ConfigMgr 2012 or NomadBranch client, NomadPackageLocator locates Nomad-enabled content on peer clients. Default location: X:\Windows\Temp\SMSTSLog\NomadPackageLocator.log
NomadBranch.Log	Records all information pertaining to the Nomad client. Package requests for software updates are logged here, as well as information regarding download details and content location. Location: X:\Windows\Temp\SMSTSLog\Logfiles

ConfigMgr OSD Conceptual Design (ViaMonstra)

The following design allows ViaMonstra to eliminate more than 95 percent of the required distribution points using a 1E Nomad-optimized design. Content only crosses the WAN once, and when available, all content is shared from other 1E Nomad peers. As you will see in this chapter, minor modifications to an existing "Gold" task sequence are required to enable this functionality.

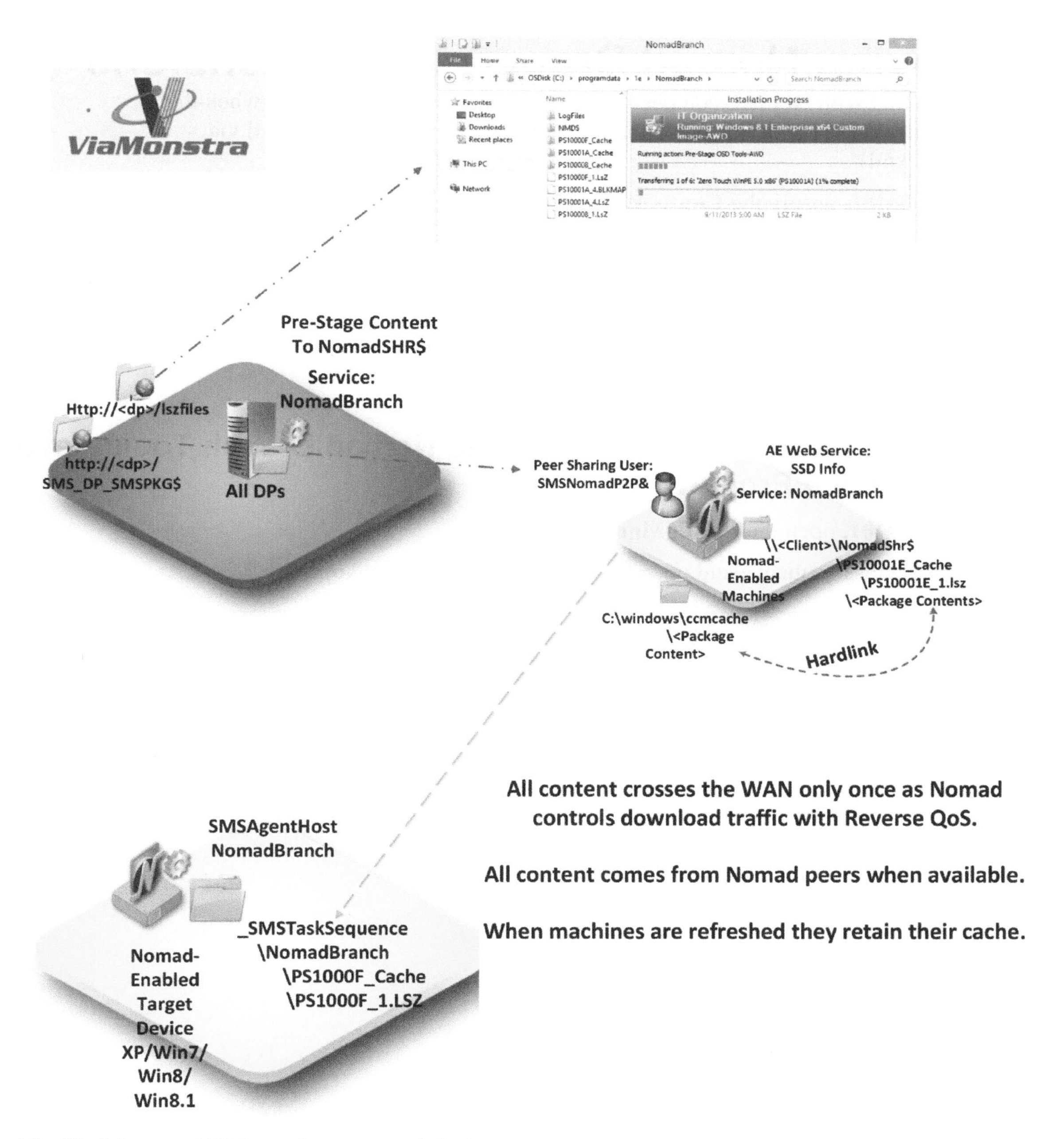

The ViaMonstra 1E Nomad conceptual design.

Deploying Nomad Branch OSD Extensions

To support OSD with Nomad, you need to install the OSD extensions, and when that is completed, update the boot image (so that the Nomad Branch files are added via osdinjection.xml).

1. On **CM01**, ensure the **ConfigMgr console** is not open.
2. Open an elevated **Command prompt** and type the following command:

   ```
   cd \labfiles\sources\NomadBranch v5.2.100.32\ConfigMgr2012
   ```
3. Type **NomadBranchTools.msi** to start the installation.
4. Accept all defaults and exit the installer when finished.

Validate that AdminUI Extensions and Nomad Branch Tools Have Been Deployed Properly

1. On **CM01**, open the **ConfigMgr console**.
2. Find a task sequence and open the properties. Notice the **Nomad** tab.

> **Real World Note:** When copying a task sequence, the Enable Nomad check box is not selected. This can be seen in the following figure. If you are copying task sequences that are Nomad-enabled, you must remember to select this option.

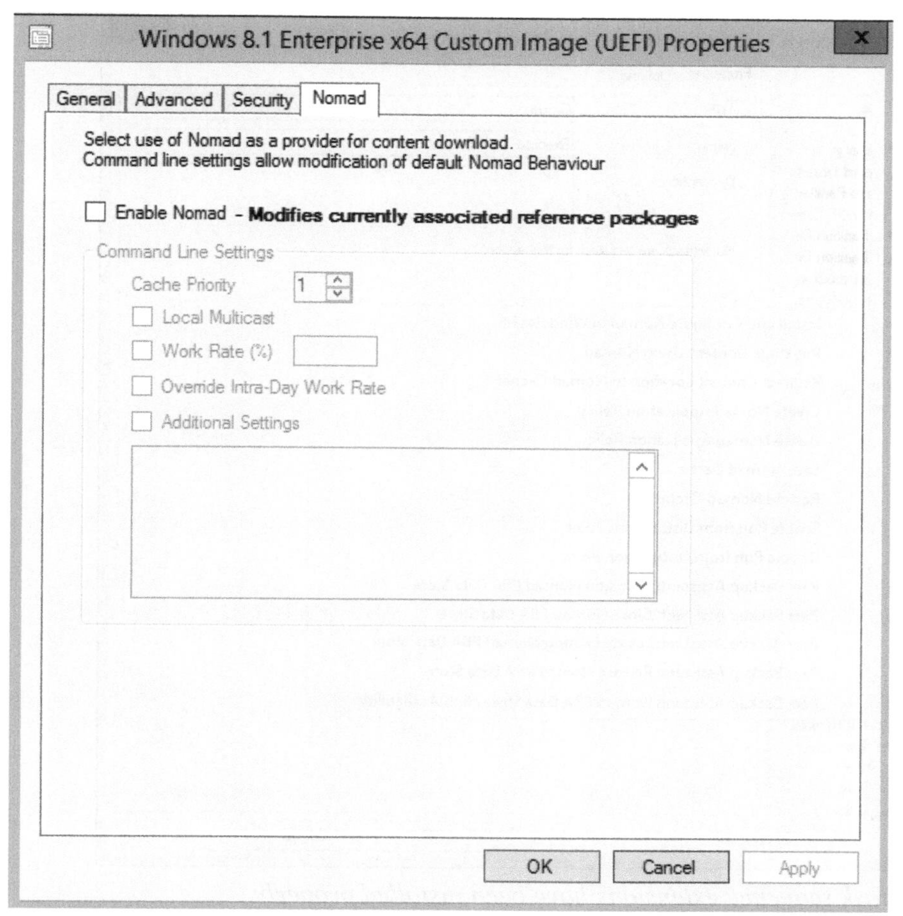

Validating that console extensions have been installed properly.

5. Now edit a task sequence to validate that the Nomad extensions are visible in the task sequence engine. After the Nomad Branch tools have been installed, the additional Nomad task sequence actions become available.

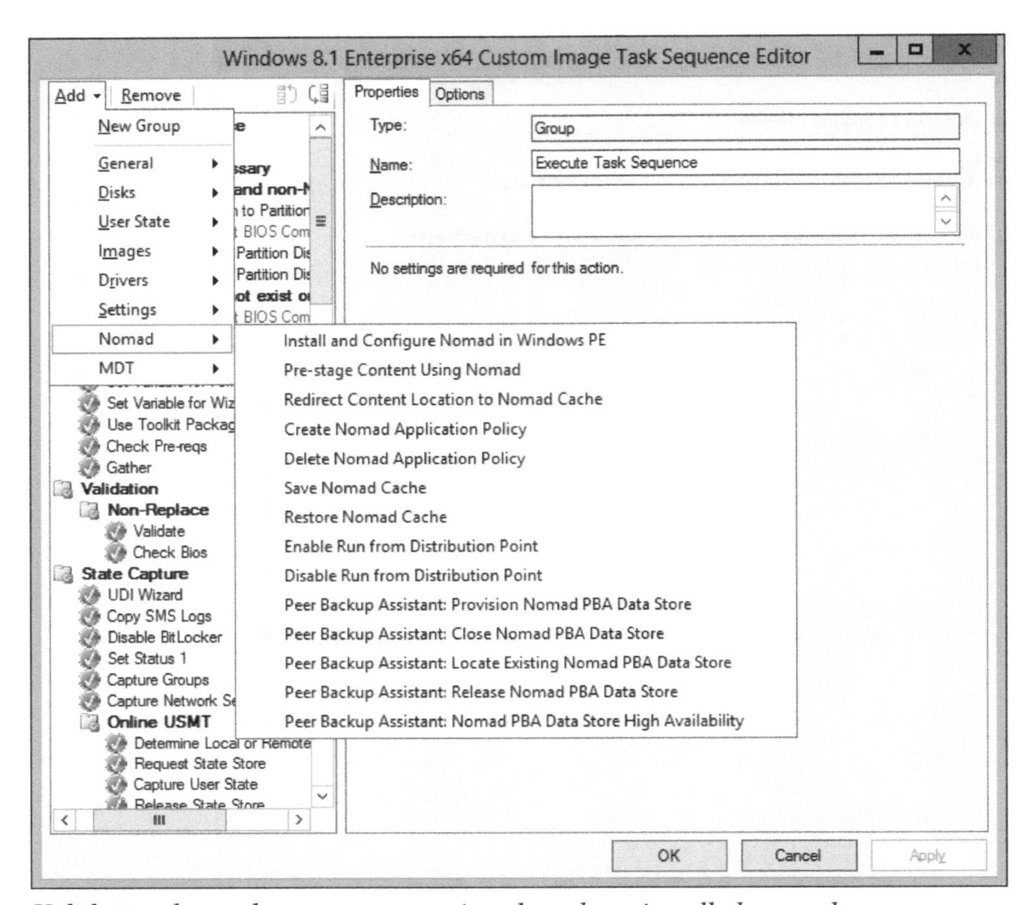

Validating that task sequence extensions have been installed properly.

Update the Boot Image

After installing the Nomad Branch OSD Extensions, you need to update the boot image in order to have the Nomad Branch OSD files injected.

1. On **CM01**, open the **ConfigMgr console**.
2. In the **Software Library** workspace, expand **Operating Systems / Boot Images**.
3. Right-click the **Zero Touch WinPE 5.0 x64** boot image, and select **Update Distribution Points**. Then complete the wizard.

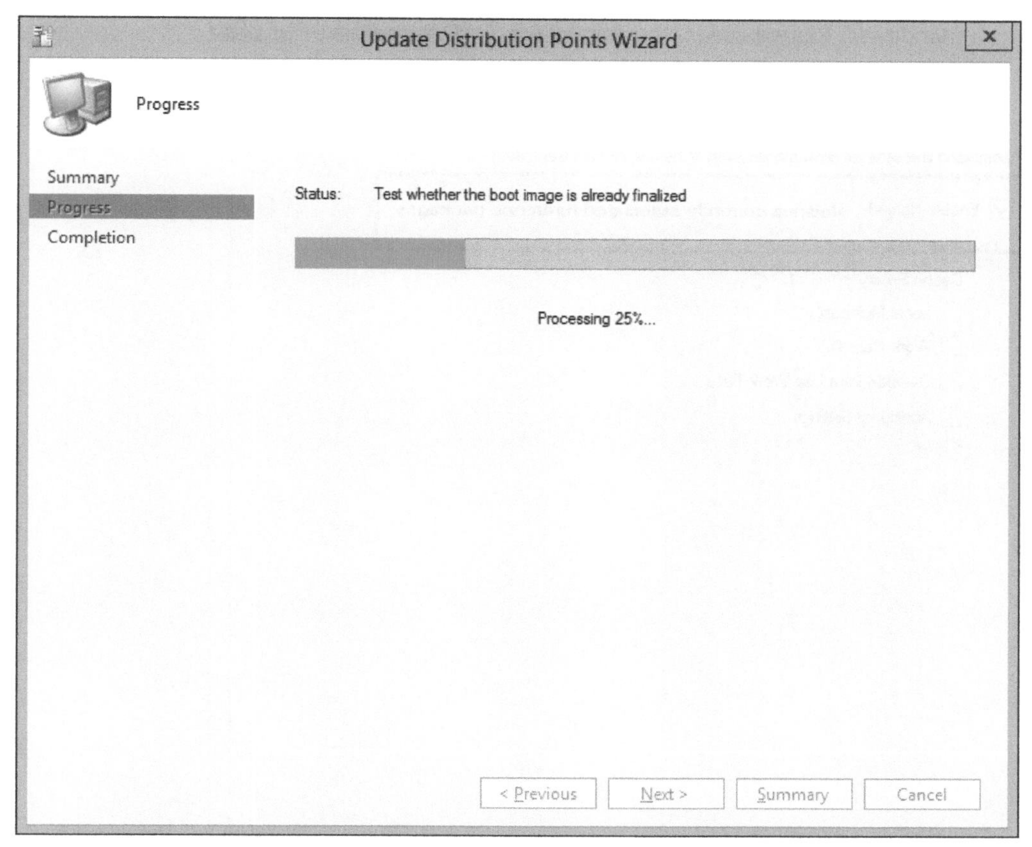

Updating the Zero Touch WinPE 5.0 x64 boot image with Nomad Branch OSD files.

Extend an Existing Task Sequence with Nomad

In order to use Nomad for OSD, you must first extend the Task Sequence Editor with the Nomad console extensions (installer). When the **Enable Nomad** check box is selected on a task sequence, Nomad is presented to the Task Sequence Execution Manager as an alternate content provider. This enables Nomad to respond to content requests as required during the deployment.

Real World Note: It is important to note that each time a task sequence is copied, the Enable Nomad check box is cleared. You must select it again each time a task sequence is copied.

1. On **CM01**, open the **ConfigMgr console**.
2. In the **Software Library** workspace, expand **Operating Systems / Task Sequences**.
3. Right-click **Windows 8.1 Enterprise x64 Custom Image-AWD** and click **Properties**.
4. Select the **Nomad** tab, and then select **Enable Nomad - Modifies currently associated reference packages**.

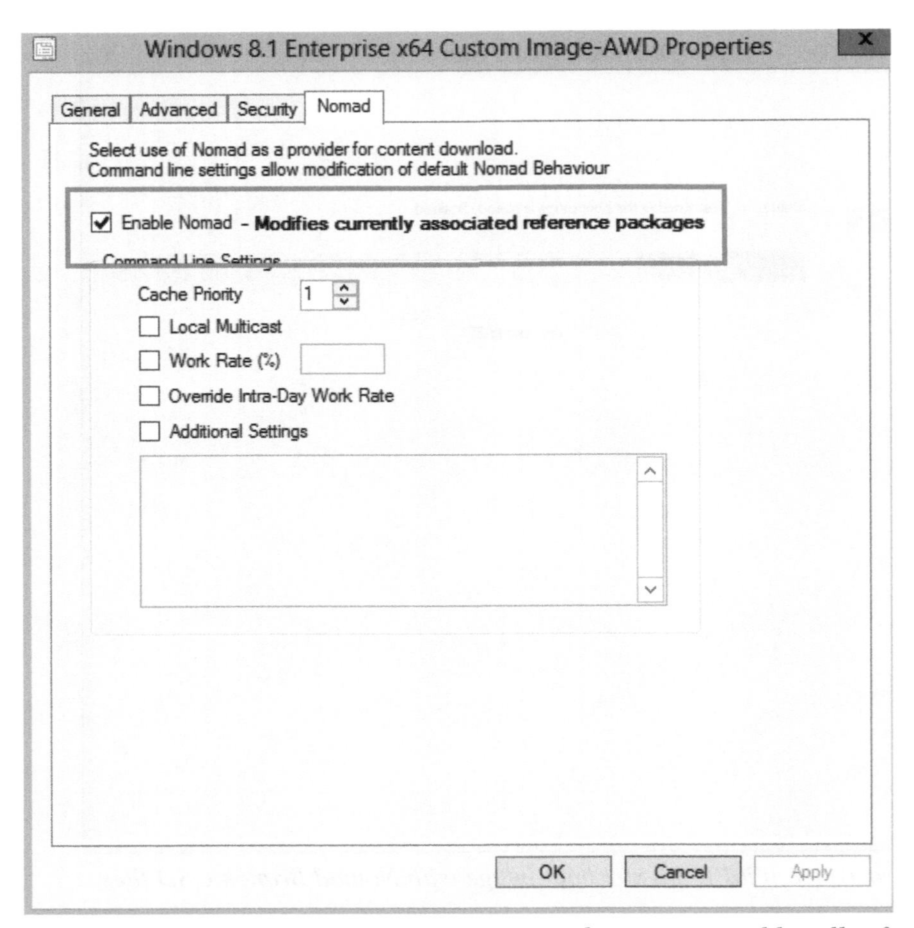

Selecting the Enable Nomad check box on a task sequence enables all reference packages.

5. Click the **General** tab and modify the task sequence description with the following, and then click **OK**:

    Version 1.0 - Base Nomad Extensions

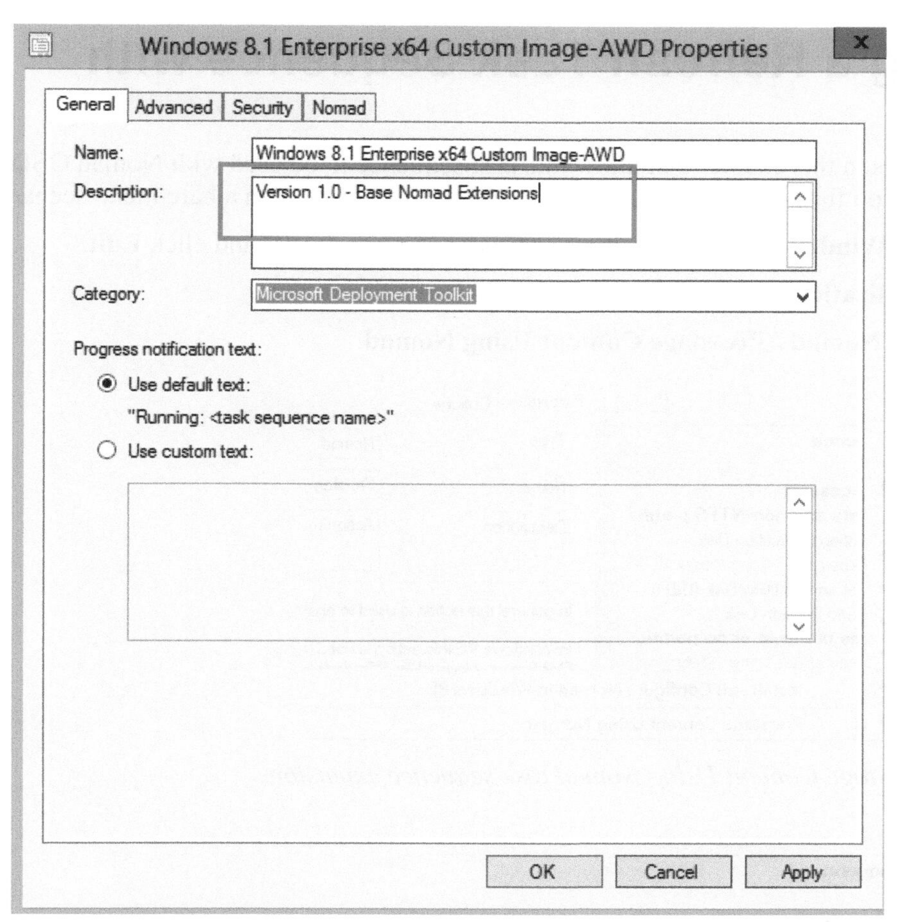

Always configure a new version number when modifying a task sequence.

Real World Note: Using the Description field for version control on a task sequence is a great way to know whether the ConfigMgr policy has updated when testing. For example, if changes have been made and the name of the task sequence remains the same, it becomes very difficult to tell which version of the task sequence is being tested. Often there will be errors that present themselves because content is not available, and this is because the policy update has not completed and there is a version mismatch of the task sequence. Using the Description field allows for quick validations of which version of a task sequence is about to be deployed.

Extending a Refresh Task Sequence with Nomad

You make extensions in this chapter that allow this task sequence to be used with Nomad OSD for a refresh scenario. You further extend this task sequence later to work with a bare metal scenario.

1. Right-click **Windows 8.1 Enterprise x64 Custom Image-AWD** and click **Edit**.
2. In the **Initialization** group, select **Set Variable for Wizard**.
3. Click **Add / Nomad / Pre-stage Content Using Nomad**.

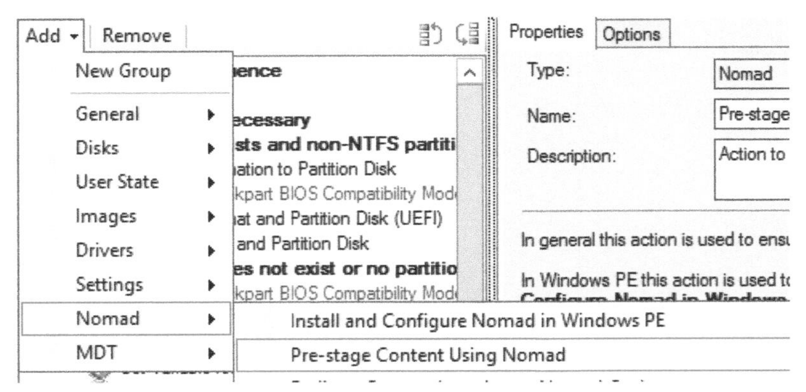

Adding the Pre-stage Content Using Nomad task sequence extension.

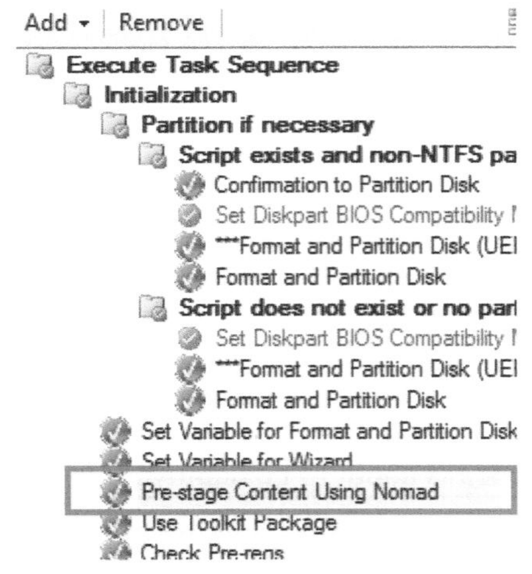

Reviewing the Pre-Stage Content Using Nomad task sequence extension.

4. Configure the following settings:
   - Name: **Pre-Stage OSD Tools-AWD**
   - References:
     - **User State Migration Tool for Windows 8**
     - **Configuration Manager Client with Hotfixes**
     - **Zero Touch WinPE 5.0 x64**
     - **Windows 8.1 Enterprise x64 Custom Image**
     - **MDT 2013**
     - **Windows 8.1 x64 Settings**

Note: Your package names could be slightly different depending on your configuration. Make sure you select all core packages used for OSD in this step.

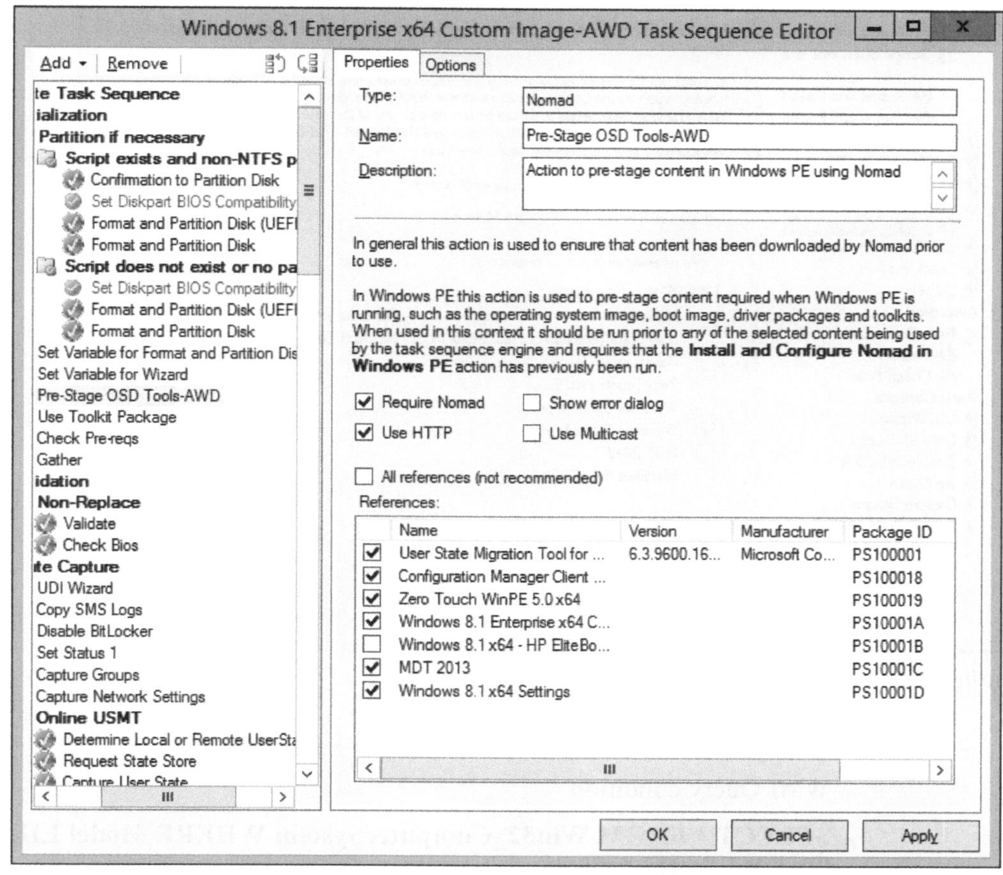

Pre-staging content using Nomad.

5. Click **Pre-stage OSD Tools-AWD**.
6. Click **Add / New Group**:

   Name: **Pre-Stage Drivers**

7. Right-click **Pre-Stage Drivers**, and then click **Add / Nomad / Pre-stage Content Using Nomad**. Use the following settings:
   - Name: **Pre-Stage HP EliteBook 8560w-AWD**
   - References: **Windows 8.1 x64 - HP EliteBook 8560w**

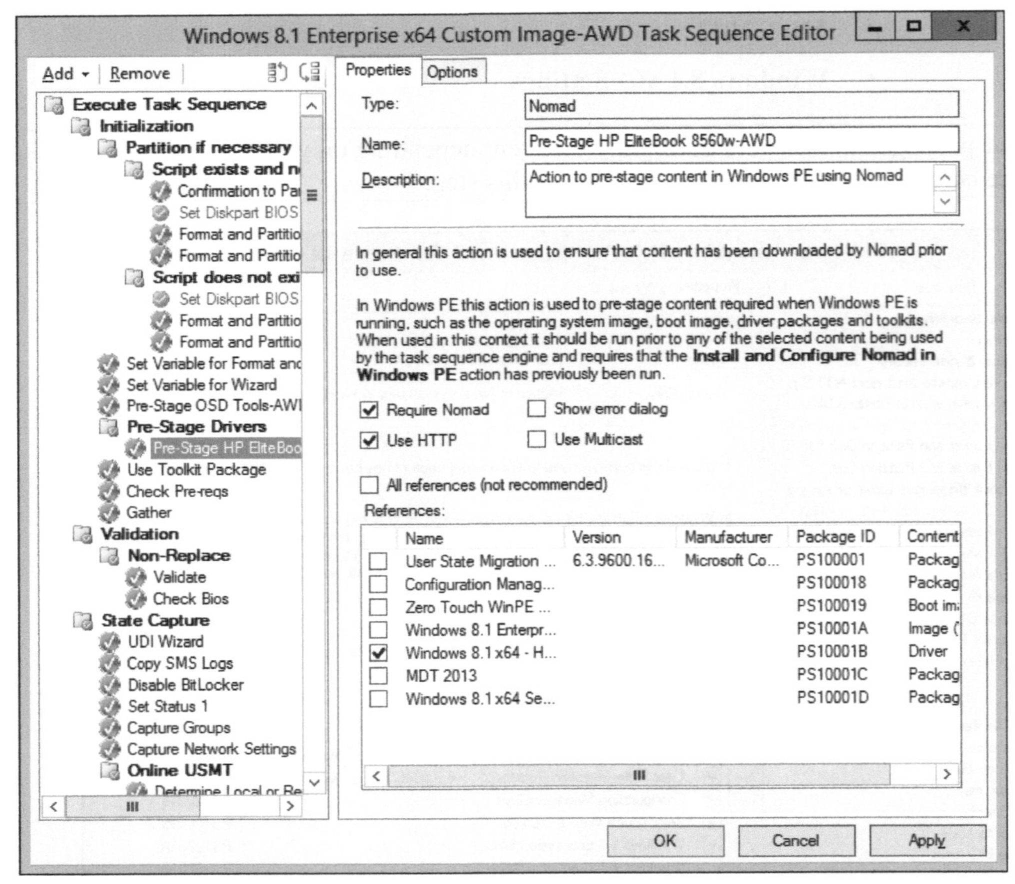

Prestaging drivers using Nomad.

   - Select the **Options tab** and then **Add Condition**. Configure the following:

     WMI Query condition

     SELECT * FROM Win32_ComputerSystem WHERE Model LIKE "%HP EliteBook 8560w%"

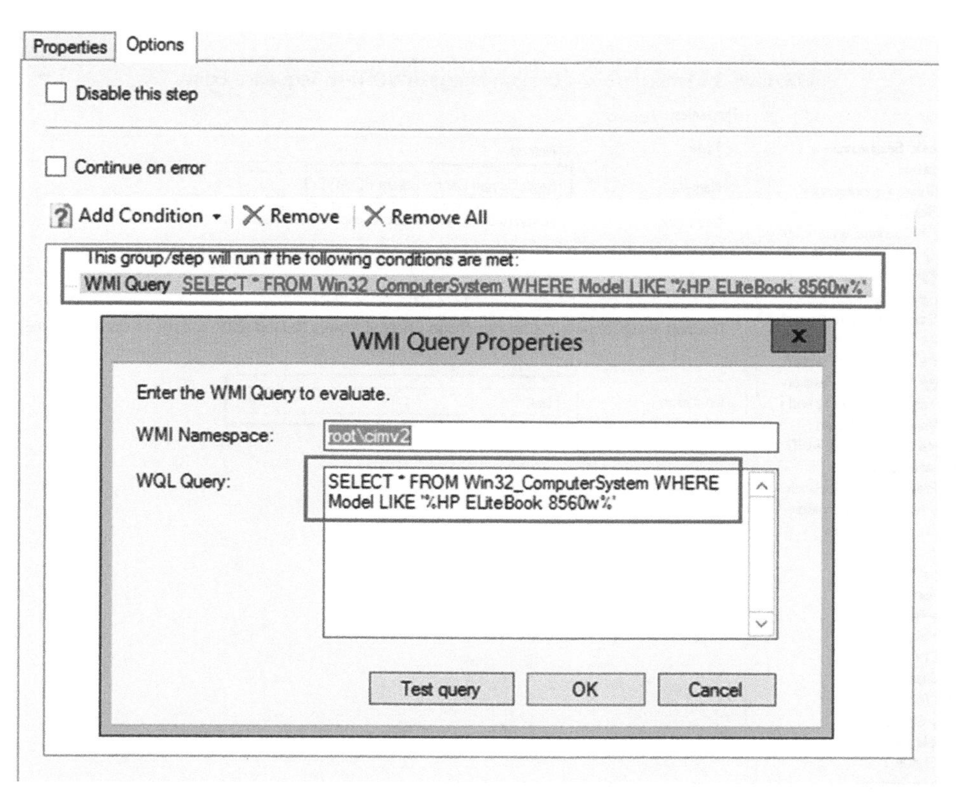

Creating a WMI query for drivers.

Real World Note: In production, this step is repeated for each driver. The reason is that you want the delivery of drivers to be dynamic per system. It doesn't make sense to prestage all drivers to every system.

8. Click **Use Toolkit Package** just under **Pre-Stage HP EliteBook 8560w-AWD**.
9. Click **Add / Nomad / Save Nomad Cache**.
10. Configure with the following settings:
    - Name: **Save Nomad Cache before PE-AWD**
    - Operation: **Link**
    - Wipe CCM Cache: Clear the check box.

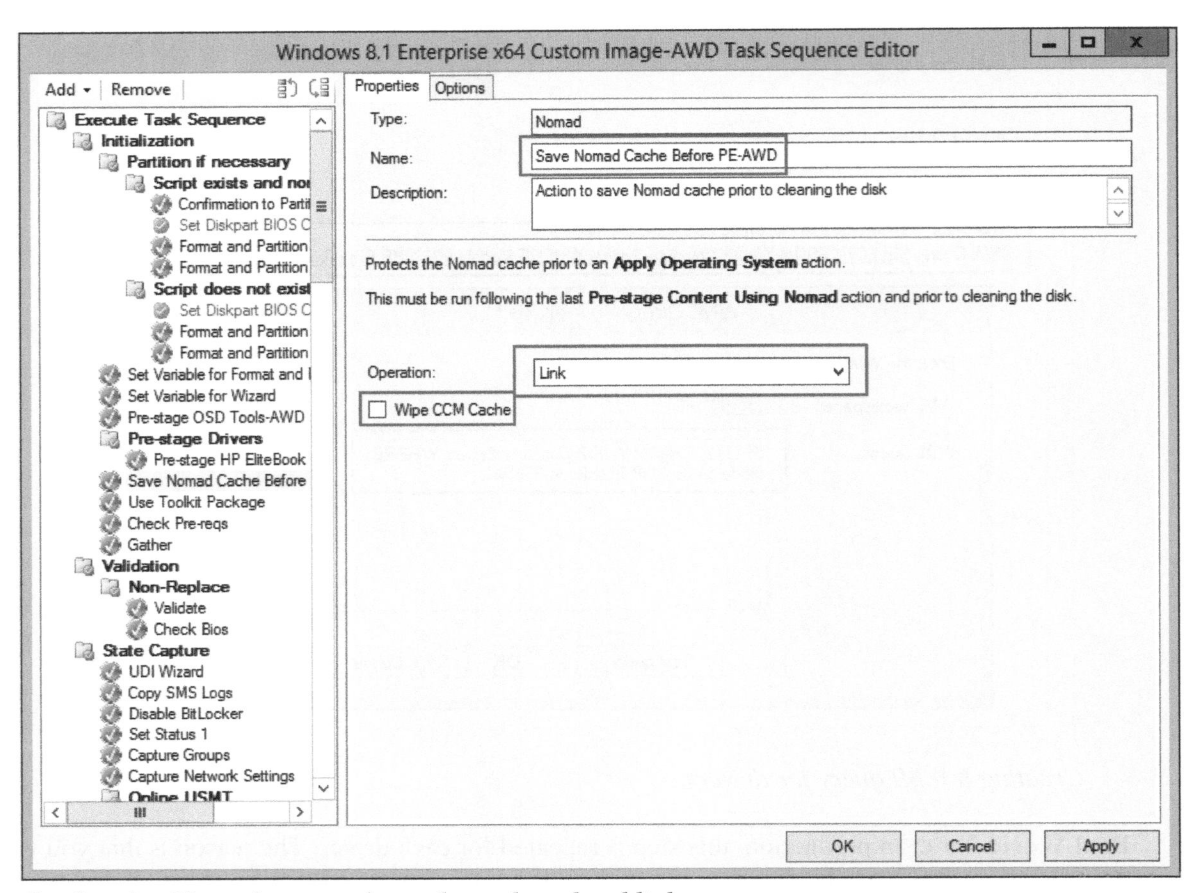

Configuring Nomad to save the cache and use hard links.

11. Click **Save Nomad Cache before PE-AWD** and move it up one level.
12. Click **Save Nomad Cache before PE-AWD**, click **Add / Nomad**, and then select **Enable Run from Distribution Point**.
13. Configure with the following setting:

    Name: **Enable Run from Distribution Point-AWD**

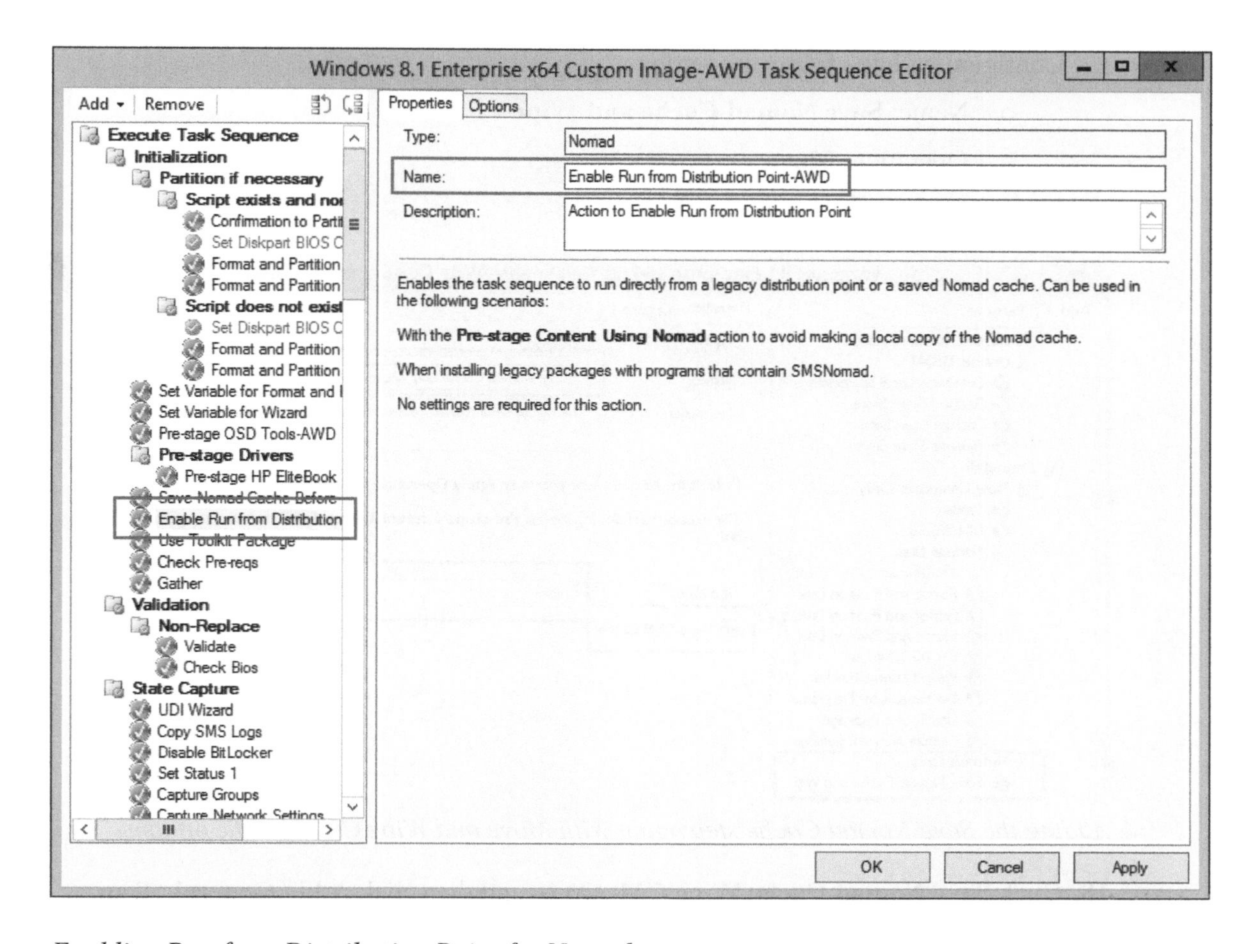

Enabling Run from Distribution Point for Nomad.

14. The steps added should look like the following image.

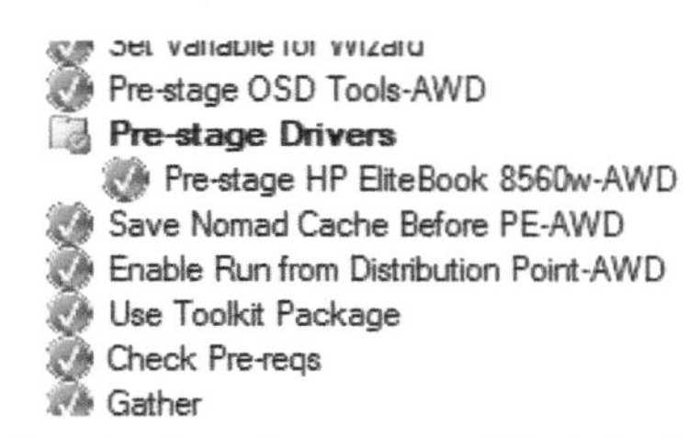

Reviewing the steps added during the task sequence creation.

15. Scroll down to the **Refresh Only** group.

16. Click **Refresh Only**, and the click **Add / Nomad / Save Nomad Cache**.

17. Configure with the following settings:
    - Name: **Save Nomad Cache and Wipe CM-AWD**
    - Operation: **Move**
    - Wipe CCM Cache: **Enabled**

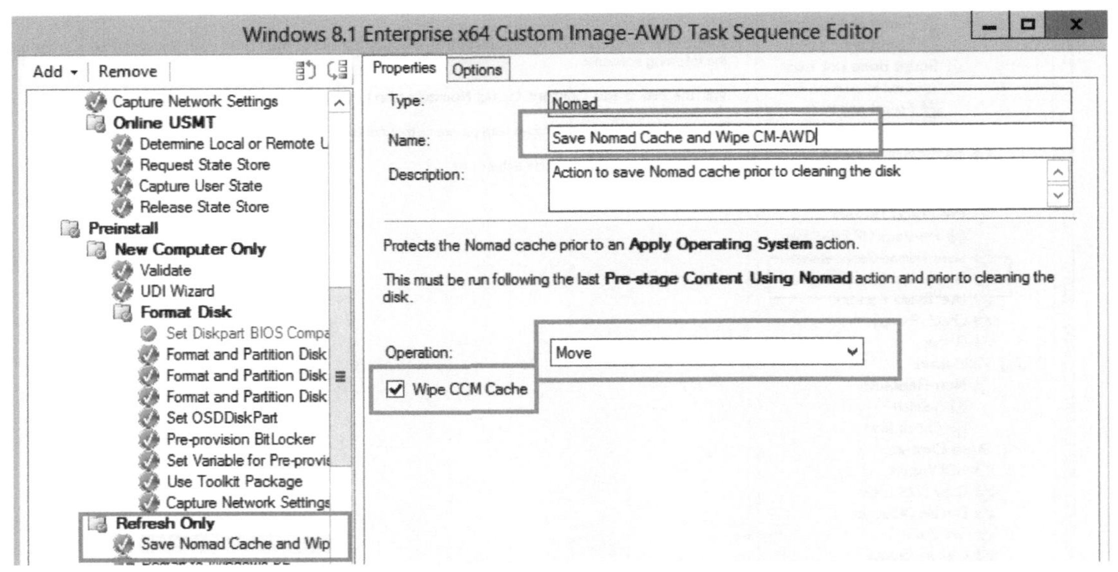

Adding the Save Nomad Cache step again with Move and Wipe CCM Cache options.

18. Click **Save Nomad Cache Wipe CM-AWD**, and then click **Add / General / Run Command Line**.
19. Configure with the following settings:
    - Name: **Rename Logfiles to Logfiles.old-AWD**
    - Command line: **cmd /c ren C:_SMSTaskSequence\NomadBranch\Logfiles Logfiles.old**

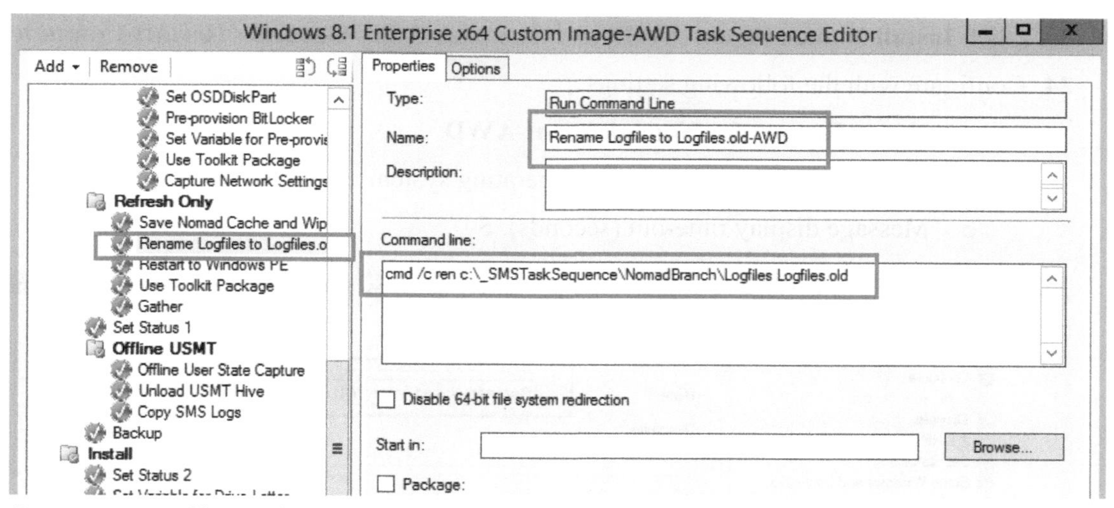

Renaming Logfiles in the Nomad path.

20. Scroll down to the **State Restore** group.
21. Click **Restart Computer**, and then click **Add / General / Install Package**.
22. Configure with the following settings:
    - Name: **Install Nomad Agent-AWD**
    - Package: **1E Software 1E Nomad Branch x64-AWD 5.2**
    - Program: **Per-system Unattended**

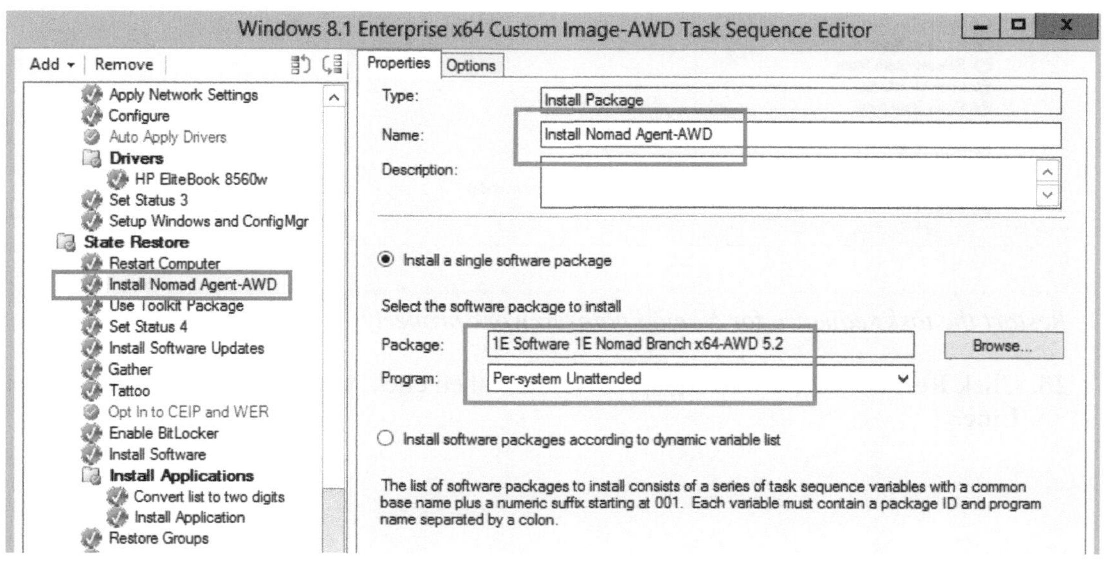

Installing the Nomad package in the task sequence.

23. Click **Install Nomad Agent-AWD**, and then click **Add / General / Restart Computer**.
24. Configure with the following settings:
    - Name: **Restart for Nomad Agent-AWD**
    - The currently installed default operating system: **Selected**
    - Message display time-out (seconds): **5**

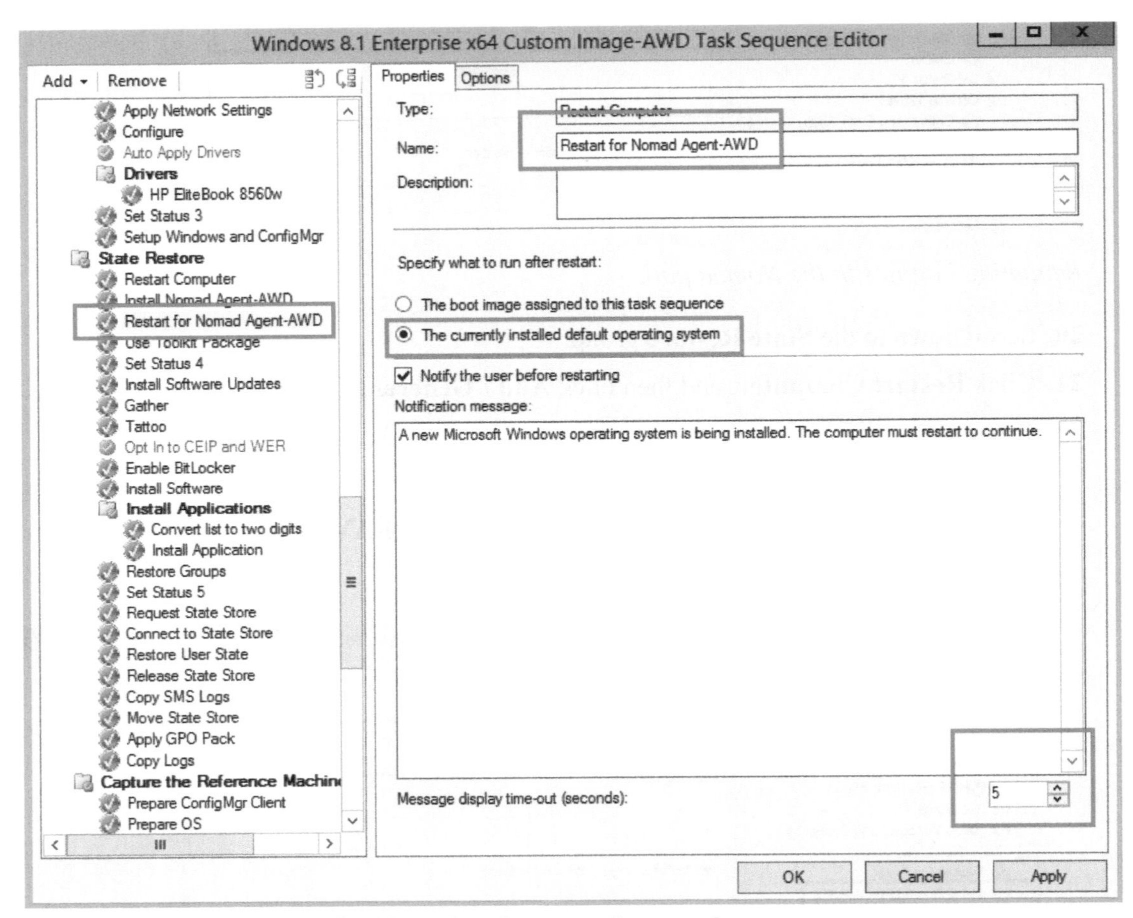

Restart the task sequence for Nomad paths to work properly.

25. Click **Restart for Nomad Agent-AWD**, and then click **Add / General / Run Command Line**.

26. Configure with the following settings:

- Properties tab
    - Name: **Remove Logfiles.old folder-AWD**
    - Command line: **cmd /c rd %configpath%\NomadBranch\Logfiles.old /s /q**
    - Description: **%ConfigPath% = _SMSTaskSequence Location**
- Options tab

    Continue on Error: **Selected**

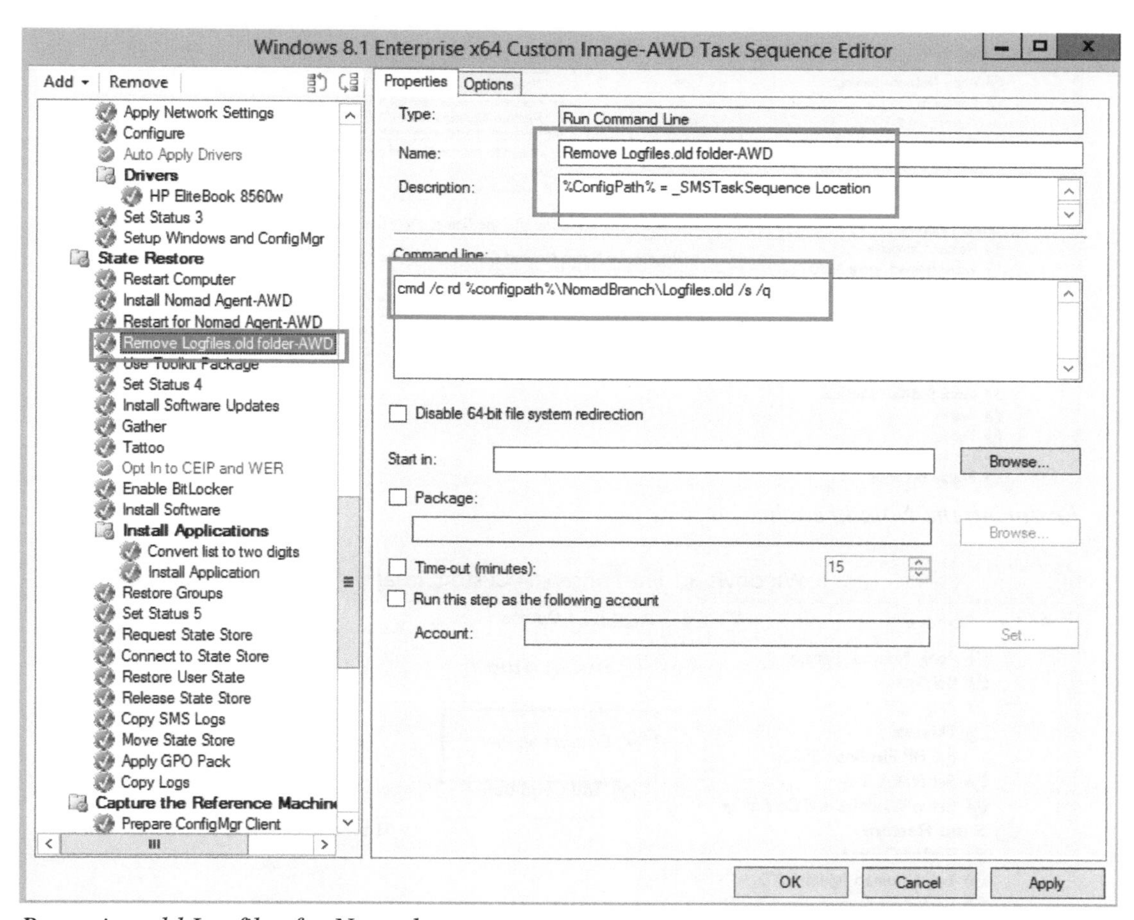

Removing old Logfiles for Nomad.

27. Click **Remove Logfiles.old folder-AWD**, and then click **Add / Nomad / Restore Nomad Cache**.

28. Configure with the following settings:

- Properties tab
  - Name: **Restore Nomad Cache-AWD**
  - Operation: **Link**
  - Activate All Content: **Selected**
- Options tab

  Continue on Error: **Selected**

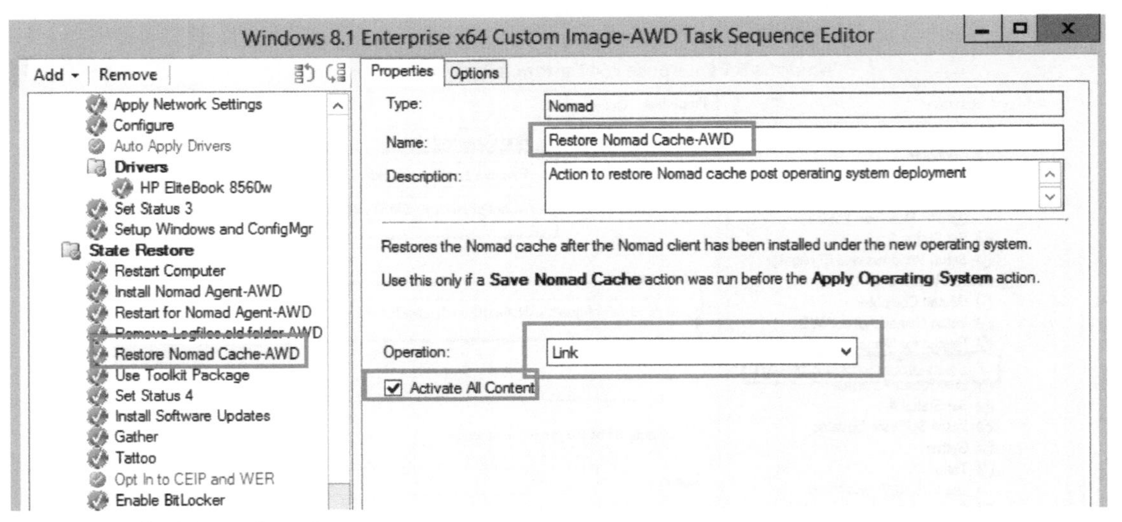

Restoring the Nomad cache.

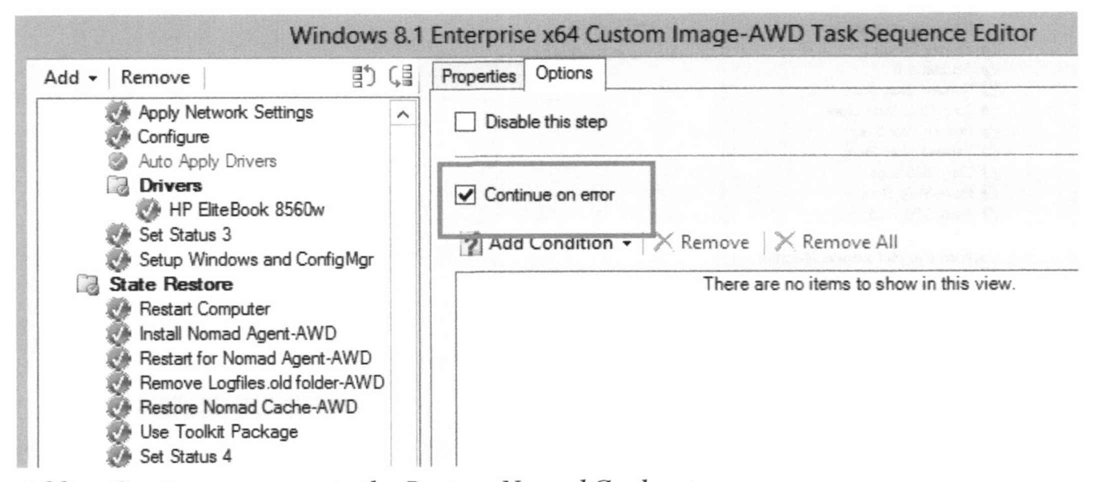

Adding Continue on error to the Restore Nomad Cache step.

Real World Note: There is a known issue with the **Restore Nomad Cache-AWD** step. If the NomadBranch.log file exists, this custom task sequence step fails. The failure is a result of trying to create a hard link over an existing file.

There are two workarounds for this issue:

1. Place **Continue on error** on the step.

2. Delete the **NomadBranch.log** before the restore step runs.

If this task sequence step fails, open X:\Windows\Temp\SMSTSLog\NBCacheActions.log.

29. Click **Restore Nomad Cache-AWD**, and then click **Add / General / Run Command Line**.
30. Configure with the following settings:
    - Name: **Reset Nomad Cache ACLs-AWD**
    - Command Line:
      icacls C:\ProgramData\1E\NomadBranch* /grant "Authenticated Users ":(RX) /grant BUILTIN\Users:(RX) /T /C /Q

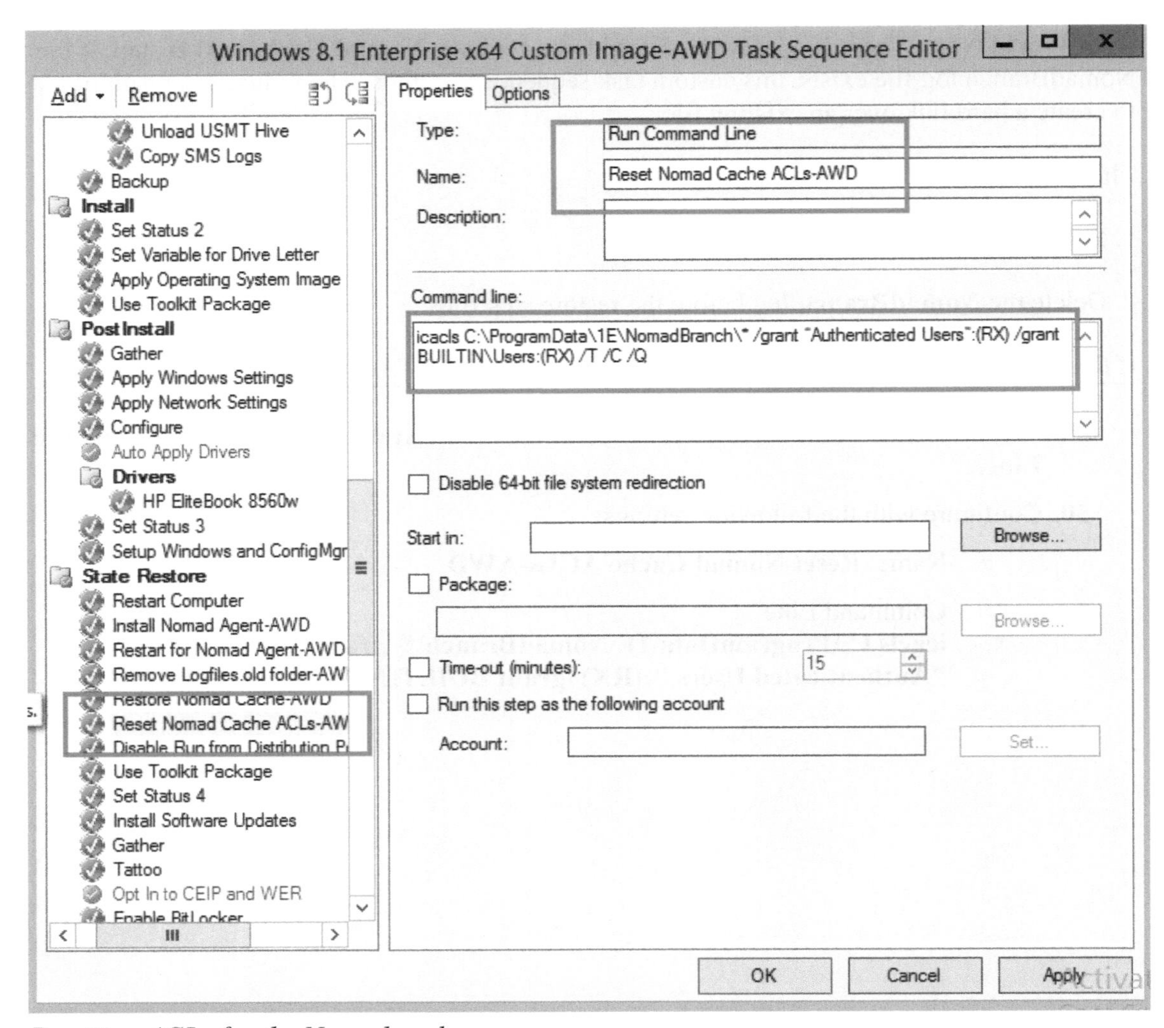

Resetting ACLs for the Nomad cache.

31. Click **Reset Nomad Cache ACLs-AWD**, and then click **Add / Nomad / Disable Run from Distribution Point**.

32. Configure with the following setting:

    Name: **Disable Run from Distribution Point-AWD**

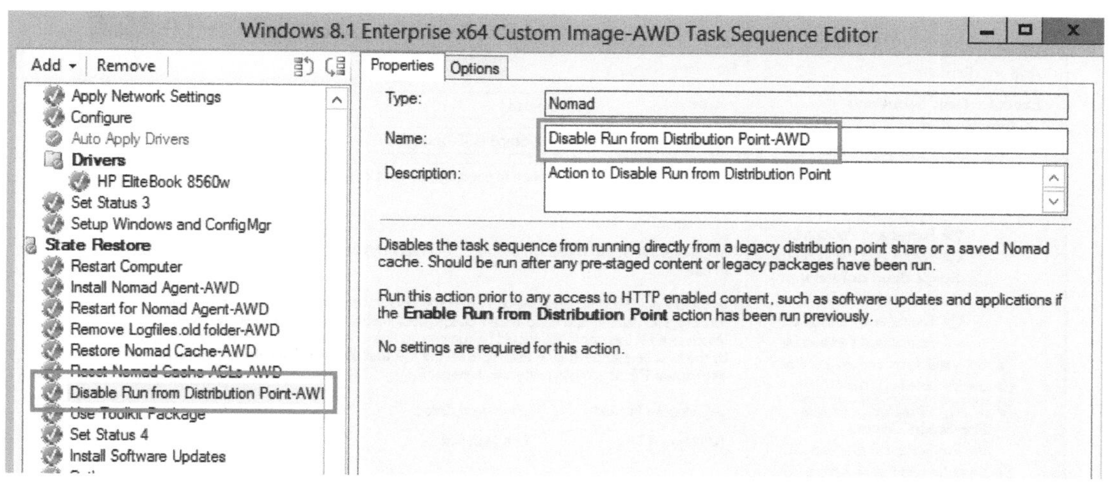

Disable Run from Distribution Point for Nomad.

33. Scroll back up to **Pre-Stage OSD Tools-AWD** and click **Apply**.

Real World Note: If you find that the reference packages are not updating in the Nomad Pre-Stage action, it is likely because you have not yet clicked Apply. Until the changes are applied, the reference package lists do not change.

34. Select the **1E Nomad Branch x64-AWD** package.
35. Click **OK**.

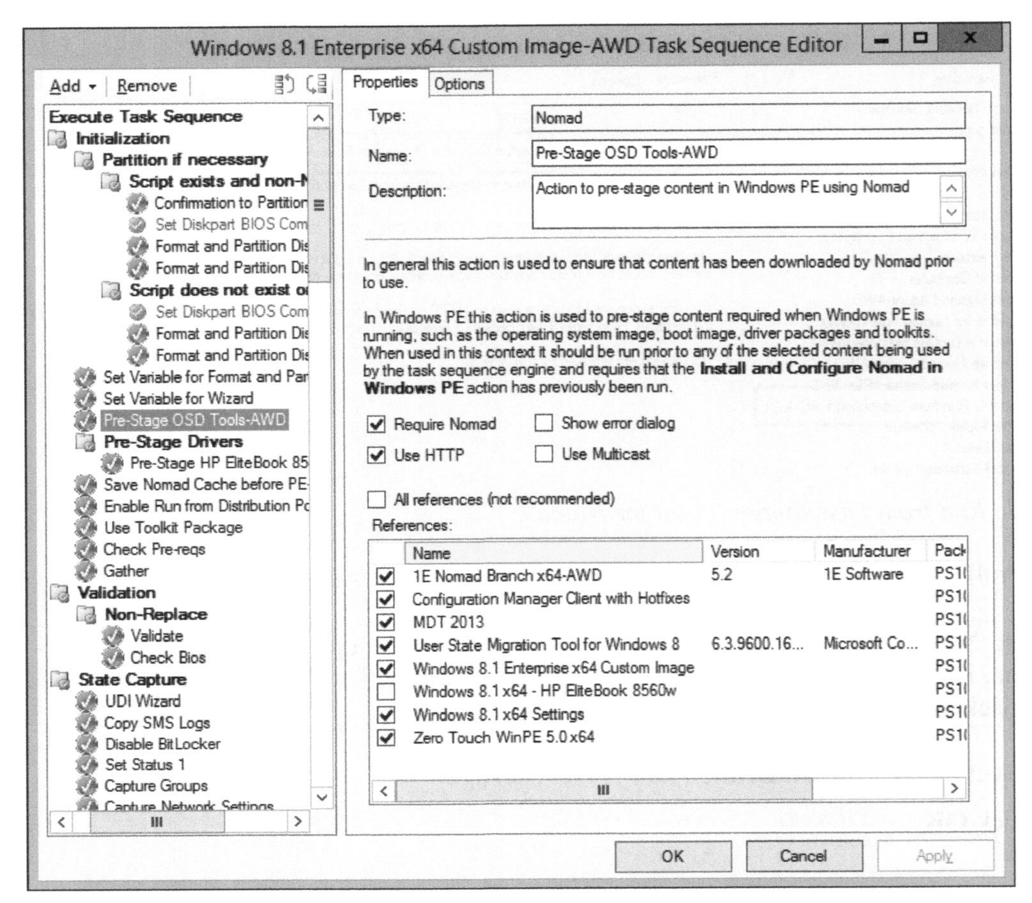

Modifying the packages to be pre-cached.

Real World Note: The preceding step added to Install Nomad Branch x64-AWD adds a reference package to the sequence. As you have not added this to the previous Pre-Stage steps, Nomad will not be aware of this package and thus will download it directly from the distribution point.

You *must* update the Pre-Stage steps every time a package is added to the sequence.

Also the Pre-Stage step has a character limitation of 255 per step. So if you have a lot of packages or applications, you must break these up into multiple steps, such as Pre-Stage Core APPS 1, Pre-Stage Core APPS2, and so forth.

The actual command line that is run for this is:

```
NomadPackageLocator.exe --NOMAD_LOCAL --RemoveHttpLocations
--RequireNomad --HideErrorDialog --RestrictPackages=<PACKAGES>
--ProcessBootImage
```

In turn, this invokes individual smsnomad.exe commands to actually prestage the content during these steps in the task sequence execution (Take note of word wrap…this is all one command):

```
smsnomad.exe --s --prestage
--pp="http://CM01.corp.viamonstra.com/SMS_DP_SMSPKG$/PS10001E
--ver4 --pkgid=PS10001E --Hash=<HASHVALUE>
```

The hash value can be found by viewing the corresponding LsZ file for the PackageID in Notepad.

This can all be tracked in the nomadpackagelocator.log file, which you can find at C:\Windows\Temp\SMSTSLog\NomadPackageLocator.log.

Deploying Base OSD Refresh Scenario with Nomad

1. Deploy the **Windows 8.1 Enterprise x64 Custom Image-AWD** task sequence with the following settings:
   - Collection: **Deploy Windows 8.1 Refresh - Base Nomad**
   - Purpose: **Available**
   - Make available to the following: **Only Configuration Manager Clients**
   - Scheduling: **<Default>**
   - User Experience: **<Default>**
   - Alerts: **<Default>**
   - Deployment Options: **Download content locally when needed by running task sequence**
2. In **Hyper-V**, take a checkpoint of **PC0004** called **Pre-Nomad-Base AWD**.
3. Log on to **PC0004** and run a machine policy refresh.
4. Ensure that **Nomad** has been deployed to **PC0004**, and if it hasn't, deploy it now.
5. Start the deployment of **Windows 8.1 Enterprise x64 Custom Image-AWD**.
6. While the deployment is starting, open the **C:\ProgramData\1E\NomadBranch** folder, as well as the **NomadBranch.log**.
7. Wait until the refresh of **PC0004** is completed before continuing.

Note: As content was not pre-cached on this subnet (the native task sequence used to deploy PC0005 did not have the Nomad integration), the traffic should go back to the distribution point CM01. You can validate this in the log files.

You should see the Nomad Pre-Stage actions start and the content begin caching locally prior to refresh.

Notice the cache files building and the .BLKMAP extension on the download that has not completed successfully. This indicates that a Nomad download is in progress and has not yet completed.

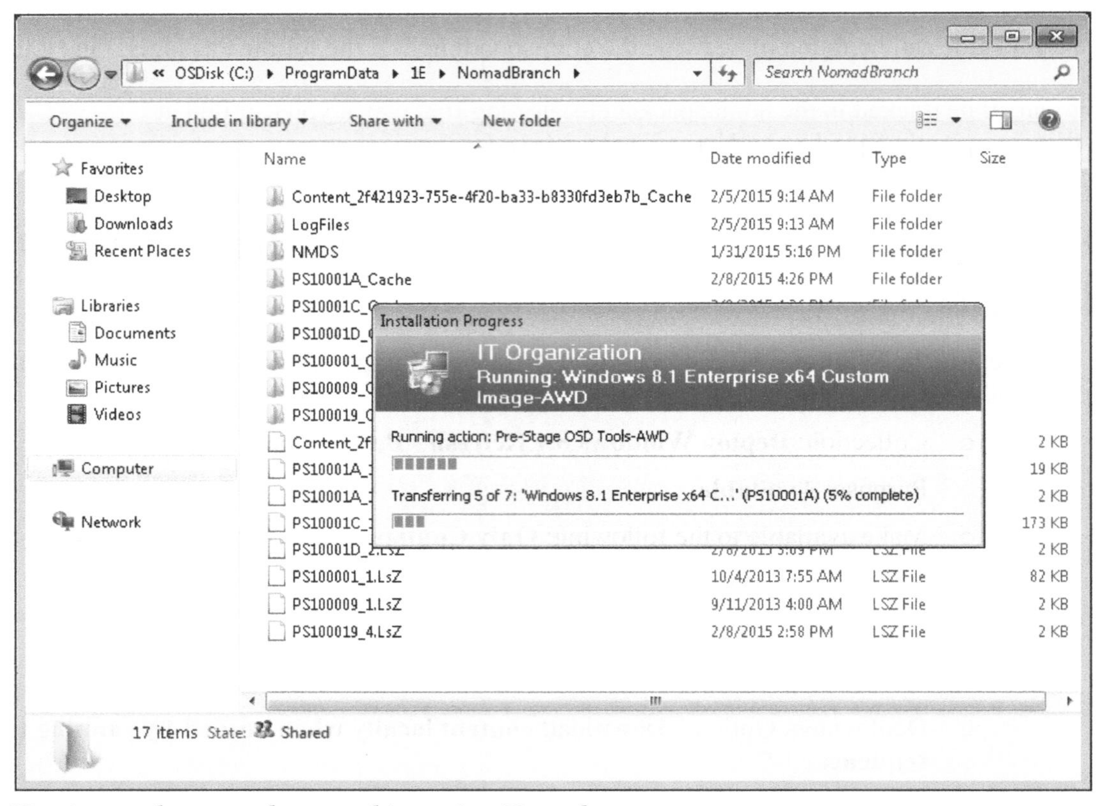

Viewing packages and pre-caching using Nomad.

Validating OSD Cache Peering

Now you need to validate that Nomad peer-to-peer is working properly for OSD packages.

1. In **Hyper-V**, take a checkpoint of **PC0002** called **Pre-Nomad-Base AWD**.
2. On **PC0002** log on as **VIAMONSTRA\Administrator**.
3. Use the **Registry Editor**, configure the **Nomad Download Monitor** to start in advanced mode by changing the **UI** value in **HKLM\SOFTWARE\Wow6432Node\1E\NomadBranch** from **0** to **1**.

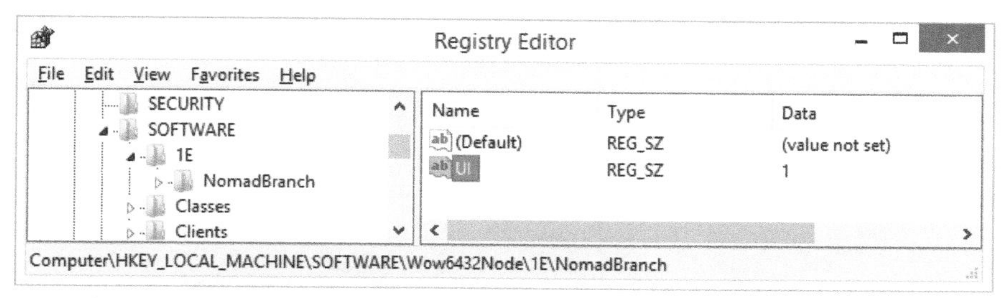

Enabling the advanced mode for the Nomad Download Monitor.

4. Start the deployment of **Windows 8.1 Enterprise x64 Custom Image-AWD**.
5. Open the **NomadBranch.log** file.

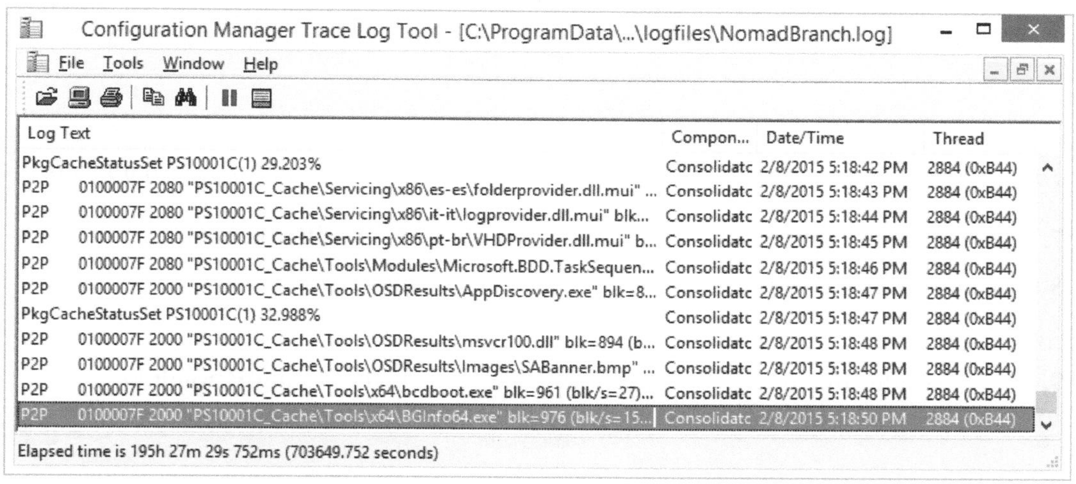

The P2P lines, indicating that content is coming from a peer. In this case PC0004.

6. Open the **Nomad Download Monitor** and view the progress of the download.

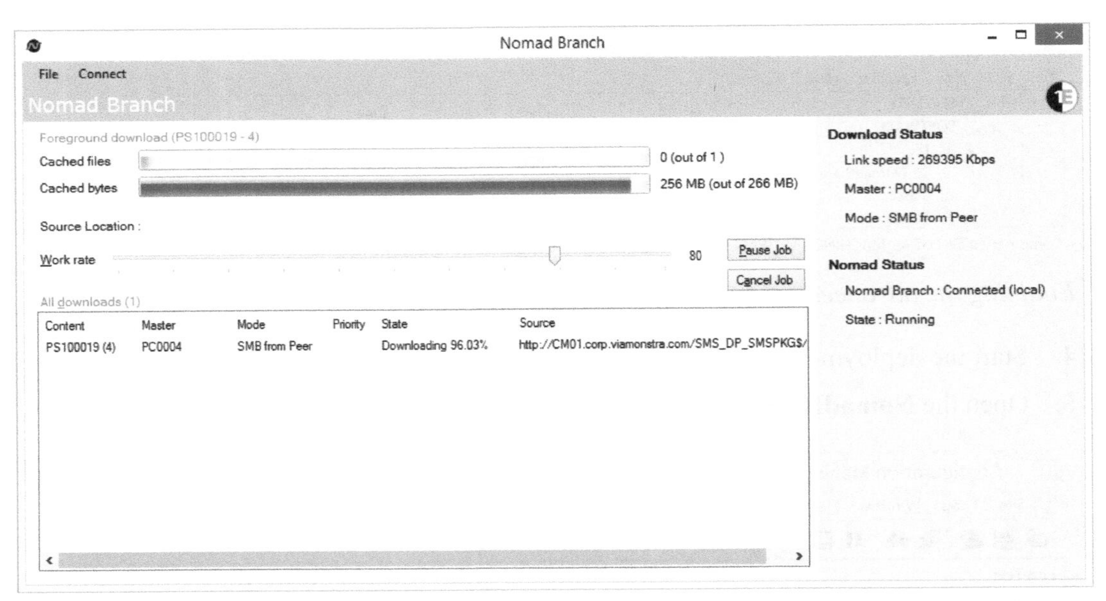

The Nomad Download Monitor (in advanced mode) showing the download from PC0004.

7. Try adjusting the work rate to **30** while viewing the **NomadBranch.log**.
8. Make note of the **(blk/s = xx)** value. What is the value?

    ____

9. Now try adjusting the work rate to **100** while viewing the **NomadBranch.log**.

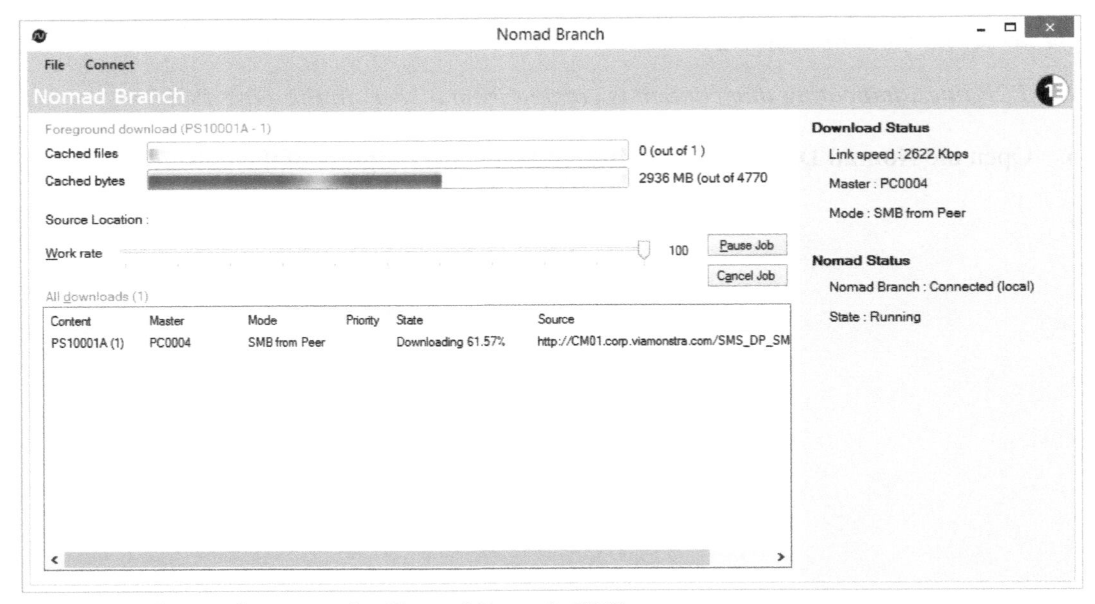

Changing the work rate in the Nomad Branch GUI.

10. Take note of the **(blk/s = xx)** value.

____

It should look something like this:

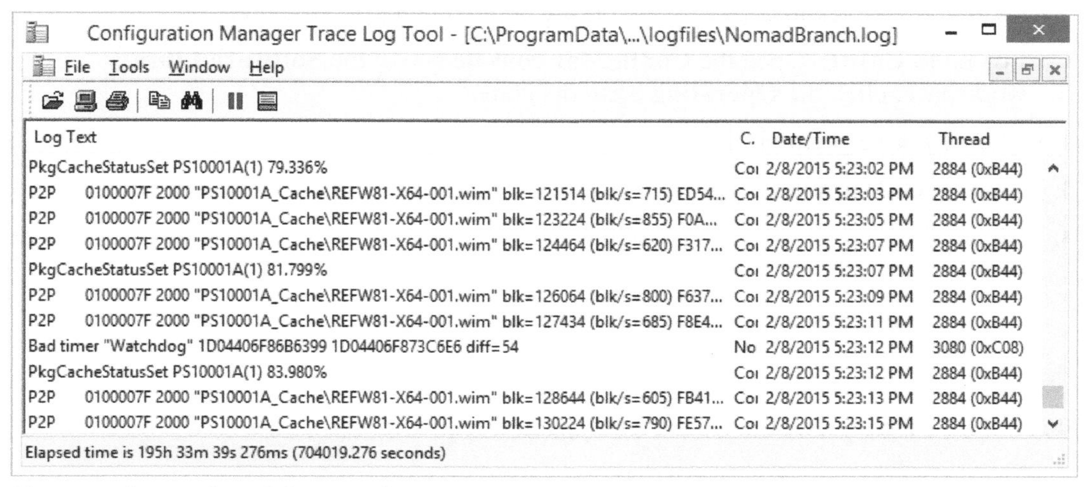

Viewing the results of the transfer using Nomad.

Real World Note: When validating the Nomad cache and peering, it is important to note that the way the task sequence was created will give back all of the prior packages that were cached in C:\ProgramData\1E\NomadBranch folder. This means that if someone needs to have one of those applications deployed after this machine is refreshed, all cached content is still valid. This dramatically reduces the amount of WAN traffic required during an OSD refresh scenario.

The steps used for this are Save Nomad Cache and Restore Nomad Cache:

Save Nomad Cache. Moves, links, or copies content from C:\ProgramData\1E\NomadBranch to _SMSTaskSequence\NomadBranch

Restore Nomad Cache. Moves, links, or copies from _SMSTaskSequence\NomadBranch to C:\Programdata\1E\NomadBranch and activates all of the content

Adding Core Packages to OSD

In this step, you add some core packages to the base Nomad task sequence. Nomad requires some simple modifications to invoke the alternate content provider in a task sequence.

First, we will make a backup copy of the working deployment task sequence:

1. Log on to **CM01**. Open the **ConfigMgr console** and in the **Software Library** workspace, click the **Operating Systems** node.
2. Click **Task Sequences**.
3. Right-click **Windows 8.1 Enterprise x64 Custom Image-AWD** and select **Copy**.
4. Right-click the new copied task sequence and click **Properties**. Rename the task sequence to the following:

   Windows 8.1 Enterprise x64-Gold-CoreApps

Windows 8.1 Enterprise x64-Gold-CoreApps

Windows 8.1 Enterprise x64-Gold-CoreApps task sequence.

5. Still in the **Windows 8.1 Enterprise x64-Gold-CoreApps Properties** dialog box, select the **Nomad** tab, select the **Enable Nomad** check box, and click **OK**.
6. Click **Windows 8.1 Enterprise x64-Gold-CoreApps** and select **Edit**.
7. Scroll down to **Install Software**.
8. Click **Install Software**, and then click **Add / New Group**.
9. Configure with the following setting:

   Name: **Install Core Packages-AWD**

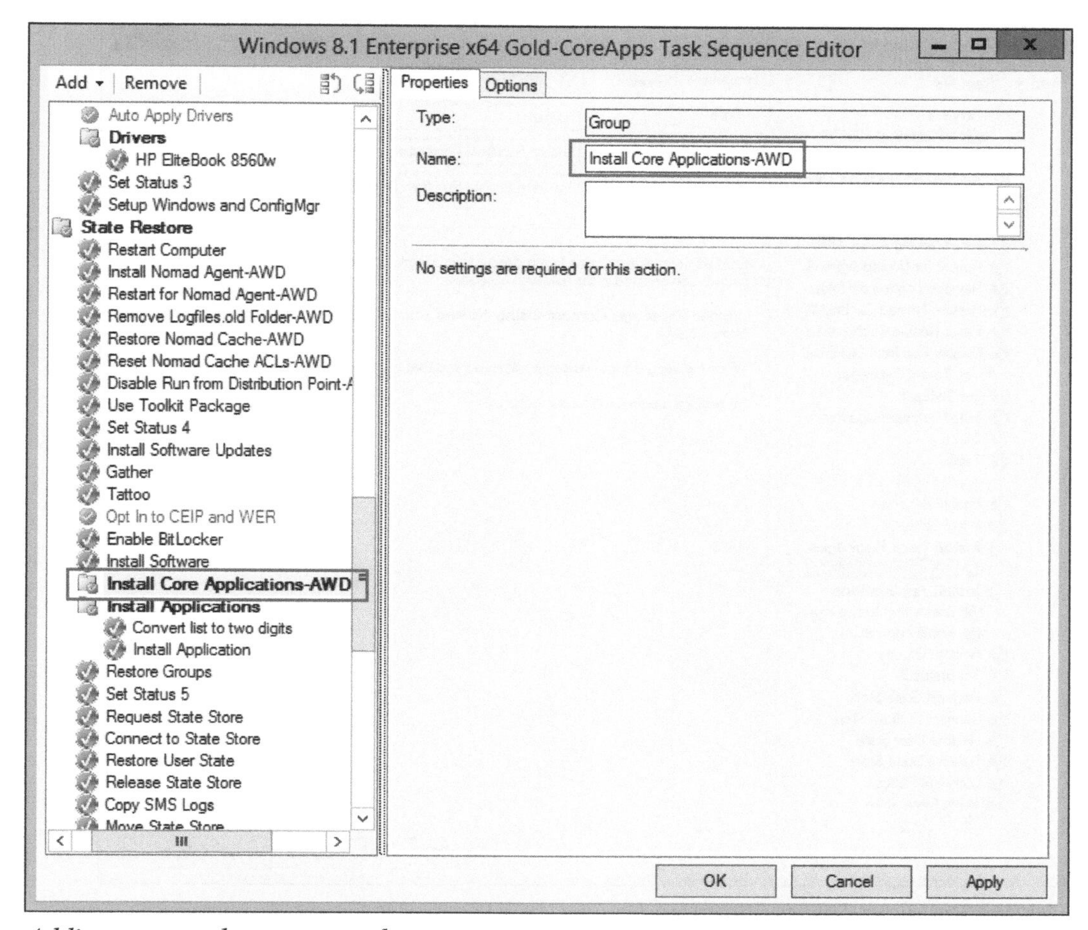

Adding core packages to a task sequence.

10. Click **Install Core Packages-AWD**, and then click **Add / Nomad / Enable Run from Distribution Point**.
11. Configure with the following setting:

    Name: **Enable Run from Distribution Point-AWD**

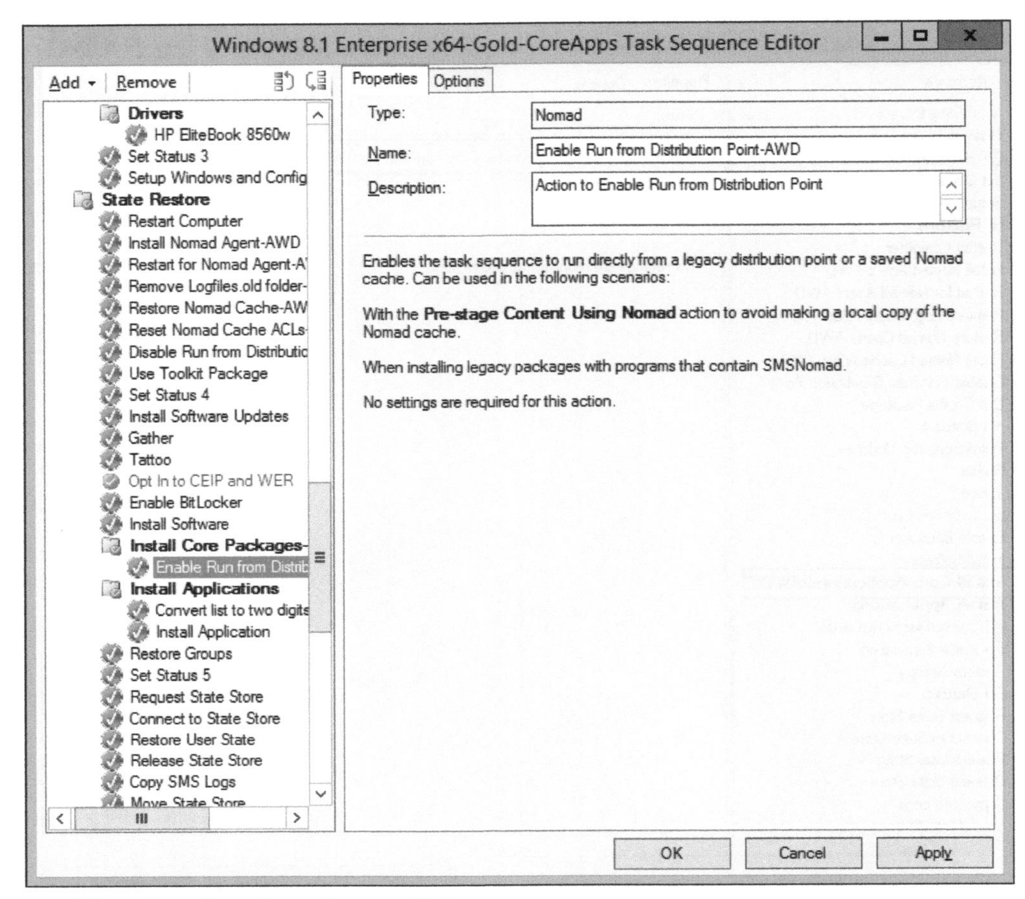

Enabling Run from Distribution Point.

12. Click **Run from Distribution Point-AWD**, and then click **Add / General / Install Package**.
13. Configure with the following settings:
    - Name: **Install Camtasia-SMSNomad**
    - Package: **TechSmith Camtasia Studio-AWD 8.0**
    - Program: **Per-system Unattended-SMSNomad**

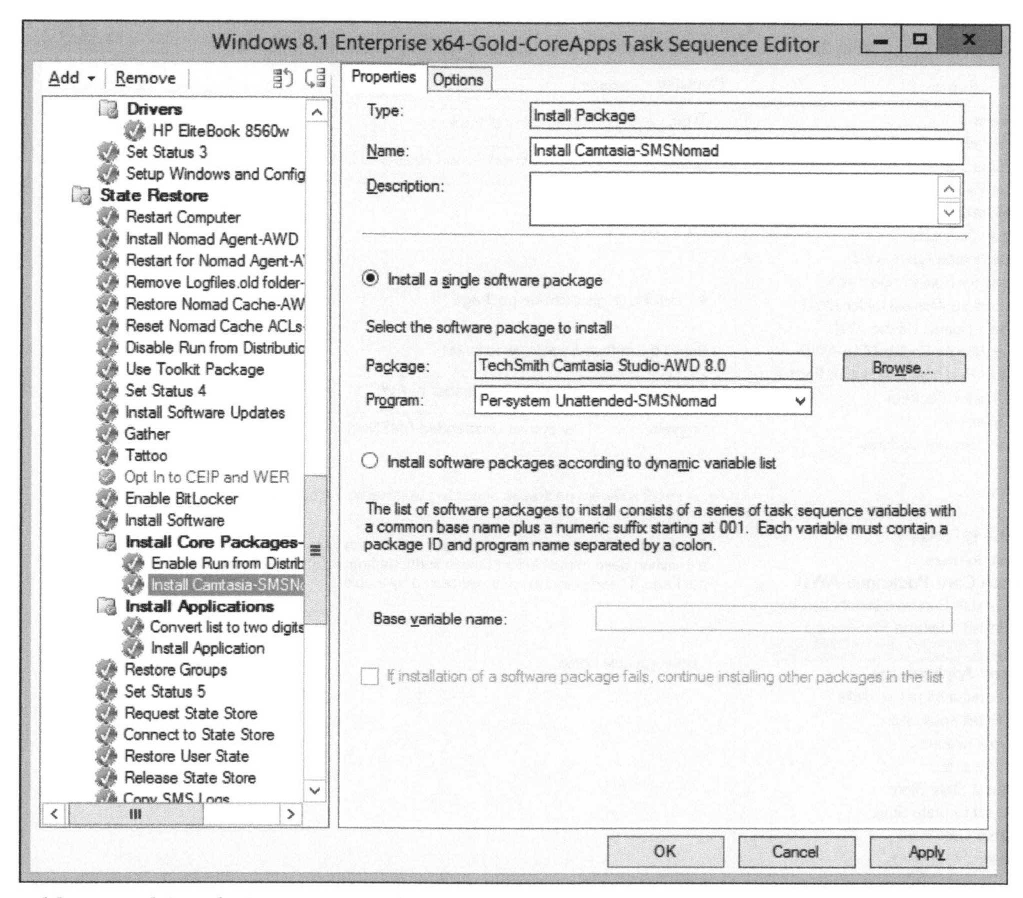

Adding TechSmith Camtasia to the task sequence.

Real World Note: The Per-system Unattended-SMSNomad program that was used in the preceding figure was created using the ConfigMgr hydration scripts as part of this book. SMSNomad.exe must be manually invoked as part of a task sequence if packages have not been pre-cached. As such, this program simply prepends SMSNomad.exe before MSIExec.exe.

14. Right-click **Install Camtasia-SMSNomad** and click **Copy**.
15. Right-click **Install Camtasia-SMSNomad** and click **Paste**.
16. Configure with the following settings:
    - Name: **Install Adobe Reader XI-SMSNomad**
    - Package: **Adobe Reader XI-AWD 11.0**
    - Program: **Per-system Unattended-SMSNomad**

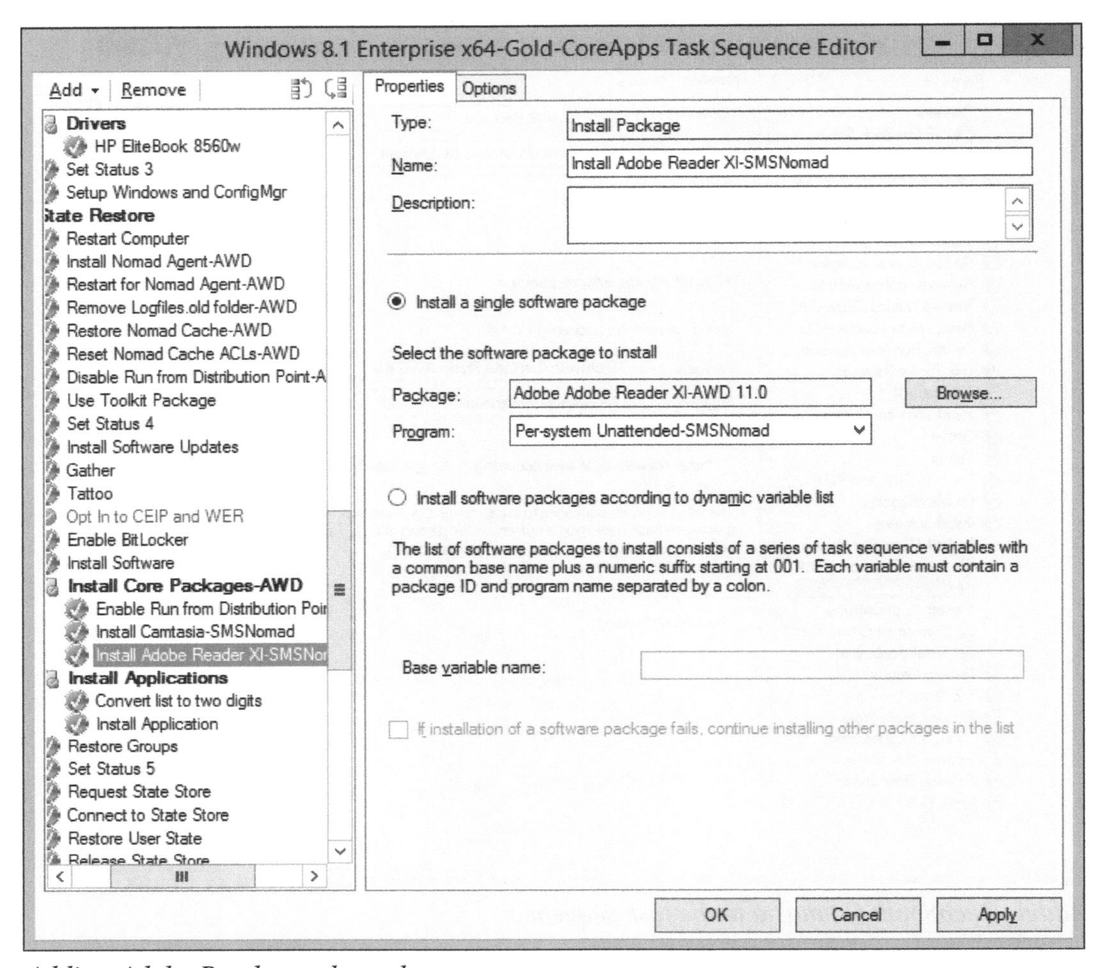

Adding Adobe Reader to the task sequence.

17. Click **Install Adobe Reader XI-SMSNomad**, and then click **Add / Nomad / Disable Run from Distribution Point**.
18. Configure with the following setting:

    Name: **Disable Run from Distribution Point-AWD**

19. Click **Apply**.
20. Scroll up to the Pre-Stage OSD Tools-AWD action, and select the following references:
    - **Adobe Reader XI-AWD**
    - **Camtasia Studio-AWD**
21. Click **OK**.

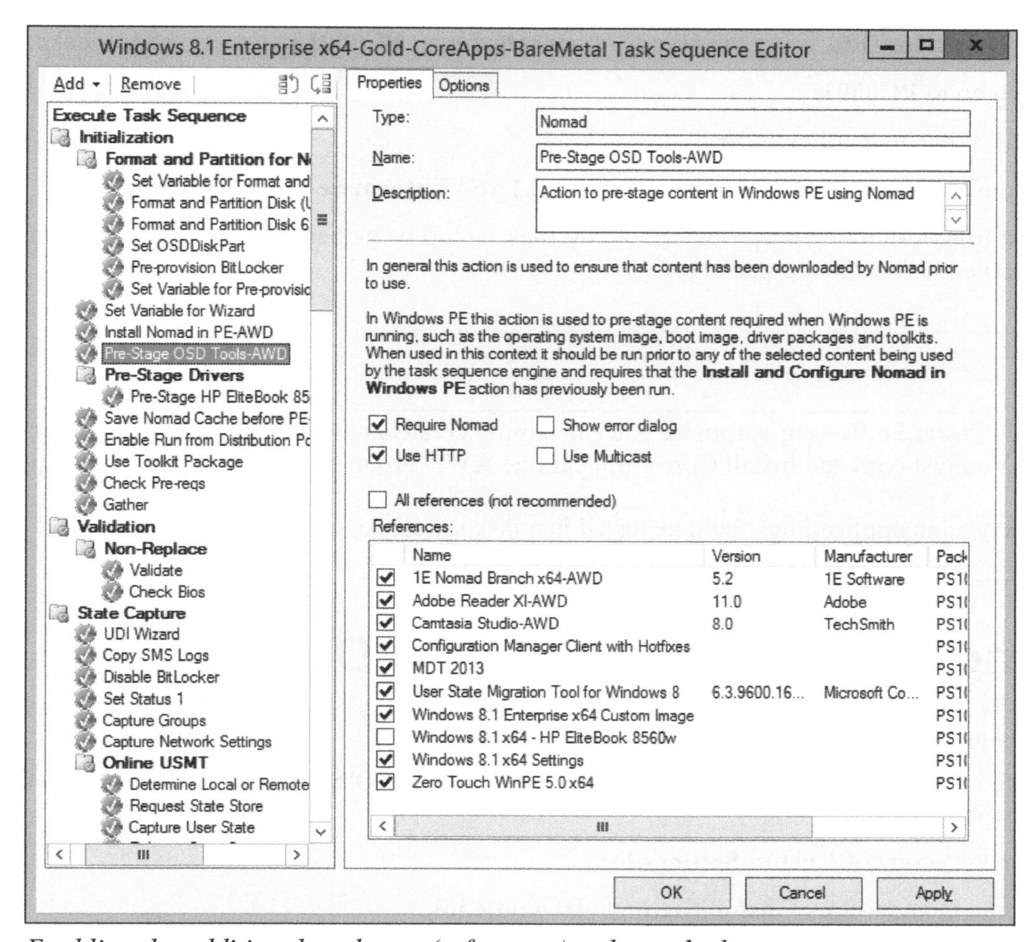

Enabling the additional packages (references) to be cached.

Deploying Core Apps OSD Refresh Scenario with Nomad

1. Deploy the **Windows 8.1 Enterprise x64-Gold-CoreApps** task sequence with the following settings:
    - Collection: **Deploy Windows 8.1 Refresh – w/Core Apps and Nomad**
    - Deployment Settings: **<Default>**
    - Scheduling: **<Default>**
    - User Experience: **<Default>**
    - Alerts: **<Default>**
    - Distribution Points: **<Default>**

2. On your **Host PC**, using the **Hyper-V console**, revert **PC0001** to the previous checkpoint.
3. Log on to **PC0001**.
4. Run a machine policy refresh.
5. From **Software Center**, install **Windows 8.1 x64 Enterprise-Gold-CoreApps**.

   For troubleshooting purposes, which log files should be gathered to troubleshoot Nomad-enabled task sequence packages?

   ____

   ____

> **Real World Note:** For testing purposes, you can simply create a new software install testing task sequence. You just copy the Install Core Applications-AWD group and run it on a test machine.
>
> Every package and application should be tested in a task sequence to ensure deployments will be successful.

Adding Dynamic Packages to OSD

In this guide, you create a new settings file and add an array of applications. When done, the settings and applications need some minor customizations to work with Nomad in OSD.

1. Log on to **CM01** and browse to **D:\SCCM_Sources\OSD\Settings\Windows 8.1 x64 settings**.
2. Create a copy of **CustomSettings.ini**.
3. Name the new copy **CustomSettings_Dynamic.ini**.

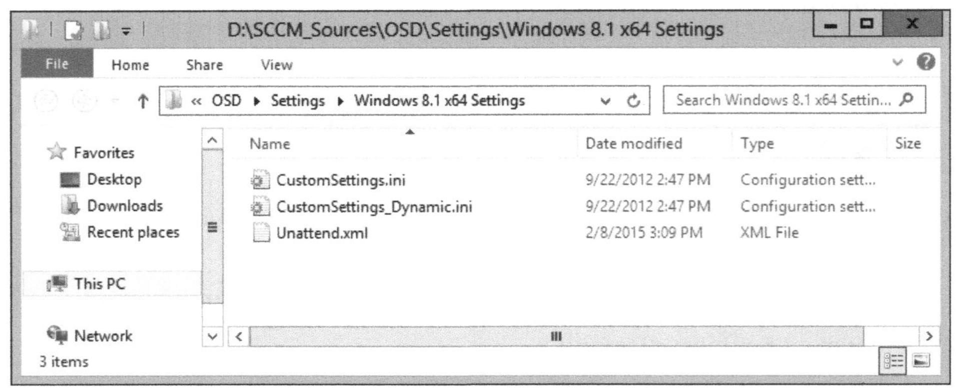

Reviewing the CustomSettings files for the dynamic packages.

4. Open **CustomSettings_Dynamic.ini** with **Notepad** and leave the file open.

5. Open the **ConfigMgr console** and browse to **Software Library / Application Management / Packages / AWD**.

6. Make note of the **Package IDs** for the following packages, as in the example in the following figure:

   - **Adobe Reader XI-AWD** ________________
   - **Camtasia Studio-AWD** ________________
   - **CMTrace-AWD** ________________

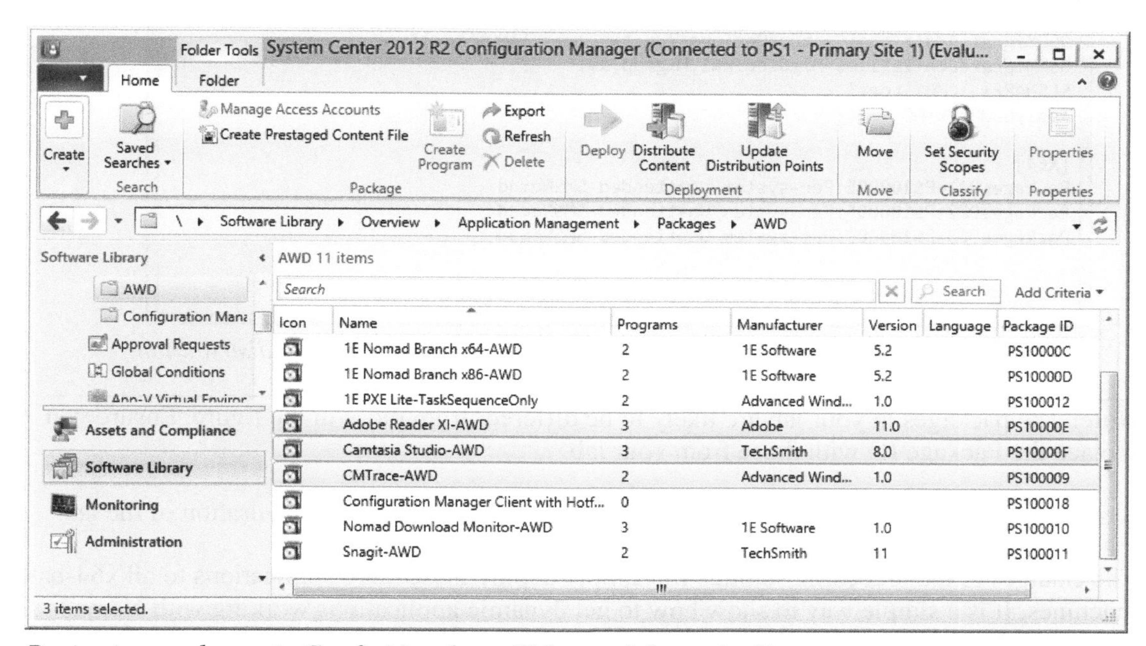

Reviewing packages in ConfigMgr that will be used dynamically.

7. Make note of the **-SMSNomad** programs for these three applications.

   Can you find the one package that has a different install string?

   ____

   Why is this program different?

   ____

8. Now return to **CustomSettings_Dynamic.ini**, make the modifications shown in the following figure, and save the file.

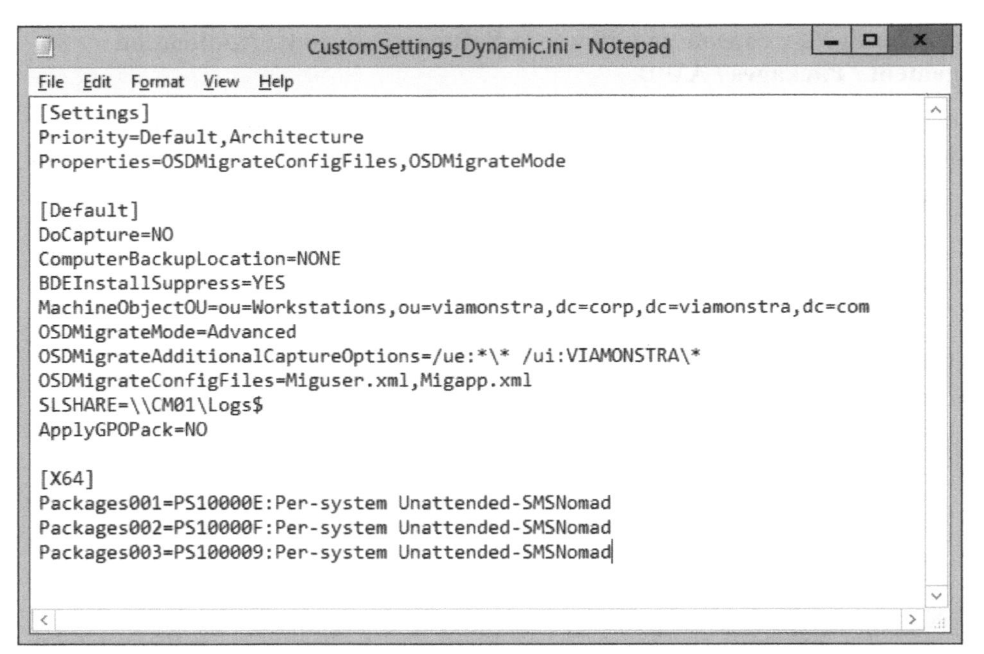


```
[Settings]
Priority=Default,Architecture
Properties=OSDMigrateConfigFiles,OSDMigrateMode

[Default]
DoCapture=NO
ComputerBackupLocation=NONE
BDEInstallSuppress=YES
MachineObjectOU=ou=Workstations,ou=viamonstra,dc=corp,dc=viamonstra,dc=com
OSDMigrateMode=Advanced
OSDMigrateAdditionalCaptureOptions=/ue:*\* /ui:VIAMONSTRA\*
OSDMigrateConfigFiles=Miguser.xml,Migapp.xml
SLSHARE=\\CM01\Logs$
ApplyGPOPack=NO

[X64]
Packages001=PS10000E:Per-system Unattended-SMSNomad
Packages002=PS10000F:Per-system Unattended-SMSNomad
Packages003=PS100009:Per-system Unattended-SMSNomad
```

Modifying the CustomSettings_Dynamic.ini file for dynamic package distribution.

Note: The packages in your lab are likely to be different from those in the figure. Ensure you replace the Package ID with those from your lab.

Also, the -SMSNomad programs were automatically created during the hydration of the lab.

The changes to the preceding settings file simply deploy these three applications to all x64-based machines. It is a simple way to show how to get dynamic applications working with Nomad during OSD.

9. Save the **CustomSettings_Dynamic.ini** file.
10. Return to the **ConfigMgr console** and update the distribution points for the **Windows 8.1 x64 Settings** package

Windows 8.1 x64 Settings package, located in the Software Library workspace.

Use a Zero Touch Test Environment to Validate the New Settings File

1. On **PC0002**, log on as **Administrator**.
2. From the downloaded lab files, copy the content of **\ZTI Support Files\Test Environment** to **C:\MDT**.

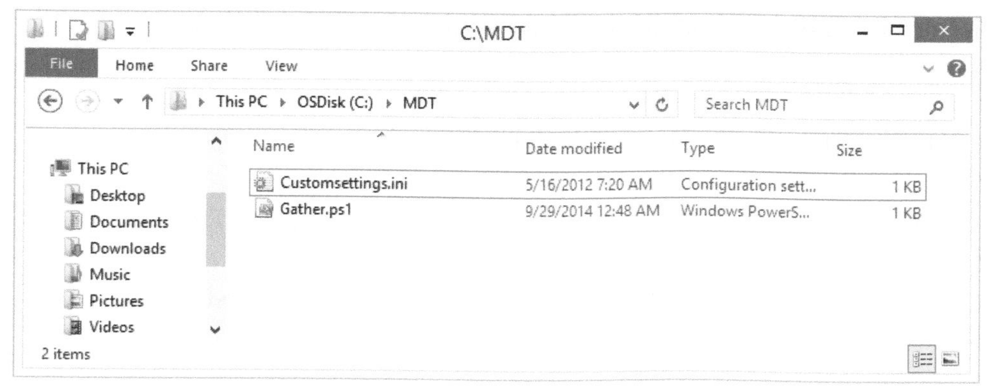

The sample files copied to C:\MDT.

3. Copy **\\CM01\SCCM_Sources$\OSD\Settings\Windows 8.1 x64 Settings\CustomSettings_Dynamic.ini** to **C:\MDT**.
4. Rename the existing **CustomSettings.ini** file to **CustomSettings_old.ini**
5. Rename **CustomSettings_Dynamic.ini** to **CustomSettings.ini**

> **Real World Note:** You can also modify the Gather.ps1 script to call a different INI file by adding the /inifile: switch to the line running ZTIGather.wsf.

6. Copy the following files from **\\CM01\SCCM_Sources$\OSD\MDT\MDT 2013\Scripts** to **C:\MDT**:
   - **ZTIDataAccess.vbs**
   - **ZTIGather.vbs**
   - **ZTIGather.xml**
   - **ZTIUtility.vbs**

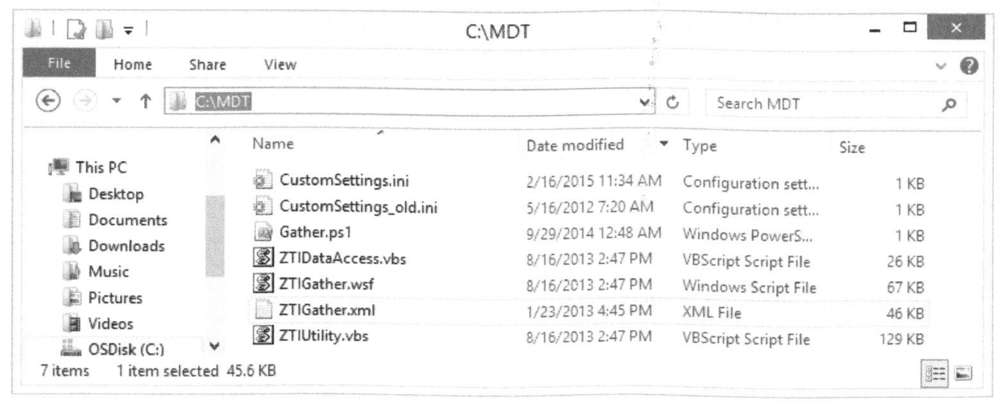

The extra MDT files copied to C:\MDT.

7. Open an elevated **PowerShell prompt** and type the following:

```
Set-ExecutionPolicy Unrestricted -Force
```

8. Change the directory to **C:\MDT** and type the following:

```
.\Gather.ps1
```

9. Using **CMTrace** (install if needed from Software Center), review **ZTIGather.log** (from the **C:\MININT\SMSOSD\OSDLOGS** folder).

10. Validate that **PACKAGES001**, **PACKAGES002**, and **PACKAGES003** have been processed as part of the **Architecture** rule, as seen in the following figure.

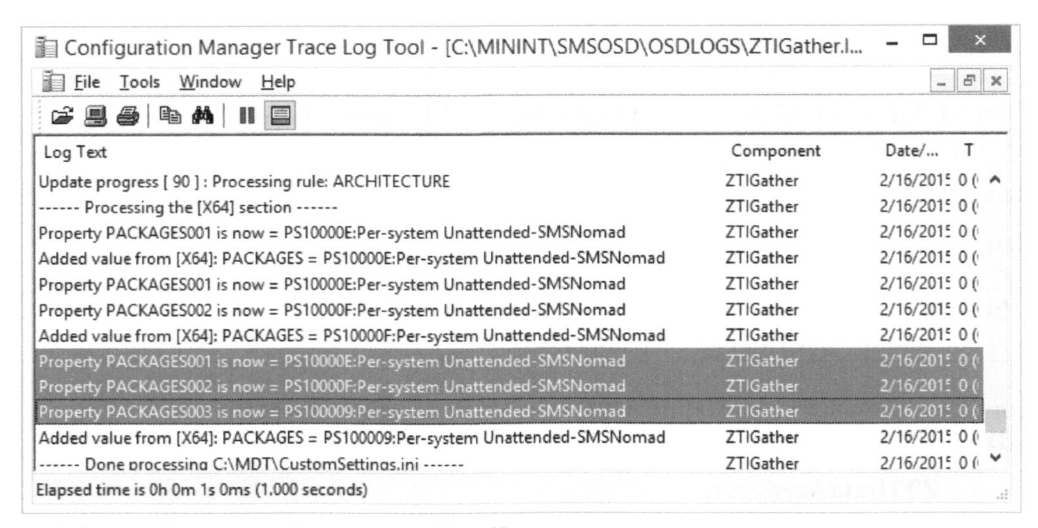

Validating the CustomSettings.ini file offline.

11. Close **CMTrace**.

Configure a New Dynamic Packages Sequence

When configuring dynamic packages for a task sequence, it is imperative that the packages use SMSNomad programs that were created earlier. This allows Nomad packages to use Nomad to find content from either peers or a distribution point during a task sequence.

1. On **CM01**, open the **ConfigMgr console**, and browse to **Software Library / Operation Systems / Task Sequences**.
2. Right-click **Windows 8.1 Enterprise x64 Custom Image-AWD** and click **Copy**.
3. Configure the copy with the following settings:
    - Name: **Windows 8.1 Enterprise x64-Gold-DynamicPackages**
    - Description: **Version 1.0 - Adding Dynamic Package Array**
    - Nomad tab: Select **Enable Nomad**.

4. Right-click **Windows 8.1 Enterprise x64-Gold-DynamicPackages** and click **Edit**.
5. Scroll down to **Enable Bitlocker** and ensure that **Enable Bitlocker** is selected.
6. Click **Add / New Group**.
7. Configure the following settings:
   - Properties tab

     Name: **Deploy Dynamic Packages-AWD**
   - Options tab

     Continue on Error: **Selected**

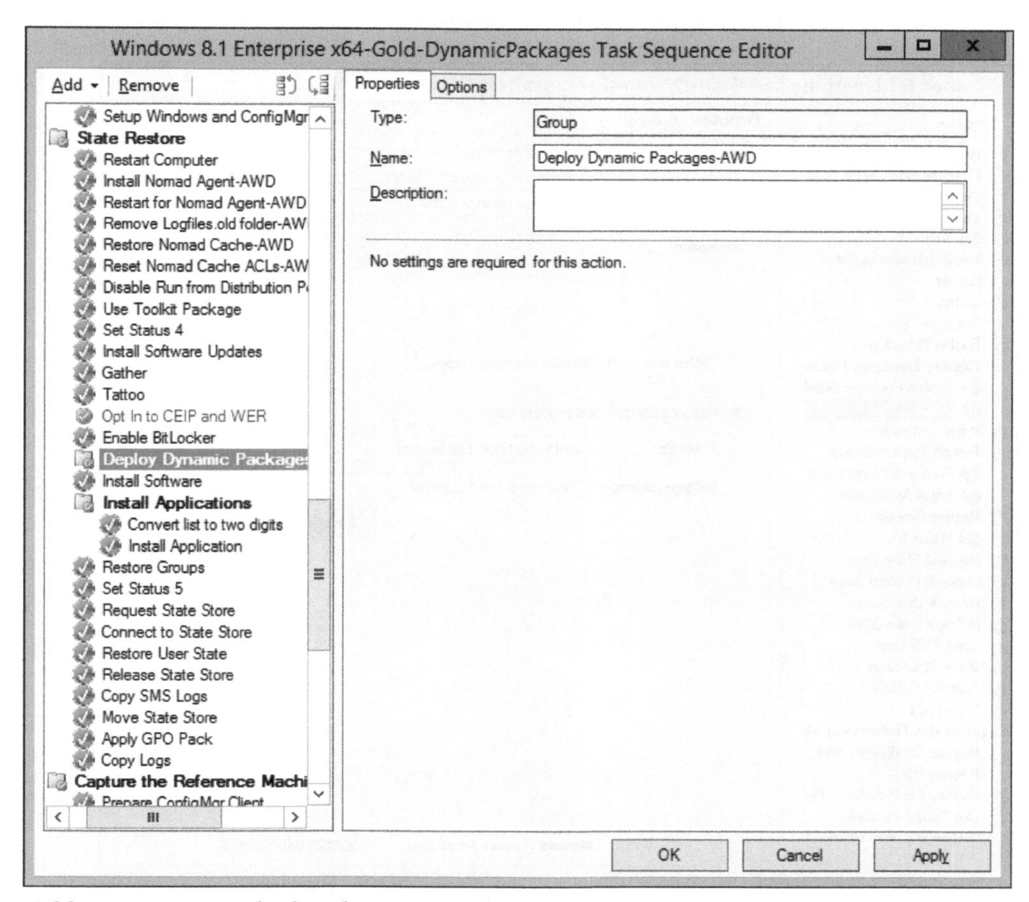

Adding a group to deploy dynamic packages.

8. Click **Deploy Dynamic Packages-AWD**, and then click **Add / Nomad / Enable Run from Distribution Point**.

9. Configure the following setting:

   Name: **Enable Run from Distribution Point-AWD**

10. Click **Enable Run from Distribution Point-AWD**, and then click **Add / MDT / Gather**.

11. Configure the following settings:

    - Name: **Gather-DynamicSettings-AWD**
    - Description: **This Step will add the array of packages from the customsettings_dynamic.ini (Architecture = x64)**
    - Rules file: **CustomSettings_Dynamic.ini**
    - Settings package: **Windows 8.1 x64 Settings**

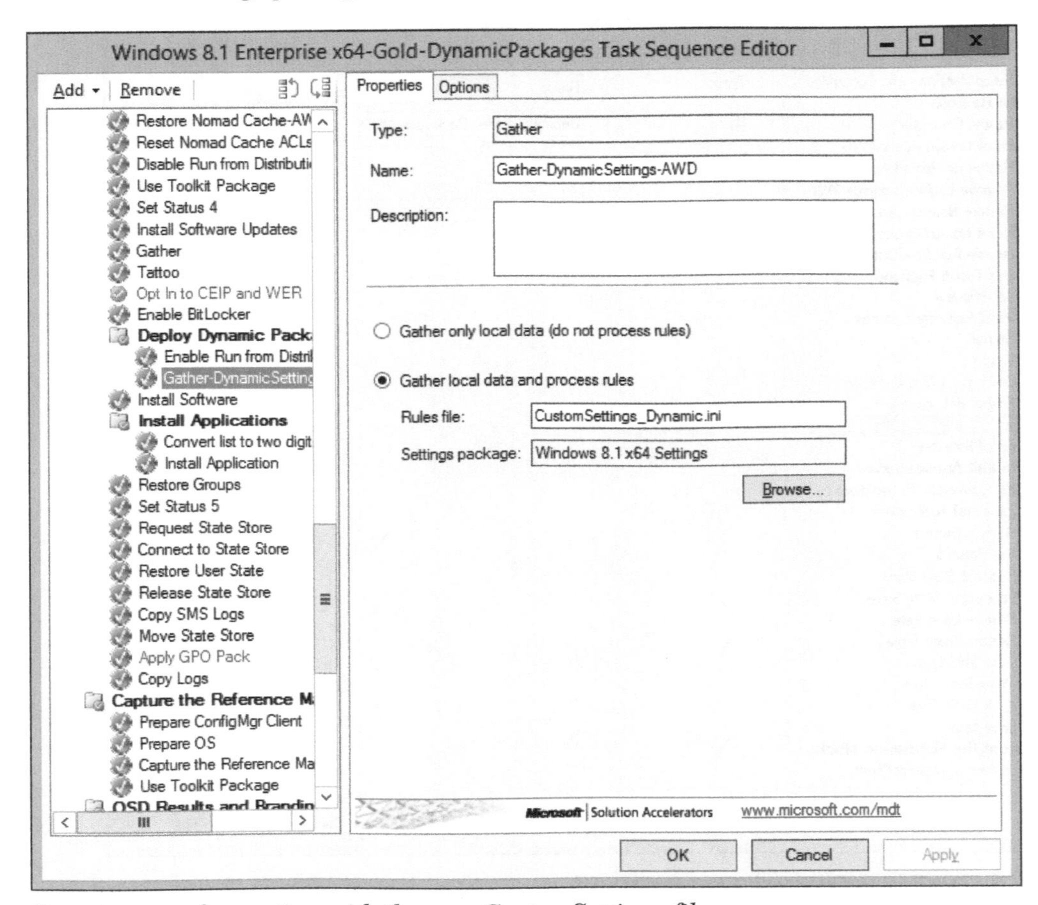

Running a gather action with the new CustomSettings file

12. Click the **Install Software** step and move it up one level.

13. Configure the follow steps for the **Install Software** step:
    - Properties tab
        - Name: **Install Software-AWD**
        - Base variable name: **PACKAGES**
        - If installation of a software package fails, continue installing other packages in the list: **Selected**
    - Options tab

        Continue on Error: **Selected**

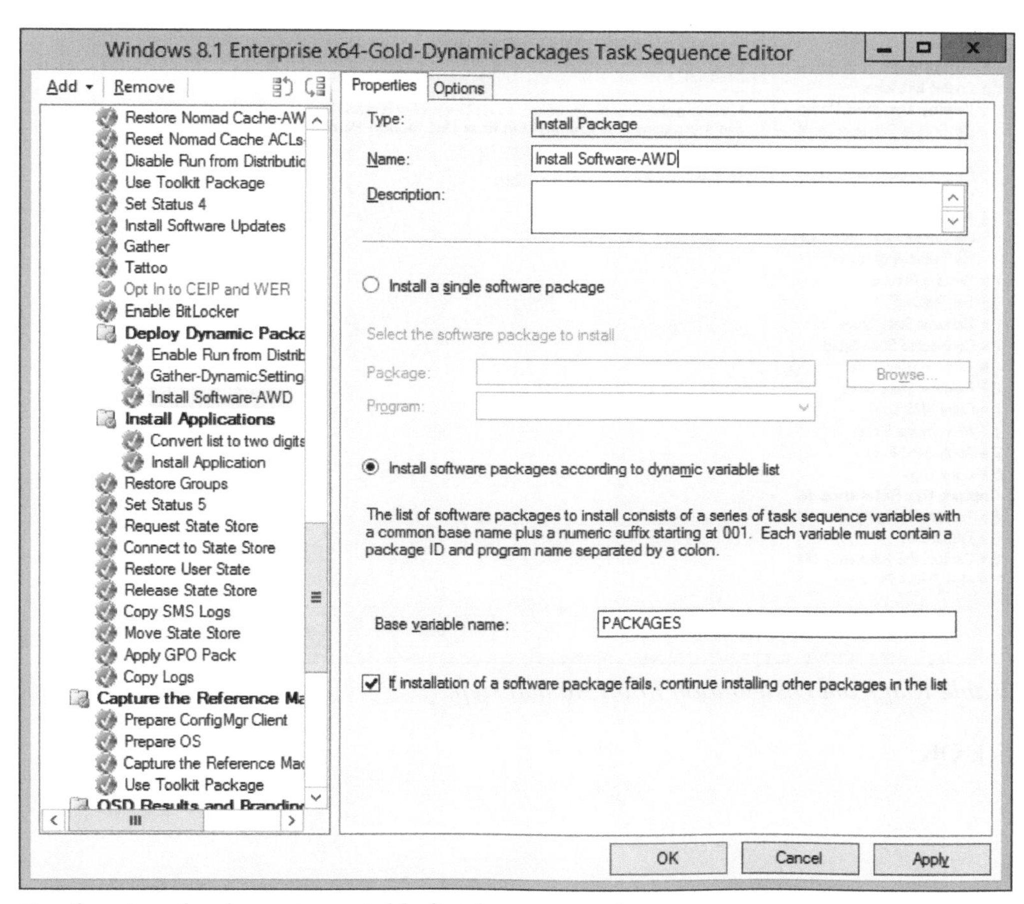

Configuring the dynamic variable list for your packages.

14. Click **Install Software**, and then click **Add / Nomad / Disable Run from Distribution Point**.

15. Configure the following settings:

Name: **Disable Run from Distribution Point-AWD**

The step should looks like the following figure.

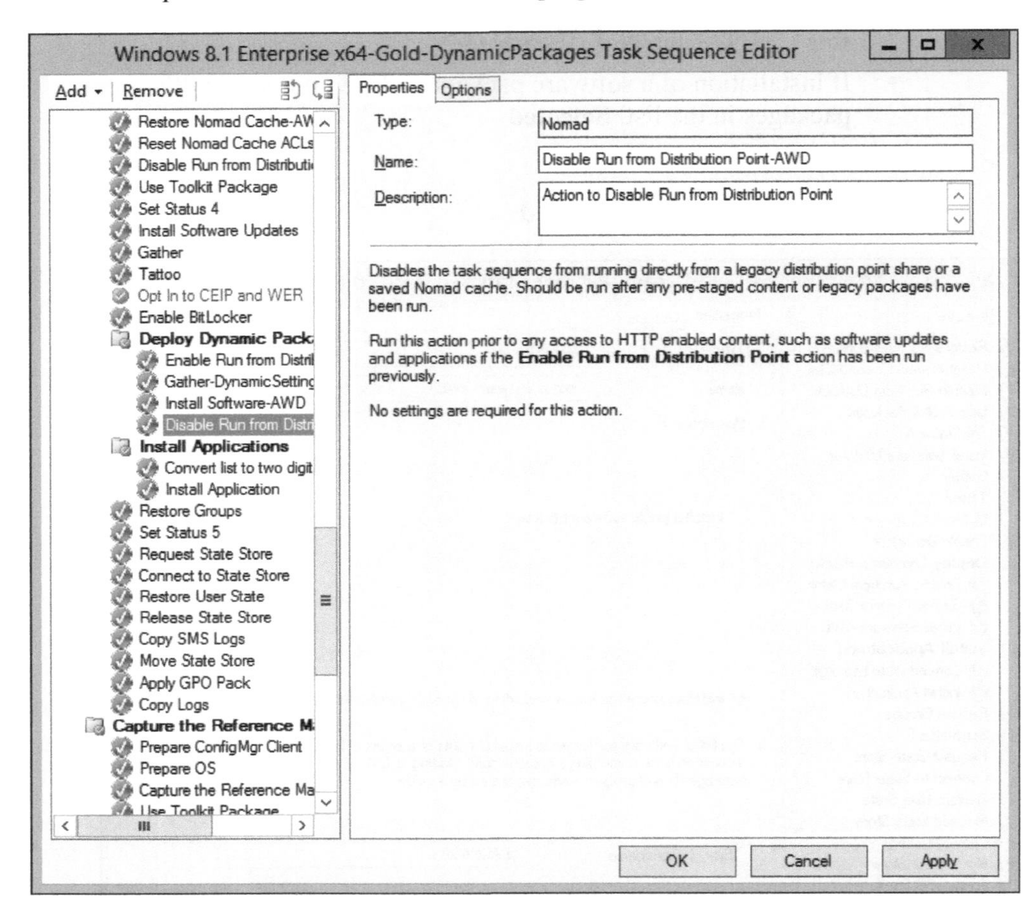

The Disable Run from Distribution Point Nomad step.

16. Click **OK**.

Deploying Refresh OSD and Dynamic Packages with Nomad

1. Deploy the **Windows 8.1 Enterprise x64-Gold-DynamicPackages** task sequence to the **Deploy Windows 8.1 Refresh - w/Core Apps Dynamic Apps and Nomad** collection with the following settings:
    - Purpose: **Available**
    - Make available to the following: **Only Configuration Manager Clients**
    - Scheduling: **<Default>**
    - User Experience: **<Default>**
    - Alerts: **<Default>**
    - Deployment Options: **Download content locally when needed by running task sequence**
2. On the **Host PC**, using the **Hyper-V console**, take a checkpoint of **PC0004** called **Pre-Nomad-Base AWD + Dynamic Apps**.
3. Log on to **PC0004** run a machine policy refresh.
4. Start the deployment of **Windows 8.1 Enterprise x64-Gold-DynamicPackages**.
5. While the deployment is starting, open **NomadBranch.log**.

Creating a Pre-Cache Task Sequence

You can use a pre-cache task sequence to get content out to branch locations before OSD installs. This would normally occur one to two weeks prior to the actual rollout. It is possible to create a single task sequence that deploys and pre-caches. For this example, you simply create a copy of one of the Gold task sequences and set it up to Pre-Cache Only. You then deploy it to the pre-cache collection.

Real World Note: Exercise extreme caution with these steps. It is not considered a best practice to use a deployment task sequence as the same pre-cache task sequence. We are showing these steps to showcase how the overall process works. In production, you must take care with these steps because if something does get configured incorrectly, you can end up deploying an image to the wrong machine or machines.

1. On **CM01**, open the **ConfigMgr console** and browse to **Software Library / Operation Systems / Task Sequences**.
2. Right-click **Windows 8.1 Enterprise x64-Gold-CoreApps** and click **Copy**.

3. Configure the copy with the following settings:
   - Name: **Windows 8.1 Enterprise x64-Gold-PreCache**
   - Description: **Version 1.0 - Adding NeverTrue Variables to prevent Execution of the Sequence**
   - Nomad tab: Select **Enable Nomad**.
4. Right-click **Windows 8.1 Enterprise x64-Gold-PreCache** and click **Edit**.
5. Click **Execute Task Sequence**.
6. Click **Options**.
7. Click **Add Condition / Task Sequence Variable**.
8. Configure the following settings:
   - Variable: **NeverTrue**
   - Condition: **equals**
   - Value: **True**

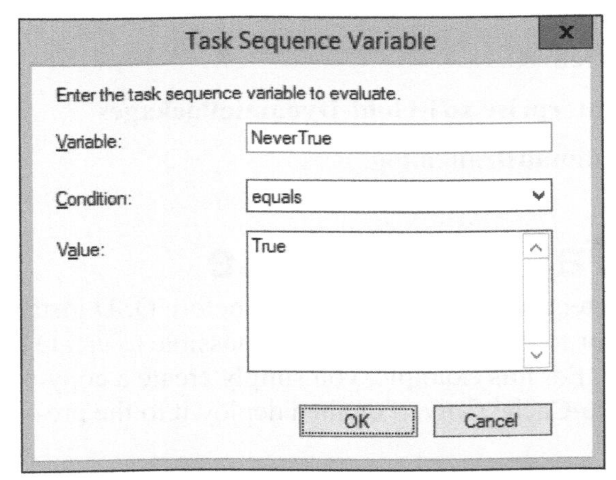

Creating a value that will always fail for a task sequence.

9. Close the task sequence by clicking **OK**.

Prepare PC0005

In the next section, you deploy the pre-cache task sequence to the previously deployed PC0005, a machine currently without the Nomad agent. In these steps, you prepare PC0005 for that.

1. On **PC0005**, log on as **VIAMONSTRA\Administrator**, change the computer name to **PC0005**, and reboot.
2. On **CM01**, deploy the **1E Nomad Branch x64-AWD / Per-system Unattended** program to the **Deploy Nomad Branch X64** collection. Make the deployment **Available**.
3. On **CM01**, in the **Assets and Compliance** workspace, wait until **PC0005** is listed in the **All Systems** collection.
4. Add **PC0005** to the **Deploy Nomad Branch X64**, **Deploy Nomad Download Monitor** and **Deploy CMTrace** collections.
5. On **PC0005**, refresh the machine policy, and using **Software Center**, install **1E Nomad Branch x64-AWD 5.2**, **Nomad Download Monitor-AWD 1.0** and **CMTrace-AWD 1.0**.
6. Using the **Registry Editor**, make sure the **Nomad Download Monitor** starts in advanced mode by verifying that the **UI** value in **HKLM\SOFTWARE\Wow6432Node\1E\NomadBranch** is set to **1**.
7. Using the **Configuration Manager** control panel applet, set the ConfigMgr 2012 client cache size to **20** GB.

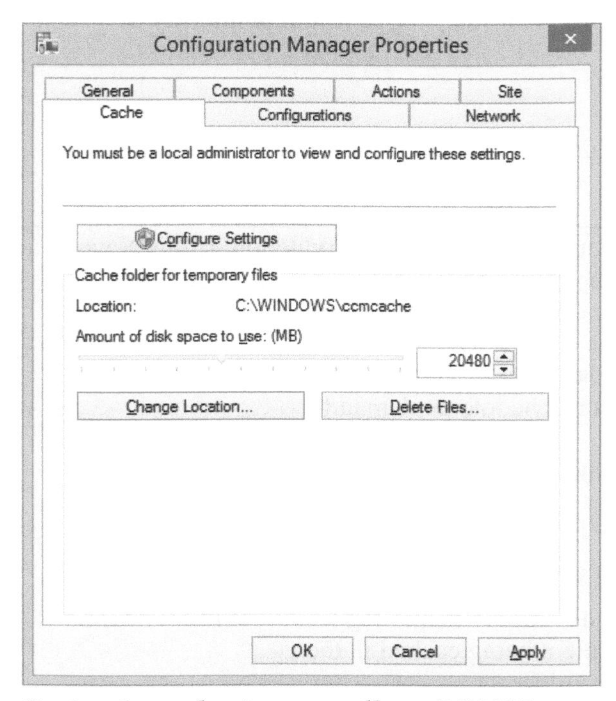

Setting the cache size manually on PC0005.

Deploying Pre-Cache Task Sequence

In this guide you deploy the pre-cache task sequence to PC0005 and monitor the content download.

1. On **CM01**, edit the direct members of the **Deploy Nomad OSD Pre-Cache** collection. Remove all existing clients and add only **PC0005**.
2. Deploy **Windows 8.1 Enterprise x64-Gold-PreCache** to the **Deploy Nomad OSD Pre-Cache** collection with the following settings:
    - Purpose: **Required**
    - Make available to the following: **Only Configuration Manager Clients**
    - Assignment schedule: **As Soon as possible** and **every 1 hours**

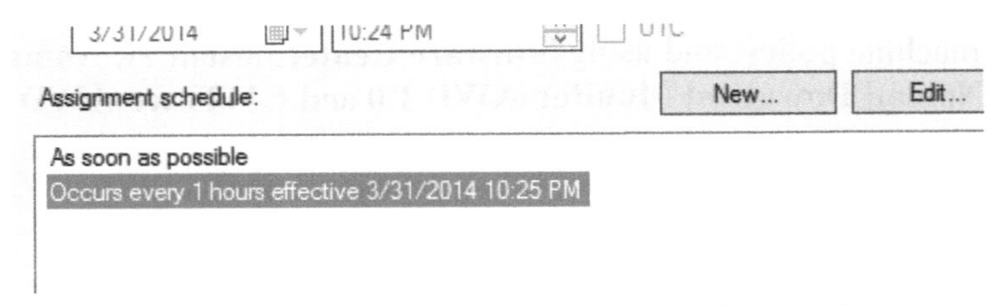

Configure the rerun schedule for the pre-caching task sequence.

- User Experience: **Allow users to run the program independently of assignments**
- Alerts: **<Default>**
- Deployment Options: **Download all content locally before starting task sequence**

> **Real World Note:** This can be a very dangerous configuration in production. If this NeverTrue variable is changed, it would be possible to deploy a mandatory (required) assignment to unwanted machines. Extreme caution must be exercised with this step.
>
> A one hour schedule has been configured for lab purposes only. In production, this could be configured to update once a week or even just reschedule on demand.

3. In **Hyper-V**, take a checkpoint of **PC0005** called **Nomad Pre-Cache**.
4. Log on to **PC0005** and run a machine policy refresh.
5. Start the deployment of **Deploy Windows OSD Pre-Cache**.
6. While the deployment is starting, open **NomadBranch.log** and **Nomad Download Monitor**. You can also review the content being cached in the **C:\ProgramData\1E\NomadBranch** folder.

Now, any subsequent deployments on this subnet will be able to download content from PC0005 (as well as any other client having the content).

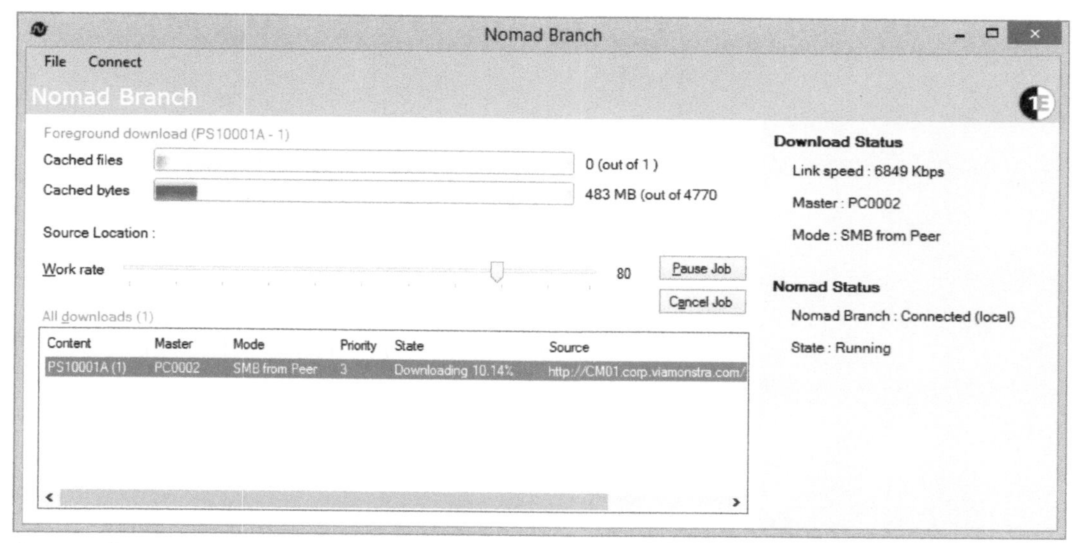

Pre-caching content on PC0005, in this case content is coming from PC0002.

Chapter 10

1E Nomad for OSD Bare Metal Scenario with Nomad Using SCCM PXE

Up to this point, you have been dealing with refresh task sequences configured for Nomad. Not only did you not have to concern yourself with a PXE boot point (more on that later), but you also had the ability to use Nomad to cache all your packages while in Windows. However, when provisioning a new machine, there isn't an existing OS, functioning ConfigMgr client, or an installation of NomadBranch. So the question arises, how do you use Nomad to download packages in Windows PE without a functioning ConfigMgr or Nomad client?

The answer is a connectionless peer-to-peer client. 1E provides a task sequence step to install a light version of Nomad for use specifically in WinPE. It uses a special configuration to establish connections to peers on the same subnet that has required content cached. It then uses the NomadPackageLocator application to locate available content.

Using Nomad in Windows PE

The process for using Nomad for bare metal deployments is fairly involved, yet logical. Because there is no functioning ConfigMgr client or a full Nomad installation, all actions surrounding the acquisition and installation of packages inside the task sequence require placing custom instructions that alter the task sequencer to use peer content locations instead of a distribution point.

There are a few things to keep in mind when performing bare metal deployments with Nomad:

- The Install and Configure Nomad in WinPE action needs to run before any other Nomad-enabled actions. It is standard practice for us to add this step at the top of the task sequence before any other package (read: MDT) is called.
- WinPE is executed in a RAM drive. This means that if/when a restart occurs, any and all information that has been cached to the hard drive is purged.
- Partitioning/formatting a hard drive must take place before packages are cached.
- All packages requiring download via Nomad must be prestaged to the machine prior to execution. This is performed using a custom 1E task sequence action.

Note: Prestaging Nomad-enabled packages in advance is not required if the package's program is appended with SMSNomad.exe. This will be discussed in further detail with respect to deploying dynamic applications created via the application model.

- Packages that are prestaged using Nomad, even in WinPE, are saved to C:\ProgramData\1E\NomadBranch. In order for the task sequencer to have visibility and access to these downloaded packages, they must be moved to the protected _SMSTaskSequence folder using the Save Nomad Cache custom task sequence action.
- Due to the way that ConfigMgr is designed to download copies of packages from a distribution point, calling a package that has been prestaged using Nomad forces the task sequencer to create a local copy of the package. In order to prevent this from happening, steps to enable and disable running from a distribution point need to be placed around the package install. These are also custom 1E task sequence actions that trick the task sequencer into thinking that it is running the package directly from a distribution point, when in reality the package is being run from the _SMSTaskSequence folder.

SCCM PXE with Nomad Log Files

The logs discussed in Chapter 9 are still applicable here, so we won't repeat them again. The addition of a PXE-enabled distribution point provides us with a new log file to view that is vital in troubleshooting issues when machines fail to PXE boot:

Log Name	Description
SMSPXE.log	Provides details about the PXE-enabled distribution point including client connection requests. Location: <ConfigMgrInstallationPath>\SMS_CCM\Logs

ConfigMgr PXE (Native) Conceptual Design (ViaMonstra)

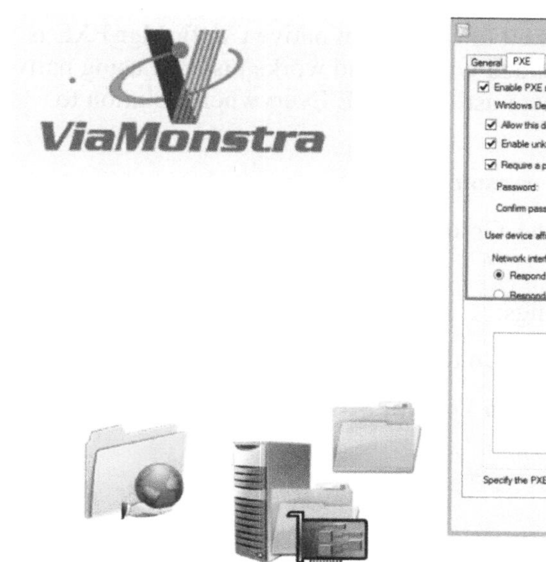

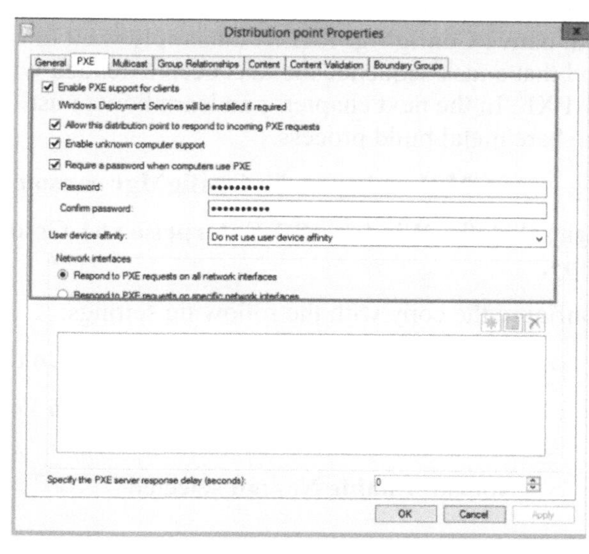

Bare metal imaging using native ConfigMgr PXE enabled DPs.

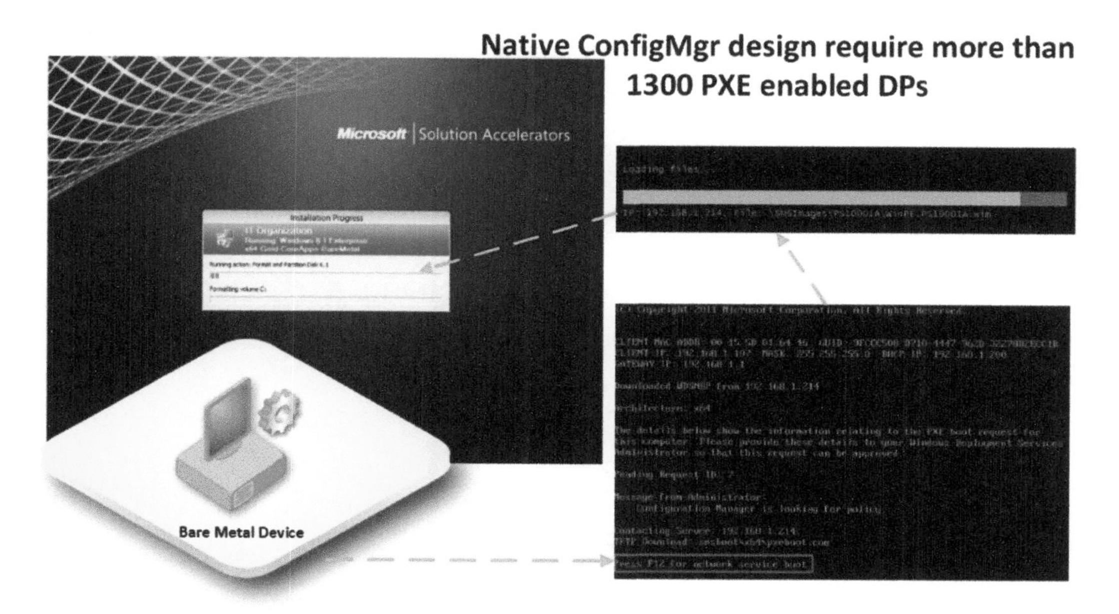

The ViaMonstra ConfigMgr PXE (native) conceptual design.

Extending a Refresh Task Sequence – Bare Metal PXE

In this guide, you extend the Windows 8.1 Enterprise x64-Gold-CoreApps sequence and enable it to work with native ConfigMgr PXE. You simply want to ensure that native ConfigMgr PXE is working and that a task sequence that has been extended with Nomad works just fine using native ConfigMgr PXE. In the next chapter, you learn how to use 1E's PXE Everywhere solution to simplify the bare metal build process.

1. Log on to **CM01** and open the **ConfigMgr console**.
2. Right-click the **Windows 8.1 Enterprise x64-Gold-CoreApps** task sequence and click **Copy**.
3. Configure the copy with the following settings:
    - Name: **Windows 8.1 Enterprise x64-Gold-CoreApps-BareMetal**
    - Description: **Version 1.0 - Cleaning up Format Steps and Adding Nomad for PE BareMetal**
    - Nomad: **Enable Nomad** selected

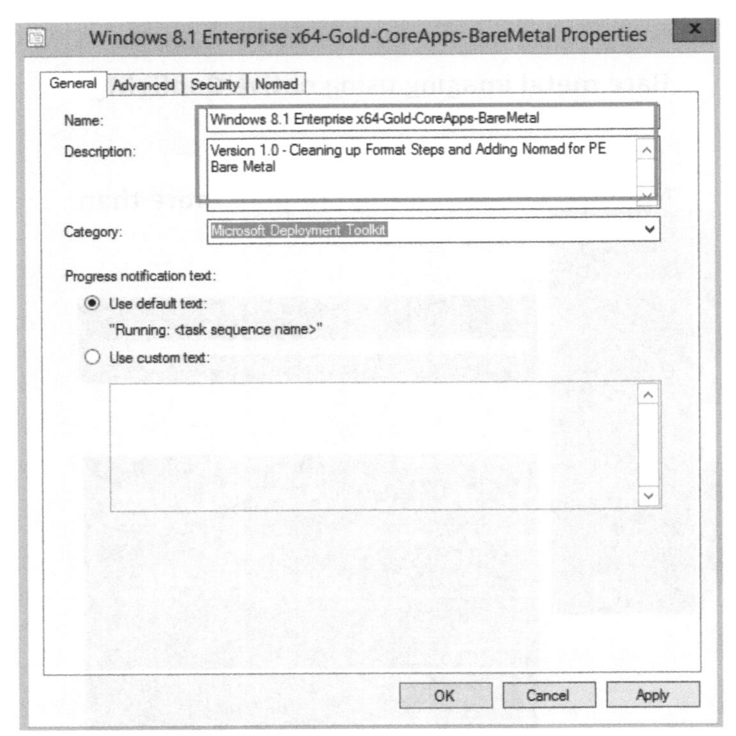

Creating a bare metal task sequence from an existing Gold task sequence.

4. Click **Windows 8.1 Enterprise x64-Gold-CoreApps-BareMetal** and click **Edit**.

5. In the **Initialization** group, select **Set Variable for Wizard**.
6. Click **Add / Nomad / Install and Configure Nomad in WinPE**.
7. Configure with the following settings:
   - Name: **Install Nomad in PE-AWD**
   - License key: This can be obtained from 1E. A trial key will not work here.
   - Workrate: **80**
   - P2P port: **1779**
   - SpecialNetShare: **8240** (0x2030)
   - P2PEnabled: **6** (0x6)
   - CompatibilityFlags: **2** (0x2)
   - MulticastSupport: **0**
   - Disable Firewall: **Selected**
   - Log file size: **<Default>**
   - Enable Single Site Download: **<Default>**

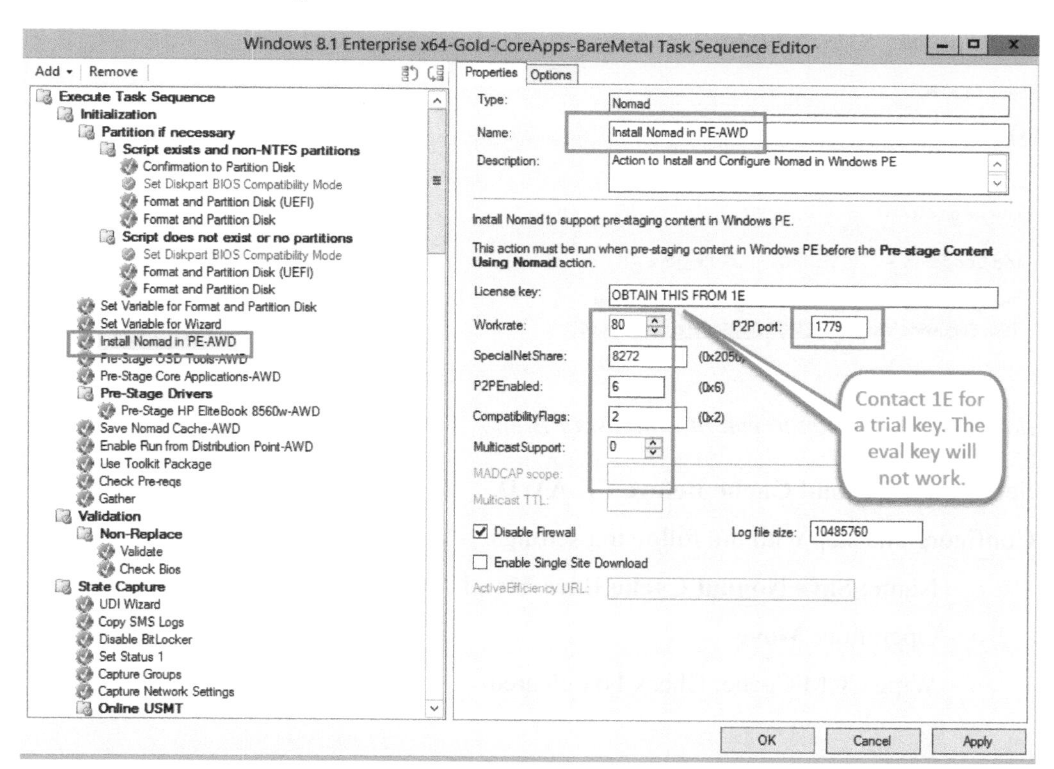

Adding steps to install Nomad in Windows PE.

8. Click the **Install Nomad in PE-AWD Options** tab.
9. Click **Add Condition**, and select **Task Sequence Variable**.
10. Configure with the following settings:
    - Variable: **_SMSTSinWinPE**
    - Condition: **equals**
    - Value: **True**

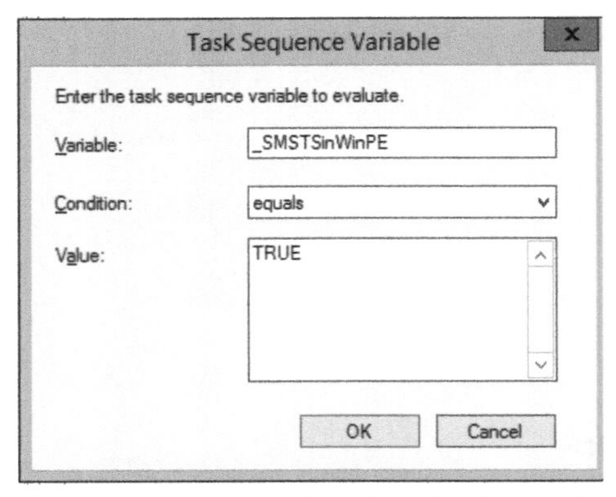

Configuring the _SMSTSinWinPE values.

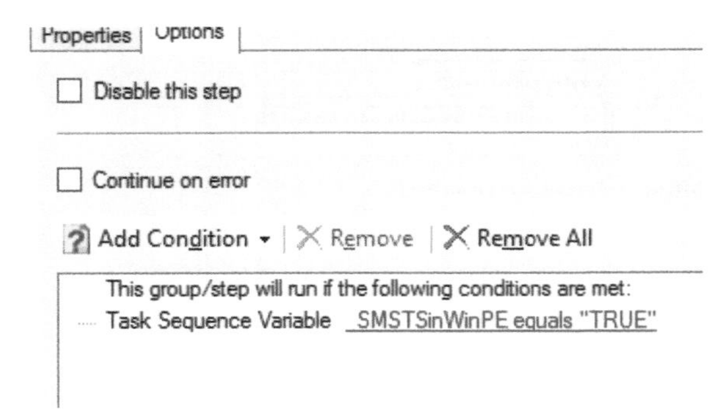

Validating the condition to run in Windows PE.

11. Select **Save Nomad Cache Before PE-AWD**.
12. Configure this step with the following settings:
    - Name: **Save Nomad Cache Bare Metal-AWD**
    - Operation: **Move**
    - Wipe CCM Cache: Check box cleared

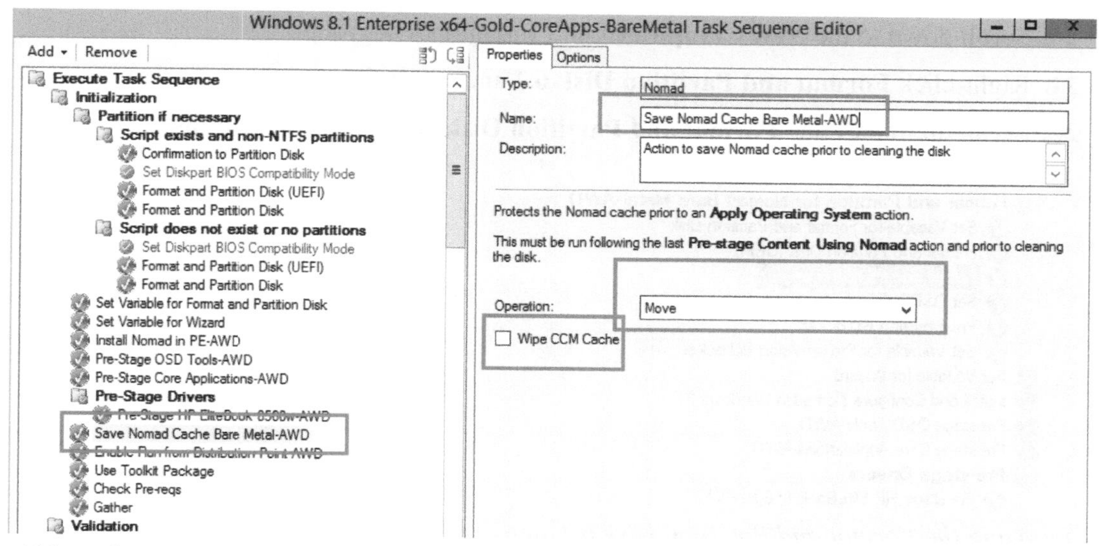

Adding the step to save the Nomad cache during the bare metal PXE process.

13. Right-click the **Partition if necessary** group and click **Delete**.
14. Click the **Initialization** group, and then click **Add / New Group**.
15. Configure this step with the following setting:

    Name: **Format and Partition for Nomad Bare Metal-AWD**

16. Click **Set Variable for Format and Partition Disk** and move it up one level.

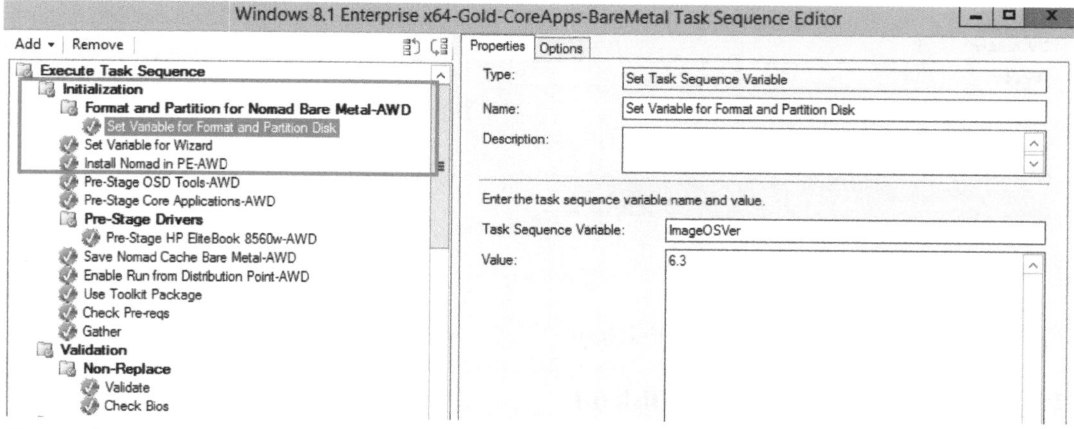

Fixing format and partition steps for bare metal.

17. Scroll down to the **New Computer Only / Format Disk** group.
18. Right-click **Format and Partition Disk (UEFI)** and select **Copy**.
19. Scroll up again, right-click **Set Variable for Format and Partition** and select **Paste**.

20. Scroll down to the **New Computer Onl / Format Disk** group.
21. Right-click **Format and Partition Disk 6.1** and select **Copy**.
22. Scroll up, right-click **Format and Partition Disk (UEFI)** and select **Paste**.

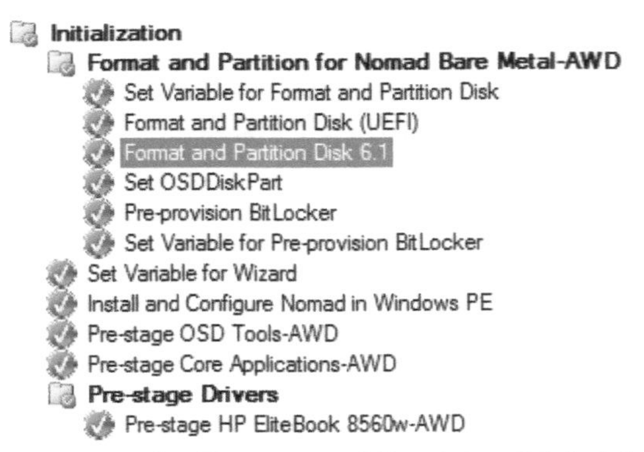

Inserting the Format and Partition Disk 6.1 step.

23. Click the **Format and Partition (UEFI)** step.
24. Delete the first three volumes.

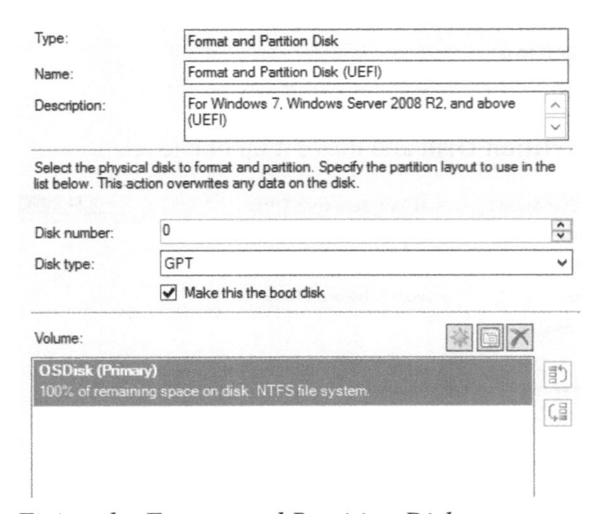

Fixing the Format and Partition Disk step.

25. Click **Format and Partition Disk 6.1**.
26. Click **BDEDrive** and click **Properties**.
27. Select **Do not assign a drive letter to the partition** and click **OK**.

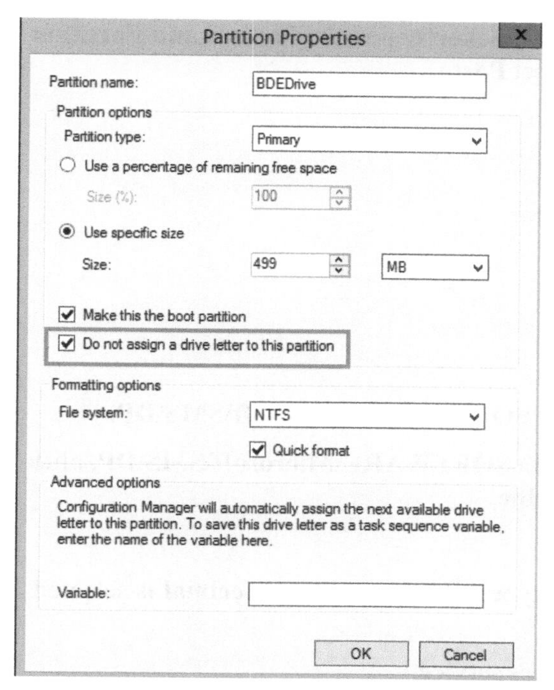

Fixing the BDEDrive drive letter assignment.

28. Scroll down to the **New Computer Only / Format Disk** group.
29. Right-click **Set OSDDiskPart** and select **Copy**.
30. Scroll up, right-click the **Format and Partition Disk 6.1** step in the **Format and Partition Nomad Bare Metal-AWD** group and select **Paste**.
31. Scroll down to the **New Computer Only / Format Disk** group.
32. Right-click **Pre-Provision BitLocker** and click **Copy**.
33. Scroll up, right-click the **Set OSDDiskPart** step in the **Format and Partition Nomad Bare Metal-AWD** group and select **Paste**.

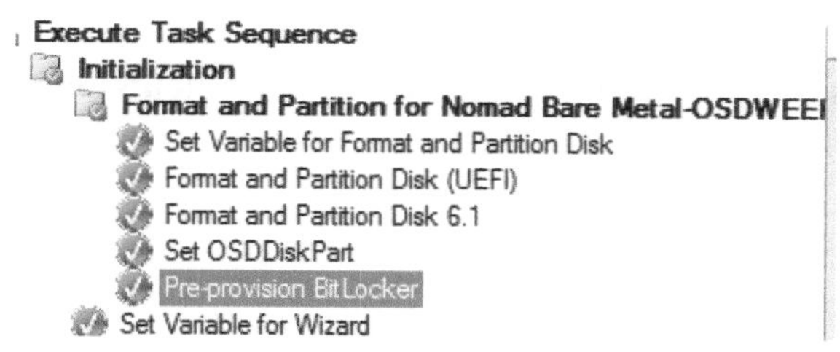

Inserting the Pre-provision BitLocker step.

34. Scroll down to the **New Computer Only / Format Disk** group.
35. Right-click **Set Variable for Pre-provision BitLocker** and select **Copy**.

36. Scroll up, right-click the **Pre-provision BitLocker** step in the **Format and Partition Nomad Bare Metal-AWD** group and select **Paste**.
37. Scroll down to the **New Computer** section.
38. Delete the **Format Disk** group.
39. Click **OK** to close the Task Sequence Editor.

Speed Up PXE Booting

1. On **CM01,** open **Regedit**.
2. Browse to **HKEY_LOCAL_MACHINE\SOFTWARE\Microsoft\SMS\DP**.
3. Right-click **HKEY_LOCAL_MACHINE\ SOFTWARE\Microsoft\SMS\DP**, click **New**, and then click **DWORD (32-bit) value**.
4. Type **RamDiskTFTPBlockSize**.
5. Double-click **RamDiskTFTPBlockSize**, type **4000,** ensure **Hexadecimal** is selected, and then click **OK.**
6. Restart the **Windows Deployment Services** service.

Real World Note: Making this change speeds up PXE boot times by four to five times if your hardware models and network supports it.

Deploying Windows 8.1 x64 Custom Image Bare Metal – Nomad Integrated

1. On **CM01**, open the **ConfigMgr console**.
2. Deploy **Windows 8.1 Enterprise x64-Gold-CoreApps-BareMetal** to the **All Unknown Computers** collection with the following settings:
    - Purpose: **Available**
    - Make available to the following: **Only Configuration Manager Clients, media, and PXE**
    - Scheduling: **<Default>**
    - User Experience: **<Default>**
    - Alerts: **<Default>**
    - Deployment Options: **Download content locally when needed by running task sequence**

Testing Native ConfigMgr PXE Using the Bare Metal Task Sequence

1. On the **Hyper-V** host machine, create a **Generation 1** Hyper-V virtual machine with the following settings:
    - Name: **PC0006**
    - Location: **D:\VMs**
    - Generation: **Generation 1**
    - Memory: **1024 MB**
    - Network: **AWD_Internal**
    - Hard disk: **<default>**
    - **Install an operating system from a network-based installation server**
2. Turn on **PC0006**, and press **F12** when prompted.
3. After WinPE booted, type in a password of **P@ssw0rd**.
4. Deploy the **Windows 8.1 Enterprise x64-Gold-CoreApps-BareMetal** task sequence.
5. When deployment starts, press **F8** and type **CMTrace.exe**.
6. When you see the task sequence reaching the Pre-Stage OSD Tools-AWD action, open the **X:\Windows\Temp\SMSTSLog\NomadBranch.log** file.

Note: If the deployment fails with error code 2 (0x00000002) when the task sequence tries to install the Nomad Agent, make sure you updated the boot image after installing the Nomad Branch OSD extensions on the site server.

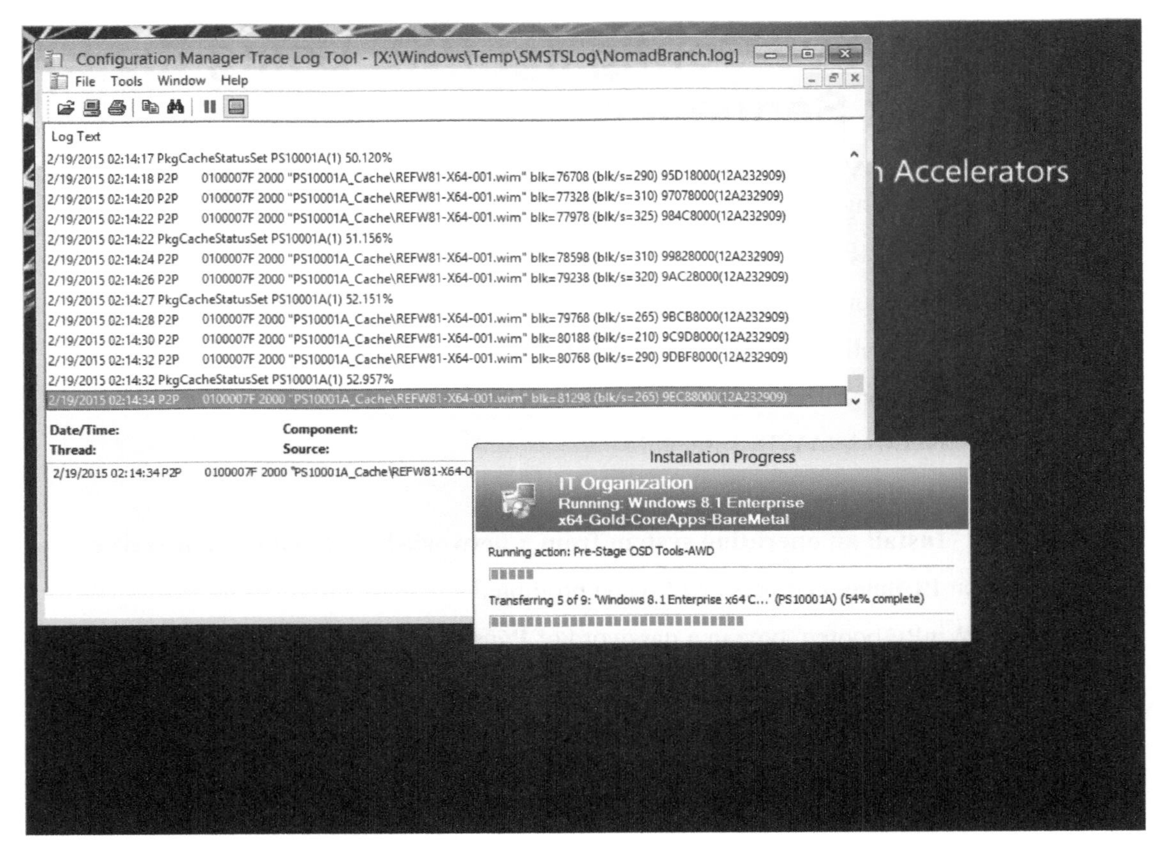

Deploying PC0006 via SCCM PXE, with content being staged from local peers.

Chapter 11

Nomad PXE Everywhere

Because you are removing remote distribution points with the implementation of Nomad, you need to address the associated removal of a PXE service point. To do this, you once again use unutilized resources on peer workstations to provide a boot image for PXE requests. A TFTP location is created on acceptable workstations, and a special boot image is deployed to the clients using a task sequence.

PXE Everywhere Key Concepts

There are three main components to the PXE Everywhere solution. A server-side application that has read access to the ConfigMgr database, a client that listens for TFTP boot image requests, and the modified boot image that is delivered to the machine.

PXE Central

Regardless of the size of a customer's environment, there is always only one PXE Central Server in an enterprise. For organizations with fewer than 100,000 devices, this is most often deployed on the primary site server. The purpose of the PXE Central Server is to validate that the client requesting a boot image actually has an operating system deployment sequence deployed to it: When a PXE Everywhere client receives a boot image request from a specific MAC address, it sends a request to the PXE Central Server via an HTTP request. PXE Central, through the use of a stored procedure, then checks the ConfigMgr database for the appropriate collection membership and corresponding OSD sequence. When this has been confirmed, an HTTP reply message is returned to the PXE Everywhere workstation, approving the requesting client use of the boot image.

PXE Lite Local

One of the confusing parts about PXE Everywhere is that although the product has undergone multiple rebranding efforts since its creation, the actual client installer remains PXELiteLocal. A lightweight application, PXELiteLocal participates in subnet elections for TFTP master selection and monitors any boot images in the TFTPRoot.

PXE Everywhere Boot Image

To create a boot image that can be deployed from machines external to the ConfigMgr site hierarchy, you take an existing Boot.wim and modify it to include the components that are dynamically added to boot images when they are deployed from a PXE enabled distribution point: the management point, distribution point, and site connection information. In a default ConfigMgr 2012 environment, the distribution point dynamically updates a file, variables.dat, in the boot image with client-specific information on how to connect to ConfigMgr 2012 without a functioning ConfigMgr 2012 client. In order to provide values that are applicable to any PXE client, regardless of location, you statically populate the variables.dat file.

PXE Log Files

As you might expect, most of the log files that pertain to PXE Everywhere are located on the PXE Everywhere client; however, there's also an important log file on the PXE Central Server that is a critical reference point when troubleshooting PXE boot issues.

Log Name	Description
WebService.log	Server-side log that stores information pertaining to client task sequence validation requests. When a machine requests a boot image from a PXE Everywhere client, this log shows the client connecting and confirming an OSD sequence for the requesting machine's MAC address. Location: C:\Program Files (x86)\1E\PXECentral
CreateBCD.log	Client log that is created when CreateBCD is run during the PXE Everywhere task sequence execution to populate the TFTPRoot Location: C:\ProgramData\1E\PXELite\TFTPRoot\Images\<BootImageID>
PXELiteServer.log	Client log that stores all PXE Everywhere information on the client, including TFTP requests, subnet elections, master selection, connectivity to PXECentral, and the delivery of boot images Location: C:\ProgramData\1E\PXELite

1E_GetPXEAction Stored Procedure

During the PXE boot process there is a stored procedure called 1E_GetPXEAction that is used to determine whether a valid PXE deployment is available for the client. If there is not a valid PXE deployment, then a PXEAbort is issued to the client attempting to boot.

Deploying PXE Central

PXE Central is a web service that interacts with the ConfigMgr database. It also adds a stored procedure to the ConfigMgr database called 1E Get PXE Action. This is what checks for a machine's advertisement status and determines whether it has a valid PXE boot job. If it does have one, then it instructs the PXE local workstation to deliver the Boot.wim to the requesting machine. If not, it instructs the PXE local workstation to issue a PXEAbort to the requesting machine.

The following steps install and configure the PXE Central web service and stored procedure on CM01.

1. Obtain a copy of **PXE Everywhere** from 1E and download it to **C:\Labfiles\Sources** on **CM01**.
2. Log on to **CM01** and browse to **C:\Labfiles\Sources\PxeLite v2.2.0.26**.
3. Double-click **PXELiteCentral.msi**.
4. Use the following values for the installation:
   a. On the **Welcome** page, click **Next**.

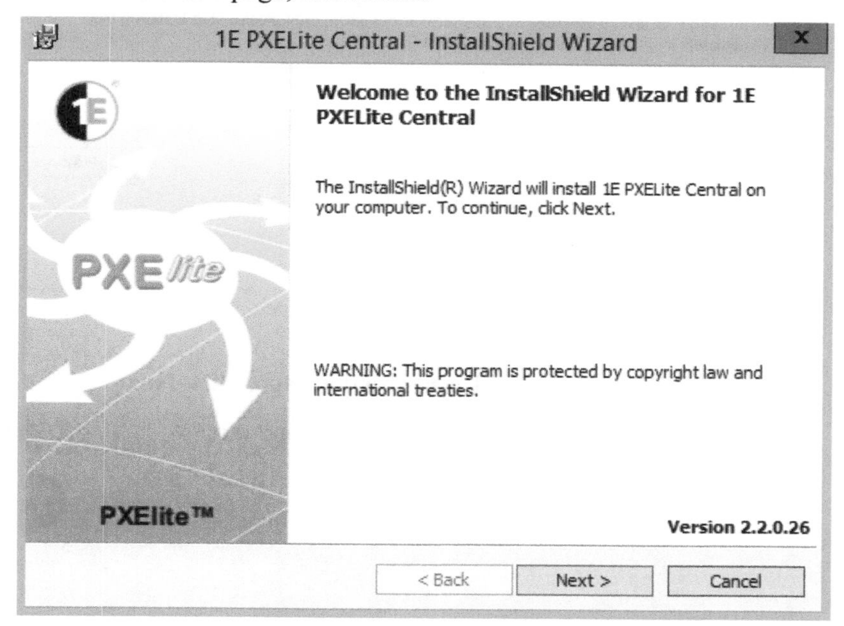

b. On the **License Agreement** page, accept the terms and click **Next**.

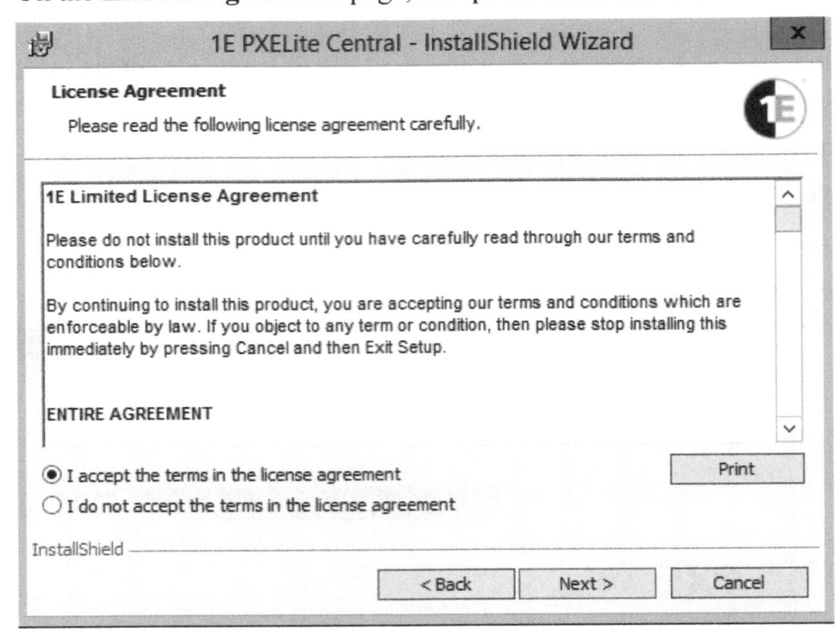

c. On the **PXE Lite Central Prerequisites** page, click **Next**.

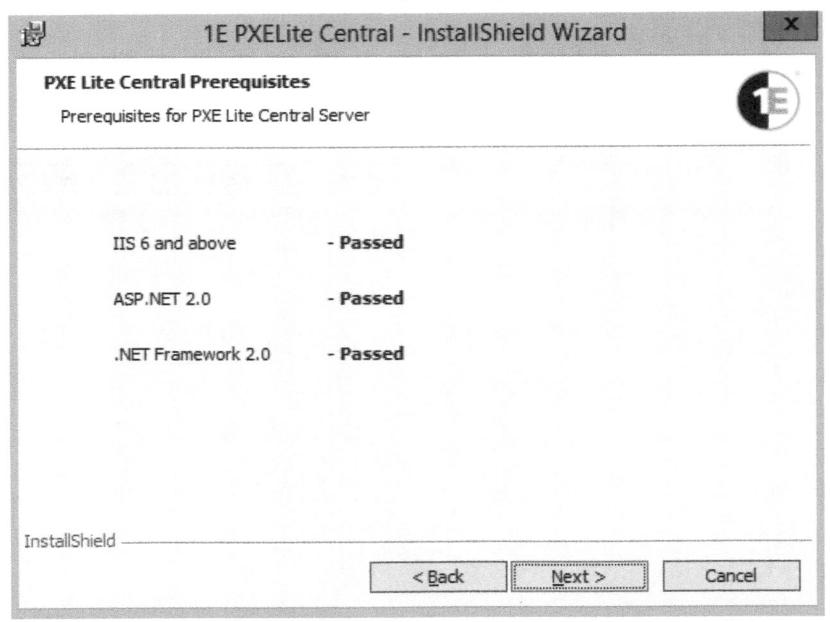

d. On the **Custom Setup** page, keep the defaults and click **Next**.

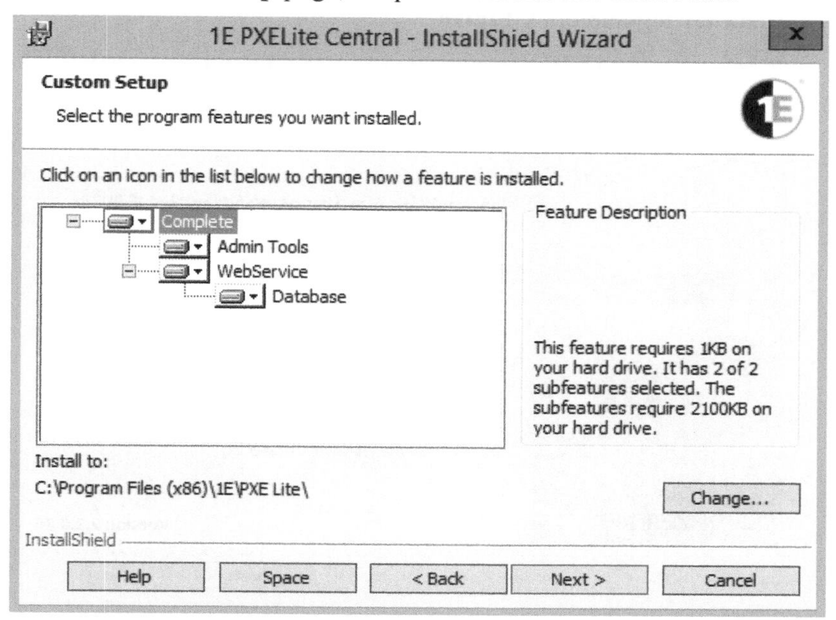

e. On the **Ready to Install the Program** page, click **Install**.

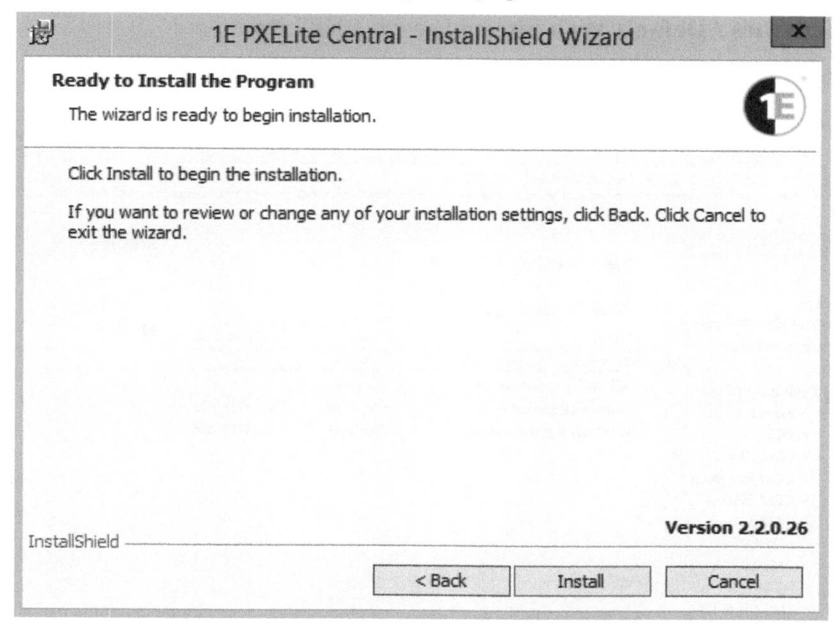

f. On the **InstallShield Wizard Completed** page, select **Show the Windows Installer log** and click **Finish**.

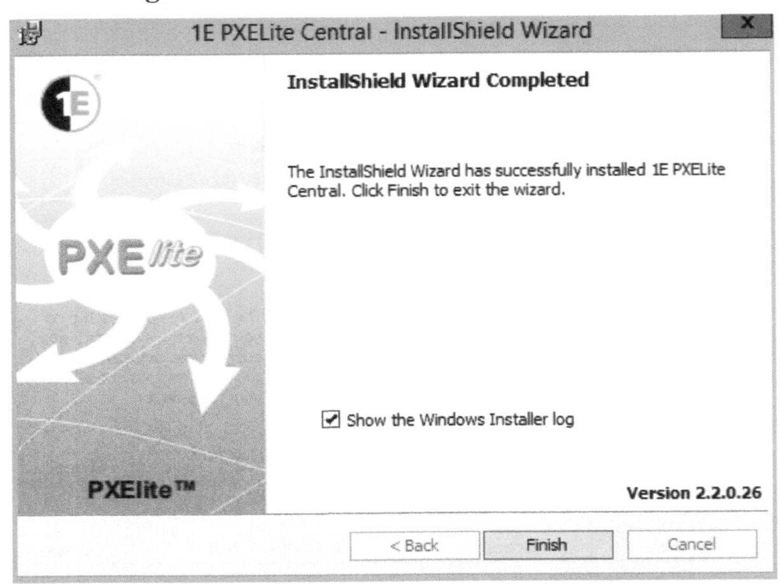

5. After reviewing the Windows Installer log file, launch **IIS Manager**.
6. Expand **Sites / Default Web Site** and select **PXELite**.
7. Double-click **Authentication** and disable **Anonymous Authentication**.

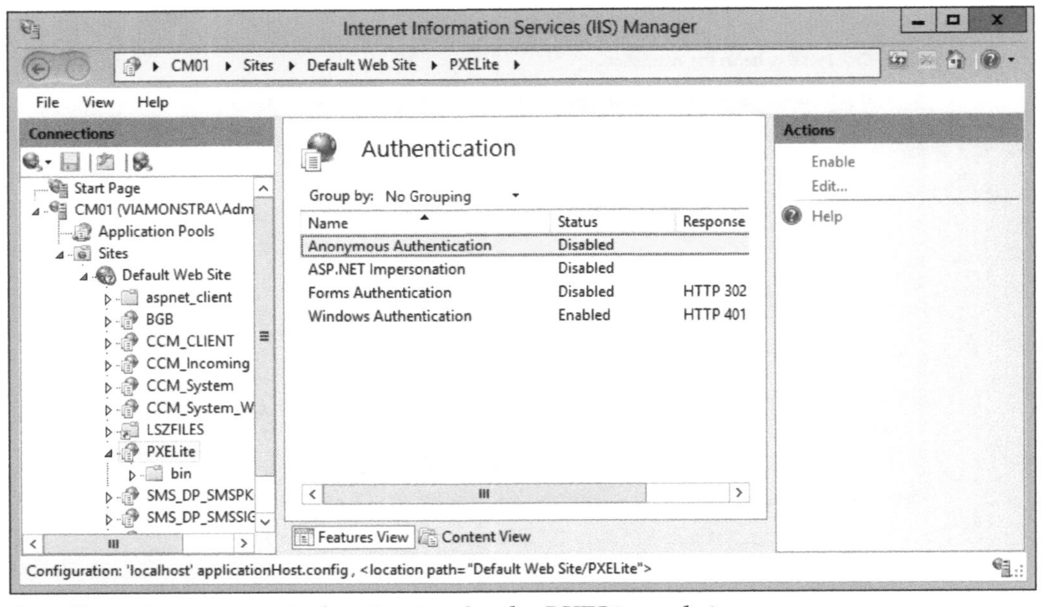

Disabling Anonymous Authentication for the PXELite website.

Note: The preceding step is important and one that we often see missed in customer environments. If Anonymous Authentication is not disabled, PXE Everywhere clients will receive SOAP errors when attempting to validate active deployments for a TFTP boot request. This is because PXE Everywhere attempts to access ConfigMgr using the NT AUTHORITY\IUSR account instead of NT AUTHORITY\NETWORK SERVICE.

8. Click **Application Pools** and double-click **PXELite**.
9. Change the **Managed pipeline mode:** to **Classic**, and click **OK**.

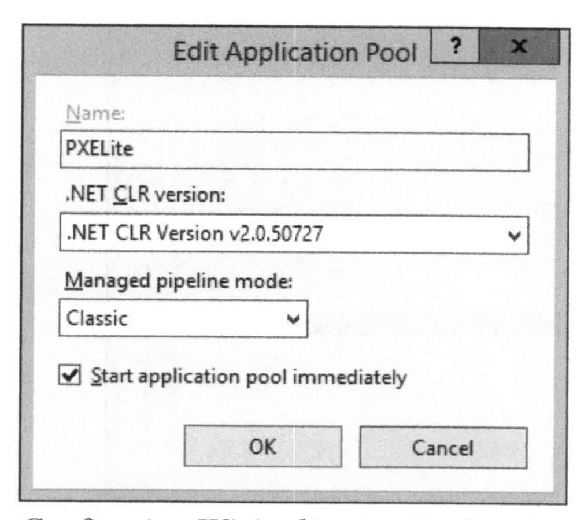

Configuring IIS Application Pool settings for the PXE Central web service.

10. Open **SQL Server Management Studio**.
11. In the left pane, expand the top level **Security** node, right-click **Logins**, and create a new login.
12. In the **Login – New** window, search for **NETWORK SERVICE** (will expand to NT AUTHORITY\NETWORK SERVICE).
13. Still in the **Login – New** windows, select the **User Mapping** node, and Grant **NT AUTHORITY\NETWORK SERVICE** the **db_datareader** rights to the **CM_PS1** database, and click **OK**.

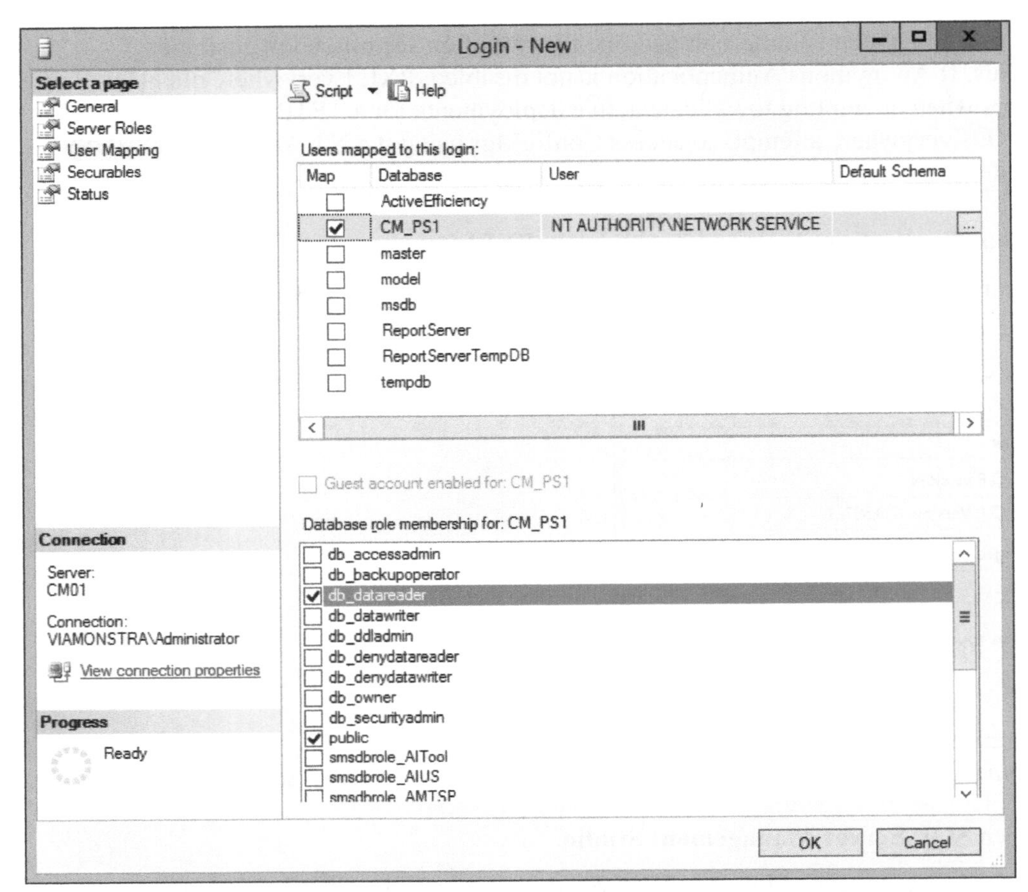

Granting db_datareader rights to the NT AUTHORITY\NETWORK SERVICE account.

14. In the left pane, expand Databases / CM_PS1 / Programmability / Stored Procedures
15. Right-click the **dbo.1E_GetPXEAction** stored procedure and select **Properties**.
16. In the **Permissions** node, click **Search**, click **Browse**, select **[NT AUTHORITY\NETWORK SERVICE]** and click **OK** twice.
17. Select **NT AUTHORITY\NETWORK SERVICE** and grant **Execute** permissions on the **1E_GetPXEAction** stored procedure.
18. Click **OK**.

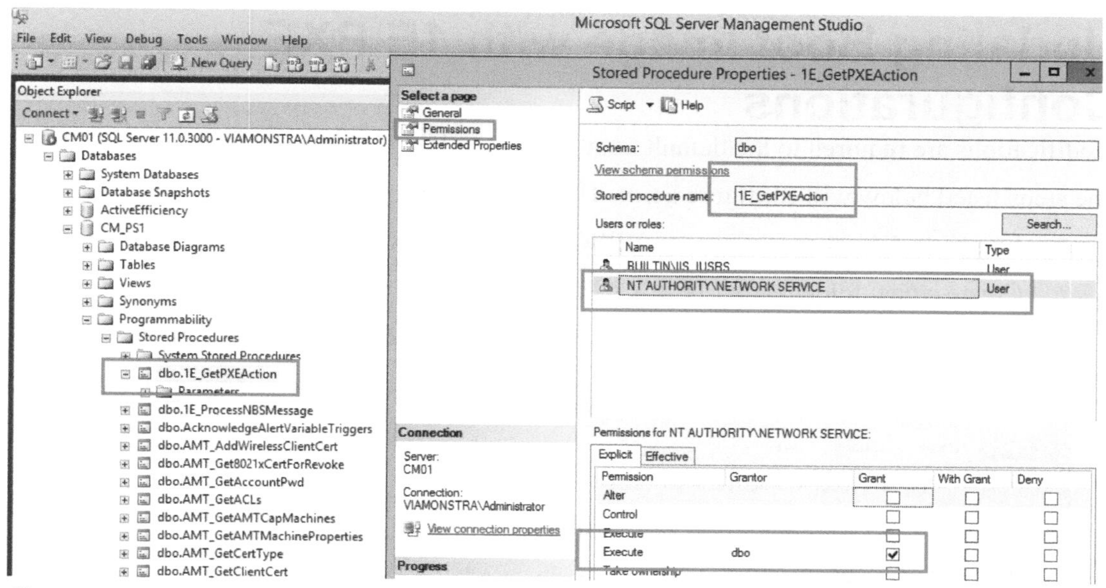

Granting Execute rights to the 1E_GetPXEAction stored procedure.

19. Validate the install by going to the following URL:

http://cm01/PXELite/PXELiteconfiguration.asmx

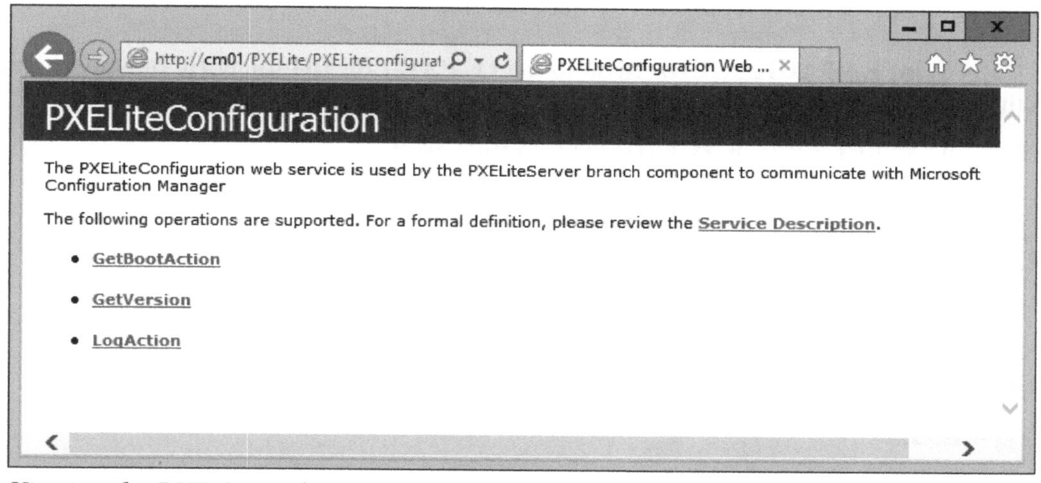

Viewing the PXE Central web service.

Updating Boot Image with 1E PXE Configurations

Modifications are required to the default boot image to allow 1E PXE Local's deployment.

The steps listed below will configure a new 1E PXE Lite Boot Image.

1. Log on to **CM01** and browse to **D:\SCCM_Sources\OSD\Boot**.
2. Create a new folder called **1E PXE Lite x64**.
3. Browse to **D:\SCCM_Sources\OSD\Boot\Zero Touch WinPE 5.0 x64**.

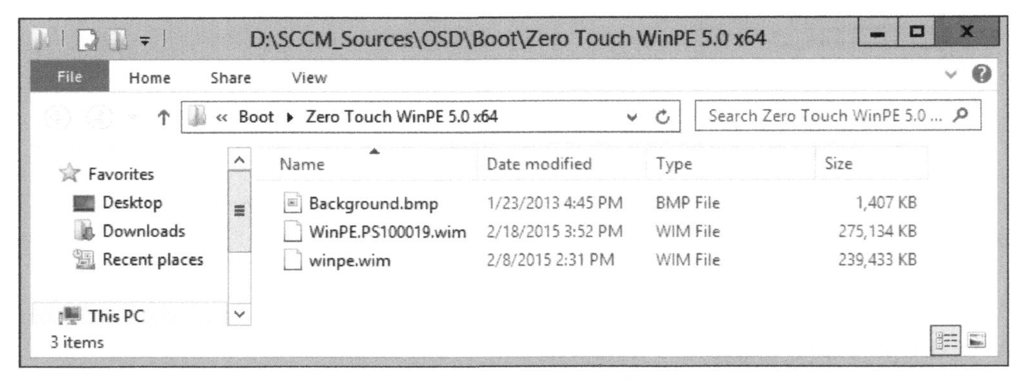

Reviewing the Zero Touch WinPE 5.0 x64 boot media.

4. Copy **WinPE.<PACKAGEID>.wim** to the **1E PXE Lite x64** folder (in our environment the Package ID was PS100019).
5. Rename **WinPE.<PACKAGEID>.wim** to **Boot.wim**.

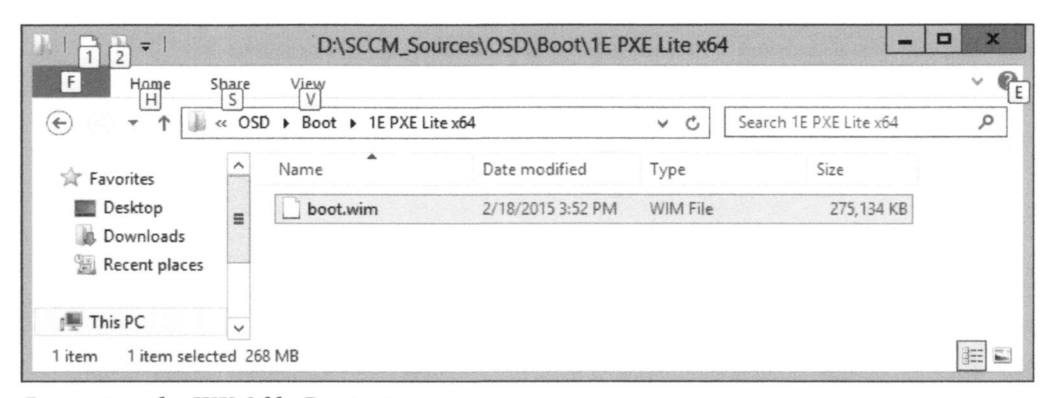

Renaming the WIM file Boot.wim.

6. Open the **ConfigMgr console** and browse to **Software Library / Operating Systems / Boot Images**.
7. Right-click **Boot Images** and click **Add Boot Image**.

8. Configure with the following settings:
   - Path: **\\CM01\SCCM_Sources$\OSD\Boot\1E PXE Lite x64\boot.wim**
   - Boot Image: **1 - Microsoft PE (x64)**

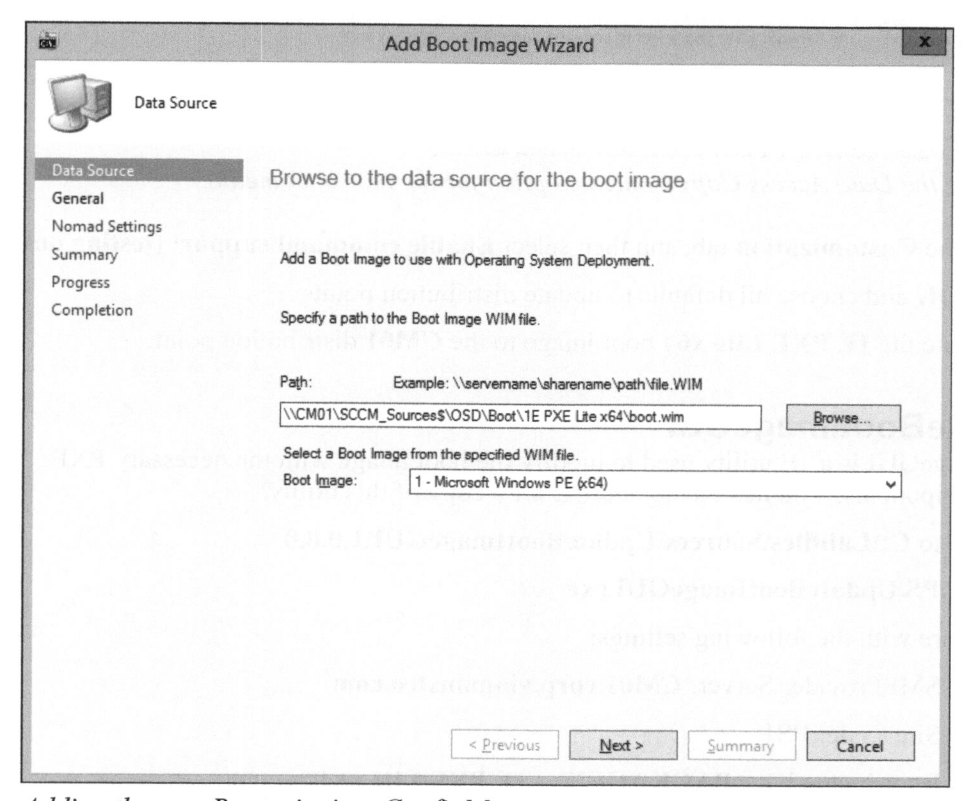

Adding the new Boot.wim into ConfigMgr.

   - Name: **1E PXE Lite x64**
   - Version: **1.0**
   - Nomad Settings: **Enable / Cache Priority 5**

9. Right-click **1E PXE Lite x64**, and click **Properties**.
10. Click the **Data Access** tab, and select **Copy the content of this package to a package share on the distribution points**.

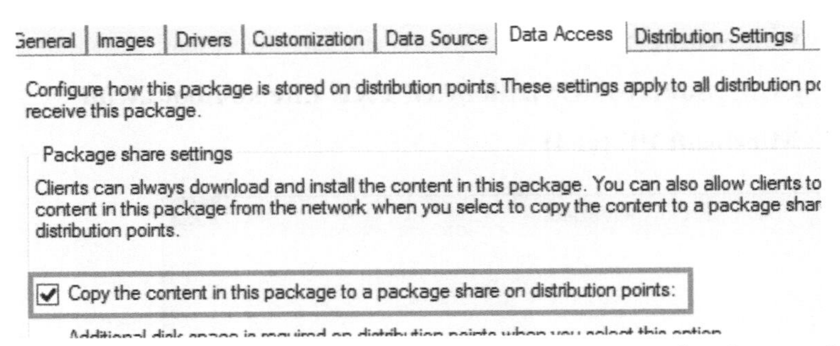

Configuring the Data Access Copy Contents option for the new boot media.

11. Select the **Customization** tab, and then select **Enable command support (testing only)**.
12. Select **OK** and choose all defaults to update distribution points.
13. Distribute the **1E PXE Lite x64** boot image to the **CM01** distribution point.

Run UpdateBootImageGUI

UpdateBootImageGUI is a 1E utility used to modify the boot image with the necessary PXE Everywhere components. You need to contact 1E for a copy of this utility.

1. Browse to **C:\Labfiles\Sources\UpdateBootImageGUI\1.0.0.0**.
2. Run **1E.PS.UpdateBootImageGUI.exe**.
3. Configure with the following settings:
    - SMSProvider Server: **CM01.corp.viamonstra.com**
    - Site Code: **PS1**
    - Boot Image ID: **<PACKAGEID - 1E PXE Lite x64 >**
    - WIM File Path\Name: **\\CM01\SCCM_Sources$\OSD\Boot\1E PXE Lite x64\boot.wim**
    - Distribution Points: Select **CM01.corp.viamonstra.com**.
    - Management Points: Select **http://CM01.CORP.VIAMONSTRA.COM**.
    - Certificate Expiry: **<Default>**
    - PXE Boot Password: **P@ssw0rd**
    - Certificate Path: **<blank>**
    - Certificate Password: **<blank>**

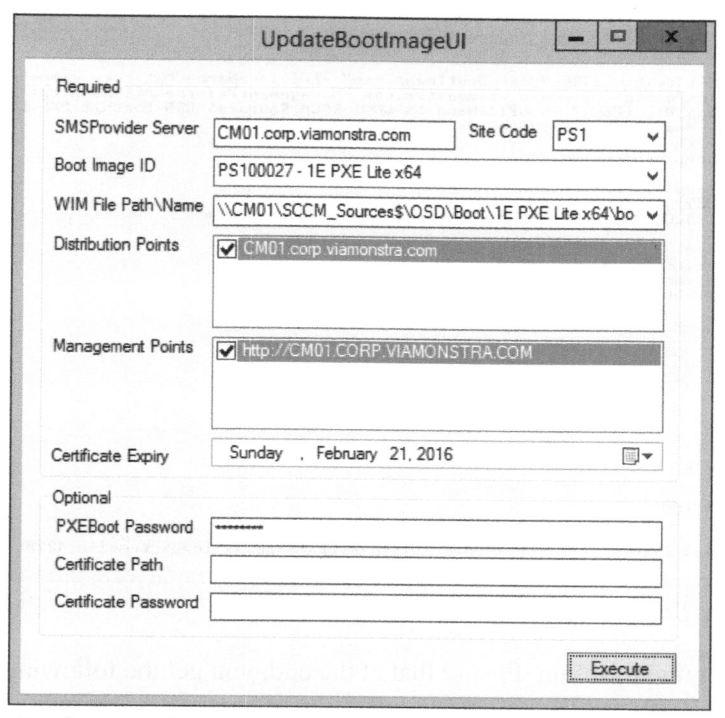

Configuring the 1E Update Boot Image utility.

4. Select **Execute**.

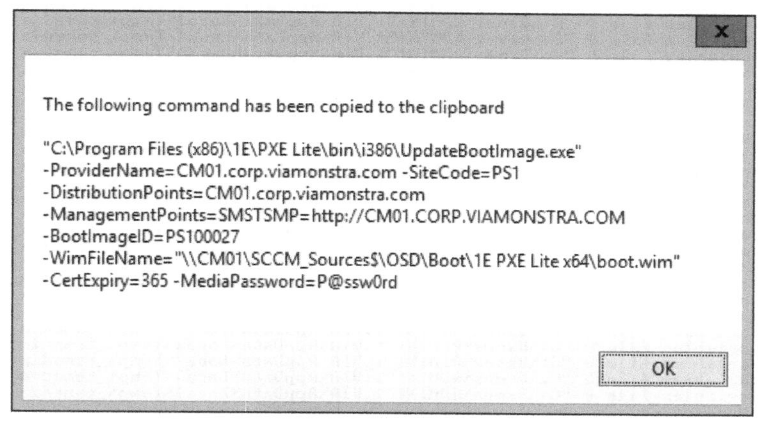

Viewing the results of Update Boot Image.

5. Open an elevated **Command prompt**.
6. Paste the command from the clipboard and press **Enter**.

```
Administrator: Command Prompt

C:\>"C:\Program Files (x86)\1E\PXE Lite\bin\i386\UpdateBootImage.exe" -ProviderName=CM01.corp.viamon
stra.com -SiteCode=PS1 -DistributionPoints=CM01.corp.viamonstra.com -ManagementPoints=SMSTSMP=http:/
/CM01.CORP.VIAMONSTRA.COM -BootImageID=PS100027 -WimFileName="\\CM01\SCCM_Sources$\OSD\Boot\1E PXE L
ite x64\boot.wim" -CertExpiry=365 -MediaPassword=P@ssw0rd
Updating ConfigMgr Boot Media for PXE Lite:
  Provider Name            = 'CM01.corp.viamonstra.com'
  Site Code                = 'PS1'
  Distribution Points      = 'CM01.corp.viamonstra.com'
  Boot Image ID            = 'PS100027'
  WIM Filename             = '\\CM01\SCCM_Sources$\OSD\Boot\1E PXE Lite x64\boot.wim'

  Media Password           = 'P@ssw0rd'
  Certificate (PFX) Path = '(use self-signed)'
  Certificate Password     = '(no password)'
  Management Points        = 'SMSTSMP=http://CM01.CORP.VIAMONSTRA.COM'
  Certificate Expiration = '365'
INITIALIZATION: 0/0, 0/100
COPYING PS100027: 0/0, 100/100
setup: 0/0, 0/100
getmpinfo: 0/0, 45/100
stagesmsdata: 0/0, 10/100
BEGIN_GEN: 0/4, 10/100
WRITEPASS: 0/4, 30/100
stagesmsbins: 0/4, 45/100
StageBootImagePackage: 0/4, 0/100
stagebootimage: 0/0, 100/100
StageBaseFiles: 1/4, 0/100
setup: 1/4, 0/100
StageSelfSignedCertificate: 2/4, 0/100
StageManifest: 3/4, 0/100
stagesmsdata: 3/4, 10/100
writeiso: 0/0, 0/100 Found variables file @ "C:\Users\ADMINI~1.VIA\AppData\Local\Temp\_tsmedia_4220\
stage\sms\data\Variables.dat"
```

Reviewing the output of Update Boot Image.

7. The command takes a few minutes to run. Ensure that at the end, you get the following output: **CreateBootMedia Returns OK**.

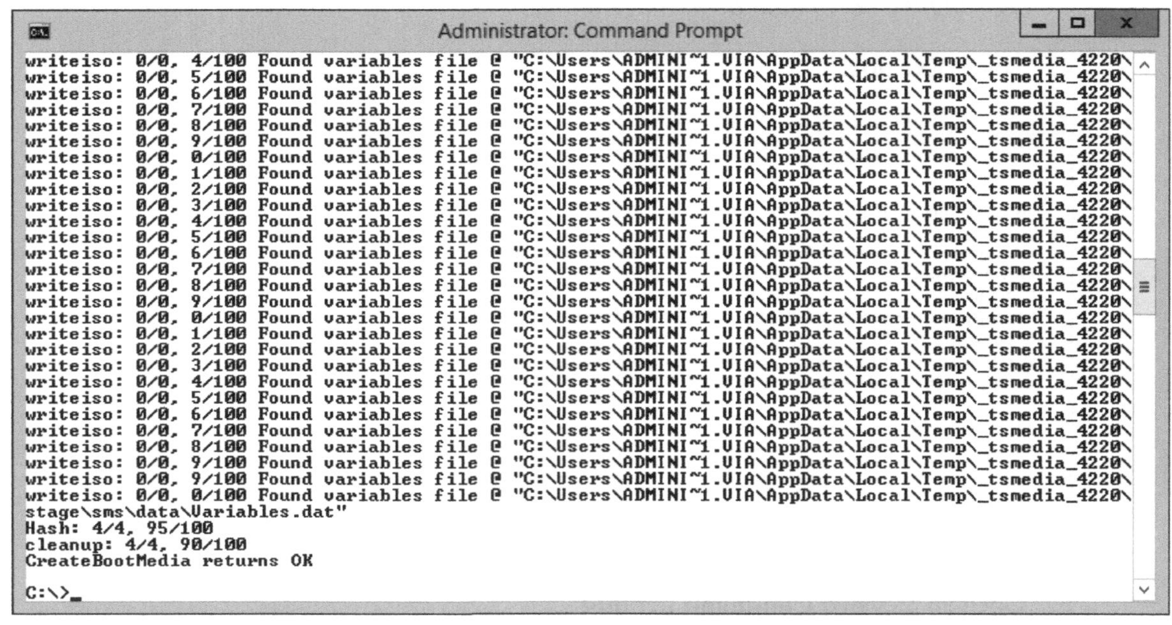

Ensuring that the final value is CreateBootMedia returns OK.

8. In the **ConfigMgr console,** update the **1E PXE Lite x64** boot image again.

Deploying PXE Lite Manually

In order to configure PXE Lite on the local workstation, there are a few key requirements:

1. Create a new boot image. **Already done**.
2. Extract PXE TFTP files from the default Boot.wim file that comes with ADK.
3. Install PXELite.msi on the target machine.
4. Create a simple task sequence to deploy the Boot.wim to the target machine.
5. Using CreateBCD.exe, copy the Boot.wim to the new TFTP root folder in the PXE Lite Install directory.

This process is fully automated later in the chapter, but to understand all of the components, you first do this manually. The following steps get PXE Lite working on a single machine for testing purposes. In this guide we assume you have downloaded the book sample files to CM01.

1. Log on to **CM01**.
2. Extract the TFTP PXE files from the default Boot.wim in ADK, by running following command in an elevated Command prompt:

   ```
   C:\labfiles\Scripts\ExtractADKFiles.cmd D:\ADKFiles
   ```

   The following figure shows the output from the script.

> **Real World Note:** The preceding script works for both WAIK and ADK deployments. The files required are in the same locations.

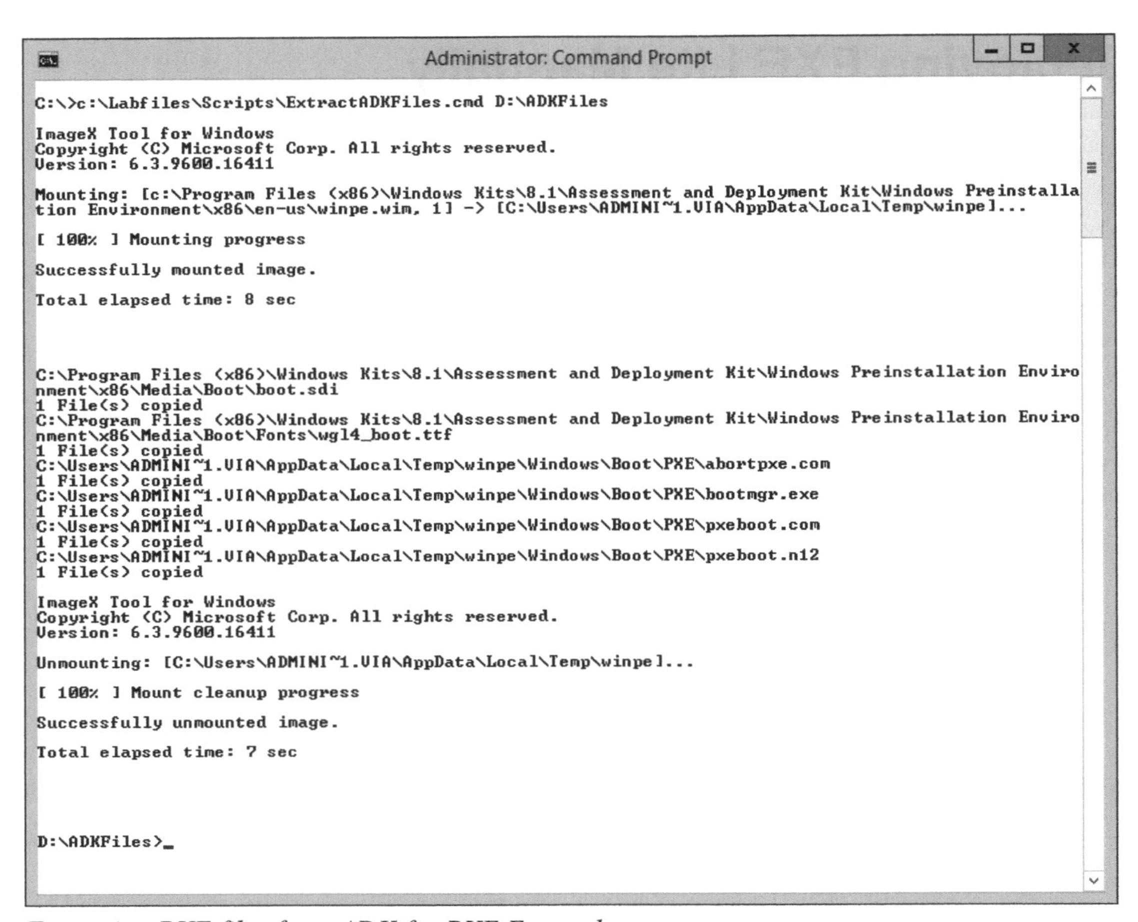

Extracting PXE files from ADK for PXE Everywhere.

3. Log on to **PC0003**.
4. Copy the **PXELite v2.2.0.26** installation files (the full folder) to **C:\Labfiles\Sources**.
5. Launch **C:\Labfiles\Sources\PXELite v2.2.0.26\PXELiteLocal.msi**.

6. Use the following values for the installation:

   a. On the **Welcome** page, click **Next**.

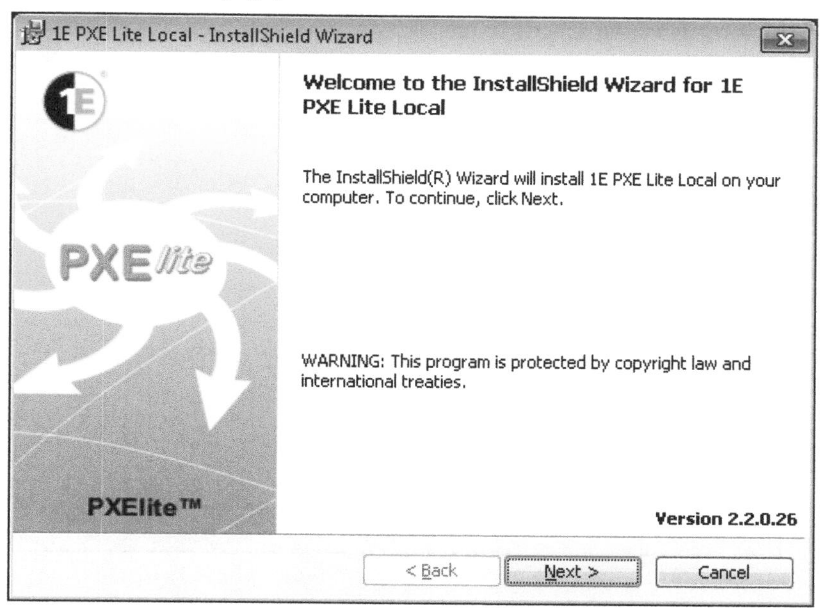

   b. On the **License Agreement** page, accept the terms and click **Next**.

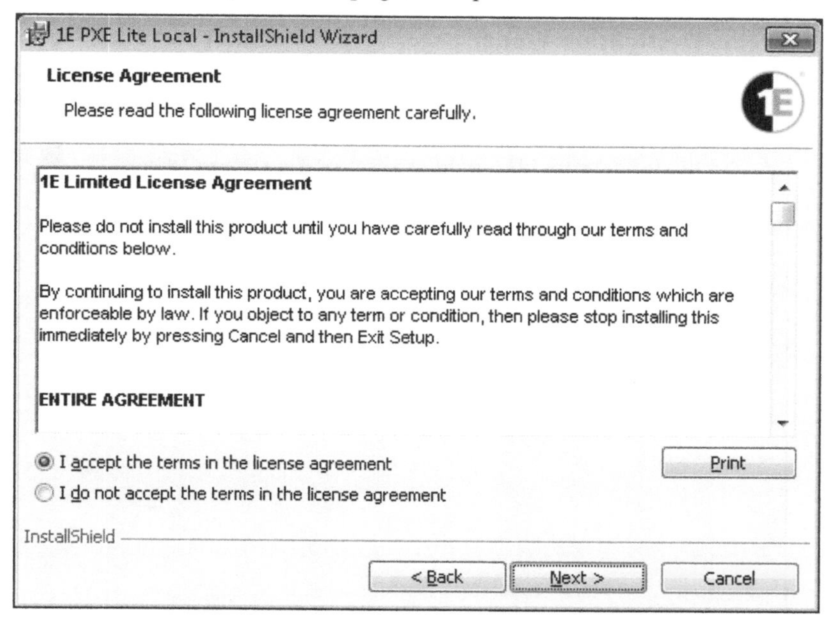

c. On the **User Information** page, keep the defaults and click **Next**.

1E PXE Lite Local - InstallShield Wizard
User Information
Enter the following information to personalize your installation.
User Name:
ViaMonstra
Organization:
ViaMonstra
License Key:
InstallShield
< Back
Next >
Cancel

Note: 1E PXE Everywhere (Lite) comes with a built-in 10-day trial key. If no key is provided during the setup, this evaluation key is used. If you have a real key, you can use that one.

d. On the **Destination Folder** page, keep the default and click **Next**.

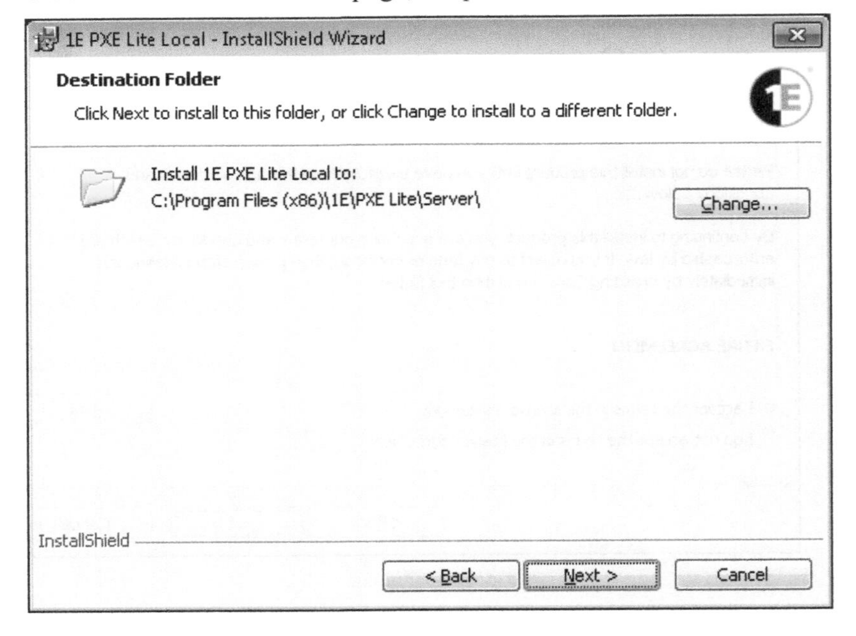

e. Configuration: **http://CM01/PXELite/PXELiteConfiguration.asmx**

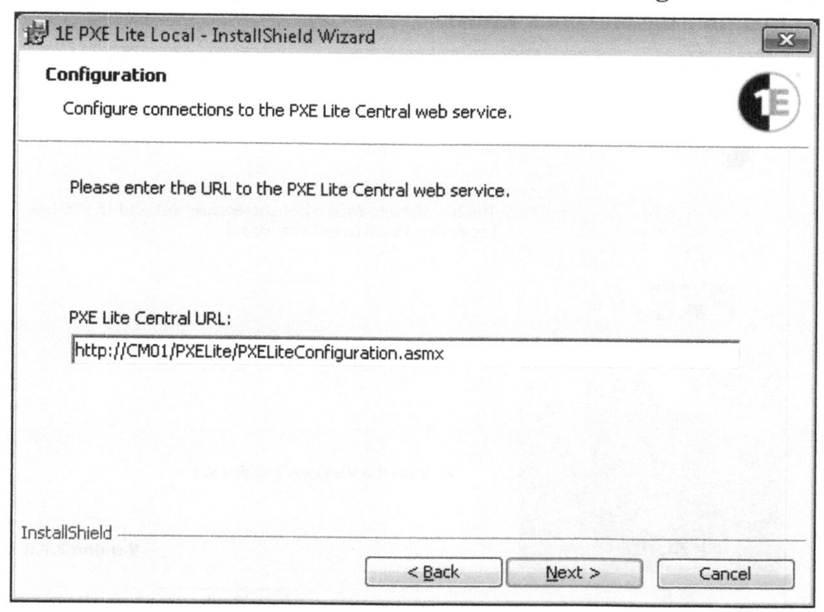

f. On the **Ready to Install the Program** page, click **Install**.

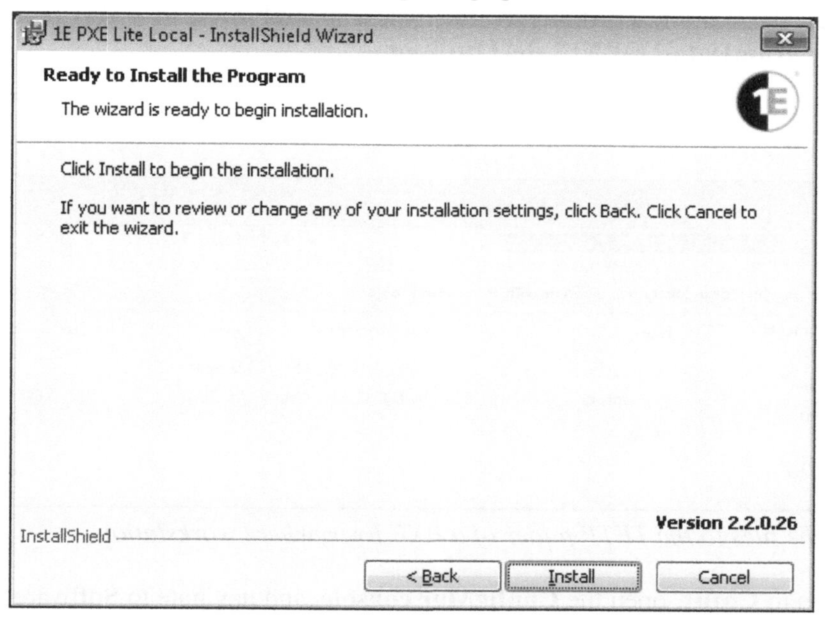

g. On the **InstallShield Wizard Completed** page, select **Show the Windows Installer log** and click **Finish**.

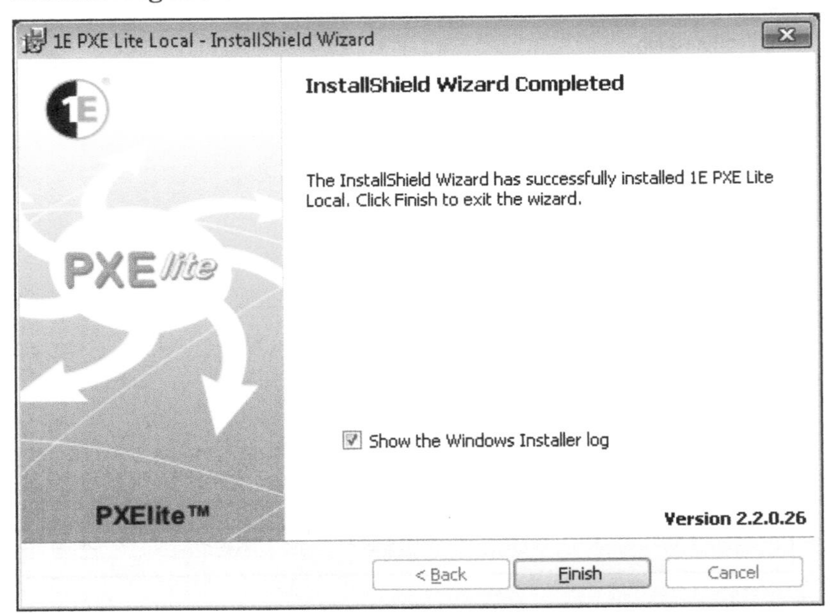

7. Review the Windows Installer log, then close it and browse to **C:\ProgramData\1E\PXELite\TftpRoot**.
8. Copy the contents of **\\CM01\D$\ADKFiles** to **C:\ProgramData\1E\PXELIte\TftpRoot**.

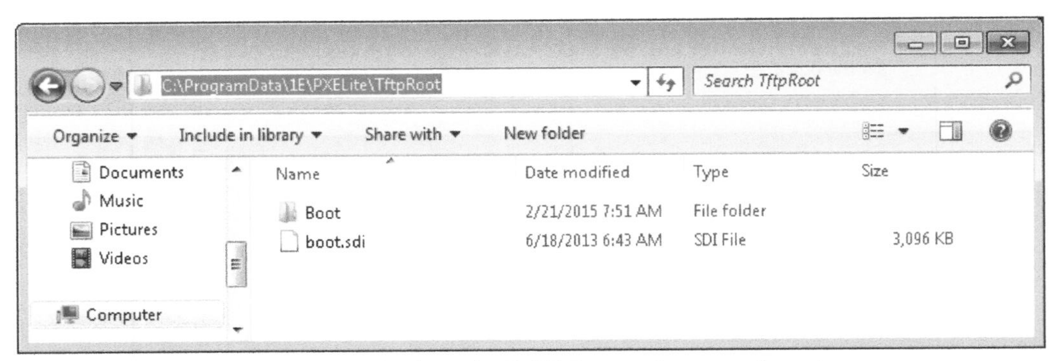

Copying the files to the TFTP folder of a PXE Everywhere workstation.

9. Log on to **CM01**, open the **ConfigMgr console**, and navigate to Software Library / Operating Systems / Task Sequences.

10. Right-click **Task Sequences**, and select **Create Task Sequence**. Use the following settings:
    - Create a new task sequence: **Create a new custom task sequence**
    - Task Sequence Name: **Deploy PXE Lite**
    - Description: **Version 1.0**
    - Boot Image: **1E PXE Lite x64**
    - Nomad Settings: **Select Enable Nomad / Cache Priority = 5**
11. Right-click the **Deploy PXE Lite** task sequence and click **Edit.**
12. Click **Add / New Group**.
13. Configure this step with the following setting:

    Name: **Deploy PXE Lite x86**
14. Click **Add / New Group**.
15. Configure this step with the following settings:
    - Name: **Deploy PXE Lite x64**
    - Move **Deploy PXE Lite x64** up one level.

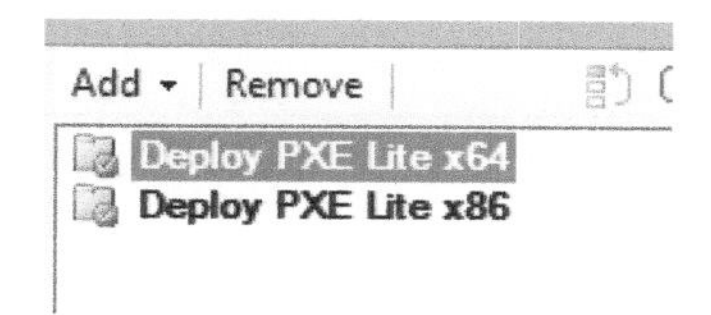

Creating new groups for the PXE Everywhere deployment task sequence.

16. Click **Deploy PXE Lite x64** and then click **Options**.
17. Configure this step with the following setting:

    WMI Query condition

    SELECT * FROM Win32_OperatingSystem WHERE OSArchitecture = "64-bit"
18. Click **Deploy PXE Lite x86** and then click **Options**.
19. Configure this step with the following setting:

    WMI Query condition

    SELECT * FROM Win32_OperatingSystem WHERE OSArchitecture = "32-bit"
20. Click **Deploy PXE Lite x64**, and then click **Add / General / Run Command Line**.

21. Configure this step with the following settings:

- Name: **CreateBCD-x64**
- Command Line:
  cmd /c "C:\Program Files (x86)\1E\PXE Lite\Server\x64\CreateBcd.exe"

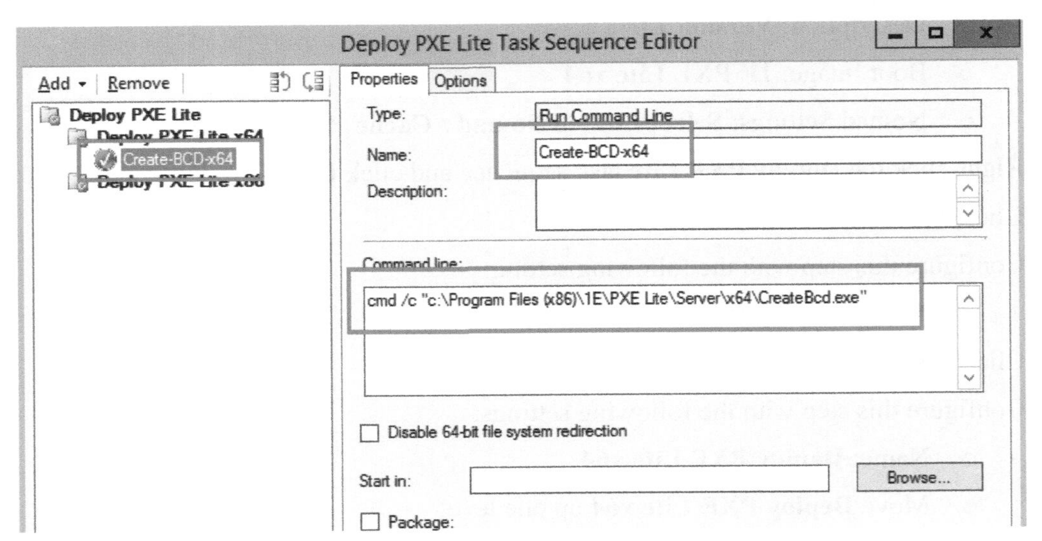

Setting up the CreateBCD.exe step.

> **Real World Note:** The CreateBCD.exe command is essential to this process as it moves the Boot.wim file for the PXE Lite TFTP server from the CCMCACHE folder to the TFTP directory on the machine.

22. Click **Deploy PXE Lite x86**, and then click **Add / General / Run Command Line**.

23. Configure this step with the following settings:

- Name: **CreateBCD-x86**
- Command Line:
  cmd /c "C:\Program Files\1E\PXE Lite\Server\i386\CreateBcd.exe"

24. Deploy **Deploy PXE Lite** to the **Deploy PXE Lite** collection with the following settings:

- Purpose: **Available**
- Make available to the following: **Only Configuration Manager Clients**
- Scheduling: **<Default>**
- User Experience: **<Default>**
- Alerts: **<Default>**
- Deployment Options: **Download all content locally before starting task sequence**

Real World Note: This task sequence to deploy PXE Lite must be configured to download all content locally before starting the task sequence. The reason for this is that there is a boot image attached to the task sequence and it is required to be in the cache. After it is in the cache, the 1E CreateBCD.exe command moves the boot image into the TftpRoot folder. If this option is not set, the CreateBCD step will fail.

25. Log on to **PC0003** and run a machine policy refresh.
26. From **Software Center**, install **Deploy PXE Lite**.
27. Using **CMTrace**, open **C:\ProgramData\1E\PXELite\CreateBCD.log** and ensure there are no errors.

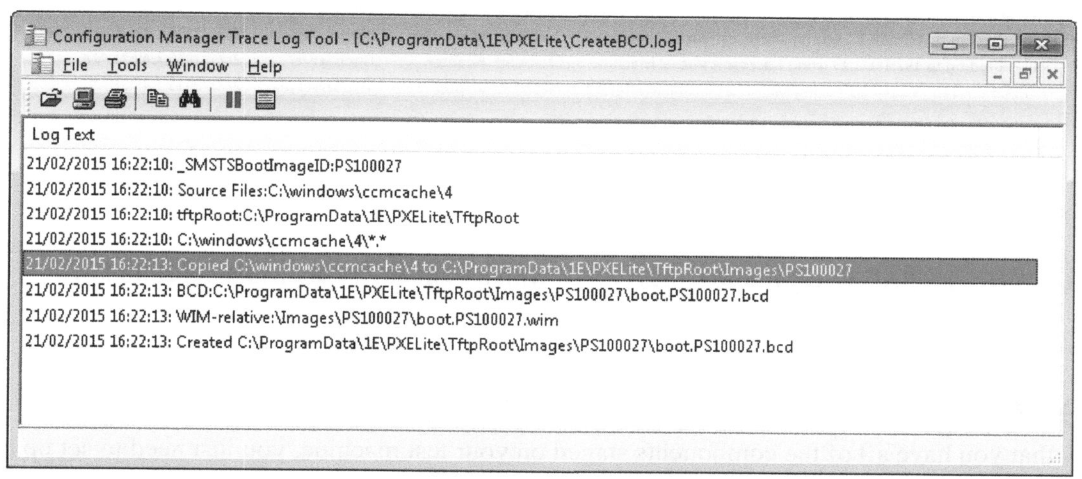

Reviewing the results after running the Deploy PXE Lite task sequence.

28. Using **CMTrace**, open **C:\ProgramData\1E\PXELite\PXELiteServer.log**.

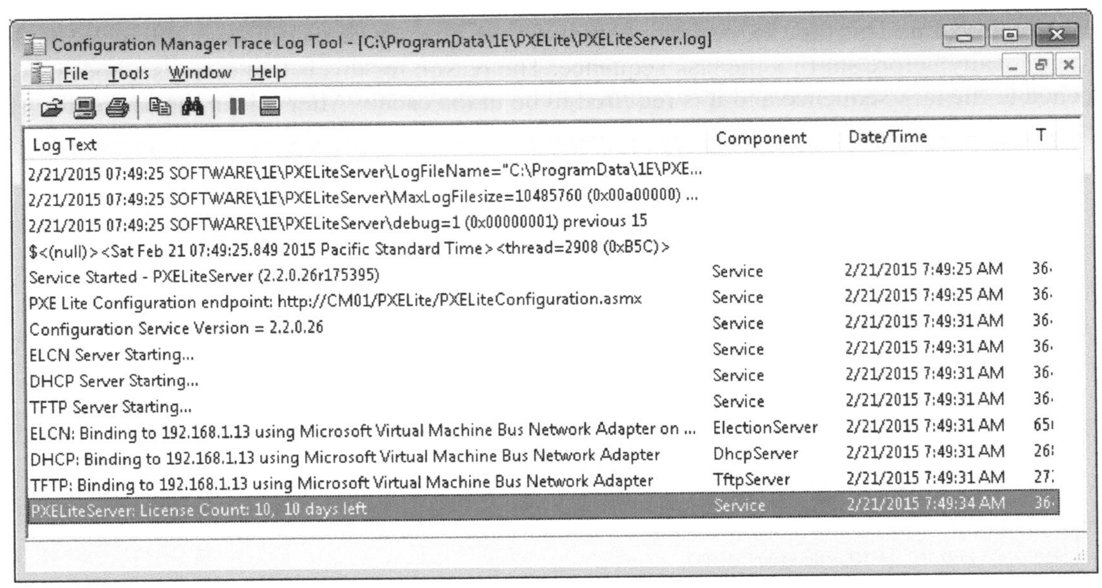

Validating in the PXELiteServer.log that the PXE Lite service is running.

Note: Again, 1E PXE Everywhere (Lite) comes with a built-in 10-day trial key. If no key is provided during the setup, this evaluation key is used.

Testing the PXE Lite Manual Deployment

Now that you have all of the components staged on your test machine, you just need to set up a PXE-enabled deployment. For this guide, you use PC0007, a newly created unknown ConfigMgr client. Because you are on the same subnet as the ConfigMgr server CM01, you disable the ConfigMgr PXE role at this time and then test the deployment.

In this exercise, you take the existing bare metal task sequence that was created earlier and swap out the boot image for the newly created PXE Lite boot image and perform some testing.

1. Log on to **CM01** and open the **ConfigMgr console**.
2. Right-click the **Windows 8.1 Enterprise x64-Gold-CoreApps-BareMetal** task sequence nd then click **Properties**.
3. Click **Advanced**.
4. Change the boot image to **1E PXE Lite x64** and click **OK**.

Real World Note: Due to a bug in the ConfigMgr console, you may have to click the Root node when browsing for available boot images.

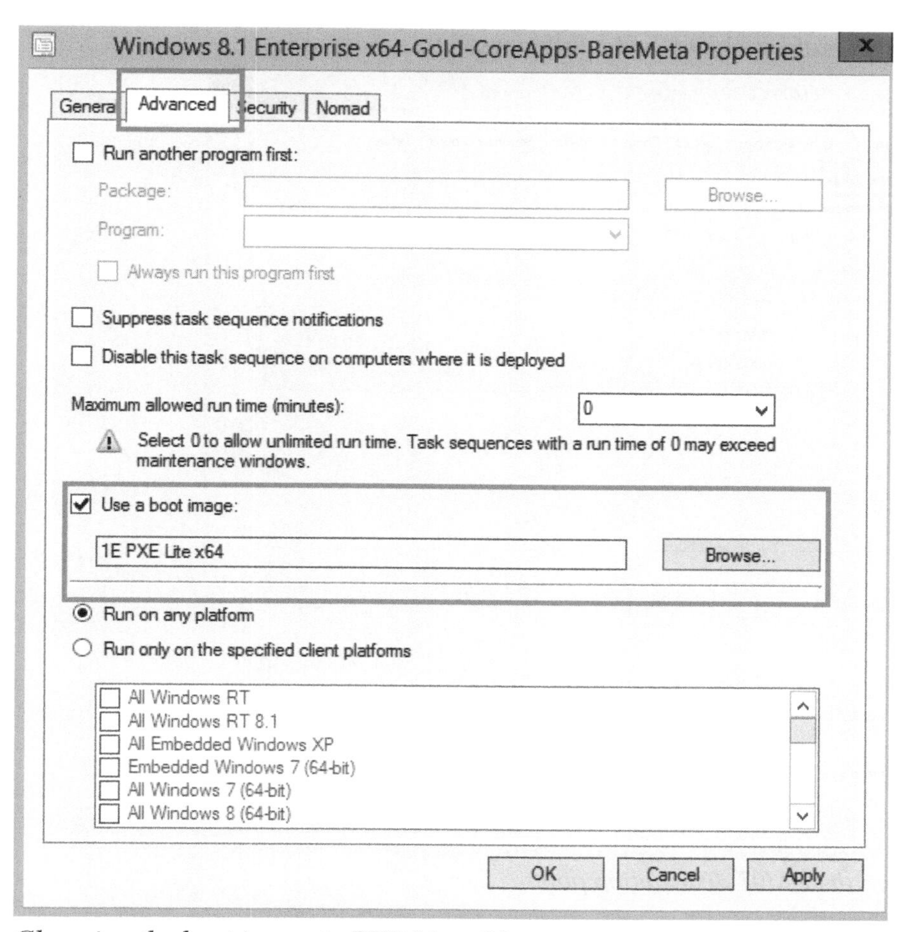

Changing the boot image to PXE Lite x64.

5. In the **Administration** workspace, in the **Distribution Points** node, right-click the **CM01** distribution point, and select **Properties**.

6. Disable the PXE role as shown in the following figure.

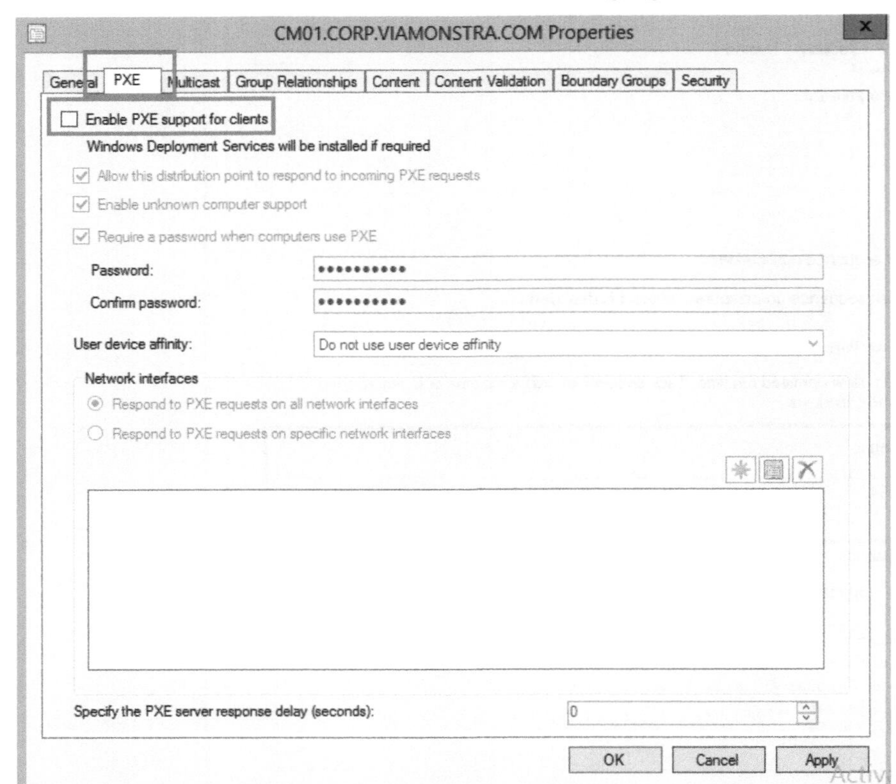

Disabling PXE on the CM01 distribution point.

7. Using **Services**, stop and disable the **Windows Deployment Service**.
8. On the **Host PC**, create a **Generation 1** Hyper-V virtual machine with the following settings:
    - Name: **PC0007**
    - Location: **D:\VMs**
    - Generation: **Generation 1**
    - Memory: **1024 MB**
    - Network: **AWD_Internal**
    - Hard disk: **<default>**
    - **Install an operating system from a network-based installation server**
9. Turn on **PC0007**.
10. Press **F12** when prompted.

```
Hyper-V
PXE Network Boot 09.14.2011
(C) Copyright 2011 Microsoft Corporation, All Rights Reserved.

CLIENT MAC ADDR: 00 15 5D A1 2E 4A  GUID: 4D867C7D-A408-4BE6-AB50-C3F3E9D5BC08
CLIENT IP: 192.168.1.103  MASK: 255.255.255.0  DHCP IP: 192.168.1.200
GATEWAY IP: 192.168.1.1

Press F12 for network service boot
_
```

PXE Booting from a PXE Everywhere client. Not the difference compared when deploying from a ConfigMgr distribution point.

11. After WinPE starts, type in a password of **P@sswrd**.
12. Deploy the **Windows 8.1 Enterprise x64-Gold-CoreApps-BareMetal** task sequence.
13. Once deployment starts, press **F8** and type **CMTrace.exe**.
14. Review the deployment by open **X:\Windows\Temp\SMSTSLog\NomadBranch.log**
15. On **PC0003**, review the **C:\ProgramData\1E\PXELite\PXELiteServer** log.

Configuration Manager Trace Log Tool - [C:\ProgramData\1E\PXELite\PXELiteServer.log]

File Tools Window Help

Log Text	Component	Date/Time	T
Read Request (RRQ)	TftpSession_192.	2/21/2015 8:43:32 AM	27:
TftpSession[192.168.1.103:19622]::BeginSession	TftpSession_192.	2/21/2015 8:43:32 AM	27:
TFTP Session starting. Server IP = 192.168.1.13 (192.168.1.0), Client IP = 192.168.1.103	TftpSession_192.	2/21/2015 8:43:32 AM	27:
filename = \Images\PS100027\boot.PS100027.wim	TftpSession_192.	2/21/2015 8:43:32 AM	27:
option:blksize = 1456	TftpSession_192.	2/21/2015 8:43:32 AM	27:
File is 287717439 byte(s). Using block size of 1456 byte(s) means 197609 blocks, 191 byte(s...	TftpSession_192.	2/21/2015 8:43:32 AM	27:
TFTP session closing; waiting for final ACK.	TftpSession_192.	2/21/2015 8:45:25 AM	27:
TFTP session[192.168.1.103:19622] completed.	TftpSession_192.	2/21/2015 8:45:25 AM	27:
TftpSession[192.168.1.103:19622]::EndSession	TftpSession_192.	2/21/2015 8:45:25 AM	27:
UnregisterSession(192.168.1.103:19622)	TftpSession_192.	2/21/2015 8:45:25 AM	27:
Sent 287717439 byte(s) in 113 seconds. 0 bytes/sec.	TftpSession_192.	2/21/2015 8:45:25 AM	27:
0/197609 blocks (0%) were resent.	TftpSession_192.	2/21/2015 8:45:25 AM	27:

The PXELiteServer log on PC0003.

PXE Local Deployment Task Sequence

Now that you have seen how to manually create a PXE Lite installation on a machine, it is important to automate this for the rest of the machines. The best way to do this is to place the logic required for the installation into a single deployment task sequence. The steps in this guide help create this unified PXE Lite installation.

Again, there is a lot of confusion over the naming of the 1E PXE solution. The technical name of the product is "PXE Lite." It is sold as a solution called PXE Everywhere. "Everywhere" meaning it should be deployed on every machine that has the 1E Nomad agent deployed, thus creating a true multi-master peer-based PXE solution that provides maximum availability through the distributed installation.

During the hydration of this lab, a 1E PXE Lite package is created with two install programs.

1. Log on to **CM01** and open the **ConfigMgr console**.
2. Review the **1E PXE Lite** package created using the hydration scripts.

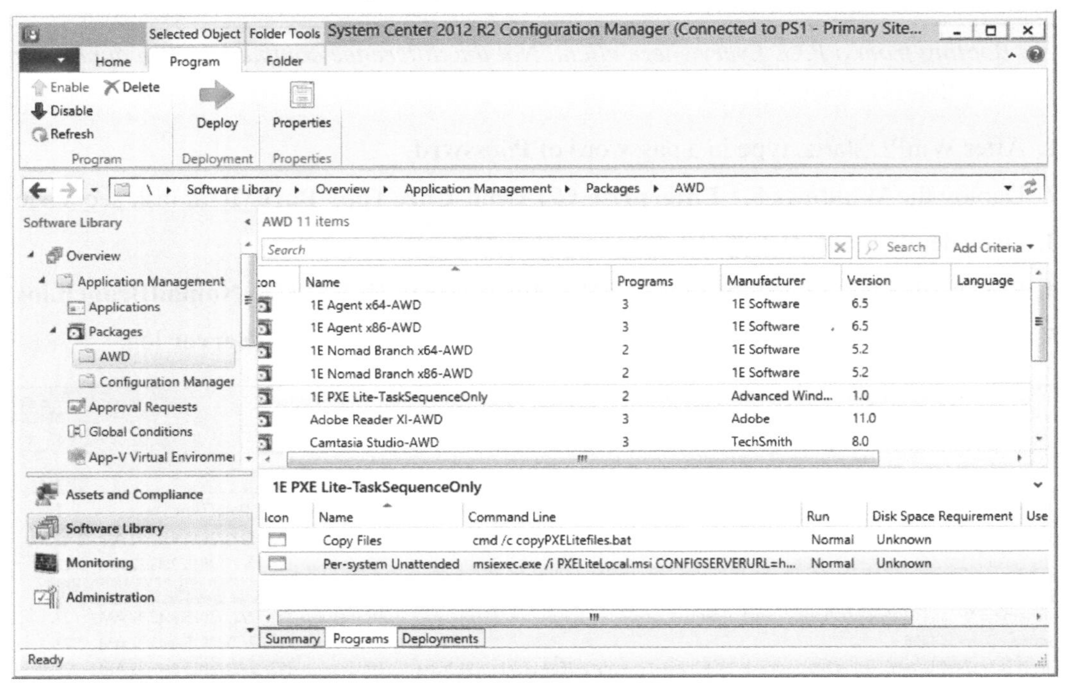

The hydrated 1E PXE Lite-TaskSequenceOnly package.

3. Review the install properties of the **Per-system Unattended** program.

> **Note:** The PIDKEY=<YOURPIDKEY> property has been left out of this install string. Therefore, each PXE Lite installation will have a 10-day trial key. For production, you should always make sure that the PIDKEY value is set on each 1E product installation where applicable.
>
> The CONFIGERVERURL= value points to the PXE Central web service on CM01.

4. Review the install properties of the **Copy Files** program.

   The CopyPXELitefiles.bat script (provided in the book sample files) simply copies the extracted ADK files from the earlier exercise into the TFTP folder of the PXE Lite machine.

```
if not exist "%ALLUSERSPROFILE%\Application
Data\1E\PXELite\TftpRoot" echo y |
md "%ALLUSERSPROFILE%\Application Data\1E\PXELite\TftpRoot"
xcopy boot.sdi "%ALLUSERSPROFILE%\Application
Data\1E\PXELite\TftpRoot\" /Y
xcopy boot\*.* "%ALLUSERSPROFILE%\Application
Data\1E\PXELite\TftpRoot\boot\" /Y /E
if not exist "%ALLUSERSPROFILE%\Application
Data\1E\PXELite\TftpRoot\Images" echo y | md
"%ALLUSERSPROFILE%\
Application Data\1E\PXELite\TftpRoot\Images"
```

5. In the **ConfigMgr console**, locate the **Deploy PXE Lite** task sequence and click **Edit**.
6. Click **Deploy PXE Lite x64**, and then click **Add / General / Install Package**.
7. Configure this step with the following settings:
   - Name: **Deploy PXE Lite x64-AWD**
   - Description: **Deploys PXE Lite Package**
   - Package: **Advanced Windows Deployment 1E PXE Lite-TaskSequenceOnly**
   - Program: **Per-system Unattended**
8. On the **Deploy PXE Lite x64-AWD** action, in the **Options** tab, click **Add Condition** and then select **Installed Software**. Browse for the **C:\Labfiles\Sources\PXELite v2.2.0.26\PXELiteLocal.msi** file and click **OK**.

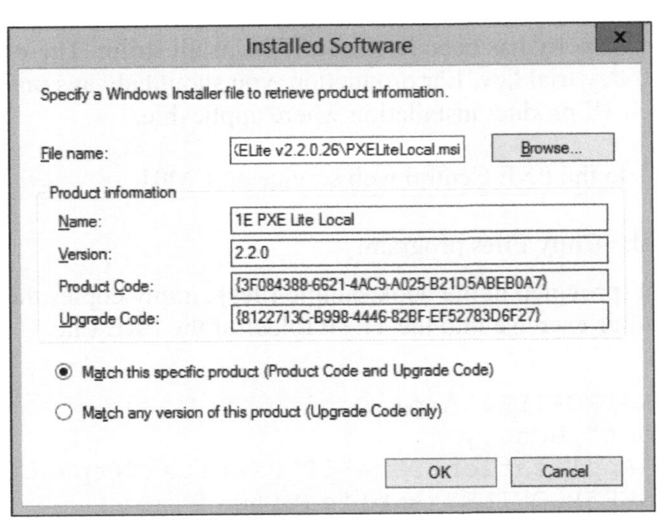

Configuring the Deploy PXE Lite x64-AWD to install only if not installed already.

Note: It may be necessary to make modifications to the Boot.wim from time to time. As a result, you will have to update the contents of the Boot.wim files on the PXE Lite machines in the field. The preceding step allows you to deploy the same task sequence as a required deployment in order to deploy updated boot images.

9. Click **Deploy PXE Lite x64**, and then click **Add / General / Install Package**.
10. Configure this step with the following settings:
    - Name: **Copy PXE Files From Cache**
    - Description: **Copies TFTP Files from Cache to PXE TFTP Directory**
    - Package: **Advanced Windows Deployment 1E PXE Lite-TaskSequenceOnly**
    - Program: **Copy Files**
11. Right-click the **Deploy PXE Lite x64-AWD** action and select **Copy**. Then select the **Deploy PXE Lite x86** group and select **Paste**.
12. In the **Deploy PXE Lite x86** group, move the **Deploy PXE Lite x64-AWD** action up one level, and then change the name to **Deploy PXE Lite x86-AWD**.
13. In the **Deploy PXE Lite x64** group, right-click the **Copy PXE Files From Cache** action and select **Copy**. Then, in the **Deploy PXE Lite x86** group, select the **Deploy PXE Lite x86-AWD x64-AWD** action and click **Paste**.

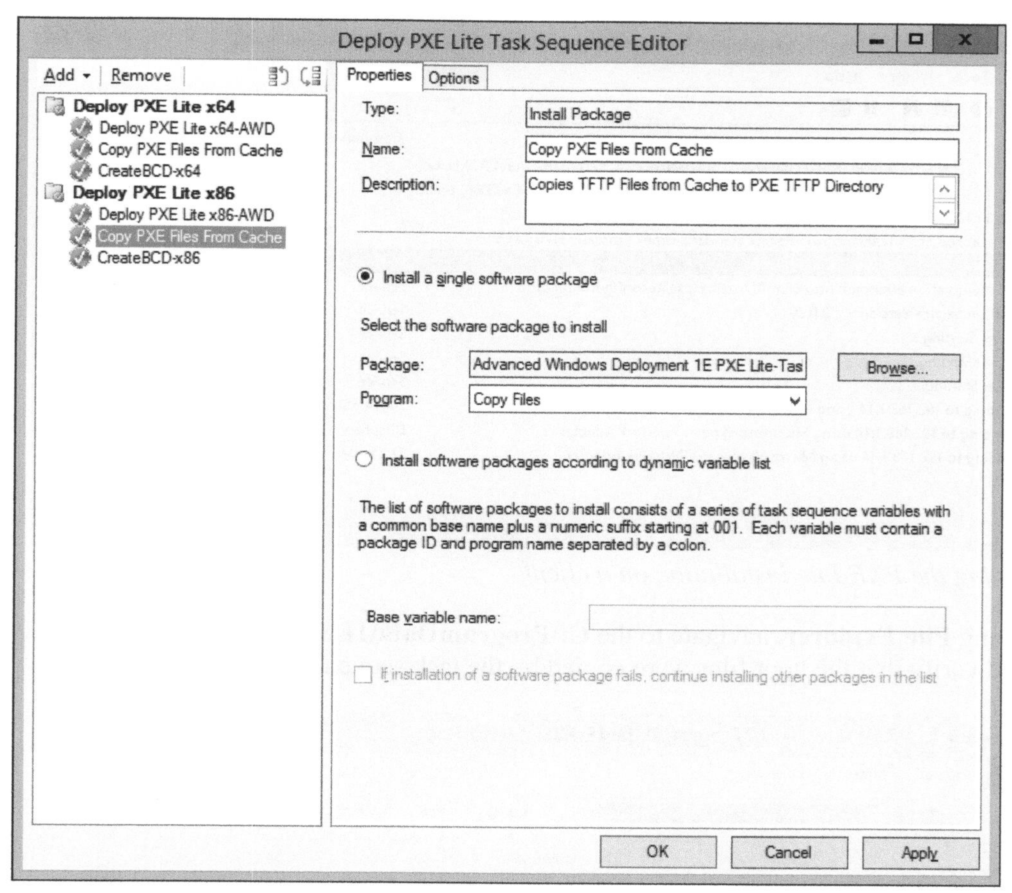

Configuring the PXE Everywhere deployment task sequence (Deploy PXE Lite).

14. Save the task sequence changes by clicking **OK**.

Deploying PXE Local Deployment Task Sequence

Because you modified an existing task sequence with an existing deployment, you just need to ensure that your client performs a policy retrieval prior to executing your updated task sequence.

1. Log on to **PC0004** and run a machine policy refresh. From **Software Center**, install the **Deploy PXE Lite** task sequence.
2. Using **CMTrace,** view the **C:\ProgramData\1E\NomadBranch\Logfiles\NomadBranch.log** file to watch the download process. After the download completes and the task sequence engine starts running, check out **C:\ProgramData\1E\PXELite\PXELiteServer.log** to ensure that PXE Lite installs successfully and the service starts.

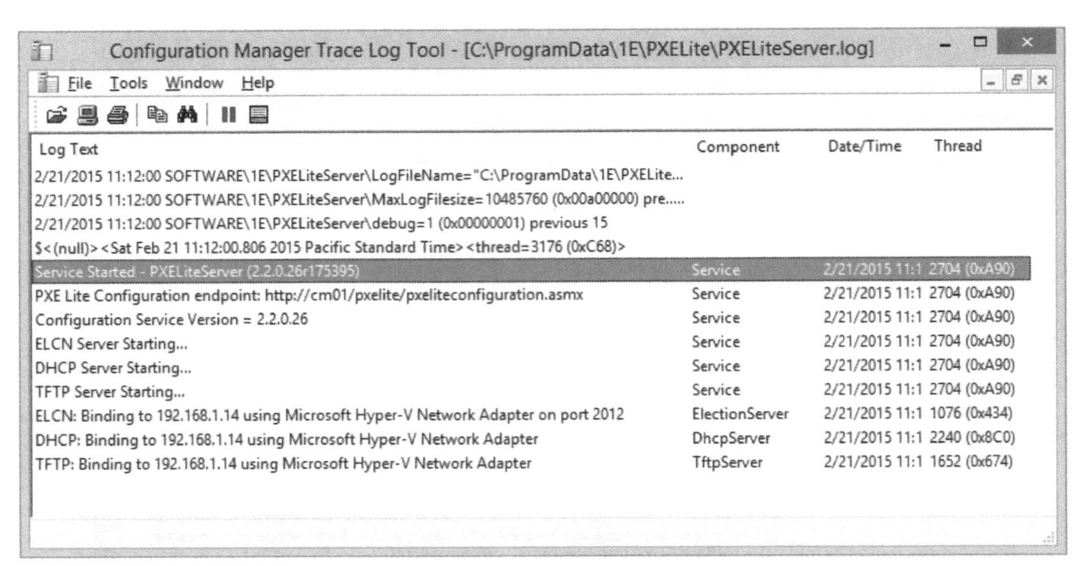

Validating the PXE Lite installation on a client.

3. Using **File Explorer**, navigate to the **C:\ProgramData\1E\PXELite\TftpRoot** folder, and verify that the boot files were copied by the task sequence.

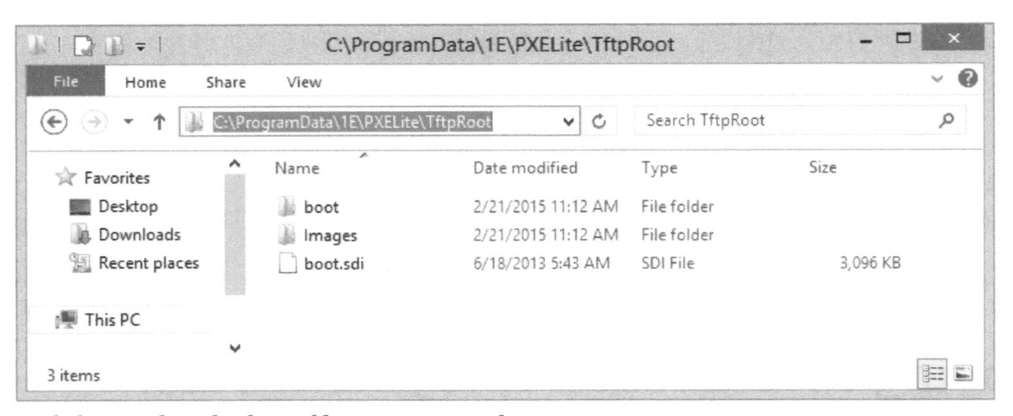

Validating that the boot files were copied.

Speeding Up the PXE Lite TFTP Transfer Speed

As is the case with disk volumes, block size plays an important role in the TFTP process of delivering PXE images. You want to maximize the size of data blocks that are transferred to the PXE-booting client, without going too big and possibly causing stability issues on some networks. This reduces the amount of time it takes to deliver that initial boot image by half.

You utilize a CreateBCD.exe switch to increase the TFTP block size.

1. On **CM01**, select the **Deploy PXE Lite** task sequence and choose **Edit** from the ribbon.
2. Select the **CreateBCD-x64** step and modify it to include **-TFTPBlockSize=16384**.
3. Repeat the preceding step for the **CreateBCD-x86** action.

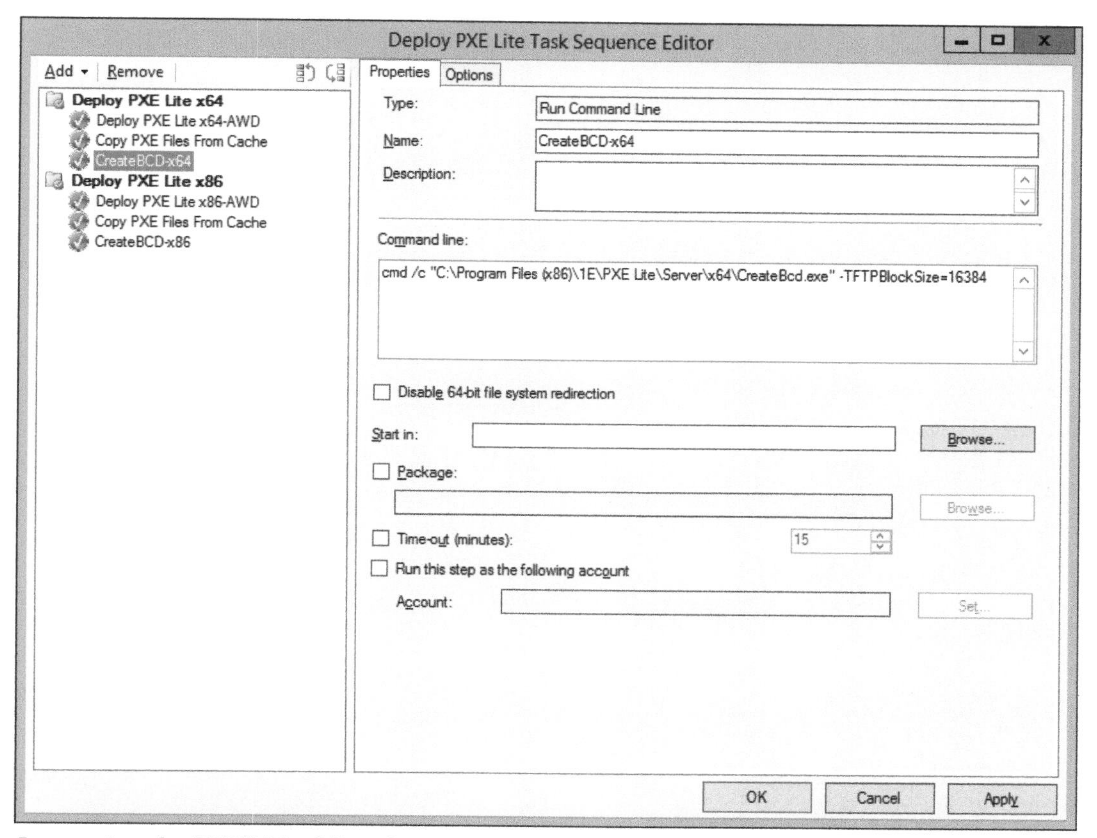

Increasing the TFTPBlockSize for PXE Everywhere clients.

Note: Not all hardware may support using 16 kb block size. If you run into any issues, try to lower to 8 kb (8192) and see if that does the trick.

Chapter 12

Nomad for OSD Replace (PBA)

When reimaging a workstation, using hard links is the preferred method for storing state migration data, as storing it locally to the _SMSTaskSequence folder is much faster than transferring that data over the LAN. However, for situations in which customers are switching disk encryption providers and do not have the ability to disable or decrypt the drive, or when machines are being replaced, hard links cannot be used. This forces the operation to store migration data off-host. With the removal of distribution points for software distribution with Nomad, a service gap is created for workstation replace scenarios and refresh sequences that require disk repartitioning. There's no longer a state migration point at every location to store user state data. To mitigate this loss in functionality, 1E invented a method, called Peer Backup Assistant, to use peer workstations to securely store migration data during the PC refresh process. Following the same concepts as Nomad, Peer Backup Assistant uses dynamic selection of host clients, eliminating the need to maintain computer associations in the ConfigMgr console.

Nomad PBA Key Concepts

Full Integration

Peer Backup Assistant is built into the Nomad product and is enabled through the same location in the Windows registry. All processes surrounding user state migration as they pertain to PBA are included in the Nomad task sequence actions, which replace the built-in USMT management actions. Encryption and retention levels, as configured in ConfigMgr, are recognized and maintained by Nomad throughout the state migration process.

Dynamic Selection

Peer Backup Assistant uses the now familiar election process within Nomad to select an appropriate workstation to store migration data, known as a PBA host. The workstation being imaged, the PBA client, initiates the PBA election process. Nomad clients that are configured to be a PBA host respond, allowing the client to select the optimal host as determined by a list of criteria, such as USMT estimate and available PBA space on a potential host. Selected host computer names are then fed into the task sequence engine and stored in the %NMDS_Remote% variable, which in turn is referenced by the OSDStateStore path variable that is part of the refresh/replace steps. As these references are dynamically created and maintained during the task sequence execution process, there is no longer a requirement to also maintain computer association memberships for machine replacements in ConfigMgr.

The USMTEstimate variable is used to provide the approximate size of a USMT file when created. This allows PBA to select an acceptable host that has enough disk space to store the file during OSD. If the value for the USMTEstimate is 500, for example, PBA will not attempt to back up the USMT file to a machine with only 300MB of free space.

The value for the USMTEstimate can be statically assigned for all deployments, or dynamically added during task sequence execution by running ScanState.exe with the /p switch.

High Availability Peer Backup Assistant

A popular (and valid) concern with using peer workstations to store state migration data is the likely event that a PBA host becomes unavailable during task sequence execution. Imagine having a PBA host machine's hard drive fail during an OS migration, right about the time the client is applying the new operating system. All that user's local data is now gone, and despite what company policy strictly dictates, business-critical data wasn't stored on corporate file servers. The potential losses for this disaster could be in the millions if it affects the right, or wrong, user. We've seen this happen time and time again over the years, when laptops are used as primary storage, and regardless of how sophisticated hard drives become, it's still a single point of failure.

Configuring the task sequence to use High Availability Peer Backup Assistant instructs the PBA host to copy the client's migration data to another PBA-enabled workstation at the site. 1E provides several configurable options in the task sequence engine for this process, such as the ability to ensure migration data has been copied to a specific number of workstations prior to wiping the client's partitions. When the new operating system and all applications have been installed on the client, it broadcasts another election looking for its migration data. All site workstations that have a copy of the requested migration file reply, triggering the dynamic selection process as previously detailed.

Real World Note: Peer Backup Assist also can be integrated to use ActiveEfficiency to span subnets in a single site. This feature is very similar to Nomad's Single Site Download. This feature is called Single Site PBA.

Nomad PBA Configuration (Registry Keys)

By default, Nomad clients do not participate in elections to store user state migration data. However, it is easily enabled through the addition of a switch into the install string or a modification in the Windows registry.

Registry Key	HKEY_LOCAL_MACHINE\SOFTWARE\1E\NomadBranch\NMDS
Value Name	MaximumMegaByte
Data Type	REG_DWORD
Data Value	102400
Description	Any value other than 0 enables the client to participate in elections to store Peer Backup Assistant content. The defined value equates to the amount of HDD space that can be used for migration data. This machine will be permitted to store up to 100 GB of migration data.

There are a half dozen other options that can be configured here, but are only configured for specific environmental situations.

Nomad PBA Log Files

Because Peer Backup Assistant is built into Nomad, all log actions are stored in the NomadBranch.log file. It is a completely server-less feature and so does not communicate with ConfigMgr site servers.

During task sequence execution, results of the Nomad actions for Peer Backup Assistant are conveniently located in the smsts.log file. As the Peer Backup Assistant process revolves around state migration, we also like to monitor the scanstate.log and loadstate.log files because they contain pertinent status information.

Nomad PBA Share Requirements

When a Nomad client is elected as a PBA host, it creates a local account that is used for the purpose of transferring that specific MIG file. It then adds this local account to the NomadSHR$ share. To permit this, client workstations must not have policies set that prevent the creation of local accounts.

Enabling PBA on Target Workstation

1. Log on to **PC0004**.
2. Open **Regedit** and browse to **HKLM\Software\1E\NomadBranch\NMDS.**
3. Modify **MaximumMegaByte** to **Decimal 10000**.

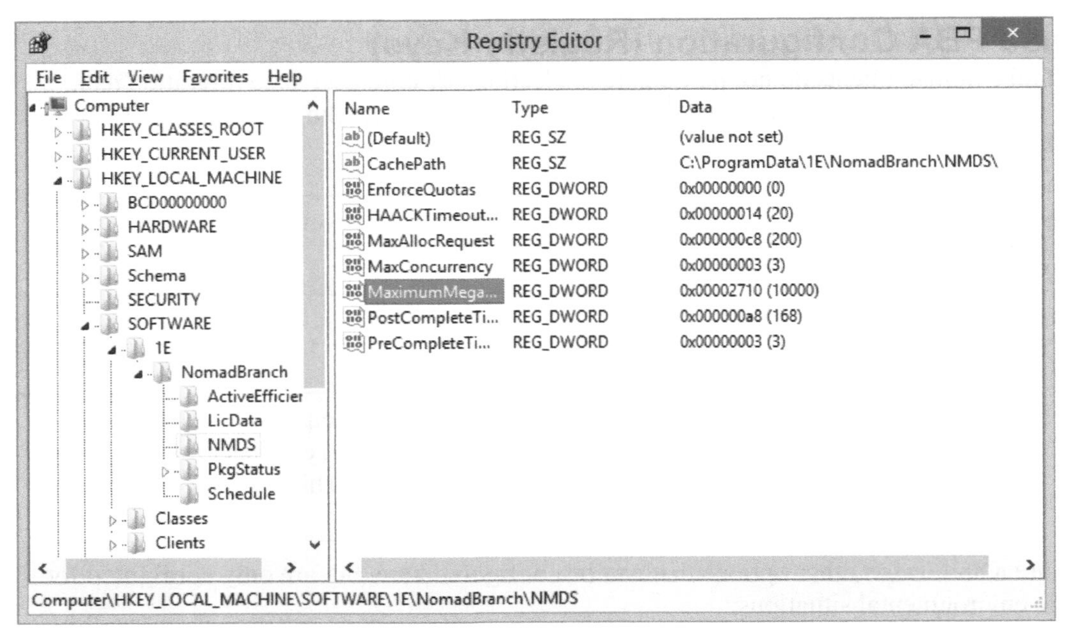

Nomad PBA registry keys.

Real World Note: When using PBA in a production environment, scripts normally are run ahead of the OS rollout to enable specific machines as PBA peers. A selection process should be considered, and desktops should have a higher preference over laptops. It is possible to have PBA (USMT) data stored on a laptop that leaves the network.

For this scenario in Nomad 5.2, 1E has released High-Availability PBA. You find guidance on configuring this feature later in this chapter.

By default, this MaximumMegaByte value is set to 0, which in essence disables the machine as a PBA peer.

Extending the Backup Only Task Sequence for PBA

When using ConfigMgr to replace a computer, you use two task sequences. The first performs a backup on the old computer, which is actually created from the Client Replace Task Sequence in the templates list, hereafter referred to as "backup only." The second task sequence is a normal bare metal deployment task sequence, used to deploy the new computer and configured to restore the backup at the end of the process.

Real World Note: When having third-party disk encryption installed, the replace scenario may be used on the same machine. You simply run the two sequences on the same machine.

1. Log on to **CM01** and open the **ConfigMgr console**.
2. In the **Software Library** workspace, expand **Operating Systems**, right-click **Task Sequences**, select **Create MDT Task Sequence**, and create a new task sequence using the following settings:
    a. Choose Template: **Client Replace Task Sequence**
    b. Task Sequence Name: **PBA Backup Only-AWD**
    c. Boot Image: **Zero Touch WinPE 5.0 x64**
    d. MDT Package: **MDT 2013**
    e. USMT Package: **Microsoft Corporation User State Migration Tool for Windows 8 6.3.9600.16384**
    f. Settings Package: **Windows 8.1 x64 Settings**
3. Click **PBA Backup Only-AWD** and click **Properties**. In the **Nomad** tab, enable **Nomad** and click **OK**.
4. Click the **PBA Backup Only-AWD** task sequence and click **Edit**.
5. Scroll down to the first **Gather** action.
6. Create a new group named **Online USMT-PBA-AWD**.
7. Remove the **Request State Store** step.
8. Scroll down and remove the **Release State Store** step.

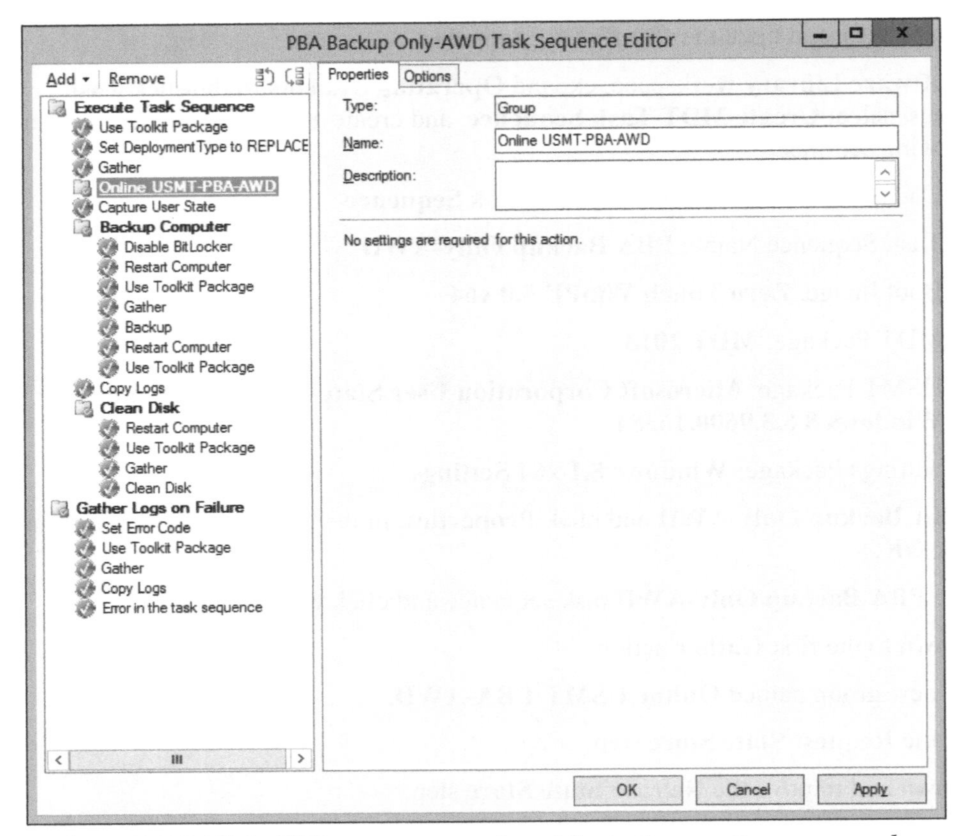

Online USMT-PBA-AWD group created, and State Store actions removed.

9. Click **Online USMT-PBA-AWD**, and then click **Add / General / Set Task Sequence Variable**.
10. Configure this step with the following settings:
    - Name: **Configure USMT Estimate-AWD**
    - Description: **For LAB purposes only**
    - Task Sequence Variable: **USMTEstimate**
    - Value: **20**

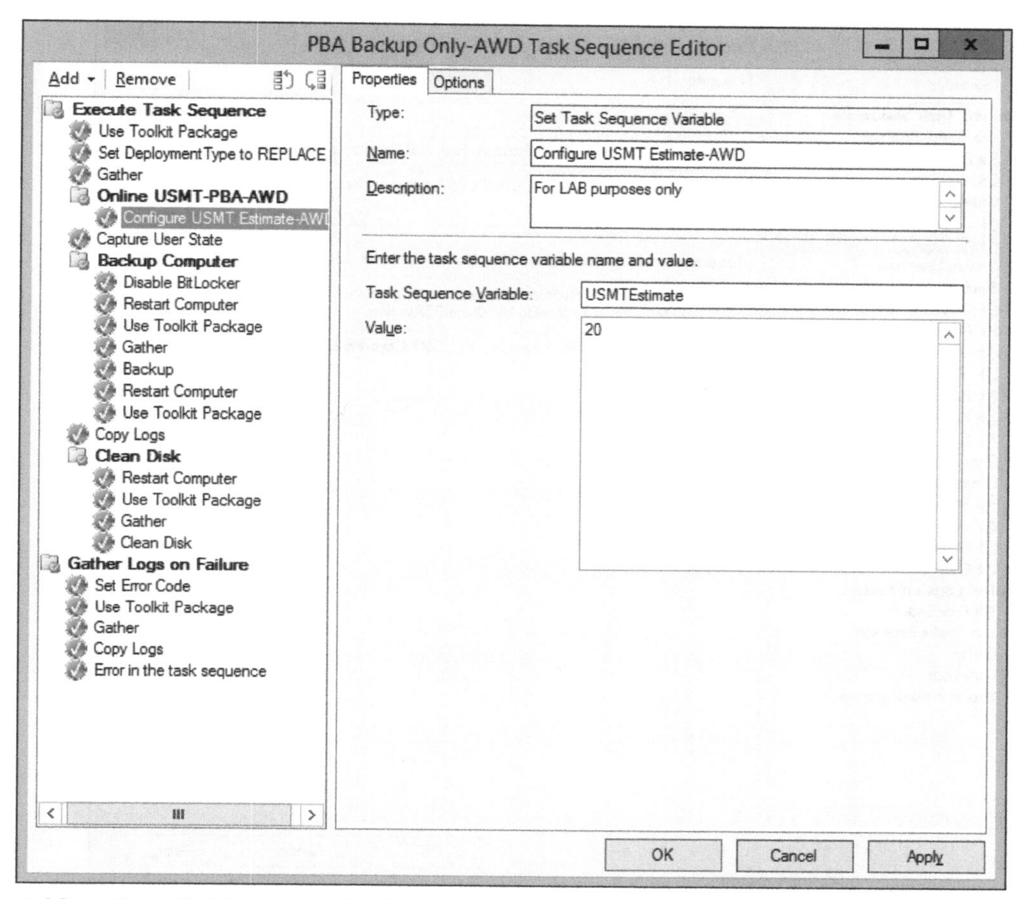

Adding the USMT estimate for Nomad PBA.

11. Click **Configure USMT Estimate-AWD**, and then click **Add / Nomad / Peer Backup Assistant: Provision Nomad PBA Data Store**.
12. Configure this step with the following settings:
    - Name: **PBA: Provision Nomad PBA DataStore-AWD**
    - Cache space (MB): **100**

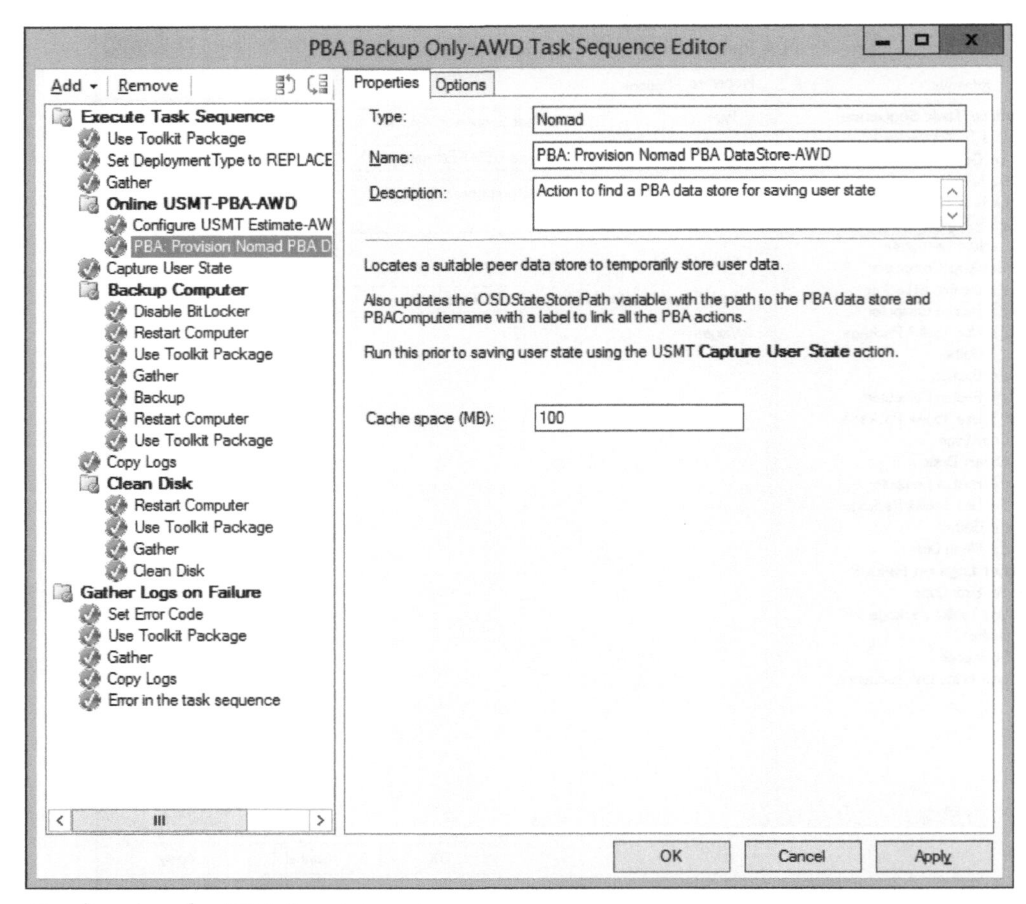

Configuring the PBA Provision step.

13. Right-click **Capture User State**, and then click **Move Up**.
14. Click **Capture User State**, and then click **Add / Nomad / Peer Backup Assistant: Close Nomad PBA Data Store**.
15. Configure this step with the following setting:

    Name: **PBA: Close Nomad PBA Data Store-AWD**

16. Click **OK**.

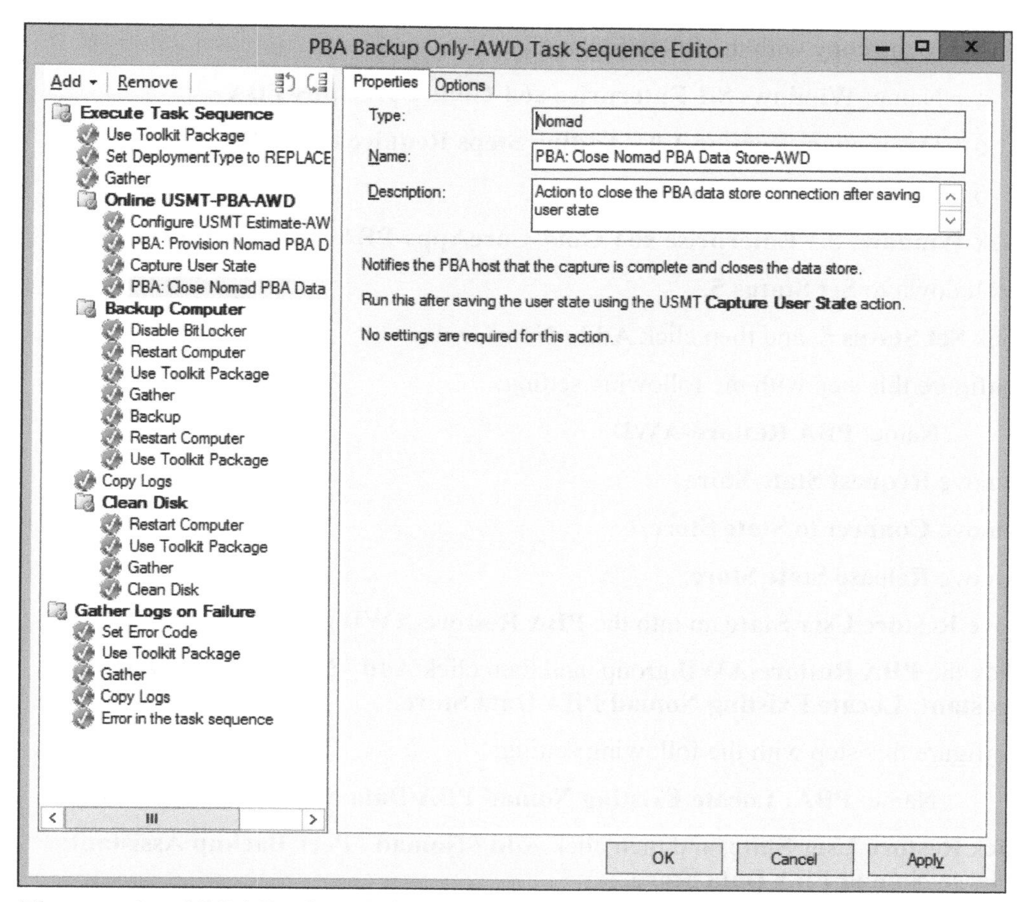

The completed PBA Backup Only task sequence.

Extending the Bare Metal Task Sequence for PBA

When the backup only task sequence is created, you need to modify the normal bare metal task sequence to restore the backup using PBA. In this guide, you take a copy of an existing bare metal task sequence and modify it.

1. Log on to **CM01** and open the **ConfigMgr console**.
2. Right-click the **Windows 8.1 Enterprise x64-Gold-CoreApps-BareMetal** task sequence and click **Copy**.

3. Configure the copy with the following settings:
   - Name: **Windows 8.1 Enterprise x64-Gold-CoreApps-PBA**
   - Description: **Version 1.0 - Adding Steps Required for PBA**
   - Nomad tab: Select **Enable Nomad**.
4. Click **Windows 8.1 Enterprise x64-Gold-CoreApps-PBA** and click **Edit**.
5. Scroll down to **Set Status 5**.
6. Click **Set Status 5**, and then click **Add / New Group**.
7. Configure this step with the following setting:

   Name: **PBA Restore-AWD**
8. Remove **Request State Store**.
9. Remove **Connect to State Store**.
10. Remove **Release State Store**.
11. Move **Restore User State** up into the **PBA Restore-AWD** group.
12. Click the **PBA Restore-AWD** group, and then click **Add / Nomad / Peer Backup Assistant: Locate Existing Nomad PBA Data Store**.
13. Configure this step with the following setting:

    Name: **PBA: Locate Existing Nomad PBA Data Store-AWD**
14. Click **Restore User State**, and then click **Add / Nomad / Peer Backup Assistant: Release Nomad PBA Data Store**.
15. Configure this step with the following setting:

    Name**: PBA: Release Nomad PBA Data Store-AWD**

Note: Adding the Peer Backup Assistant: Release Nomad PBA Data Store step deletes the backup from the peer client. If you want to keep the data after a successful restore, you can remove this action. By default the peer then keeps the backup for seven days (configurable via the PostCompleteTimeoutHours registry key).

16. Click **OK**.

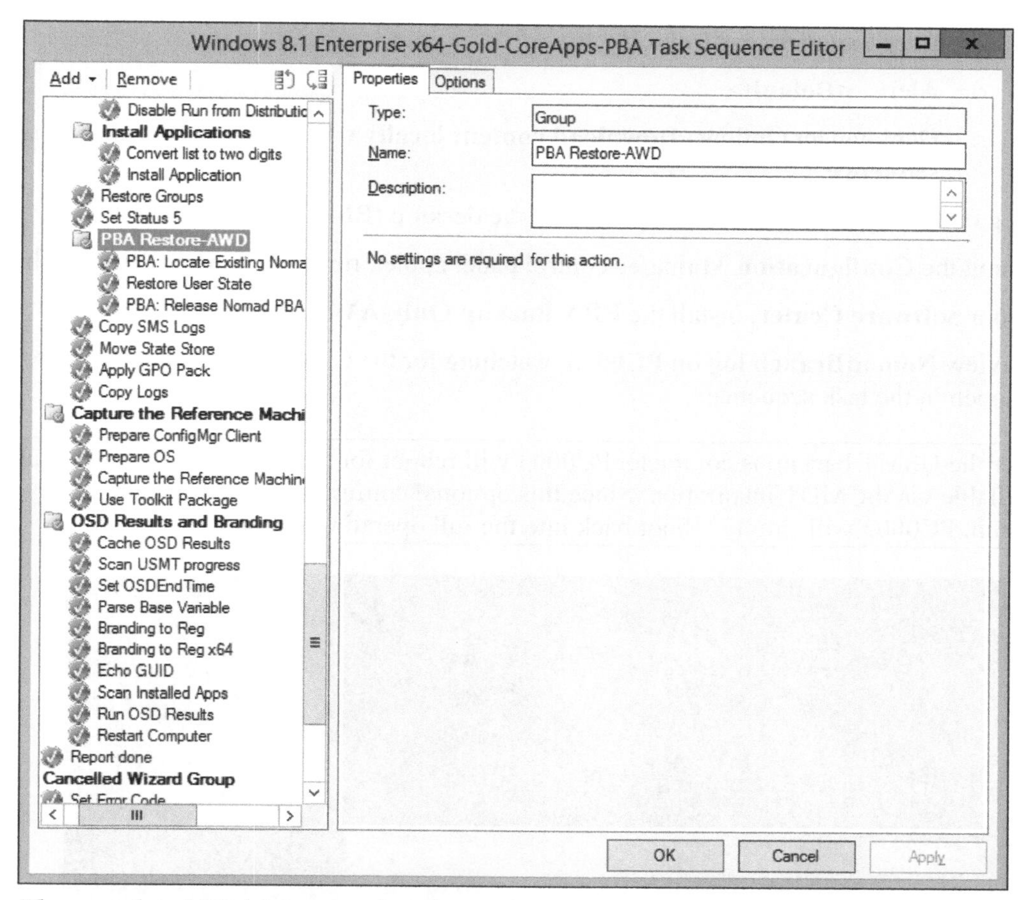

The completed PBA bare metal task sequence.

Deploying the PBA Backup Only Task Sequence

In this guide, you deploy and run the backup only task sequence on PC0003 and verify that the USMT backup is being stored on PC0004, the machine you configured for PBA earlier.

1. On **CM01**, using the **ConfigMgr console**, in the **AWD** folder, create a device collection named **Deploy PBA Backup Only**. Use **All Systems** as limiting collections, and add **PC0003** as a direct member.
2. Deploy the **PBA Backup Only-AWD** task sequence to the **Deploy PBA Backup Only** collection with the following settings:
    - Purpose: **Available**
    - Make available to the following: **Only Configuration Manager Clients**
    - Scheduling: **<Default>**

- User Experience: **<Default>**
- Alerts: **<Default>**
- Deployment Options: **Download content locally when needed by running task sequence**

3. Log on to **PC0003** and create some files to the desktop (BMP, TXT and RTF files).
4. Using the **Configuration Manager** control panel applet, run a machine policy refresh.
5. From **Software Center**, install the **PBA Backup Only-AWD** task sequence.
6. Review **NomadBranch.log** on **PC0003**, watching for the Capture User State action to happen in the task sequence.

> **Note:** After the USMT backup is complete, PC0003 will reboot for the optional full WIM backup option available via the MDT integration. Since this optional configuration in not enabled in your configuration, PC0003 will simply reboot back into the full operating system.

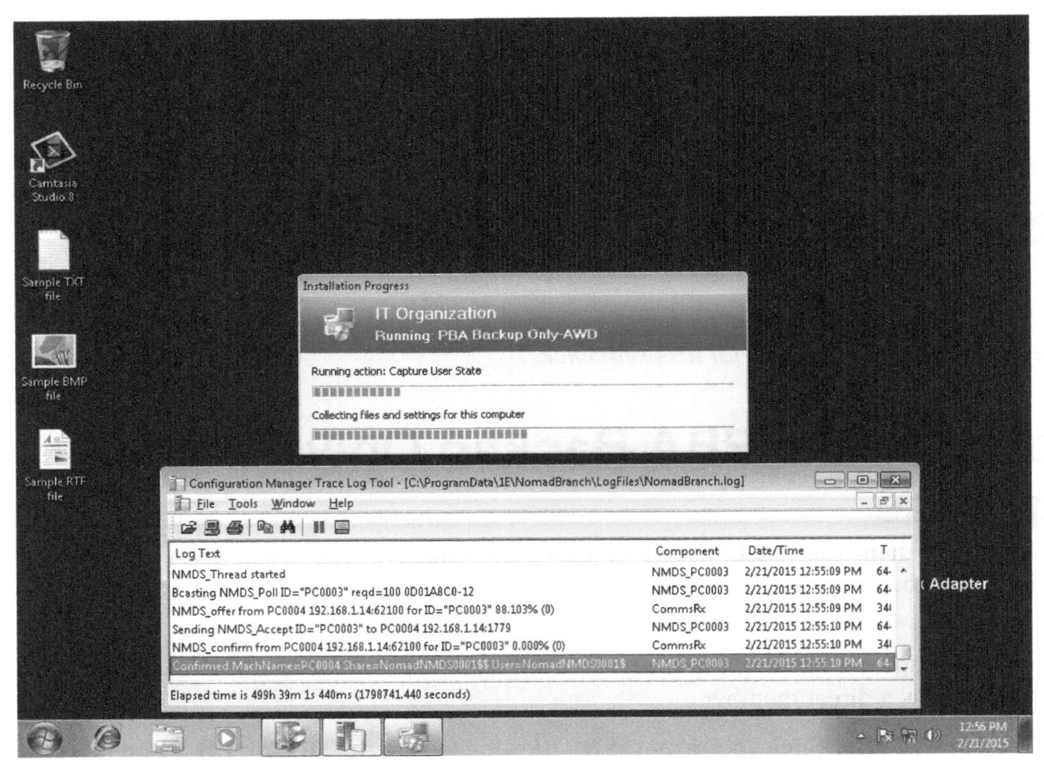

Validating that the USMT backup is redirecting to a peer (PC0004) using Nomad PBA.

7. On **PC0004**, open **HKLM\SOFTWARE\1E\NomadBranch**.
8. Expand the newly created **NMDS_State** key.

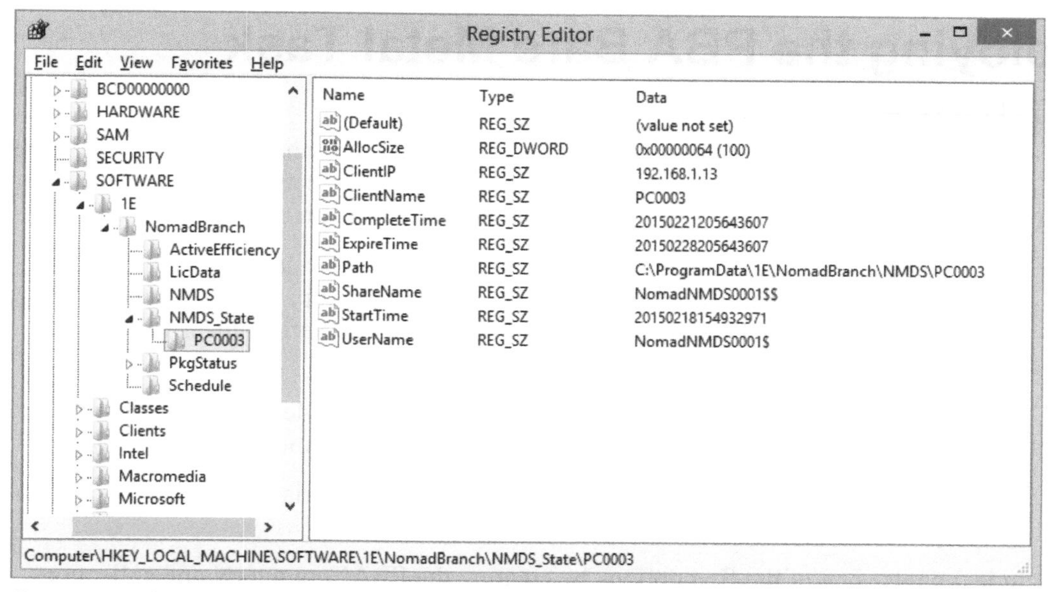

Reviewing the registry values created by Nomad PBA.

9. Browse to **C:\ProgramData\1E\Nomadbranch\NMDS**.
10. Review the **PC0003\USMT** data.

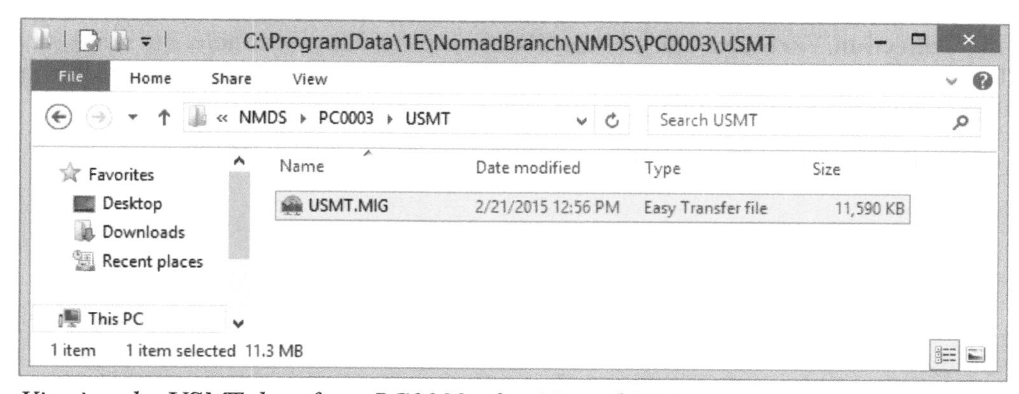

Viewing the USMT data from PC0003 after Nomad PBA.

Deploying the PBA Bare Metal Task Sequence

After you have verified that the backup was created on PC0003, you are one final step from being able to deploy the new computer using the bare metal task sequence configured for PBA. The final step is connecting the old machine with the new machine, and this can be done in three ways:

- Have the task sequence prompt for which backup (computer name) to restore, via an empty collection variable, a script that prompts for the backup; via a custom HTA page; or via a customized UDI wizard pane. The variable used to define this is named PBAComputerName.
- Use the native ConfigMgr computer association feature, and develop either a script or a web service that reads that information and sets the PBAComputerName variable.
- Extend the MDT database to use the PBAComputerName variable, and use the database to configure which backup to restore.

In this guide, you use one of the first options by creating the PBAComputerName collection variable, but don't set a value. This forces ConfigMgr to prompt for it at deployment time.

1. Log on to **CM01** and open the **ConfigMgr console**.
2. In the **Assets and Compliance** workspace, right-click the **All Unknown Computers** collection and select **Properties**.
3. In the **Collection Variables** tab, add the **PBAComputerName** variable, but don't set a value (clear the **Do not display this value in the Configuration Manager console** check box and leave the **Value** text box empty).

Adding the PBAComputerName empty variable.

4. Click **OK**.
5. Deploy the **Windows 8.1 Enterprise x64-Gold-CoreApps-PBA** task sequence to the **All Unknown Computers** collection with the following settings:
    - Purpose: **Available**
    - Make available to the following: **Only media and PXE**
    - Scheduling: **<Default>**
    - User Experience: **<Default>**
    - Alerts: **<Default>**
    - Deployment Options: **Download content locally when needed by running task sequence**

6. On the **Host PC**, create a **Generation 1** Hyper-V virtual machine with the following settings:
   - Name: **PC0008**
   - Location: **D:\VMs**
   - Generation: **Generation 1**
   - Memory: **1024 MB**
   - Network: **AWD_Internal**
   - Hard disk: **<default>**
   - **Install an operating system from a network-based installation server**
7. Turn on **PC0008**, and press **F12** when prompted.
8. After WinPE starts, type in a password of **P@ssw0rd**.
9. Deploy the **Windows 8.1 Enterprise x64-Gold-CoreApps-PBA** task sequence.
10. In the **Edit Task Sequence Variables** dialog box, double-click **PBAComputerName**, type in **PC0003**, click **OK**, and then click **Next**.

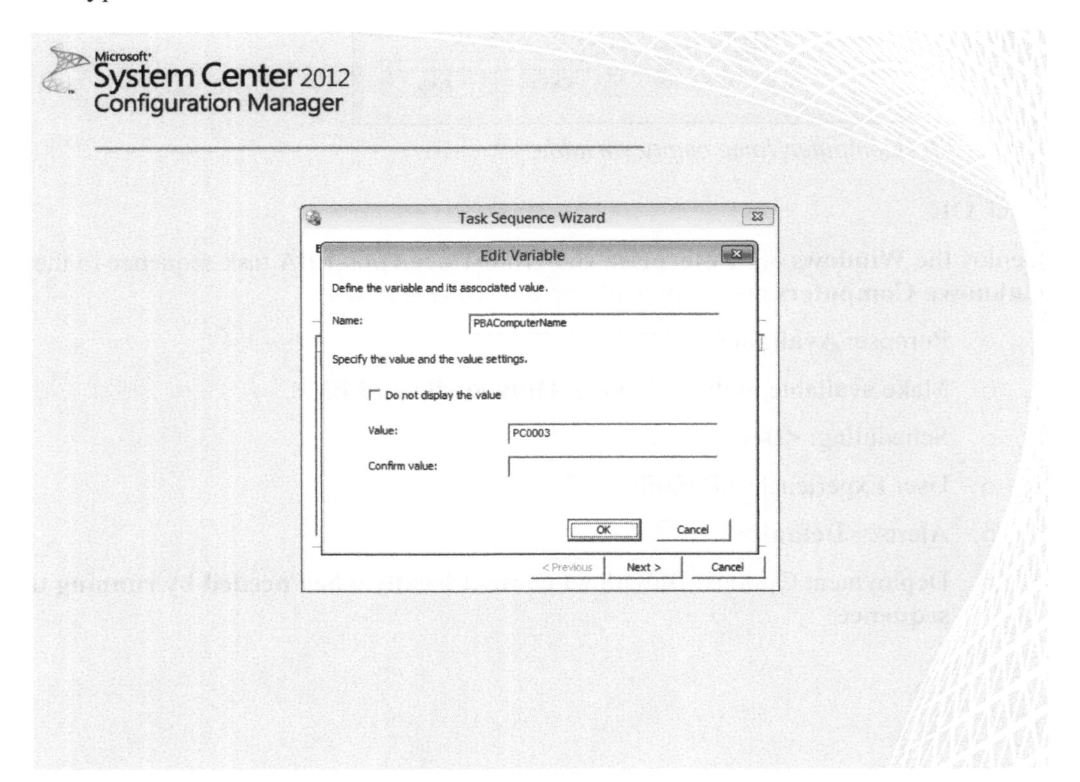

Entering which backup should be restored, in this case the backup from PC0003.

11. Allow the deployment to complete, and in the State Restore phase, look for the various restore USMT backup actions, such as the **Restore User State** action.

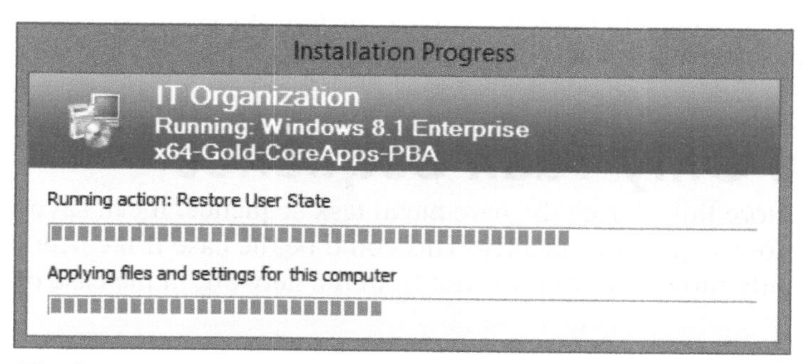

The Restore User State action running in the State Restore phase of the task sequence.

12. When the **PC0008** virtual machine is deployed, log in as **VIAMONSTRA\Administrator** and verify that the backup was restored.
13. Rename the computer on the **PC0008** virtual machine to **PC0008** (by default a MININT-XXYYZZ computer name is generated), and reboot **PC0008**.

PC0008 deployed, and the backup from PC0003 is restored.

Note: Again, with the current configuration of the task sequence, after a successful restore, the backup store is deleted from PC0004. If you want to keep the backup for a while (by default seven days), even after a successful restore, you need to remove the Peer Backup Assistant: Release Nomad PBA Data Store action from the task sequence.

The PBA Restore Only Task Sequence

In the event that the PBA USMT restore fails during the bare metal task sequence, it can save you some time just to rerun the PBA restore step independently. This could be the case if the peer hosting the USMT data is inadvertently turned off, or removed from the network in the case of a laptop hosting PBA USMT data.

Running a restore only job is also efficient when you want to minimize the downtime for users when replacing their computers. With this sequence, you can use the following optional scenario when replacing computers:

1. Use the normal (non-PBA) bare metal task sequence to deploy a new computer on a staging network.
2. Ask the user to have a coffee break or go for lunch.
3. Run the backup only task sequence on the old computer.
4. Turn off the old computer, unplug the network cable, and plug in the new computer.
5. Run the restore only task sequence on the new computer.

In this, and the following guide, you take a new backup from PC0003 and then restore it to the already deployed PC0008. To have the task sequence ask you which backup to restore when you start it in running Windows, you use a script included in the book sample files.

The script for prompting was originally developed by Nickolaj Andersen and David Green, and we modified it to use the PBAComputerName variable instead of OSDComputerName. Nickolaj and David graciously allowed us to include the script in the book sample files. For more scripts and other info related to ConfigMgr and OSD, check out Nickolaj's blog at http://scconfigmgr.com and David's blog at http://tookitaway.co.uk.

1. Log on to **CM01** and copy the **PromptForPBAComputerName.ps1** sample script to D:**\SCCM_Sources\OSD\MDT\MDT 2013\Scripts**.
2. Using the **ConfigMgr console**, update distribution points for the **MDT 2013** package.

3. Right-click **Task Sequences** and select **Create MDT Task Sequence**. Use the following settings:
   - Create New Task Sequence: **Microsoft Deployment Custom Task Sequence**
   - Name: **PBA Restore Only-AWD**
   - Boot Image: **Zero Touch WinPE 5.0 x64**
   - MDT Package: **MDT 2013**
   - Settings Package: **Windows 8.1 x64 Settings**
4. Click **PBA-Restore Only-AWD** and click **Properties**.
5. In the **Nomad** tab, enable **Nomad** and click **OK**.
6. Click **PBA-Restore Only-AWD** and click **Edit**.
7. Remove the last four actions in the task sequence; then select **Gather**, and click **Add / New Group**.
8. Configure this step with the following setting:

   Name: **Restore Nomad PBA-AWD**
9. Click **Restore Nomad PBA-AWD**, and then click **Add / General / Run Command Line**.
10. Configure this step with the following settings:
    - Name**: Prompt for PBA Computer Name**
    - Command line: **"%deployroot%\tools\%architecture%\ServiceUI.exe" -process:TSProgressUI.exe %SYSTEMROOT%\System32\WindowsPowerShell\v1.0\powershell.exe -NoProfile -WindowStyle Hidden -ExecutionPolicy Bypass -File Scripts\PromptForPBAComputerName.ps1**
    - Package: **MDT 2013**

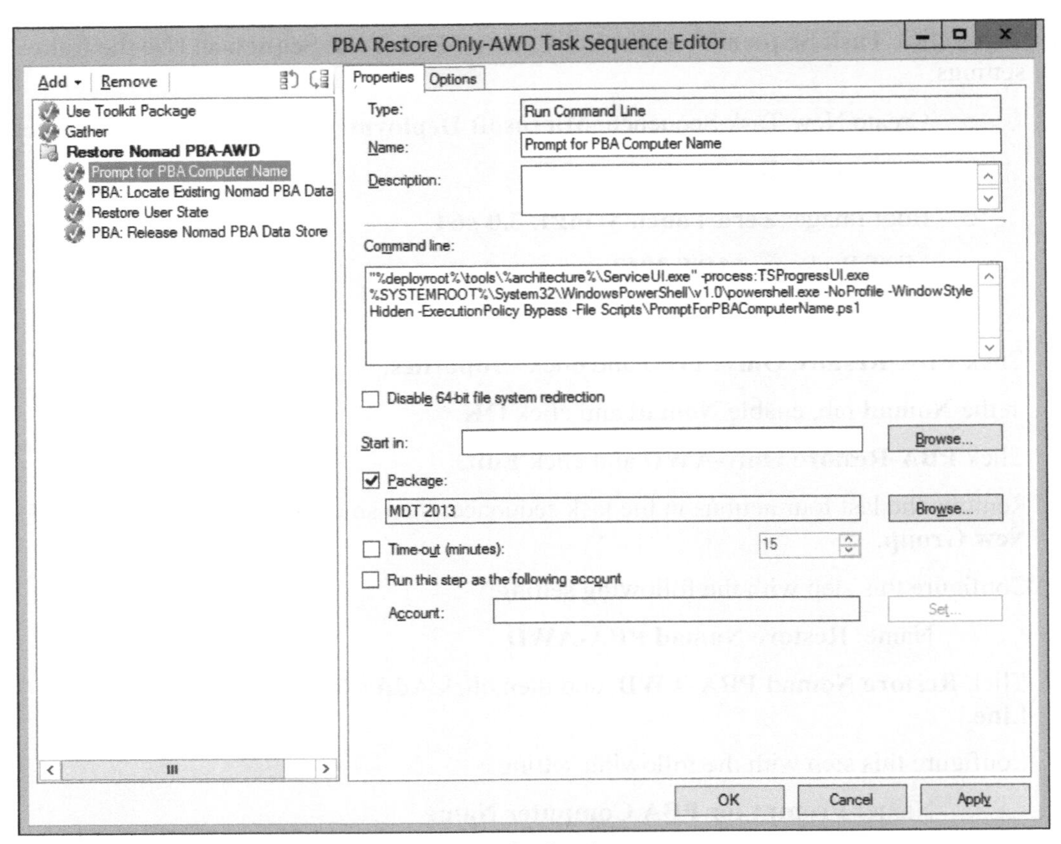

Configuring the task sequence to prompt for backup.

11. Click **Prompt for PBA Computer Name**, and then click **Add / Nomad / Peer Backup Assistant: Locate Existing Nomad PBA Data Store**. Rename the action to **PBA: Locate Existing Nomad PBA Data Store**.
12. Click **Add**, and then click **User State / Restore User State**. Browse to select the **Microsoft Corporation User State Migration Tool for Windows 8 6.3.9600.16384**.
13. Click **Add**, and then click **Nomad / Peer Backup Assistant: Release Nomad PBA Data Store**. Rename the action to **PBA: Release Nomad PBA Data Store**.

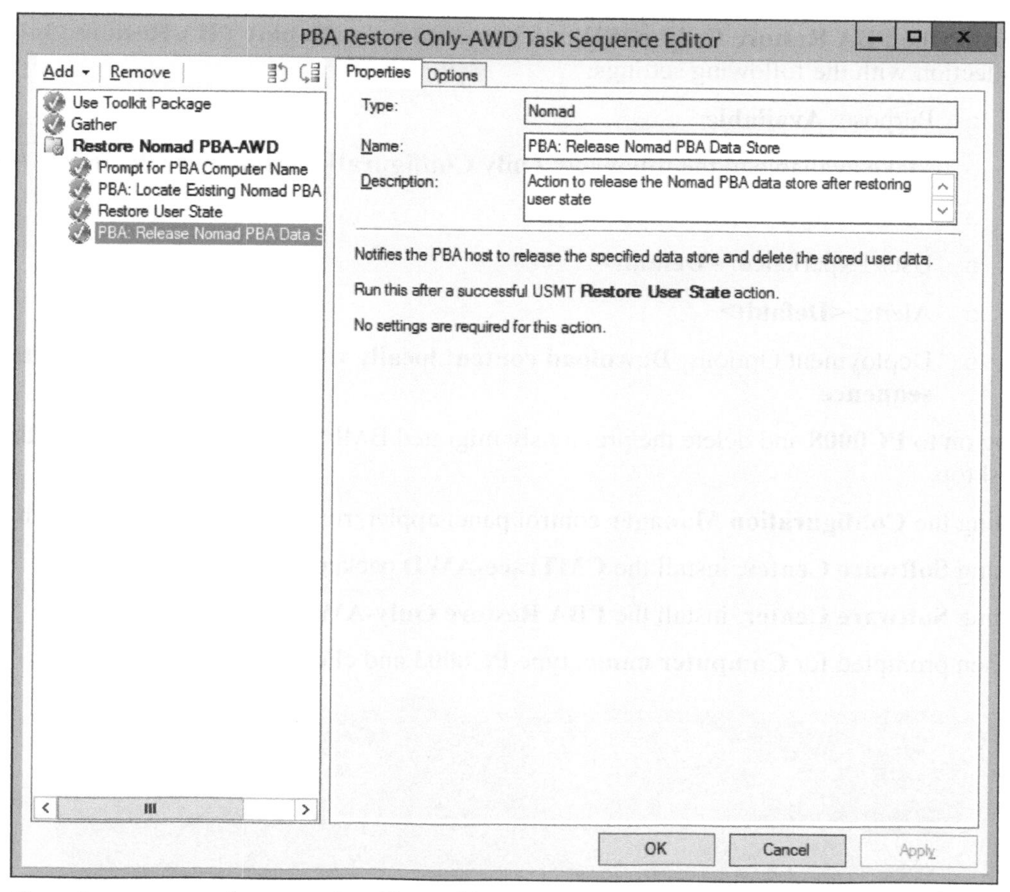

Creating a group for restoring Nomad PBA.

Deploying the PBA Restore Only Task Sequence

In this guide, you deploy and run the restore only task sequence on PC0008, and then verify that the USMT backup from PC0003 is restored successfully.

1. On **PC0003**, using **Software Center**, install the **PBA Backup Only-AWD** task sequence.
2. Review **NomadBranch.log**, and verify that the new backup was stored on **PC0004** before continuing.
3. On **CM01**, using the **ConfigMgr console**, in the **AWD** folder, create a device collection named **Deploy PBA Restore Only**. Use **All Systems** as the limiting collection, and add **PC0008** as a direct member.
4. Also add **PC0008** as a direct member to the **Deploy CMTrace** collection.

5. Deploy the **PBA Restore Only-AWD** task sequence to the **Deploy PBA Restore Only** collection with the following settings:
    - Purpose: **Available**
    - Make available to the following: **Only Configuration Manager Clients**
    - Scheduling: **<Default>**
    - User Experience: **<Default>**
    - Alerts: **<Default>**
    - Deployment Options: **Download content locally when needed by running task sequence**
6. Log on to **PC0008** and delete the previously migrated BMP, TXT, and RTF files on the desktop.
7. Using the **Configuration Manager** control panel applet, run a machine policy refresh.
8. Using **Software Center**, install the **CMTrace-AWD** package.
9. Using **Software Center**, install the **PBA Restore Only-AWD** task sequence.
10. When prompted for **Computer name**, type **PC0003** and click **OK**.

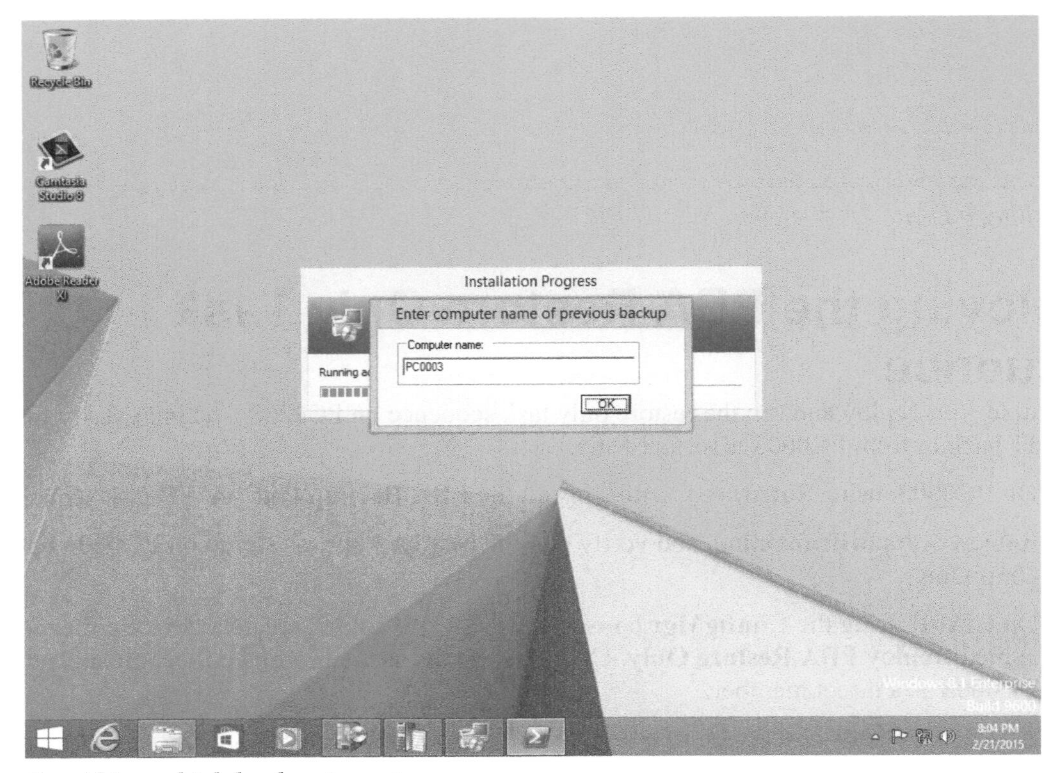

Specifying which backup to restore.

11. While running the task sequence, review the **NomadBranch.log**, and then verify that the files on the desktop were restored.

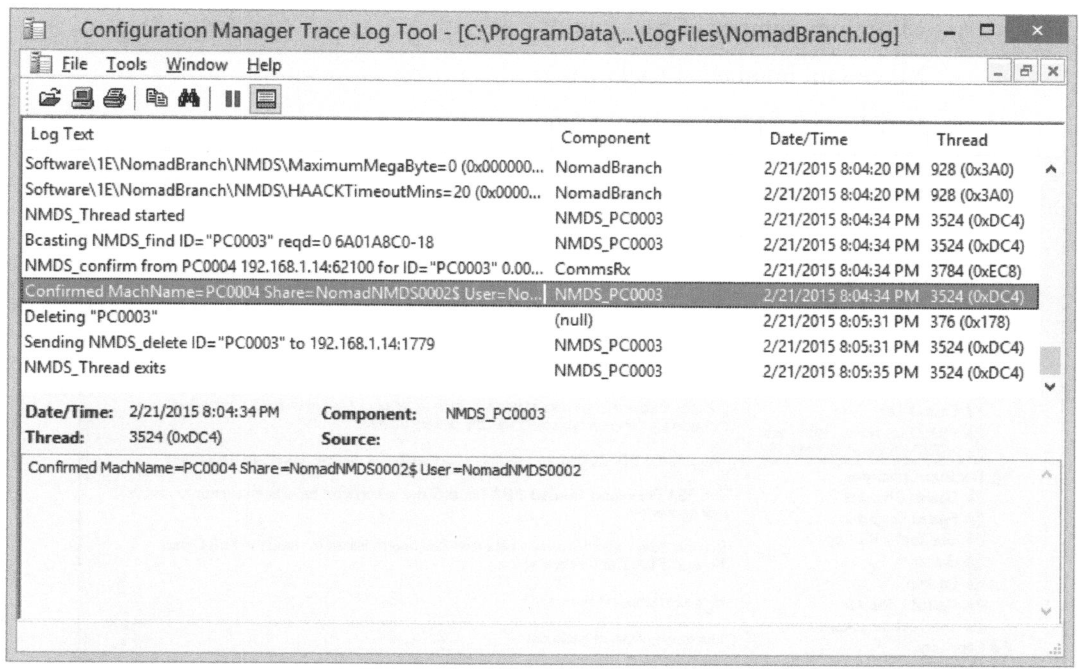

Viewing the task sequence restore process in the NomadBranch.log.

The PBA Highly Available Backup Only Task Sequence

For testing purposes, it is nice to have a PBA backup only task sequence. This helps test the PBA's functionality prior to a migration. In Nomad 5.2, PBA has the ability to store USMT data on more than one peer, thus making USMT data highly available.

1. Log on to **CM01** and open the **ConfigMgr console**.
2. Click **PBA Backup Only-AWD** and click **Copy**.
3. Configure the copy with the following settings:
    - Name: **PBA HA Backup Only-AWD**
    - Description: **Version 1.0 - Adding HA PBA Step**
4. Click **PBA HA Backup Only-AWD** and click **Edit**.
5. Click **PBA: Close Nomad PBA Data Store-AWD**, and then click **Add / Nomad / Peer Backup Assistant: Nomad PBA Data Store High Availability**.

6. Configure this step with the following settings:
    - Name: **PBA: Nomad PBA Data Store High Availability**
    - Minimum number of backups: **1**
    - Maximum number of backups: **2**
    - Synchronous backups for which to wait: **1**

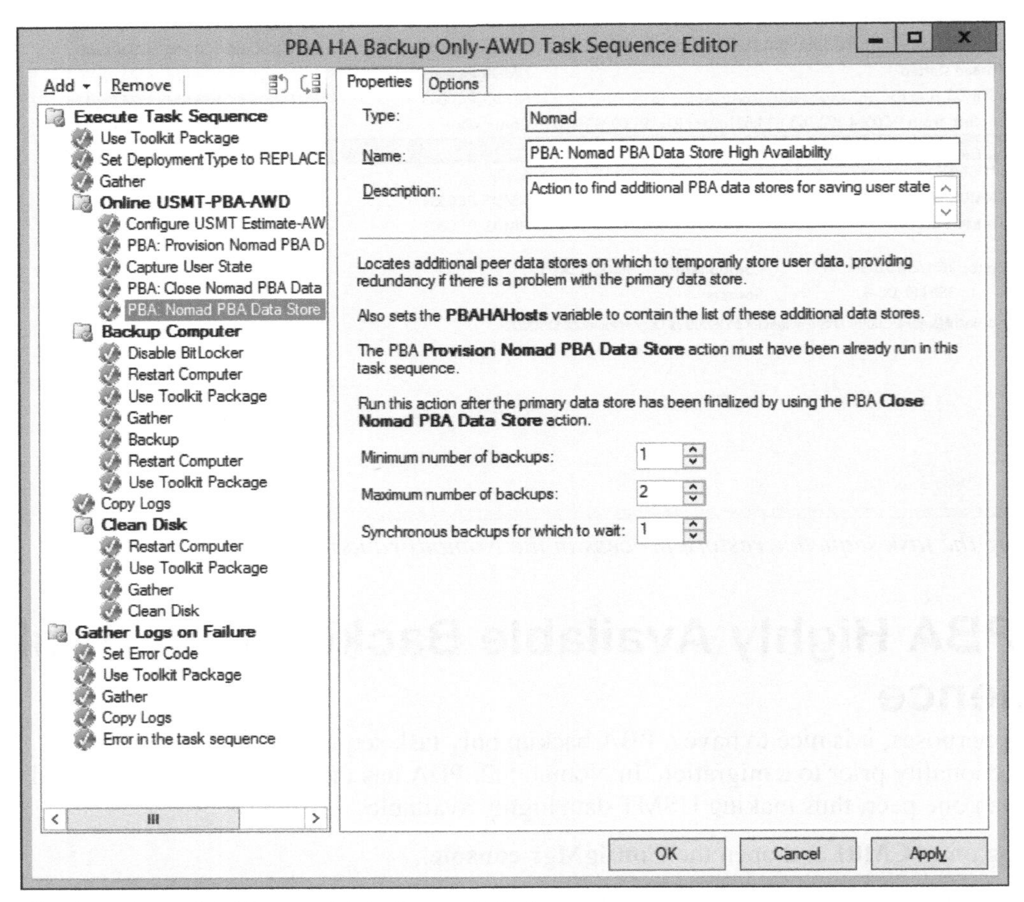

Configuring a highly available Nomad PBA step.

Chapter 13

Shopping for Self-Service OSD Refresh

As you saw in the preceding chapter, a task sequence can be built and deployed to systems by adding them to deployment collections. This process is probably one of the most complex and difficult to manage portions of a Windows deployment. In this chapter, you use a script to quickly hydrate the prerequisites for 1E Shopping. You then use 1E Shopping later in this chapter to empower end users with a self-service OSD module in the Shopping App Store (Portal). Giving users the ability to self-serve and schedule their own Windows upgrades alleviates much of the workload on the project management office that governs the upgrade.

This finished product for this chapter will be a self-service banner in the 1E Shopping Enterprise App Store (Portal).

The Welcome page of the 1E Shopping Enterprise App Store.

Shopping Key Concepts

Shopping has been designed from the ground up to help reduce operating and licenses costs pertaining to software applications. Providing the end user with a self-service portal that automatically ties into ConfigMgr, eliminates help desk tickets and manual deployment on various levels based on software distribution practices. Managerial approvals and rental options for business applications reduce license costs and help proactively manage volume license distribution. The last major feature with Shopping is the ability for users to schedule their own OS migration, which has revitalized the OSD process, drastically improved success rates, and generated significant savings for organizations that adopt the feature.

Application Approval

It is possible with 1E Shopping to configure an application-approval workflow. The built-in workflow allows for email approvals and is fully customizable. The approval workflow can be extensively configured using chains, groups, chains of groups, and so forth. Approval also can be varied by computer category or branch, allowing different geographical regions or business units to have different approval processes.

Delegated Administration

Shopping comes with two administrative models: central and branch. The *central* administration model is useful for organizations that do not require delegation. Whereas the *branch* administration model is useful where there is a distributed administrative model. Delegating administration for Shopping is performed on a per-application basis. As an example, this allows regional applications to be managed by the respective regional administrators.

Shopping for ConfigMgr Applications

ConfigMgr applications are those applications added to Shopping that are configured for use in the ConfigMgr infrastructure. Shopping simply provides a skinnable frontend app store for users to self-serve their own applications. The framework of the Shopping App Store is often compared to the Application Catalog from ConfigMgr. However, it has greater extensibility than the Application Catalog. For example, Shopping enables you to allow users to shop for task sequences, request resources not affiliated with ConfigMgr, and provide an integrated e-mail approval process for requesting software with associated licensing costs.

Shopping for Non-ConfigMgr Applications

Shopping can be configured to allow users to shop for non-ConfigMgr items. For example, Active Directory group membership, new hardware devices (Surface Pro 3 or Windows Phones), stationary, and so forth. An approval workflow can be configured for any item that the business requires.

Shopping for OSD

The ability to self-serve schedule OSD deployments is key to any successful Windows migration project. This can relieve a lot of pressure from the project management office that is managing the migration effort, as the solution provides options to schedule an OSD to run at a specific date/time. The Shopping self-service OSD interface is fully customizable and even shows end users their target applications that have been configured for their new machines. All that is required for this configuration is a working OSD task sequence in ConfigMgr.

OSD Application Mapping

One of the most sophisticated aspects of Shopping's OSD capabilities is Application Mapping. Shopping is able to reinstall applications automatically as part of the OSD task sequence. Application Mapping works with 1E AppClarity, which provides a normalized inventory of all the applications installed on each device, as well as whether the application is used or unused. This allows Shopping to vary the application that is reinstalled to be based on mapping rules on the applications that were previously present on the machine being migrated. These mapping rules can even be based on usage so that different applications are reinstalled (or no application at all) depending on whether the original application was used or not. As an example, if a user has Project Professional installed on their machine, but has not used it for more than three months, Application Mapping can be configured to replace this with a no-fee application, Project Viewer.

License Management

Shopping supports the ability to manage application licenses. This gives administrators the ability to use Shopping to track license install counts. This can be set up internally in the Shopping Admin Console and configured to integrate via synchronization from ConfigMgr using the data from the application's Add/Remove Programs entry.

Software Rental

1E defines this concept as *application rental*. As its name indicates, it is possible to rent software for a period of time. This is fully configurable by the Shopping administrator and allows for some interesting flexibility for the software asset management teams. When a rental period expires, the end user can request an extension or the software is simply uninstalled.

Real World Note: To enable an application to be rented, you must define it with an uninstall package, program, or task sequence. To enable that application to be rented again after it has been removed, you set the application to be reshoppable.

Restricting What the End User Can See

Applications available in the Shopping App Store are configured by either category level or application level permissions. These are controlled by Active Directory group membership and are easily managed via the Shopping Administration Console by simply adding the respective AD users or groups to the relevant User Categories and/or Computer Categories.

Shopping Admin Console

The Shopping Admin Console is the sole console for Shopping administrators to manage the Shopping Enterprise App Store. Access to the console is role-based and can be delegated via a security node in the console.

Shopping Receiver

The Shopping Receiver is a service that is hosted on the ConfigMgr primary site server. When applications are shopped for on the Shopping Enterprise App Store, the order is placed into a staging table in the Shopping database. The Shopping Receiver is configured to poll the Shopping database via the Shopping APIs installed on the Shopping Central Server. When an order is detected, the Shopping Receiver configures a new ConfigMgr collection and assigns a mandatory deployment to it. It then adds the target machine the user was shopping from or for into that collection. This process is really where most of the magic of the shopping solution happens.

Machine Policy Refresh Integration

The Shopping process can trigger a machine policy refresh remotely on the client machine after the Receiver has completed creating the collection, adding the client machine to it, and creating a required deployment. In order for the process to work seamlessly, it is a requirement that the Shopping Receiver service account be added to the Local Administrators group on each machine.

Real World Note: As an alternative, it is also possible to configure machine policy refreshes on clients via the Wakeup agent if it is deployed. This configuration would not require Local Administrator rights for the Shopping Receiver service account.

Shopping Installation Prerequisites

Unlike many 1E products, Shopping does require some prerequisite configuration before running the installer. Some of these changes include the creation of specific service accounts, groups, IIS features, and database permissions. Pay careful attention to these, and the installation will proceed without many issues.

Real World Note: In our experience deploying Shopping in the field, many of the issues come from missing prerequisites. Often this includes going back over the list and ensuring things are done correctly. For this guide, a hydration script has been created for the deployment. It creates all of the necessary service accounts, groups, and other settings.

Shopping AD Groups and Accounts

The Shopping Installer requires the precreation of the groups in the following table.

Group/Account	Description
Shopping Admins	This group is used to manage Shopping and has access to the Administration tab in the web interface of the Shopping Enterprise App Store.
Full Shopping Admin Access	This account/group has full administrative access to the Shopping Admin Console.
Limited Shopping Admin Access	This account can be delegated for specific purposes. Changes are made via the Full Shopping Admin user in the Shopping Admin Console.
ConfigMgr 2012 R2 Database Access	For users to add ConfigMgr applications to the console, they must have access granted to the ConfigMgr database to see a list of all available applications. This group is granted the necessary access rights during the installation.
Report Managers	This account/group has visibility to the Reporting tab in the web interface of the Shopping Enterprise App Store.
License Managers	This account/group is notified via email when an application's license threshold or maximum counts are exceeded.

Shopping Service Accounts

The Shopping installer requires the precreation of the service accounts in the following table.

Service Account	Description
Shopping Receiver	By default, the Shopping Receiver service account is set to Network Service. This is configurable depending on your environment.
Shopping Central	The Shopping Central service account is used for communication with the Shopping2 MSSQL database. Permissions for this service account are granted during the installation process.

DNS Alias

A DNS alias is recommended for the configuration of the Shopping Enterprise App Store. Typically this is configured with an easy-to-remember name like AppShop or Shopping. This ultimately becomes the name that the self-service portal is referred to by users since it's the URL they remember.

Shopping Log Files

Pertaining to 1E specific logs, there are only two that are utilized for Shopping. One is for the client, and the other for the server. When a user shops for an application, the process is heavily integrated with ConfigMgr and IIS, so there are a few other logs that are important to Shopping functionality.

Log Name	Description
MSI Logs	All 1E products are installed via a Windows Installer package. When executing these installers from a command line, append /l*v C:\Temp\1EShopping.log to the msiexec.exe string to log the installation process of a particular product.
ShoppingCentral.log	The Shopping Central log file contains information about orders placed and administrative functions. Location: C:\ProgramData\1E\shoppingcentral\shoppingcentral.log
ShopingReceiver.log	The Shopping Receiver log file can be found on the ConfigMgr primary site server. It contains all of the information about order processing, collection creation, deployment creation, collection membership addition and removal, and policy refresh status remote triggering. Often we have this log file open during real time watching the order flow during a Shopping deployment. Location: C:\ProgramData\1E\shoppingreceiver\shoppingreceiver.log
ShoppingApi.log	The ShoppingAPI.log file can be found on the Shopping Central Server. This log file is interesting to watch when Application Mapping integration features are enabled. Location: C:\ProgramData\1E\ShoppingAPI
IIS LOGS	Because Shopping is functionally a website, all the standard IIS logs also can be important when troubleshooting, as the root cause of a Shopping issue is potentially IIS itself.

As with ConfigMgr, all actions are logged in a .log file and can be viewed using CMTrace.exe.

Hydrating the Lab for 1E Shopping

To ensure that you properly configure the lab environment for ViaMonstra to use 1E Shopping, a hydration script has been created. The 1E Shopping installation requires several prerequisites before it can be successfully configured. The prerequisites for this self-service OSD scenario using 1E Shopping require the following:

1. Create the required Active Directory groups
2. Create the Shopping Central service account
3. Create the Shopping Receiver services account
4. Add CM_NAA and the Shopping Receiver service account to the Shopping Receivers group
5. Create an A Record for appshop.corp.viamonstra.com pointing to 192.168.1.210 (MDT01)
6. Install the required roles and features for 1E Shopping
7. Add the SMTP service

The steps in this guide help you with the hydration of the prerequisites for the shopping environment.

1. Log on to **CM01** as **VIAMONSTRA\Administrator**.
2. Open an elevated **PowerShell prompt** and run the following command:

   ```
   C:\labfiles\Scripts\Shopping_Hydration.ps1
   ```
3. After running the script, restart **CM01**.
4. While **CM01** is rebooting, log on to **DC01** and review the service account and groups created.
5. On **CM01**, log on again, and open the **ConfigMgr console**.
6. Click **Administration / Security / Security Roles**.
7. Right-click **Security Roles** and select **Import Security Role**.

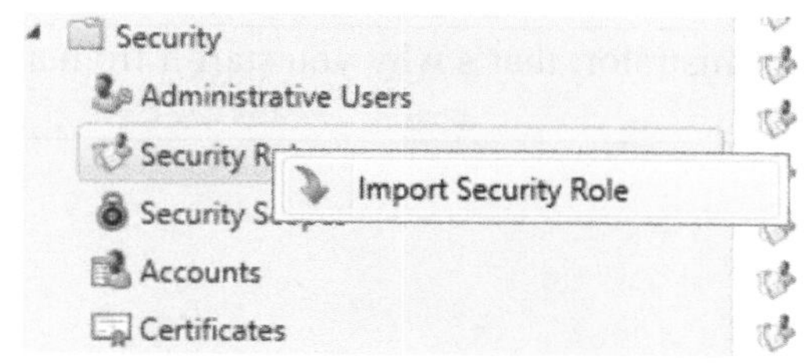

Importing the security roles for Shopping.

8. Browse to **C:\Labfiles\Sources\Shopping.v5.0.100.254\1E Shopping Receivers Security Role in ConfigMgr 2012.xml**.

Viewing the RBAC XML file downloaded from help.1e.com.

Real World Note: The RBAC .XML file can be downloaded from help.1e.com.

9. Validate that the role has been added.
10. From **Security**, right-click **Administrative Users** and then click **Add User or Group**.

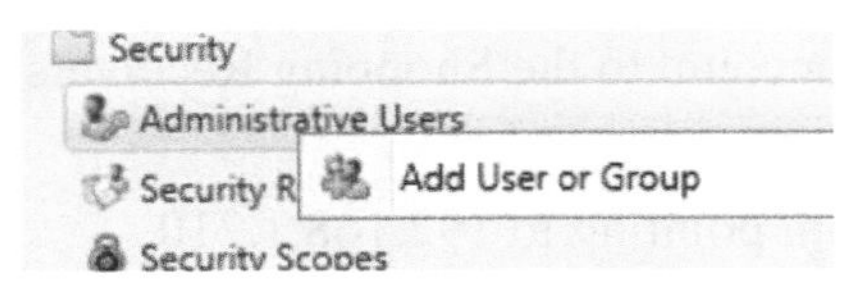

Adding a new security group for Shopping.

11. Configure with the following settings:
    - Add Group Name: **VIAMONSTRA\1E_Shopping_Receivers**
    - Role: **1E Shopping Receivers**

Installing Shopping Central

You install 1E Shopping on the MDT01 server in this guide. The Shopping Admin Console, website, and web services are installed as part of this process. Pre-requisites like Windows Authentication for IIS is already installed as part of the hydrations script you run earlier.

1. Log on to **MDT01**
2. Obtain the 1E Shopping installation files from 1E and copy them to **C:\Labfiles\Sources**.
3. Open an elevated **Command prompt**, navigate to **C:\Labfiles\Sources\shopping.v5.0.100.254** and run the following command:

```
ShoppingCentral.msi
```

Note: The Shopping Central setup must be run as Administrator, that's why you start it from an elevated command prompt.

4. Configure the setup wizard with the following options:

   a. On the **Welcome** page, click **Next**.

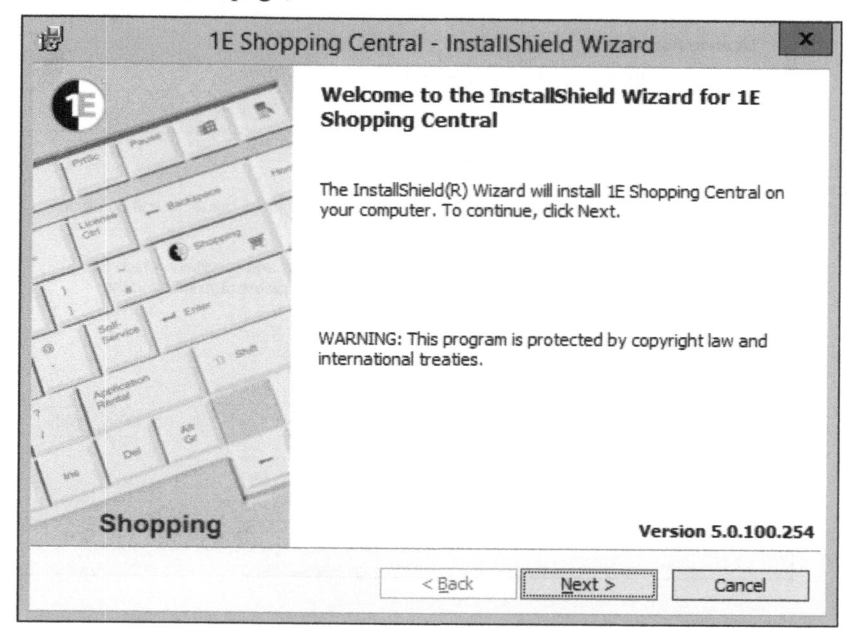

   b. On the **Shopping Prerequisites** page, click **Next**.

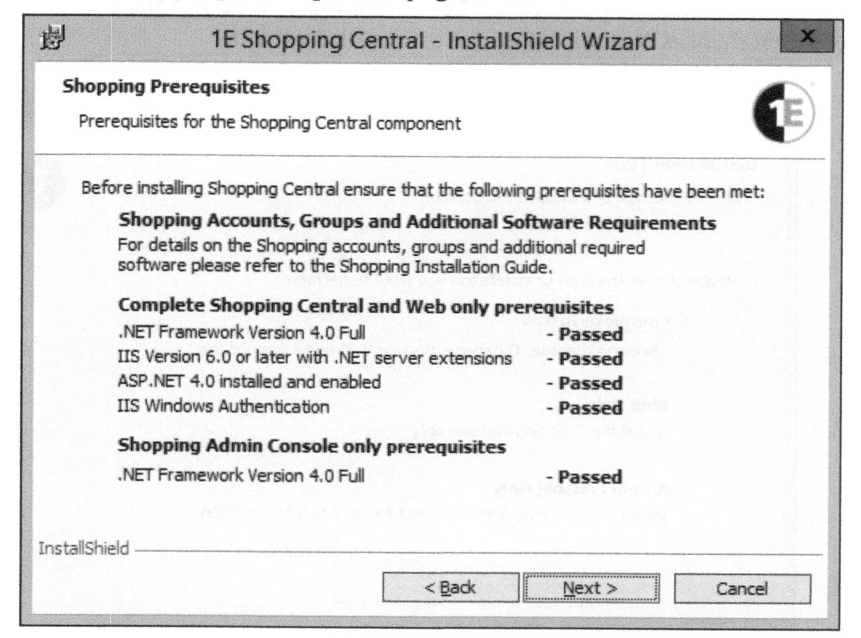

c. On the **License Agreement** page, accept the terms and click **Next**.

1E Shopping Central - InstallShield Wizard

License Agreement

Please read the following license agreement carefully.

Ref 280109
1E Limited License Agreement

Please do not install this product until you have carefully read through our terms and conditions below.

By continuing to install this product, you are accepting our terms and conditions which are enforceable by law. If you object to any term or condition, then please stop installing this immediately by pressing Cancel and then Exit Setup.

ENTIRE AGREEMENT

I accept the terms in the license agreement

I do not accept the terms in the license agreement

Print

InstallShield

< Back Next > Cancel

d. On the **Installation Type** page, select **Complete Install** and click **Next**.

Note: The Web Only installation is useful when Shopping will be installed and made available on the Internet or when there is a requirement for a tiered installation.

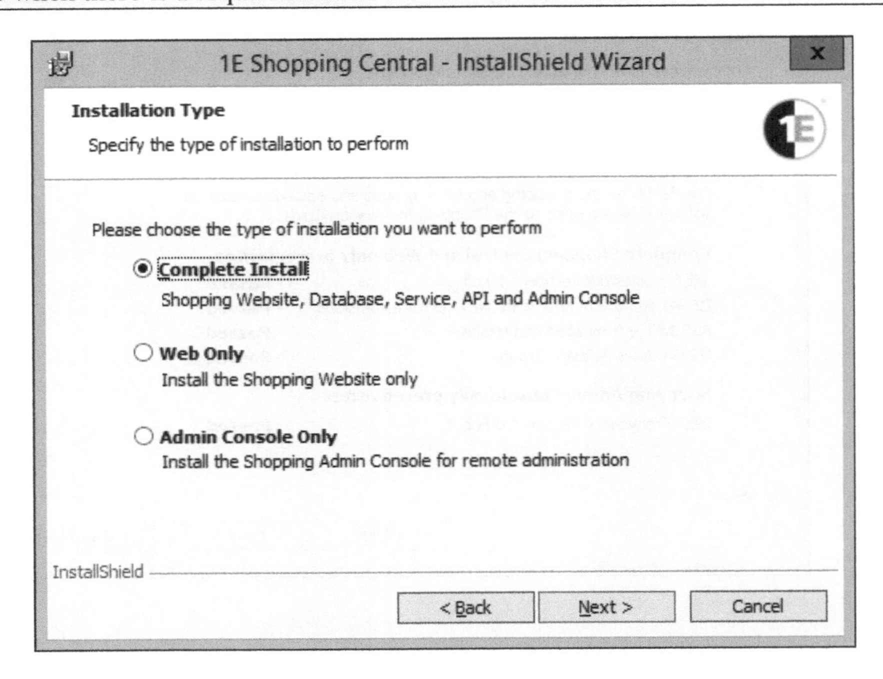

e. On the **Customer Information** page, accept the defaults and click **Next**.

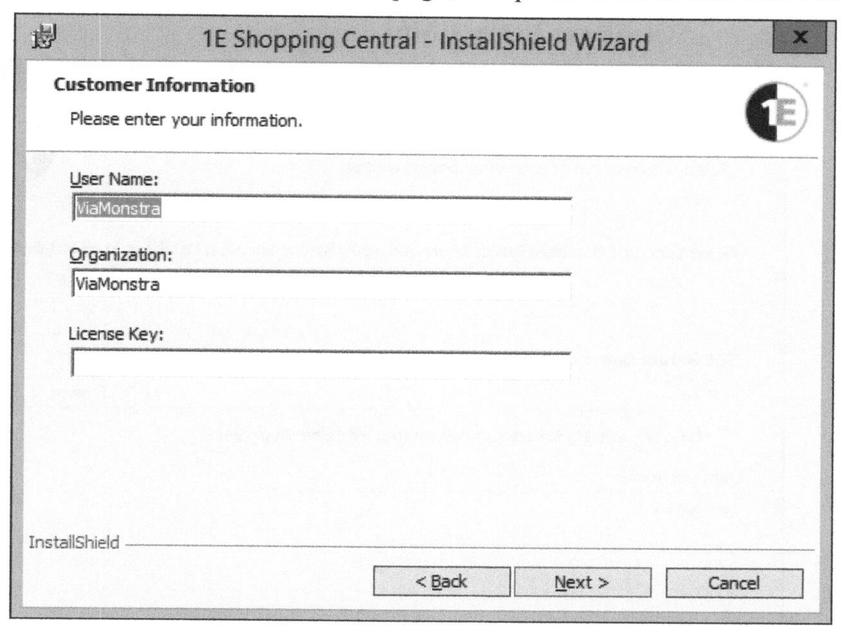

f. On the **Custom Setup** page, accept the defaults and click **Next**.

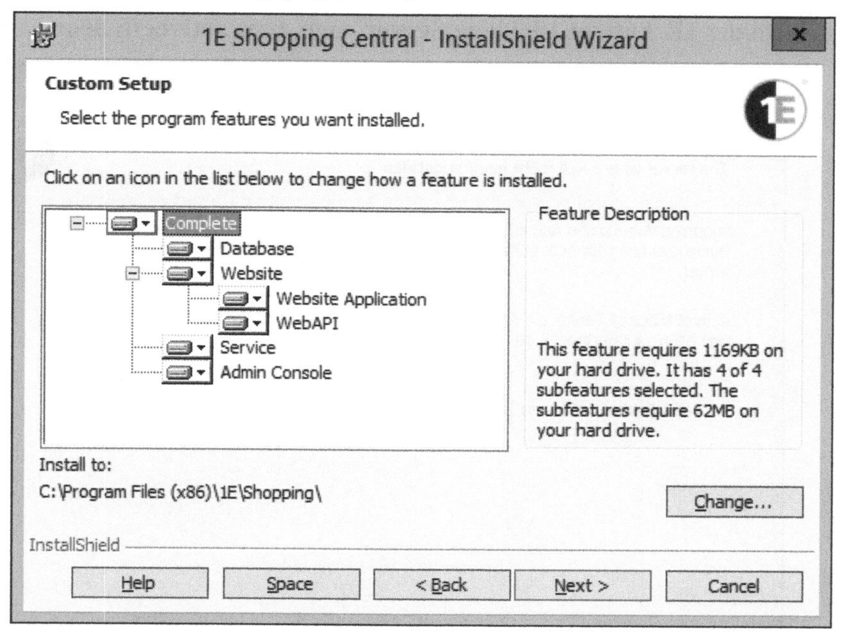

g. On the **Database Server** page, use the following setting and click **Next**:

SQL Server Name: **CM01**

1E Shopping Central - InstallShield Wizard

Database Server

Select database server and authentication method

Please select the Database Server where you would like the Shopping Database to be installed.

SQL Server Name:

CM01

Browse...

Drop any existing Shopping Database (this will delete all old data)

Database Name:

Shopping2

InstallShield

< Back Next > Cancel

h. On the **1E ActiveEfficiency Server** page, type **activeefficiency** and click **Next**.

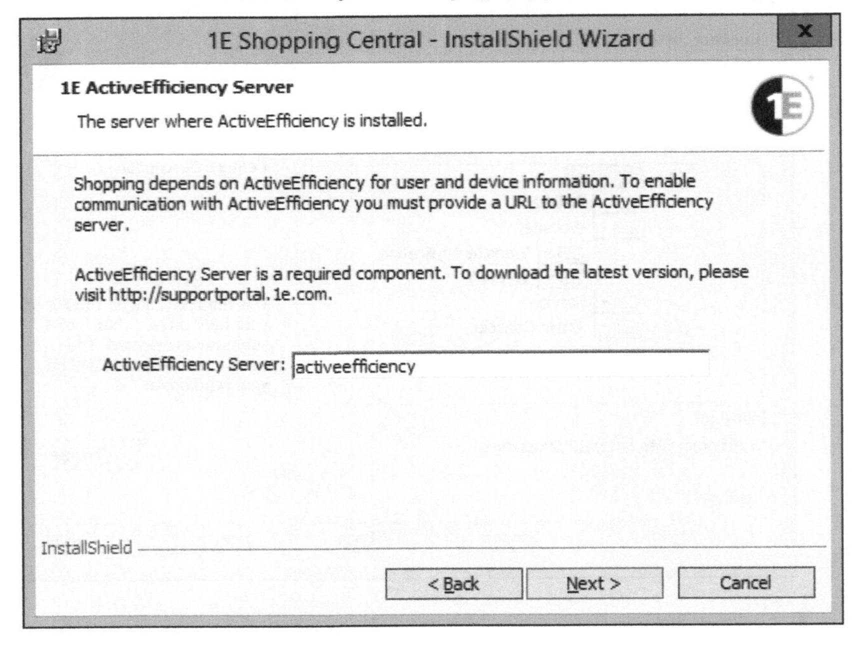

i. On the **Active Directory Integration** page, type **DC01** and click **Next**.

j. On the **Service Account** page, use the following settings and click **Next**:
   - User name: **VIAMONSTRA\Administrator**
   - Password: **P@ssw0rd**
   - Receiver: **VIAMONSTRA\1E_Shopping_Receivers**

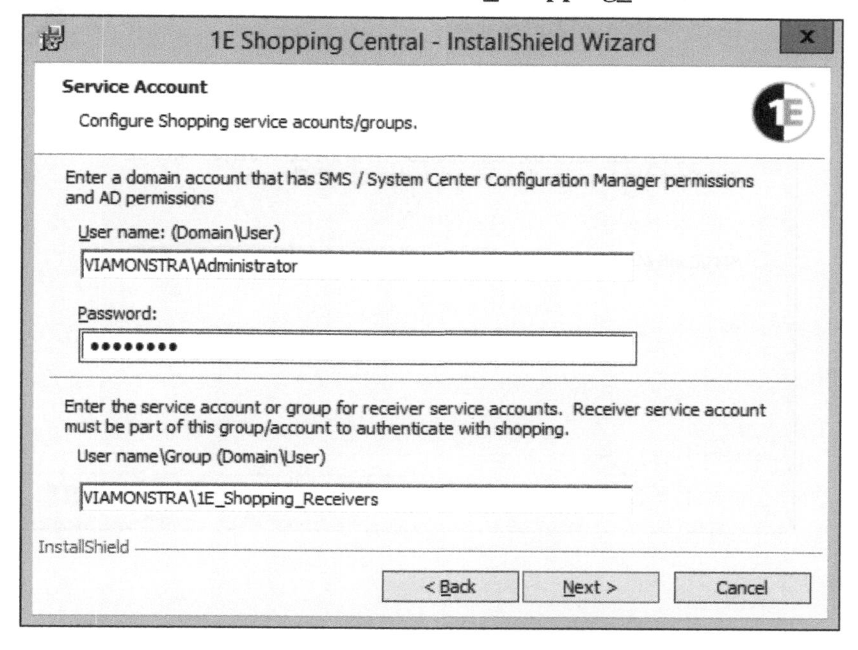

k. On the **Exchange or SMTP Server** page, type **MDT01** and click **Next**.

1E Shopping Central - InstallShield Wizard
Exchange or SMTP Server
Configure integration with the SMTP Server
Please enter the fully qualified domain name of your SMTP Server.
SMTP Server Name: MDT01
InstallShield
< Back Next > Cancel

l. On the **SMS / System Center Configuration Manager Integration** page, type **CM01** and click **Next**.

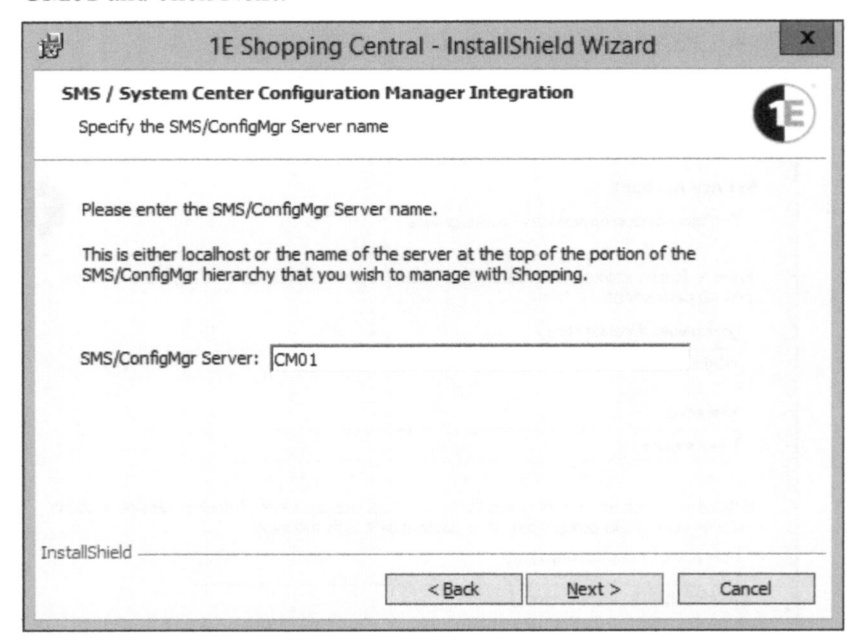

m. On the **Admin Console Node Security** page, use the following settings and click **Next**:

- Full Shopping DB Admin Access:

  VIAMONSTRA\1E_Shopping_FullDB

- Limited Shopping DB Admin Access:

  VIAMONSTRA\1E_Shopping_LimitedDB

- SMS / ConfigMgr Access:

  VIAMONSTRA\1E_Shopping_CMDB

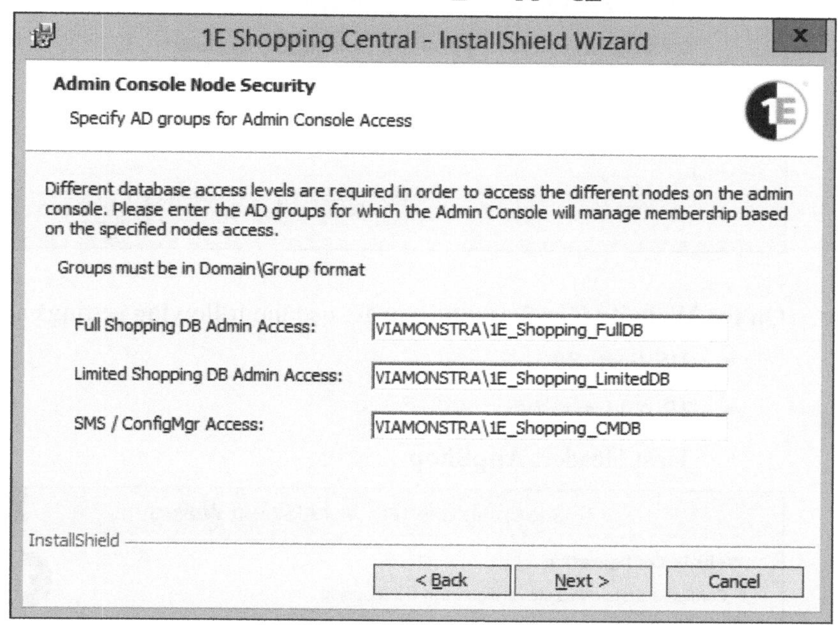

n. On the **Shopping Management Accounts** page, use the following settings and click **Next**:

- Admin account:

  VIAMONSTRA\1E_Shopping_Admins

- Reports access account:

  VIAMONSTRA\1E_Shopping_Report_Viewers

- License manager account:

  VIAMONSTRA\1E_Shopping_License_Viewers

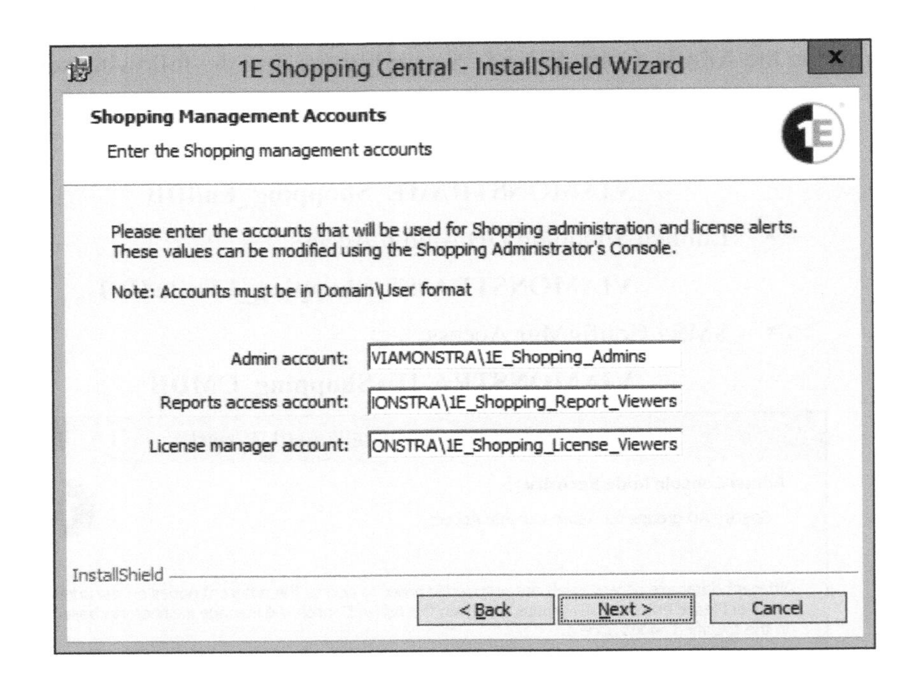

o. On the **Website Configuration** page, use the following settings and click **Next**:

- IIS Port: **80**
- IP Address: *
- Host Header: **AppShop**

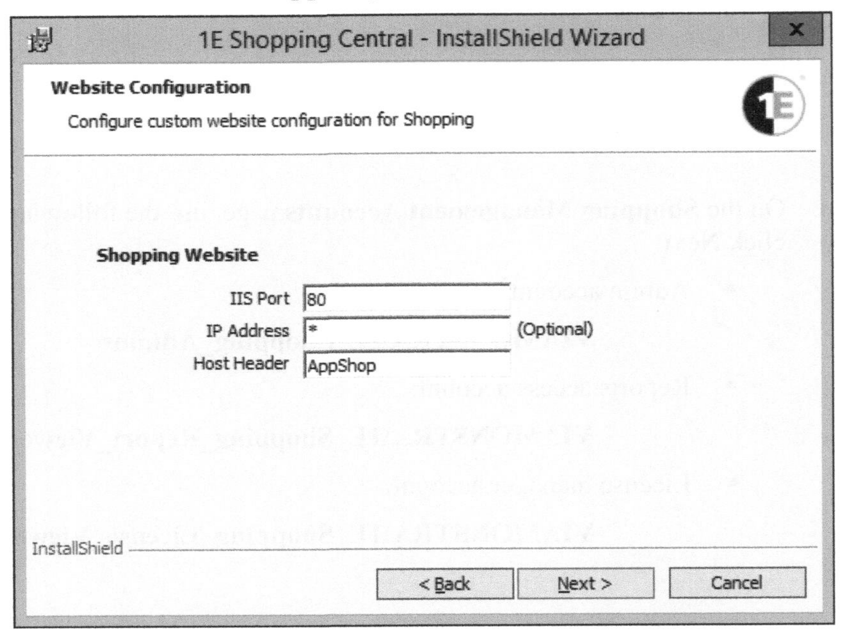

p. On the **Shopping URL Prefix** page, make sure **http://AppShop** is displayed, and click **Next**.

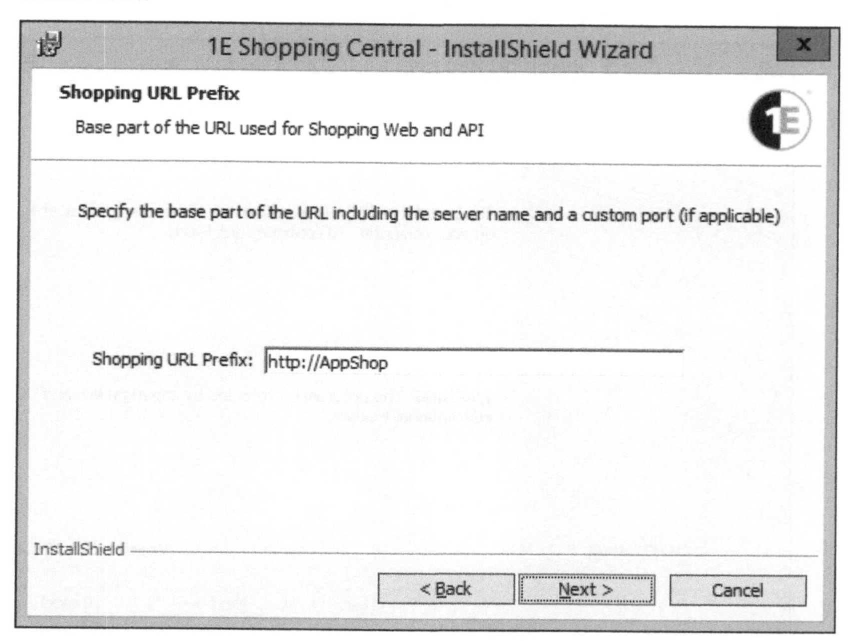

q. Accept the defaults on the remaining wizard pages.

Installing Shopping Receiver

You install the 1E Shopping Receiver on CM01 in this lab.

1. Log on to **CM01** as **VIAMONSTRA\Administrator**.
2. Obtain the 1E Shopping installation files from 1E and copy them to **C:\Labfiles\Sources**.
3. Open an elevated **Command prompt**, navigate to **C:\Labfiles\Sources\shopping.v5.0.100.254** and run the following command:

```
ShoppingReceiver.msi
```

Note: Like the Shopping Central setup, the Shopping Receiver setup must also be run as Administrator, that's why you start it from an elevated command prompt.

4. Configure setup wizard with the following settings:

   a. On the **Welcome** page, click **Next**.

   b. On the **License Agreement** page, accept the terms and click **Next**.

c. On the **Destination Folder** page, keep the default and click **Next**.

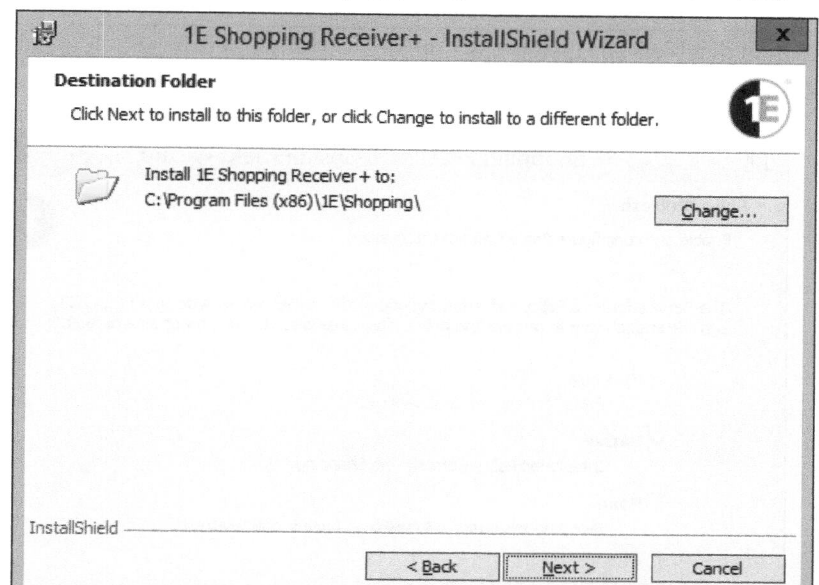

d. On the **Receiver Service Account** page, use the following settings and click **Next**:

- User name: **VIAMONSTRA\1E_Shopping_Receiver**
- Password: **P@ssw0rd**

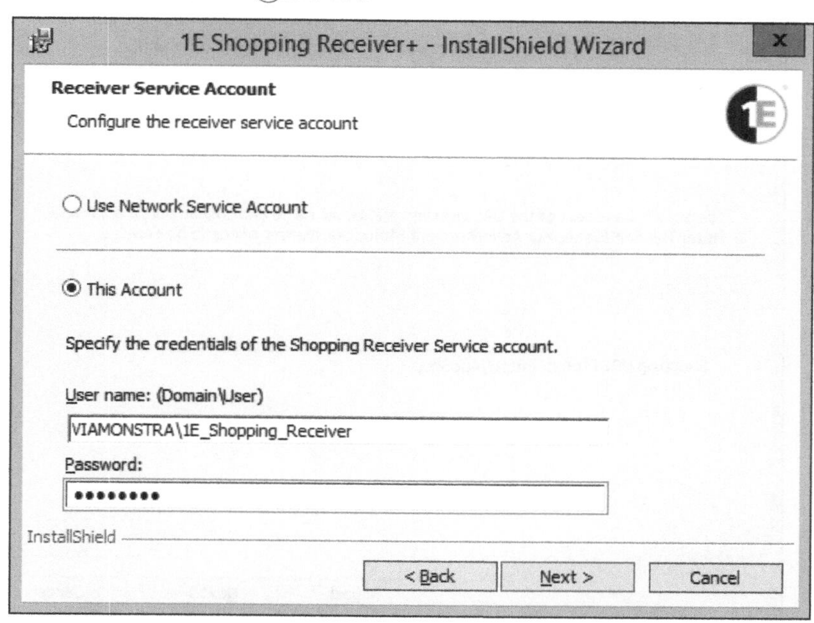

e. On the **Policy Refresh** page, accept the defaults and click **Next**.

Note: 1E Wakeup is disabled because it has not been installed in this lab. You can modify this later by editing the Shopping Receiver Config file.

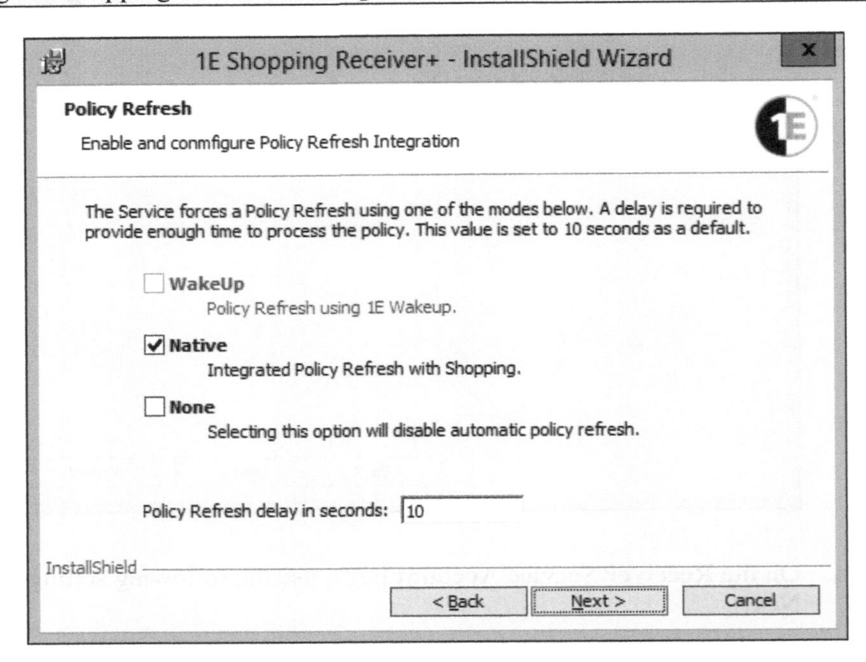

f. On the **Shopping URL Prefix** page, type **http://AppShop** and click **Next**.

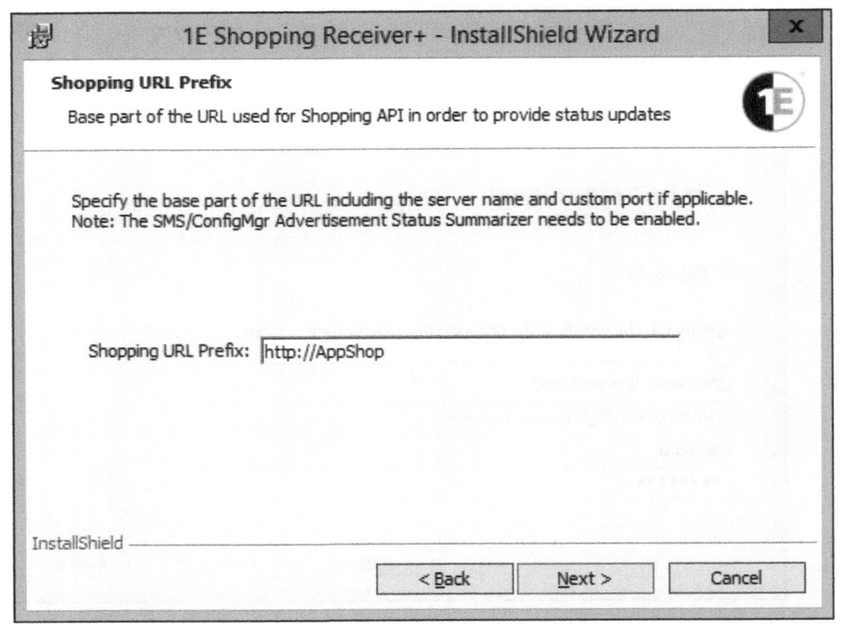

g. On the **Default Advanced Client Flags** page, select **Always download from DP** and click **Next**.

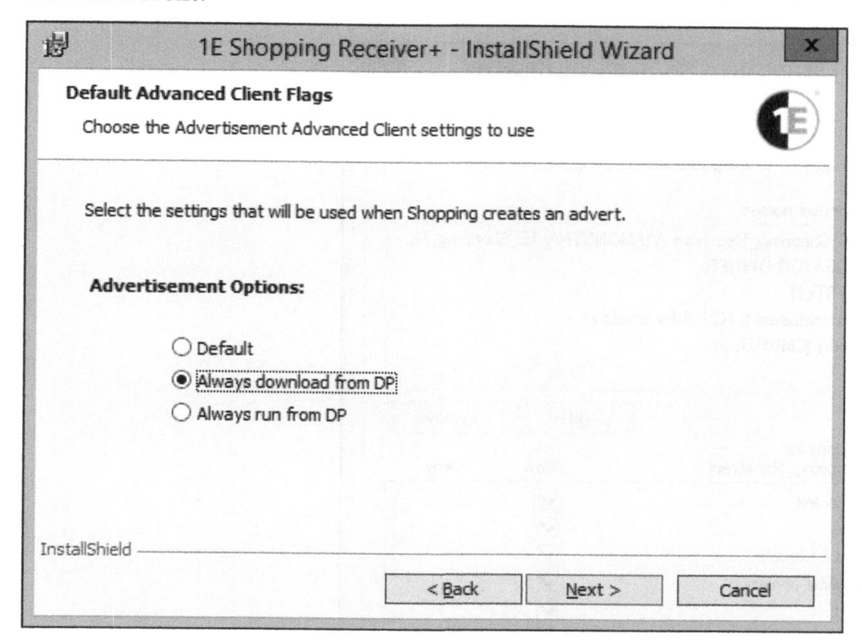

h. On the **Ready to Install the Program** page, click **Install**.

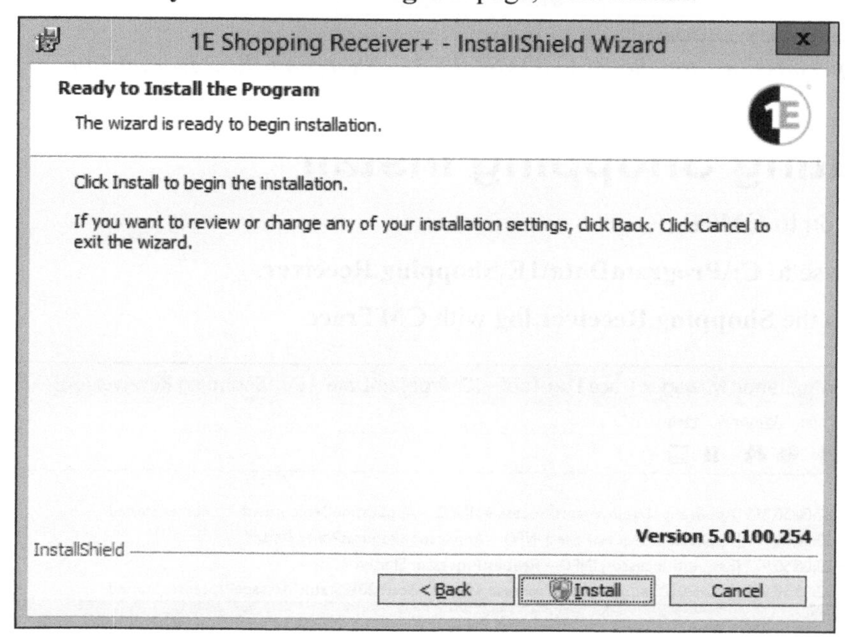

i. When setup is completed, click **Finish**.

5. Grant the **VIAMONSTRA\1E_Shopping_Receivers** group **Full control** access to the **C:\ProgramData\1E\Shopping.Receiver** folder and click **OK**.

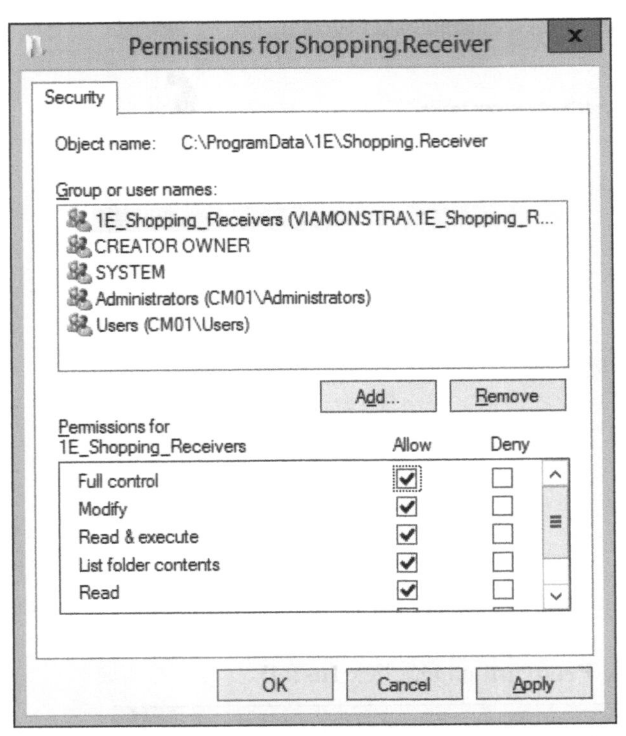

Adding permissions for the VIAMONSTRA\1E_Shopping_Receivers group.

Validating Shopping Install

1. Log on to **CM01**.
2. Browse to **C:\ProgramData\1E\Shopping.Receiver**.
3. Open the **Shopping.Receiver.log** with **CMTrace**.

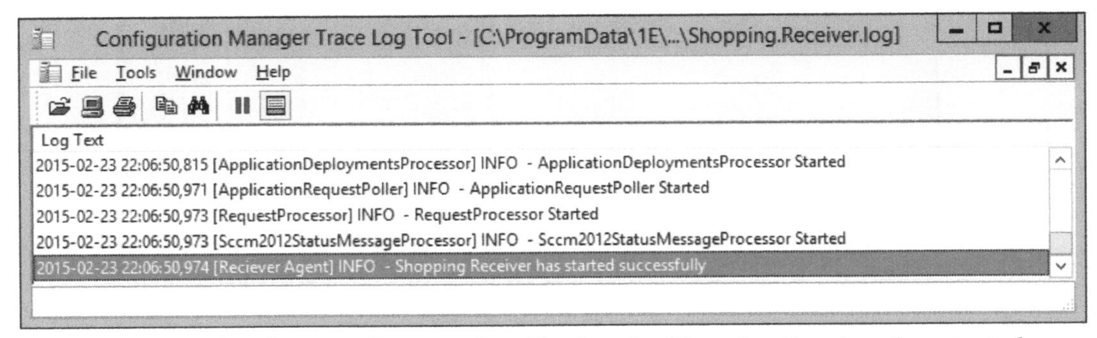

Confirming via the Shopping.Receiver.log file that the Shopping Receiver has started.

4. Ensure that the **Shopping Receiver** service has started properly.
5. Browse to **C:\Program Files (x86)\1E\Shopping\Shopping.Receiver**.
6. Open **shopping.receiver.config** from an elevated **Notepad** instance.
7. Modify the **<level value ="INFO"/>** to **ALL**.

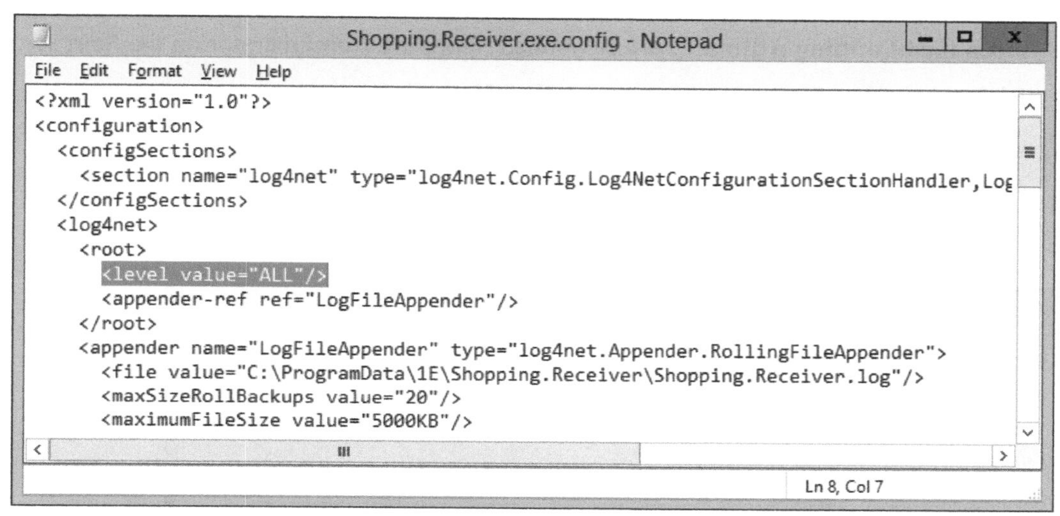

Changing the debug logging value for Shopping Receiver.

8. Return to **MDT01**.
9. Browse to **C:\inetpub\logs\LogFiles\W3SVC2**.
10. Open the most recent log file using **CMTrace**.
11. Review the log file and look for communication from **CM01 (192.168.1.214)**. This is the Shopping Receiver communicating with the Shopping Central API, searching for pending requests. The Shopping Receiver continues to poll this API, and as job orders are created inside the Shopping database, the receiver picks them off from here.

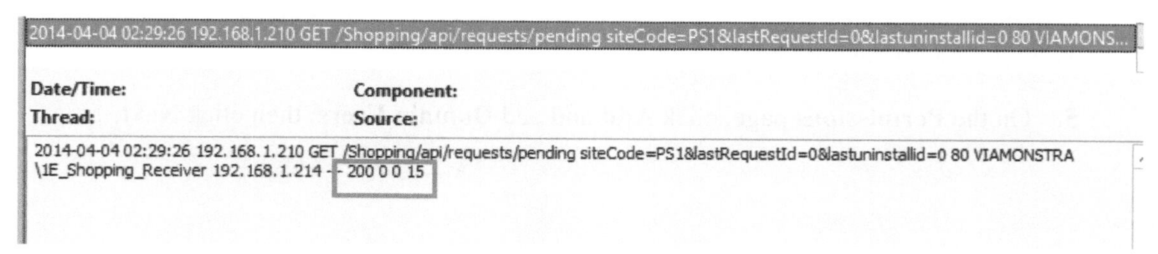

Reviewing the Shopping Central log entries in the IIS logs.

12. Open and review **C:\ProgramData\1E\ShoppingCentral\ShoppingCentral.log**.

Adding an Application to Shopping

To test 1E Shopping's configuration, add a sample application to the Shopping portal. Then you log on to a PC and try to install the application from the Shopping portal. You then verify that the collection and deployment have been created properly and the application has installed.

1. Log on to **MDT01**.
2. Open the **Shopping Admin Console** (named Shopping Administrator on the Start screen).
3. Right-click **User Categories** and select **New User Category**.
4. Configure the following settings and click **Next**:
    - Name: **NAM-Engineering Software**
    - Description: **North America Engineering Applications**

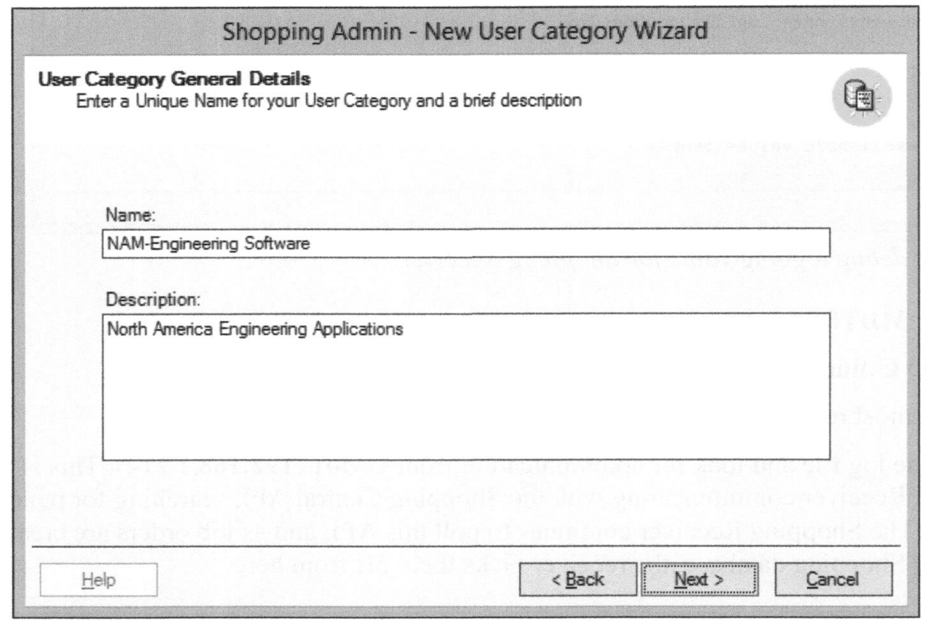

Adding a User Category in Shopping.

5. On the **Permissions** page, click **Add** and add **Domain Users**; then click **Next**.

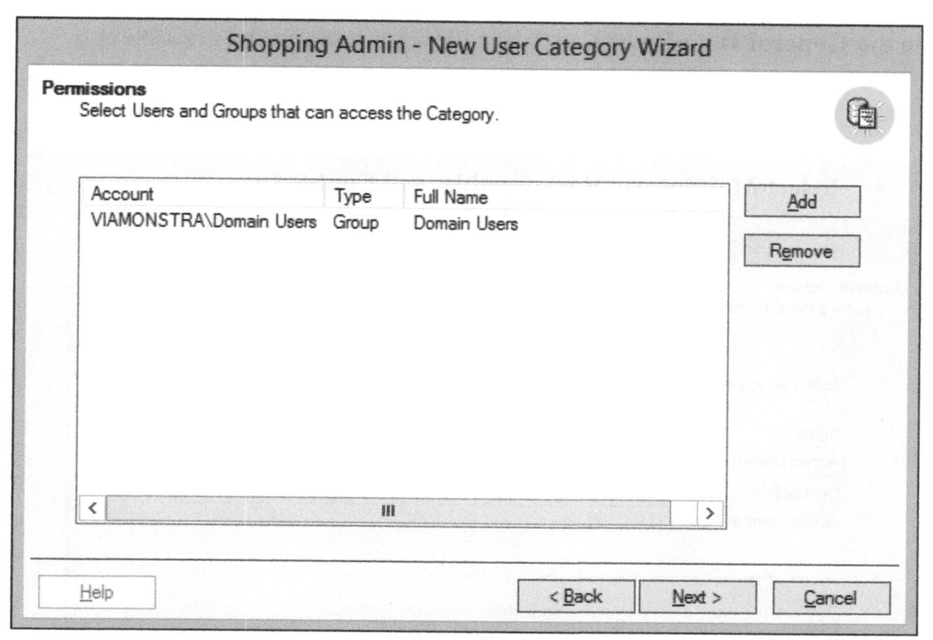

Granting rights to the application in Shopping.

6. Click **Finish**.
7. Right-click **Applications**, and then select **New ConfigMgr Application**.
8. Configure with the following options:
   a. On the **Welcome** page, click **Next**.

b. On the **General Details** page, use the following settings and click **Next**:

- Name: **Adobe Reader**
- Description: **Adobe Acrobat Reader** (Note that this can be HTML text.)
- Select **Mandatory**, **Reshoppable**, and **Enabled**

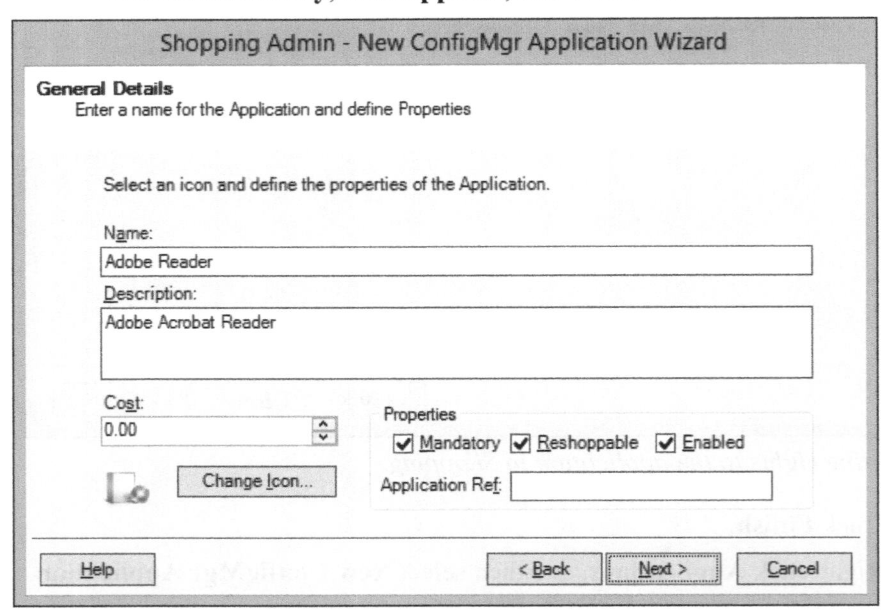

c. On the **User Categories** page, select **NAM-Engineering Software**.

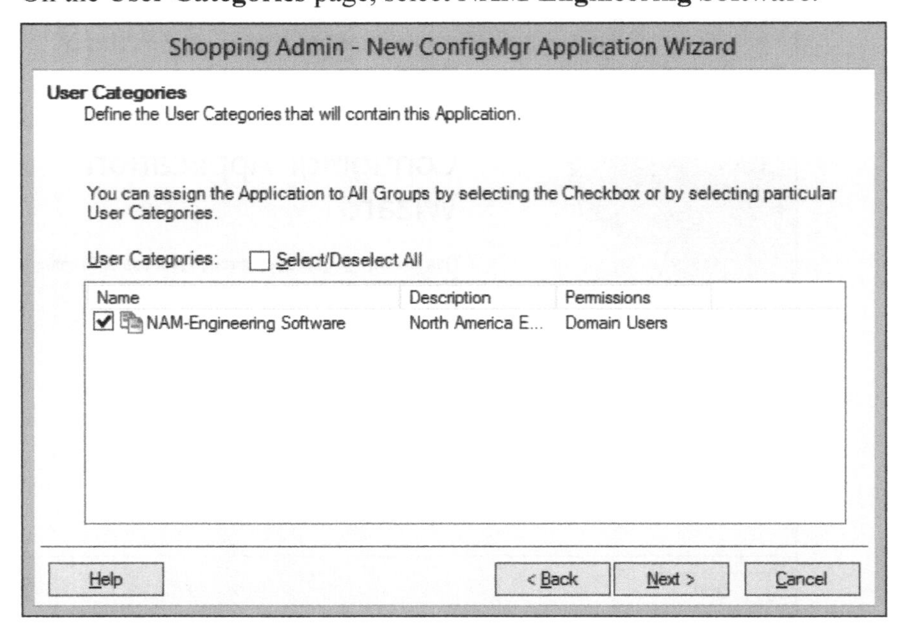

d. On the **ConfigMgr Sites** page, accept the defaults and click **Next**.

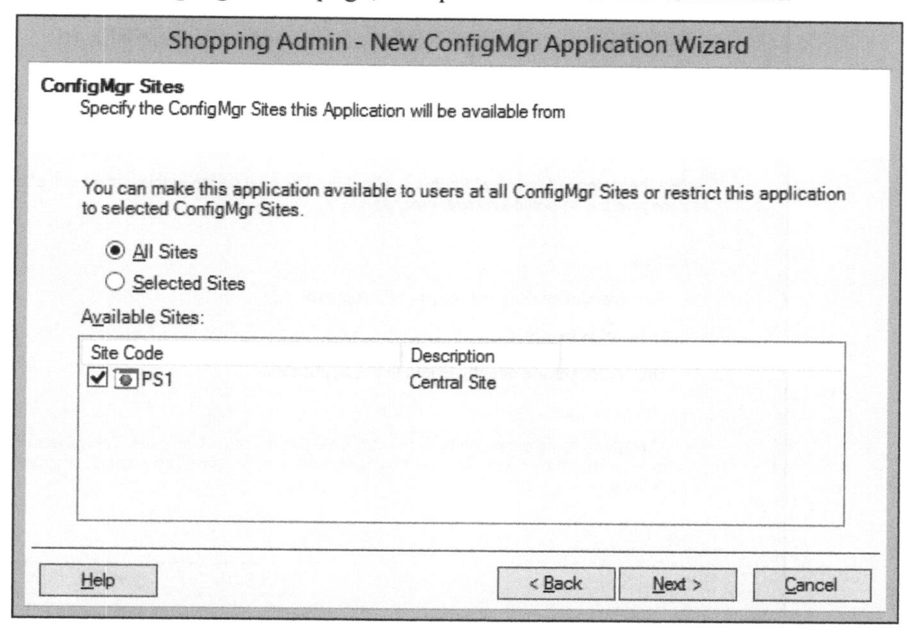

e. On the **Central or Branch Management** page, select **Central Administration** and click **Next**.

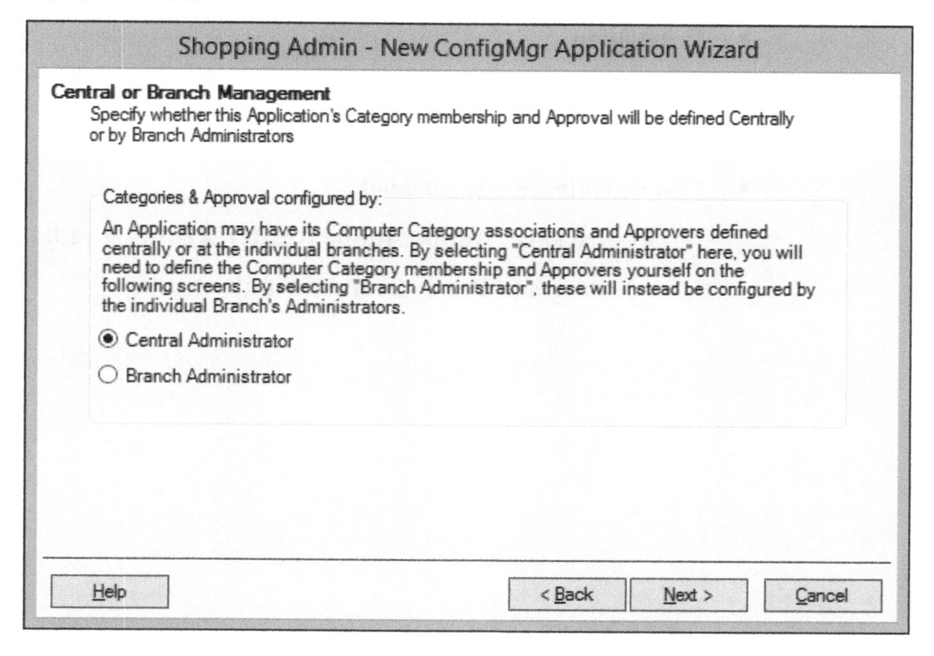

f. On the **Approval** page, select **None** and click **Next**.

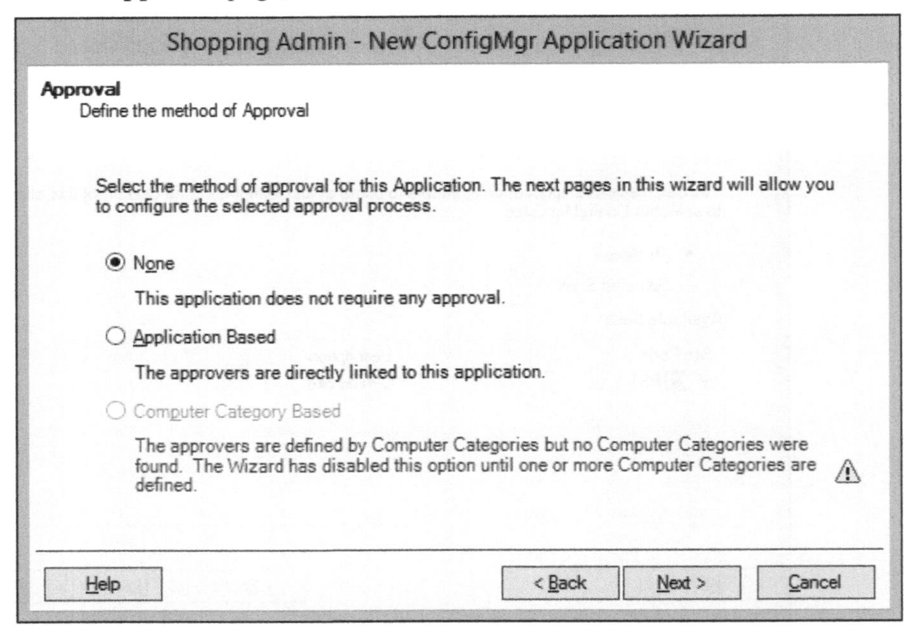

g. On the **ConfigMgr Package and Program Details** page, use the following settings and click **Next**:

- Installation
  - Package: **Adobe Adobe Reader XI-AWD 11.0**
  - Program: **Per-system Unattended**
- Can be Uninstalled: **Selected**
  - Package: **Adobe Adobe Reader XI-AWD 11.0**
  - Program: **Per-system uninstall**

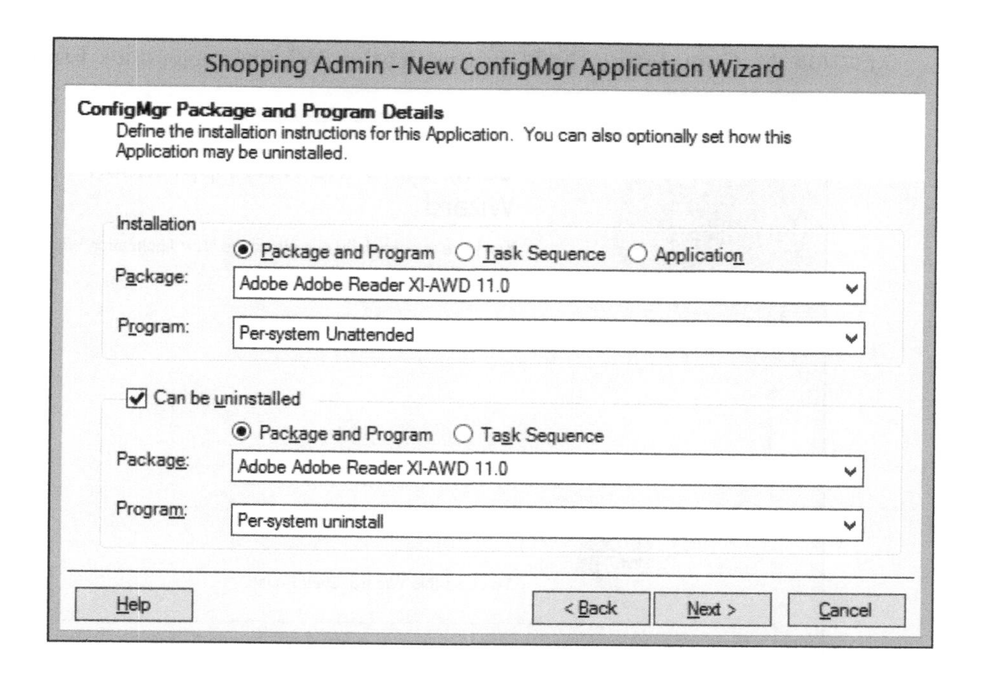

h. On the **Licensing Details** page, keep the defaults and click **Next**.

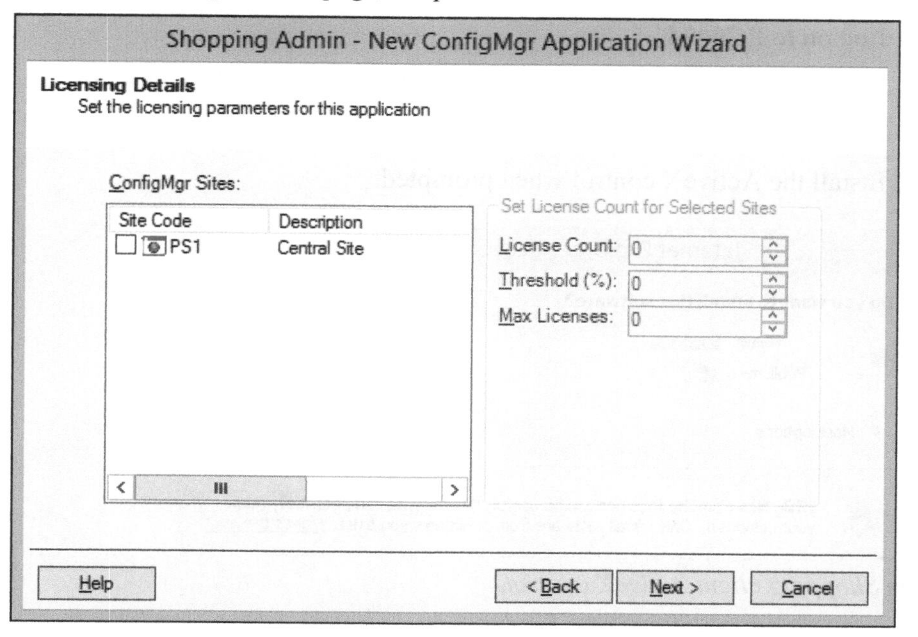

i. On the **Completing the New Application Wizard** page, click **Finish**.

9. Log on to **PC0004**.
10. Uninstall the existing Adobe Reader (installed by the task sequence).
11. Open **http://appshop/shopping**.
12. Install the ActiveX control when prompted.

The Shopping client ActiveX control.

Note: The ActiveX control for Shopping is called shoppingclientidentity.msi. This is normally packaged and deployed to clients as part of the Shopping deployment.

13. Hover over **Adobe Acrobat Reader**, and select **Request**.

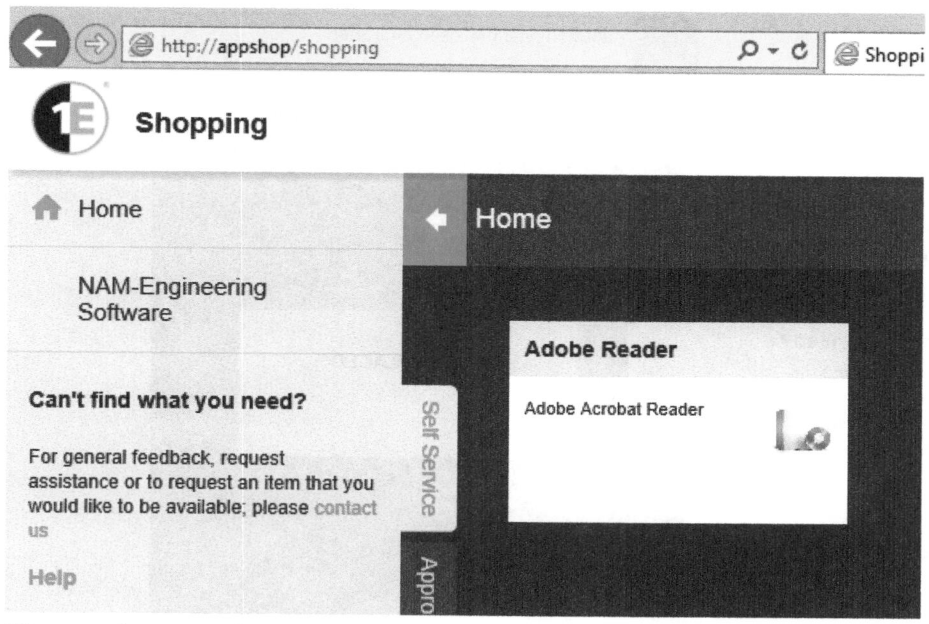

Viewing the main Shopping Enterprise App Store for the first time.

Requesting your first application in the Shopping Enterprise App Store.

The portal should now show that the order has been placed.

Validating that your order was placed.

14. Run a machine policy refresh.

Real World Note: In a production rollout, you would normally add the 1E_Shopping_Receivers group to the Local Admins group on each workstation. This allows the Shopping Receiver to trigger a machine policy refresh remotely.

15. Open **C:\Windows\CCM\Logs\execmgr.log**. Notice that the install event has been raised.

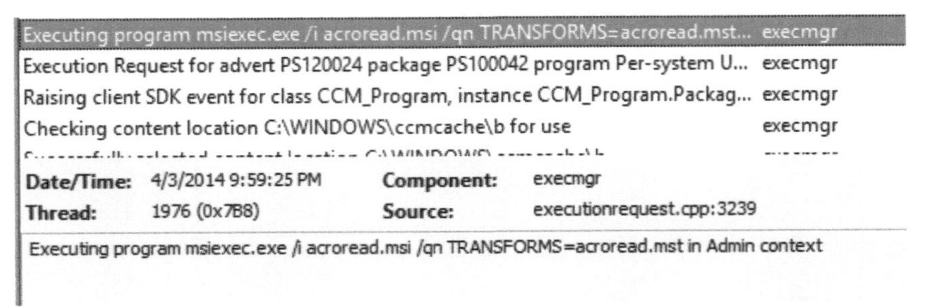

Reviewing the logs to ensure that the software is being distributed via ConfigMgr.

16. Check the desktop of **PC0004** and validate that **Adobe Reader** is there.

Validating your software install via Shopping.

17. Open **Software Center** and click **Installation Status**.

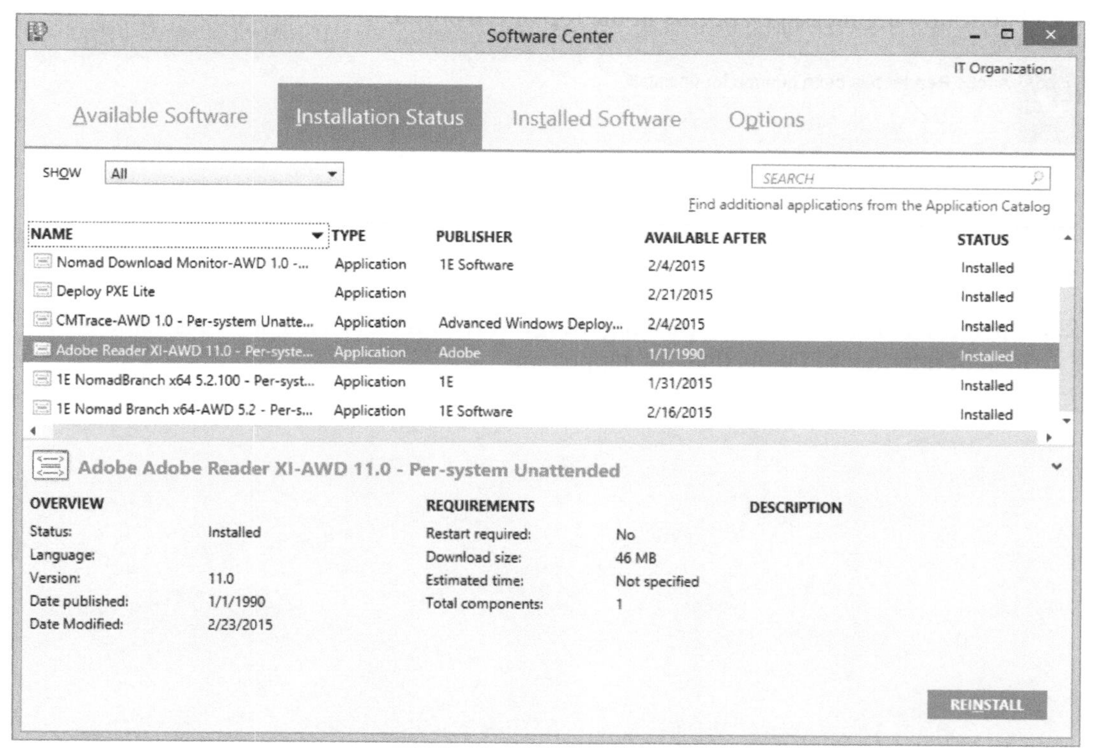

Validating that the shopped application shows up in Software Center.

18. Now try uninstalling this package. Return to **http://appshop/shopping**.
19. Select **My Software / All Orders / Uninstall**.

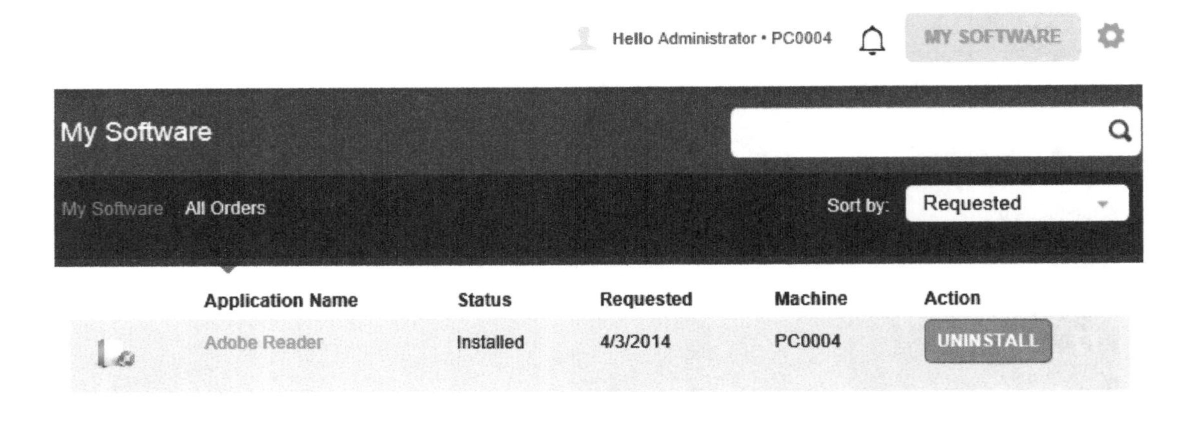

Uninstalling the application from the Shopping Enterprise App Store.

The following message appears at the top of the portal.

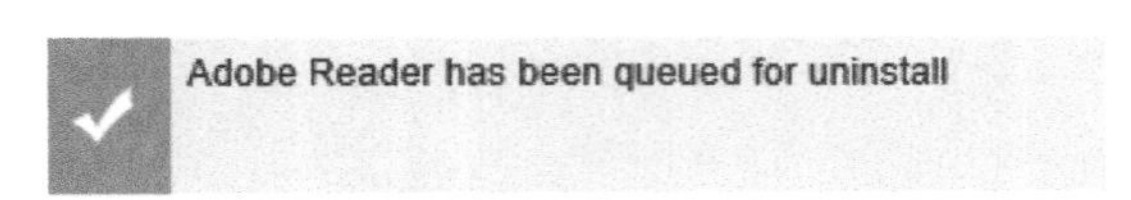

The validation screen from the Shopping Enterprise App Store.

20. Run another machine policy refresh and then open the **Execmgr.log** again.
21. Now look at what is happening on the backend. Log on to **MDT01**.
22. Open the **IIS** logs in **C:\inetpub\logs\LogFiles\W3SVC2.** This provides some great insight into the API calls that are happening.

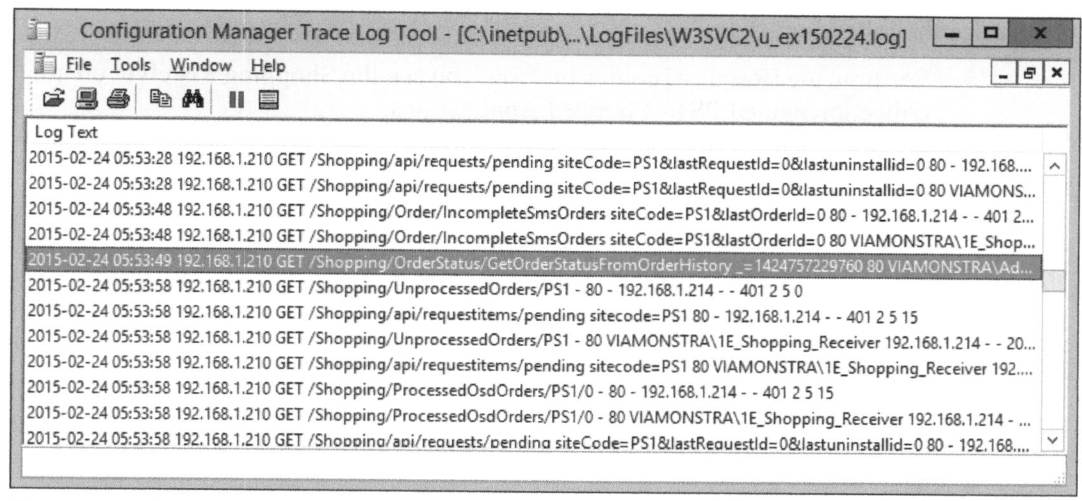

Reviewing the IIS logs for the calls to the Shopping order and API web services.

23. Open **C:\ProgramData\1E\Shopping\shopping.log**. Notice the order being placed for PC0004 for Adobe Reader.

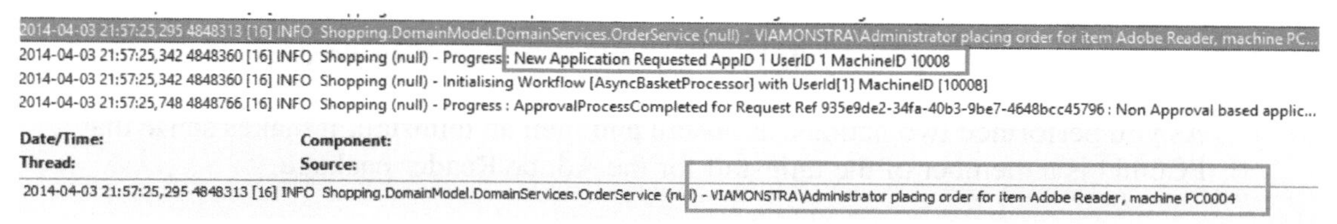

Viewing the Shopping.log file for the application request.

24. Now look at the **ConfigMgr** server **CM01** and how the **Shopping Receiver** interacts with the Shopping APIs to build the collections and deployments.

25. Log on to **CM01** and open **C:\ProgramData\1E\Shopping.Receiver**.

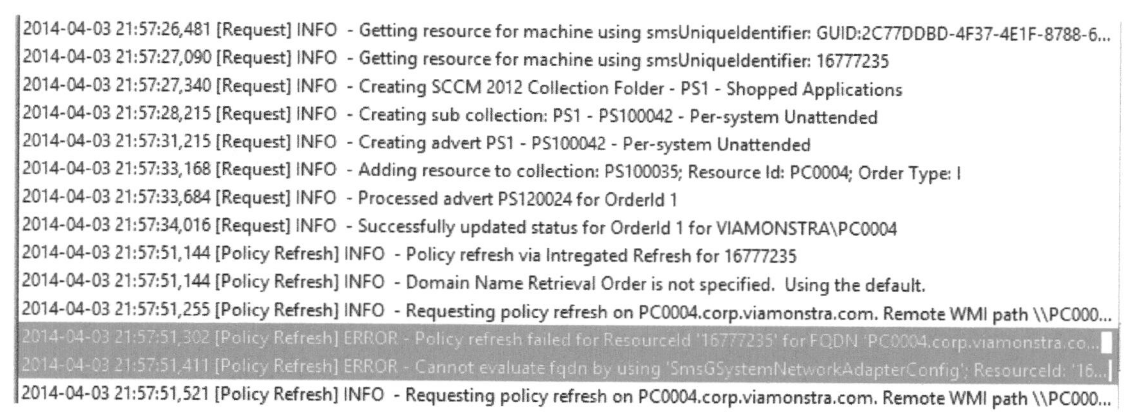

Viewing the Shopping Receiver log to validate that the order has been placed.

Notice the following:

a. See how the [Request] comes in. Now you see the Shopping Receiver creating a collection named PS1 - Shopped Applications.

b. Then it creates an install collection called PS1 - PS100042 - Per-system Unattended.

c. Next it adds PC0004 to this collection.

d. See the [Policy Refresh] error message, which occurs because the Shopping Receivers Group is not a member of Local Admins on PC0004.

26. Open the **ConfigMgr console** and browse to **Device Collections**.

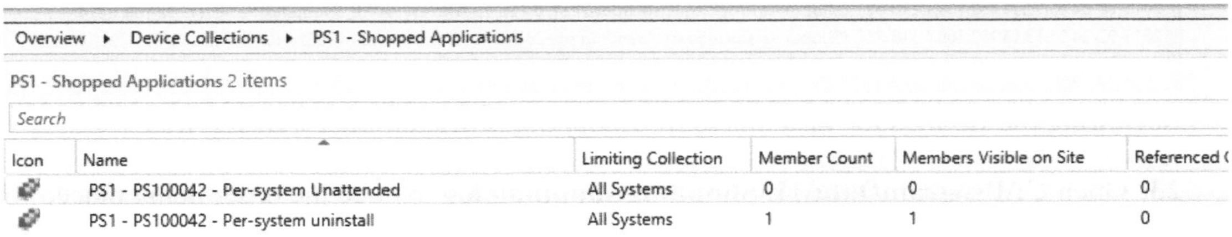

Overview ▸ Device Collections ▸ PS1 - Shopped Applications

PS1 - Shopped Applications 2 items

Search

Icon	Name	Limiting Collection	Member Count	Members Visible on Site	Referenced (
	PS1 - PS100042 - Per-system Unattended	All Systems	0	0	0
	PS1 - PS100042 - Per-system uninstall	All Systems	1	1	0

Validating the collections in ConfigMgr created by the Shopping Receiver.

As you performed two actions, an install and then an uninstall, it makes sense that PC0004 is a member of the uninstall for the Adobe Reader package.

Creating a Banner Item in the Shopping Portal

Banner items are a great way to showcase popular installs or upgrade programs that an organization could have in place. For example, a deployment of MS Office 2013 could be featured in the portal.

1. Log on to **PC0004**.
2. Open **http://appshop/shopping**.
3. Click **Administration**, and then click **Manager Banners / Create New**.

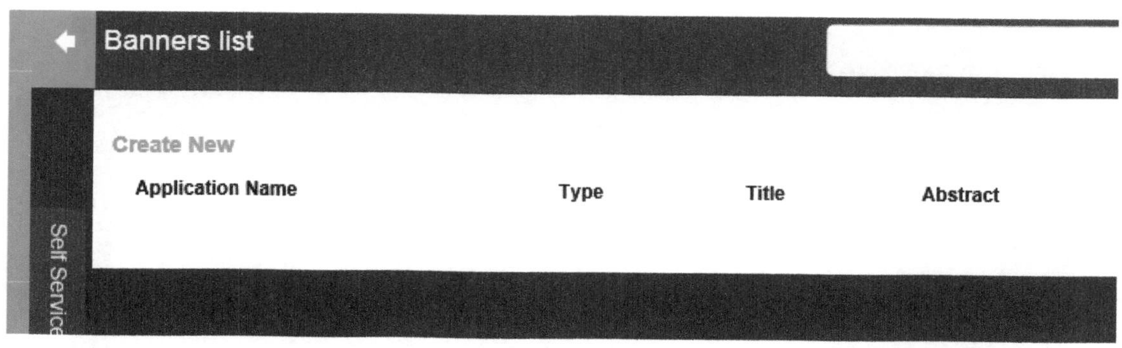

Creating a new banner item in the Shopping Enterprise App Store.

4. For **Application Name**, type **A** and then click **Adobe Reader**.

Note: When creating a new banner, don't type the full application name. Instead, select the application in the list, or you will get an error saying "Please enter a valid application Name."

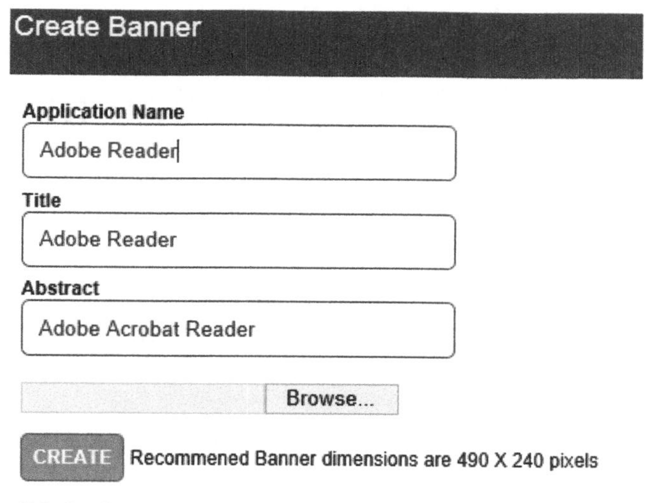

Choosing the application for the banner.

5. Type **\\MDT01\C$\Program Files (x86)\1E\Shopping\WebSite\Shopping\Assets\Uploads\Images\slide-1.jpg**.
6. Click **Create**.
7. In the top left corner, click **Home**.

Viewing the application banner in the Shopping Enterprise App Store.

Creating a Self-Service OSD Application in Shopping

Now that you can see how to create a banner item, wouldn't it be nice to allow end users to self-serve their very own OSD refresh. Well, they can, and you set it up now!

1. Log on to **CM01**.
2. In the **Deploy Windows 8.1 Refresh - Shopping Self Serve - DO NOT MOFIFY** collection, remove the existing members.

> **Note:** This collection was created as part of the lab hydration script. For production, you simply create this collection manually.

3. Locate the **Windows 8.1 Enterprise x64-Gold-DynamicPackages** task sequence.
4. Right-click **Windows 8.1 Enterprise-Gold- DynamicPackages** and click **Deploy**.
5. Create the deployment with the following settings:
   - Task Sequence: **Windows 8.1 Enterprise x64-Gold-DynamicPackages**
   - Collection: **Deploy Windows 8.1 Refresh - Shopping Self Serve - DO NOT MODIFY**
   - Purpose: **Required**
   - Make available to the following: **Only Configuration Manger Clients**
   - Assignment Schedule: **As Soon as possible**

- User Experience:
    - Software Installation: **Selected**
    - System Restart (If required to complete the installation): **Selected**
- Alerts: **<Default>**
- Deployment Options: **Download content locally when needed by running task sequence**

6. Log on to **MDT01** and open the **Shopping Admin Console** (Shopping Administration).
7. Right-click **Applications** and select **New OS Deployment**.

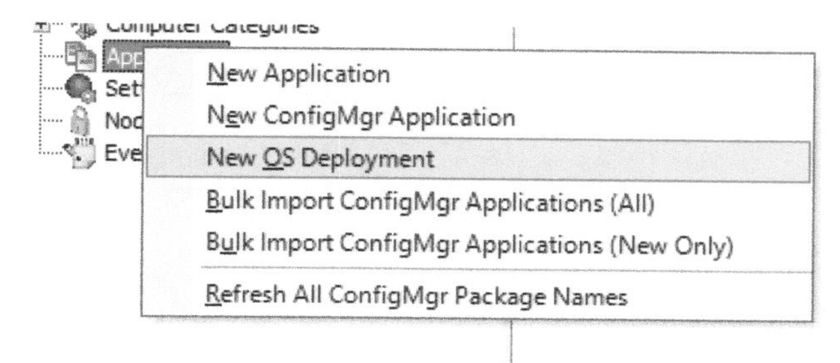

Creating a new OS deployment in the Shopping Central Admin Console.

8. Configure the OS deployment with the following settings:
    a. On the **Welcome** page, click **Next**.

b. On the **General Details** page, use the following settings and click **Next**:

- Name: **Get Windows 8.1**
- Description: **NAM Windows 8.1 Corporate OS Refresh**

c. On the **SMS/Config Mgr collection** page, use the following settings and click **Next**:

- **Deploy Windows 8.1 Refresh - Shopping Self Serve - DO NOT Modify**
- Advertisement: **Windows8.1Enterprisex64-Gold-DynamicPackages….**

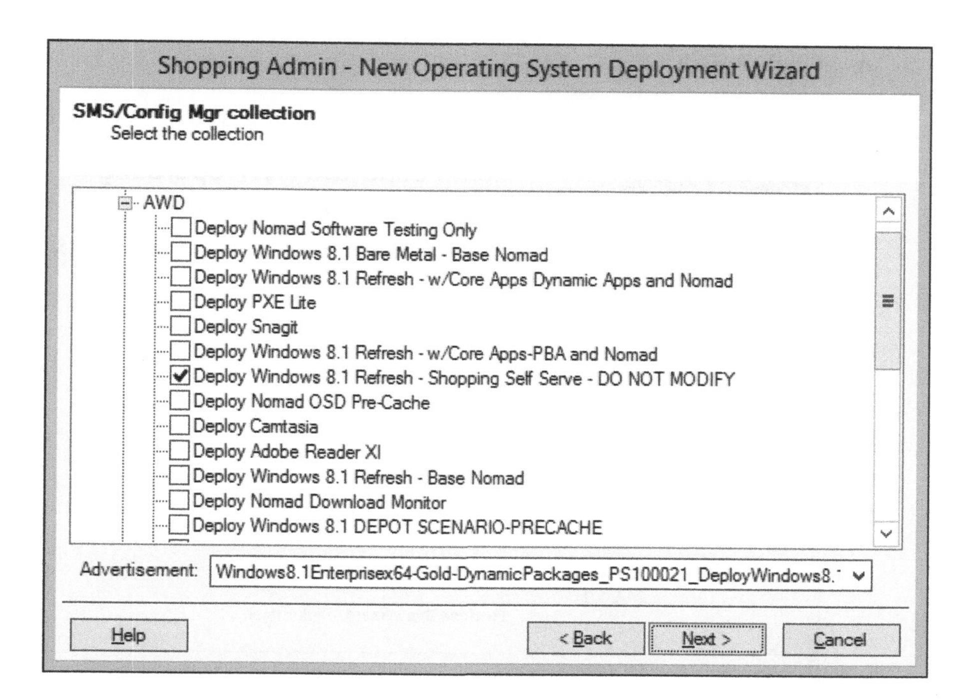

d. On the **Permissions** page, click **Add** and add **Domain Users**; then click **Next**.

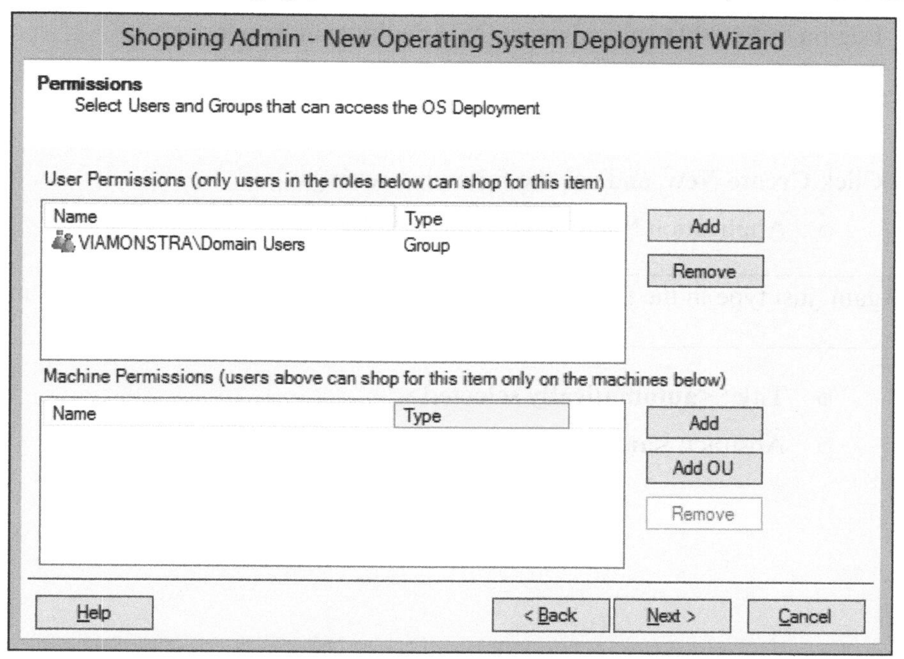

e. Click **Finish**.

9. Log on to **PC0004** and create an OSD deployment banner.
10. Open **http://appshop/shopping**.
11. Click **Administration / Manager Banners**.
12. Click **Create New**, and use the following settings:
    - Application Name: **Get Windows 8.1**

Note: Again, just type in the first characters in the name, and then select "Get Windows 8.1" from this list.

- Title: **<automatically selected>**
- Abstract: **<automatically selected>**

Create Banner

Application Name

Get Windows 8.1

Title

Get Windows 8.1

Abstract

NAM Windows 8.1 Corporate OS Refresh

Browse...

CREATE Recommened Banner dimensions are 490 X 240 pixels

P.S. Creating an OSD banner will show all available OSDs in shopping.

Creating a banner item for the OS deployment in the Shopping Enterprise App Store.

13. Click **Browse** and locate **\\MDT01\C$\Program Files (x86)\1E\Shopping\WebSite\Shopping\Assets\Uploads\Images \slide-1.jpg**.
14. Click **Create**.
15. Browse to the **Home** page and validate that the **Get Windows 8.1** banner has appeared.

Viewing the new OSD banner in the Shopping Enterprise App Store.

End User Self-Service OSD

In this guide, you perform an end-user type OSD refresh from PC0004.

1. Log on to **PC0004**.
2. Using the **Configuration Manager** control panel applet, set the ConfigMgr 2012 client cache size to **20** GB.
3. If the **C:\StateStore** folder exist (from an earlier refresh of PC0004), continue on step 5, if not skip to step 8.
4. Copy the **\\CM01\C$\Program Files (x86)\Windows Kits\8.1\Assessment and Deployment Kit\User State Migration Tool\amd64** folder to **C:**. Then rename **C:\amd64** to **C:\USMT**.
5. Delete the **C:\StateStore** folder by starting an elevated **Command prompt** and run the following commands (press **Enter** after each command):

```
cd C:\USMT
usmtutils /rd C:\StateStore
```

6. Reboot **PC0004** and log on again.
7. Open **http://appshop/shopping**.
8. Click **Launch** on the **Get Windows 8.1** banner.
9. Configure the **OSD Self-Serve Wizard** with the following settings:
   a. Introduction: Click **Next**.

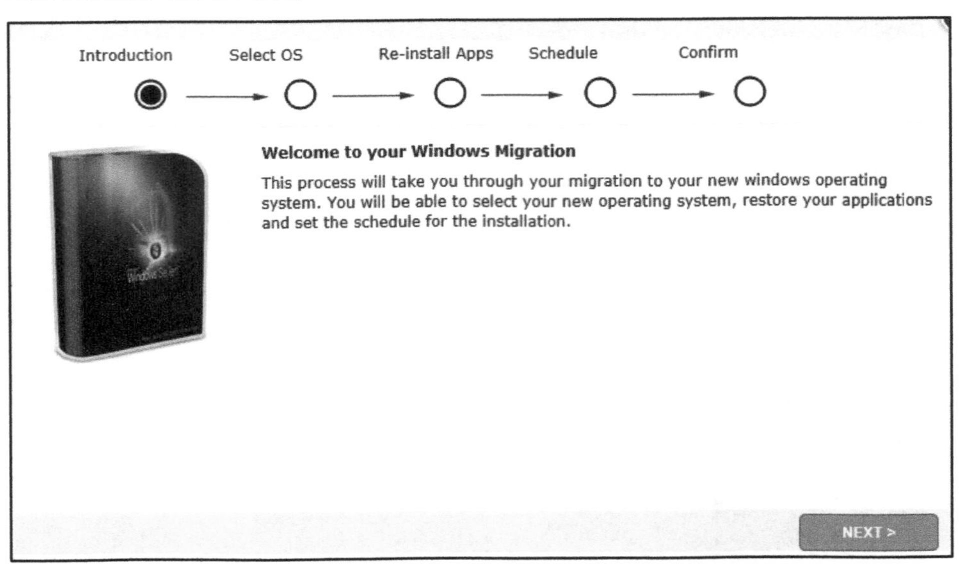

b. Select OS: Select **Get Windows 8.1**.

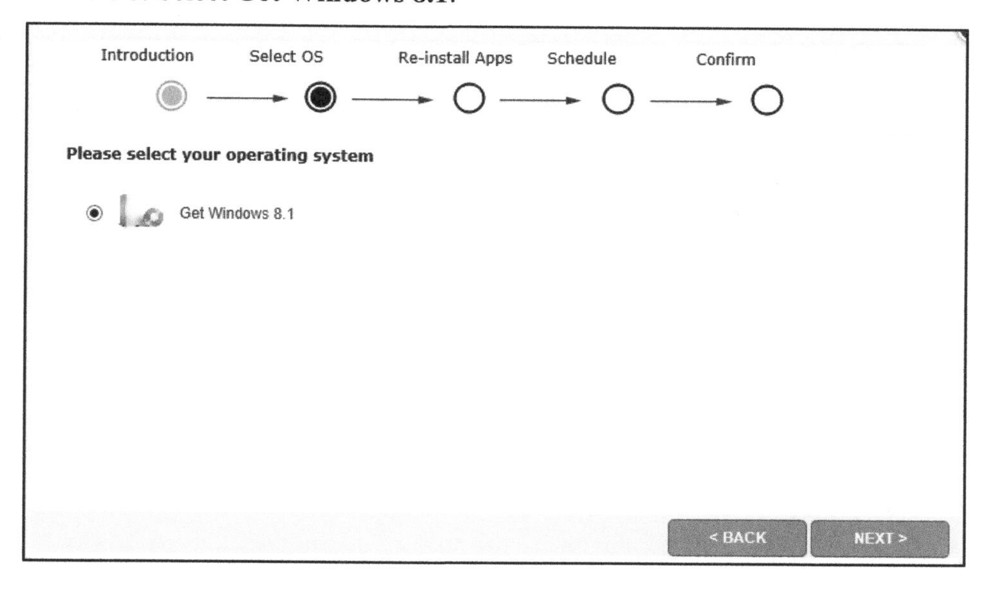

c. Re-install Apps: Click **Next**.

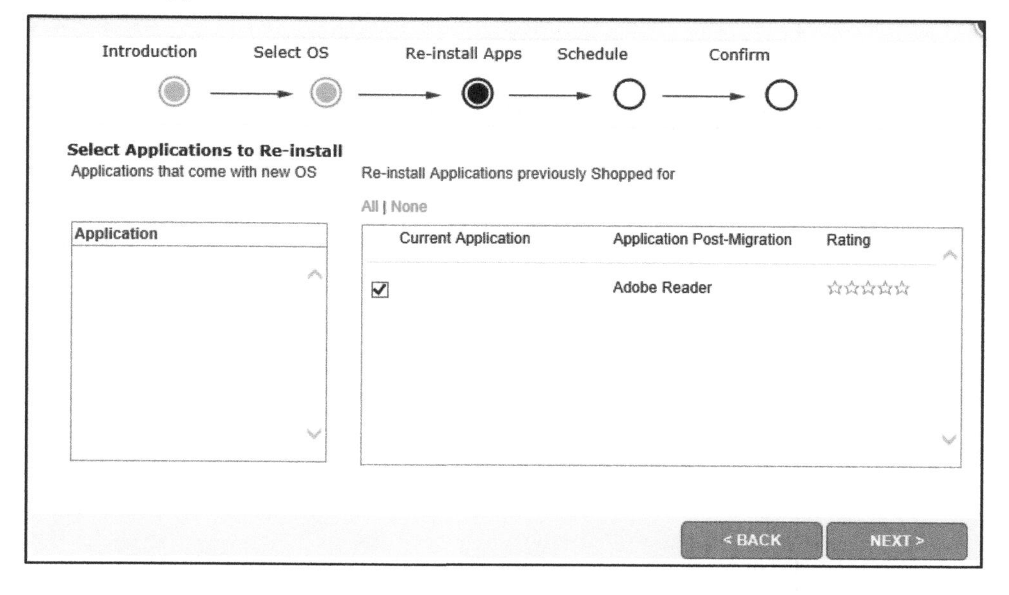

- The Application pane is a static list that can be configured to show the end user the core apps that are included in the image.
- The Current Application pane with Adobe being reinstalled shows that this application has been previously shopped.

d. Schedule: Select **Schedule Immediately**.

Real World Note: Normally you would limit the number of installs per day to prevent a burden on the service desk and desktop teams during migration.

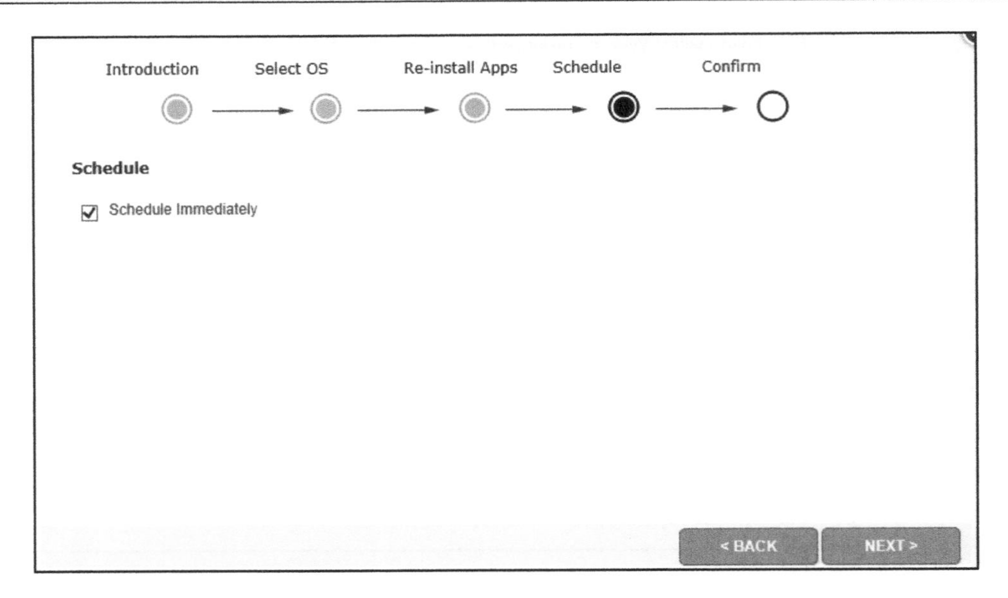

e. Confirm: Select the check box **I confirm that I have backed up my system** and then click **Finish**.

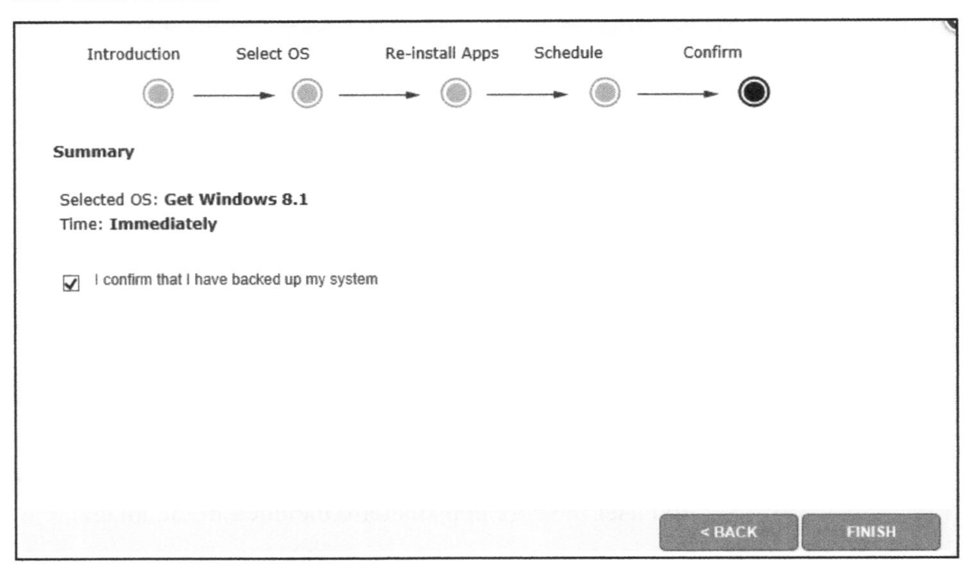

10. Perform a machine policy refresh. The refresh will commence shortly.

11. While you wait, validate that things have been created properly on CM01.

    On **CM01**, open the **ConfigMgr console** and validate that **PC0004** has been added to the **Deploy Windows 8.1 Refresh - Shopping Self Serve - DO NOT MODIFY** collection.

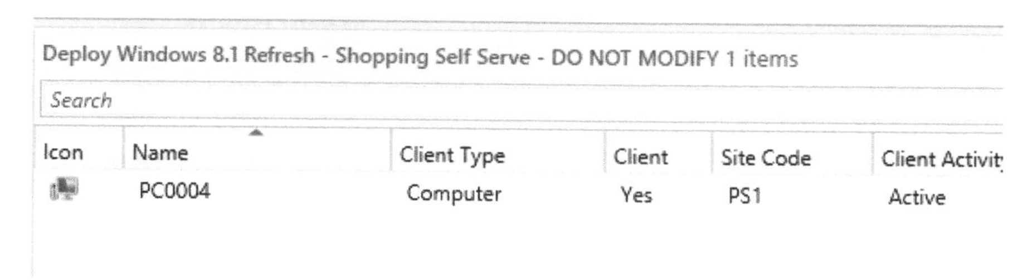

Validating that the machine has been placed into the OSD collection.

12. Open **C:\ProgramData\1E\Shopping.Receiver\shopping.receiver.log**.

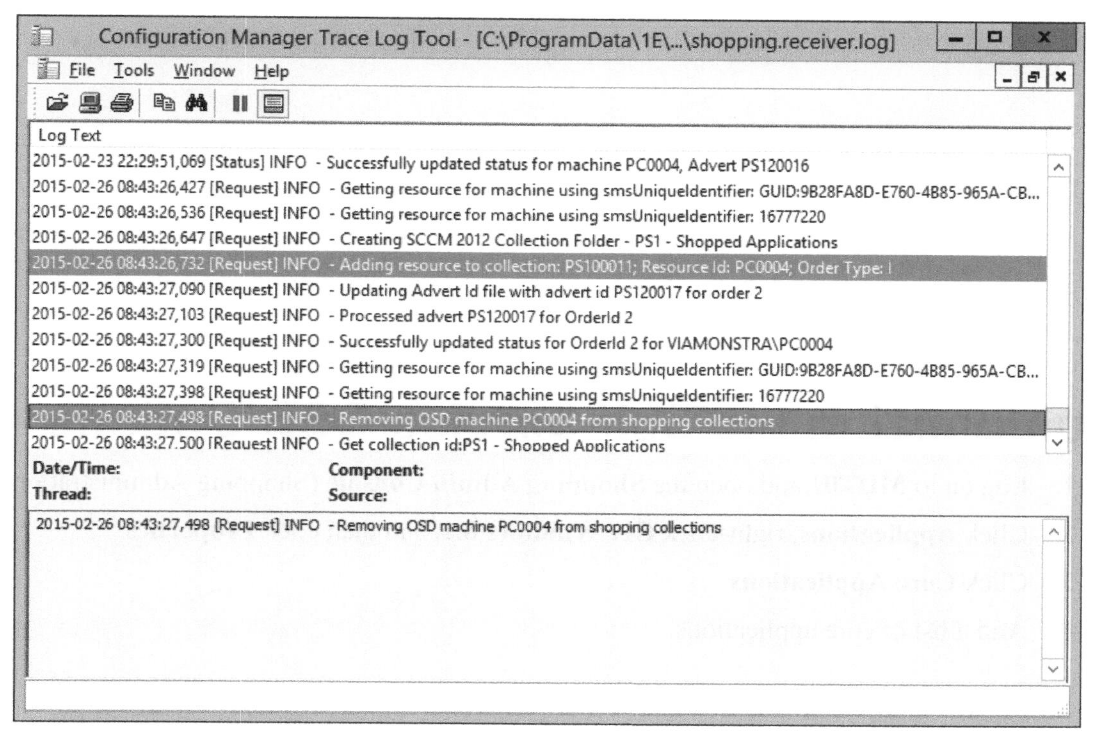

Reviewing the order in the Shopping Receiver log file.

> **Real World Note:** When a self-service Shopping order has been placed, 1E Shopping automatically removes machines from existing shopping collections.

13. **Return** to **PC0004**, and your refresh should now be in progress.

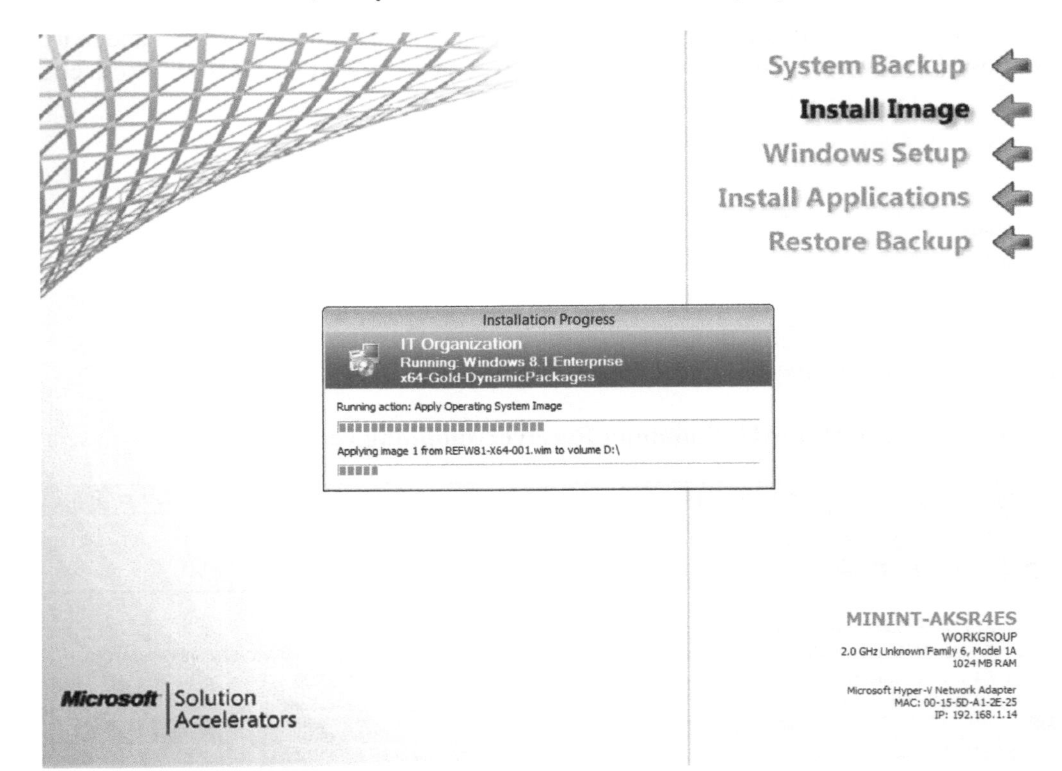

Validating that the OSD process has been initiated automatically by the end user.

Customizing the Self-Service OSD Options

1. Log on to **MDT01** and open the **Shopping Admin Console** (Shopping Administration).
2. Click **Applications**, right-click **Get Windows 8.1**, and then click **Properties**.
3. Click **Core Applications**.
4. Add a list of core applications.

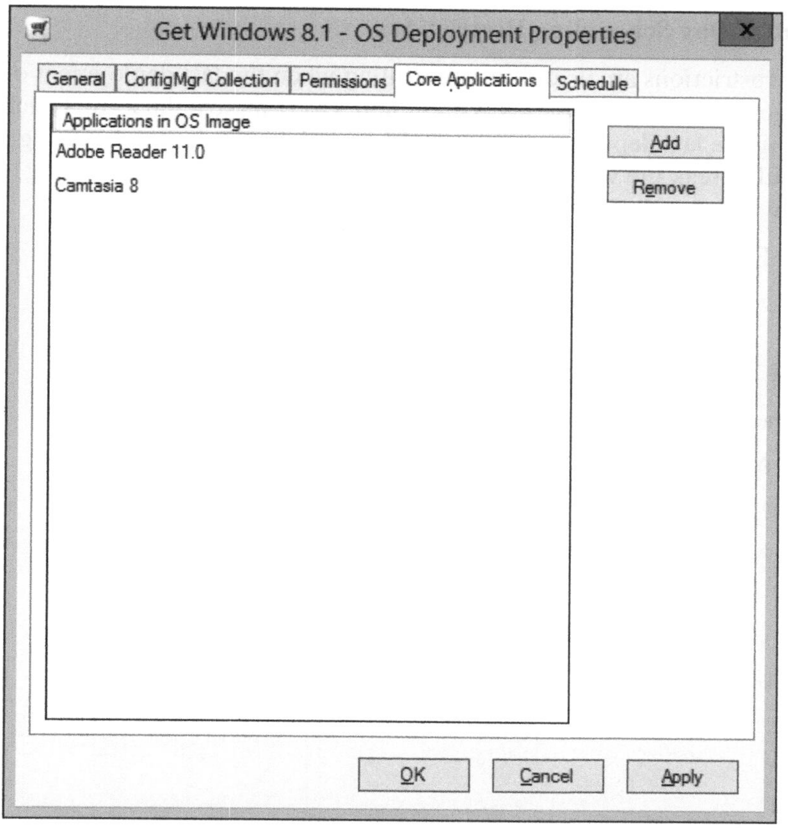

Customizing the Self-Service OSD Wizard core applications.

Real World Note: This is typically a list of applications that are automatically installed as core apps in the Gold image. This is an informative list only and doesn't have any backend functions for installing applications.

5. Click the **Schedule** tab.
6. Review the following:
   - **Maximum Deploys Per Day:**

     This is an important setting because it can help throttle the number of deployments per day and allow the service desk time to keep up with post-deployment calls.
   - **Enable Scheduling Restrictions:**

     This turns on the scheduling restrictions for a period of time and is great for limiting the number of deployments during a pilot phase. For example, 1000 machines will be deployed during a pilot deployment.

- **Enable Time of Day Scheduling Restrictions:**

  Time-of-day restrictions are useful for controlling when the last deployment of the day can go. For example, if it takes eight hours to complete the Zero Touch refresh, setting the last deployment for 8:00 PM would make sense. Anything after that would break the window, and you could have deployments running during the day.

- **Exclude the Following Days:**

  Is very useful to exclude holidays like July the 1st… (Canada Day!)

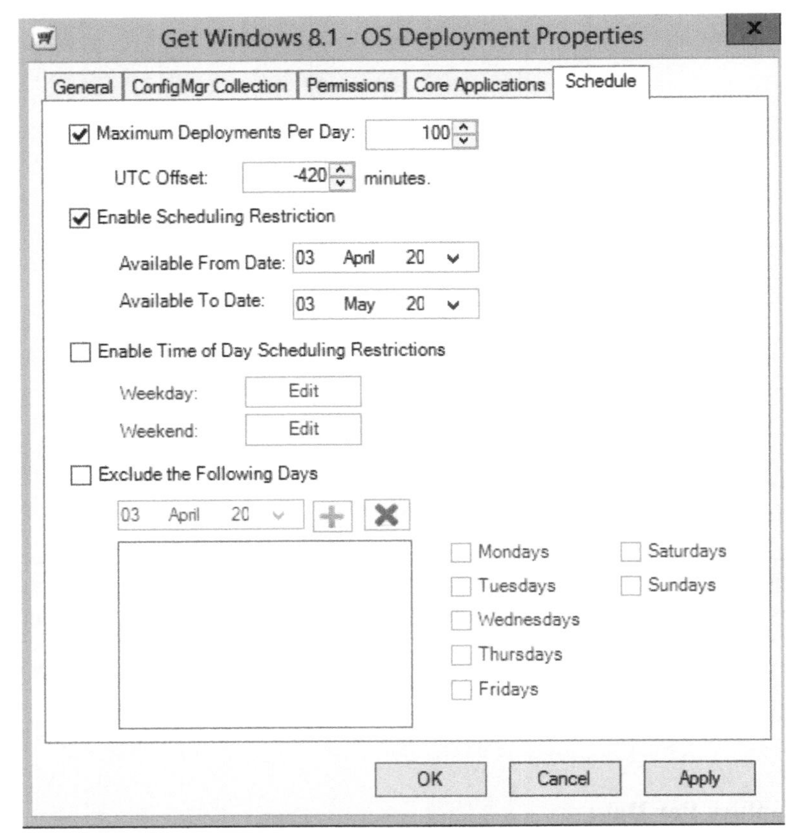

Customizing the Self-Service OSD Wizard schedule.

Appendix A

Hydrating the Lab

Here are the detailed steps for installing and configuring the initial hydration kit provided in the book sample files. This hydration kit allows you to build the same environment that is used for this book in a virtual environment based on Hyper-V in Windows Server 2012 R2.

Taking hydration to the next level, we have provided PowerShell scripts that automate the initial build of the Hyper-V environment, as well as create all necessary items inside the ConfigMgr infrastructure to allow you full functionality out of the gate.

To set up a virtual environment with all the servers and clients, you need a Windows Server 2012 R2 Hyper-V host with at least 16 GB of RAM, even though 32 GB RAM is recommended. Either way, make sure you are using SSD drives for your storage. Because we are using dynamic disks on the virtual machines, a single 240 GB SSD is enough to run all the scenarios in this book.

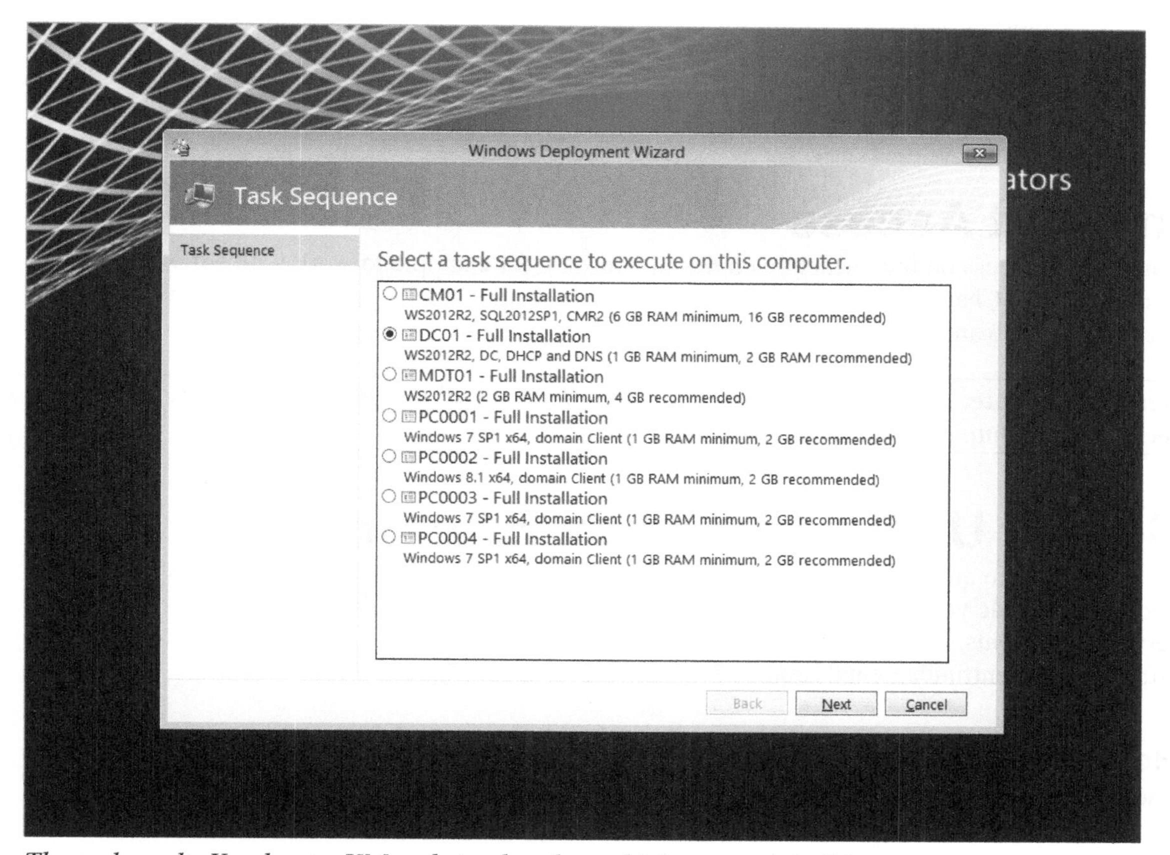

The end result: You boot a VM and simply select which server to build.

Note: The password for the accounts created by the hydration kit (including the Administrator account) is P@ssw0rd.

The Base Servers

Using the hydration kit, you build the following list of servers.

- **DC01.** Domain Controller, DNS, and DHCP
- **MDT01.** File Server
- **CM01.** SQL Server 2012 SP1 and ConfigMgr 2012 R2

The Base Clients

In addition to the servers, you also use a few clients throughout the book guides. Four clients are created in this appendix, and the others are installed as part of the book guides.

- **PC0001.** Windows 7 Enterprise SP1 x64
- **PC0002.** Windows 8.1 Enterprise x64
- **PC0003.** Windows 7 Enterprise SP1 x64
- **PC0004.** Windows 7 Enterprise SP1 x64

Internet Access

For Internet access on the virtual machines in your lab, for example to work with software updates as described in Chapter 6, we commonly use a virtual router (running in a VM) to provide Internet access to our lab and to test VMs.

Real World Note: For detailed guidance on setting up a virtual router for your lab environment, see this guide: http://tinyurl.com/usingvirtualrouter.

Setting Up the Hydration Environment

To enable you to quickly set up the servers and clients used for the step-by-step guides in this book, we provide you with a hydration kit (part of the book sample files) that will build all the servers and clients. The sample files are available for download at http://deploymentfundamentals.com.

How Does the Hydration Kit Work?

The hydration kit that you download is just a folder structure and some scripts. The scripts help you create the MDT 2013 Lite Touch offline media (big ISO), and the folder structure is there for you to add your own software and licenses when applicable. You can use trial versions for the lab software, as well. The overview steps are the following:

1. Download the needed software.
2. Install MDT 2013 Lite Touch and Windows ADK 8.1.
3. Create a MDT 2013 deployment share.
4. Populate the folder structure with your media and any license information.
5. Generate the MDT 2013 media item (big ISO).
6. Create a few virtual machines, boot them on the media item, select what servers they should become, and about two hours later you have the lab environment ready to go.

Preparing the Downloads Folder

These steps should be performed on the Windows Server 2012 R2 Hyper-V host.

Download the Software

1. On your **Windows Server 2012 R2 Hyper-V** host, create the **C:\Downloads** folder.
2. Download the following software to the **C:\Downloads** folder:
    - The book sample files (http://deploymentfundamentals.com)
    - ADK 8.1 (To download the full ADK, you run adksetup.exe once and select to download the files.)
    - BGInfo
    - ConfigMgr 2012 R2
    - ConfigMgr 2012 R2 PreReqs

> **Note:** To download the ConfigMgr 2012 R2 prerequisites, run the SMSSETUP\BIN\X64\Setupdl.exe application from the ConfigMgr 2012 R2 installation files, specify a temporary download folder, and click Download.

- MDT 2013
- SQL Server 2012 with SP1 x64 Standard (trial or full version)
- Microsoft Visual C++ 2005 SP1 runtimes (both x86 and x64)
- Microsoft Visual C++ 2008 SP1 runtimes (both x86 and x64)
- Microsoft Visual C++ 2010 SP1 runtimes (both x86 and x64)
- Microsoft Visual C++ 2012 SP1 runtimes (both x86 and x64)

Note: All the Microsoft Visual C++ downloads can be found on the following page: http://support.microsoft.com/kb/2019667.

- Windows Server 2012 R2 (trial or full version)
- Windows 7 Enterprise with SP1 x64 (trial or full version)
- Windows 8.1 Enterprise x64 (trial or full version)

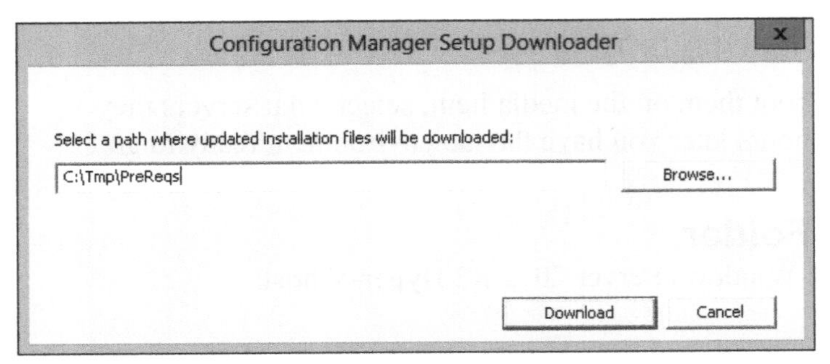

Running the Setupdl.exe to download the ConfigMgr 2012 R2 PreReqs.

Preparing the Hydration Environment

You need to have at least 75 GB of free disk space on C:\ for the hydration kit and about 200 GB of free space for the volume hosting your virtual machines. Also make sure to run all commands from an elevated PowerShell prompt.

Create the Hydration Deployment Share

1. On your **Windows Server 2012 R2 Hyper-V** host, install **ADK (adksetup.exe)**, selecting only the following components:
   - **Deployment Tools**
   - **Windows Preinstallation Environment (Windows PE)**

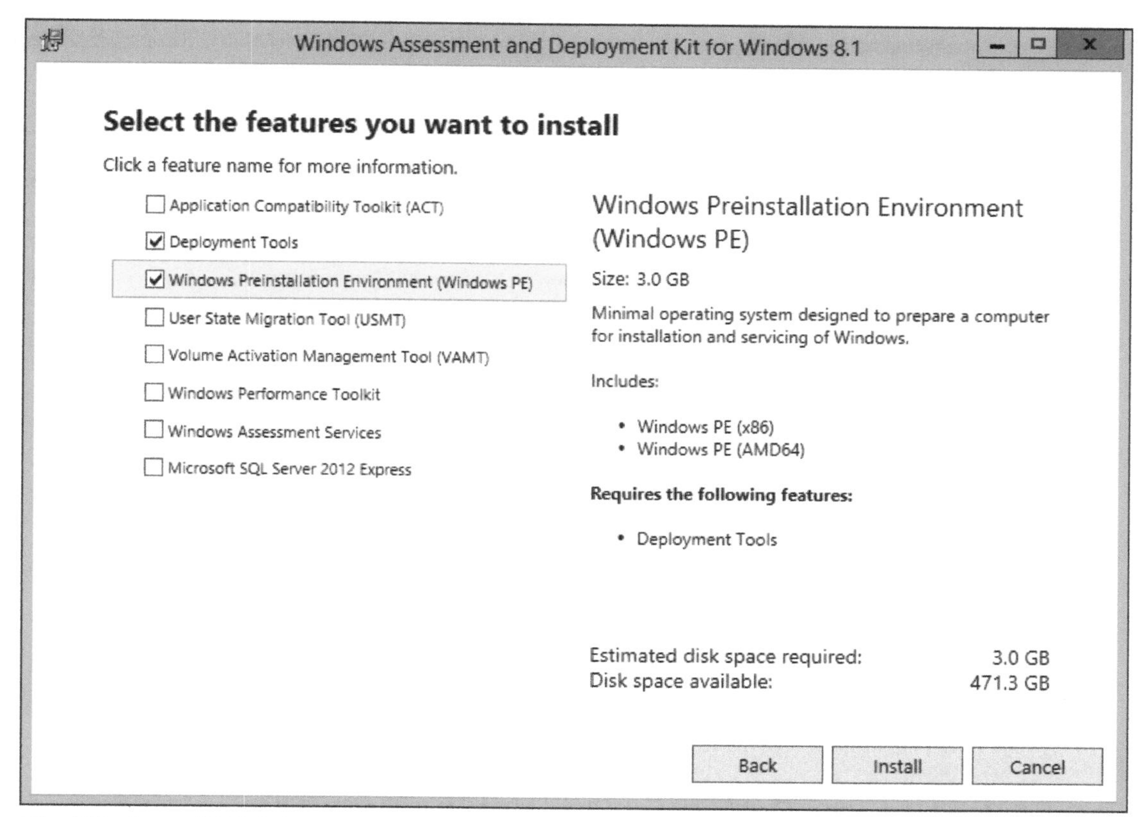

The Windows ADK 8.1 setup.

2. Install **MDT 2013** (**MicrosoftDeploymentToolkit2013_x64.msi**) with the default settings.
3. Extract the book sample files and copy the **HydrationCM2012R2-1E** folder to **C:**.
4. You should now have the following folder containing a few subfolders and PowerShell scripts:

   C:\HydrationCM2012R2-1E\Source
5. In an elevated (run as Administrator) **PowerShell** command prompt, navigate to the hydration folder by running the following command:

   ```
   Set-Location C:\HydrationCM2012R2-1E\Source
   ```
6. Still at the **PowerShell** command prompt, with location (working directory) set to **C:\HydrationCM2012R2-1E\Source**, create the hydration deployment share by running the following command:

   ```
   .\CreateHydrationDeploymentShare.ps1
   ```
7. After creating the hydration deployment share, review the added content using **Deployment Workbench** (available on the Start screen).

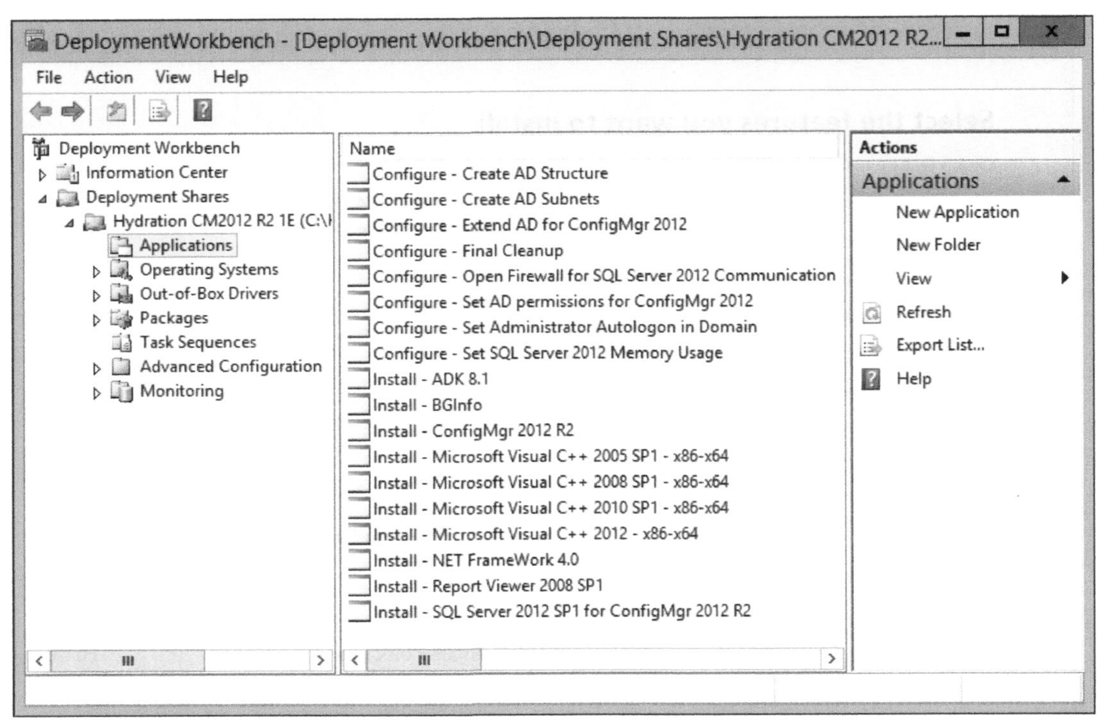

Deployment Workbench with the readymade applications listed.

Populate the Hydration Deployment Share with the Setup Files

In these steps, you copy the setup files to the correct target folder in the hydration structure.

1. On your **Windows Server 2012 R2 Hyper-V** host, copy the ADK 8.1 installation files to the following folder:

C:\HydrationCM2012R2-1E\DS\Applications\Install - ADK\Source

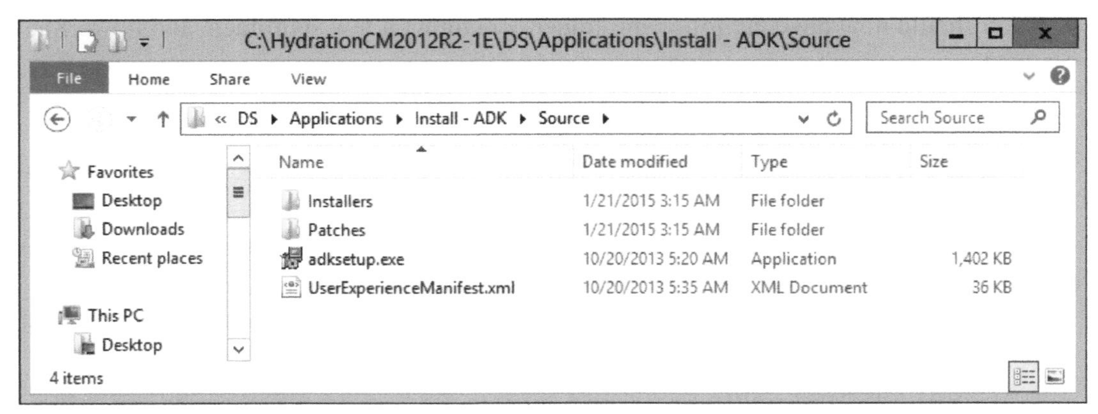

The Windows ADK 8.1 files copied.

2. Copy the **BGInfo** file (**bginfo.exe**) to the following folder:

   C:\HydrationCM2012R2-1E\DS\Applications\Install - BGInfo\Source

3. Copy the **SQL Server 2012 with SP1 x64** installation files (the content of the ISO, not the actual ISO) to the following folder:

   C:\HydrationCM2012R2-1E\DS\Applications
   Install - SQL Server 2012 SP1\Source

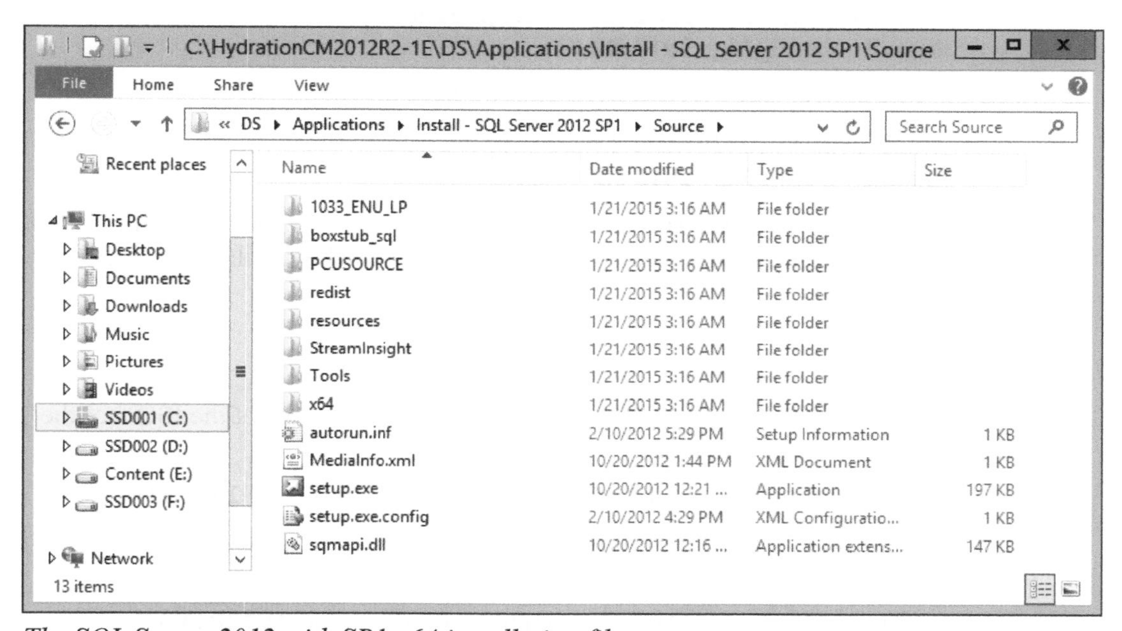

The SQL Server 2012 with SP1 x64 installation files.

4. Copy the **Microsoft Visual C++ 2005 SP1 x86** and **Microsoft Visual C++ 2005 SP1 x64** installation files **(vcredist_x86.exe and vcredist_x64.exe)** to the following folder:

   C:\HydrationCM2012R2-1E\DS\Applications
   Install - Microsoft Visual C++ 2005 SP1 - x86-x64\Source

5. Copy the **Microsoft Visual C++ 2008 SP1 x86** and **Microsoft Visual C++ 2008 SP1 x64** installation files **(vcredist_x86.exe and vcredist_x64.exe)** to the following folder:

   C:\HydrationCM2012R2-1E\DS\Applications
   Install - Microsoft Visual C++ 2008 SP1 - x86-x64\Source

6. Copy the **Microsoft Visual C++ 2010 SP1 x86** and **Microsoft Visual C++ 2010 SP1 x64** installation files **(vcredist_x86.exe** and **vcredist_x64.exe)** to the following folder:

   C:\HydrationCM2012R2-1E\DS\Applications
   Install - Microsoft Visual C++ 2010 SP1 - x86-x64\Source

7. Copy the **Microsoft Visual C++ 2012 x86** and **Microsoft Visual C++ 2012 x64** installation files **(vcredist_x86.exe** and **vcredist_x64.exe)** to the following folder:

   C:\HydrationCM2012R2-1E\DS\Applications
   Install - Microsoft Visual C++ 2012 - x86-x64\Source

8. Copy the **ConfigMgr 2012 R2** installation files (extract the download) to the following folder:

   C:\HydrationCM2012R2-1E\DS\Applications
   Install - ConfigMgr 2012 R2\Source

9. Copy the **ConfigMgr 2012 R2 PreReqs** files to the following folder:

   C:\HydrationCM2012R2-1E\DS\Applications
   Install - ConfigMgr 2012 R2\PreReqs

10. From the **C:\HydrationCM2012R2-1E\DS\Applications\Install - ConfigMgr 2012 R2\Source\SMSSETUP\BIN\X64** folder, copy the **extadsch.exe** file to the following folder:

    C:\HydrationCM2012R2-1E\DS\Applications
    Configure - Extend AD for ConfigMgr 2012\Source

11. Copy the **Windows Server 2012 R2** installation files (the content of the ISO, not the actual ISO) to the following folder:

    C:\HydrationCM2012R2-1E\DS\Operating Systems\WS2012R2

12. Copy the **Windows 7 Enterprise with SP1 x64** installation files (again, the content of the ISO, not the actual ISO) to the following folder:

    C:\HydrationCM2012R2-1E\DS\Operating Systems\W7SP1X64

13. Copy the **Windows 8.1 Enterprise x64** installation files (again, the content of the ISO, not the actual ISO) to the following folder:

    C:\HydrationCM2012R2-1E\DS\Operating Systems\W81X64

Create the Hydration ISO (MDT 2013 Update Offline Media Item)

1. On your **Windows Server 2012 R2 Hyper-V** host, using the **Deployment Workbench** (available on the **Start screen**), expand **Deployment Shares** and then expand **Hydration CM2012 R2 1E**.

2. Review the various nodes. The **Applications**, **Operating Systems**, and **Task Sequences** nodes should all have some content in them.

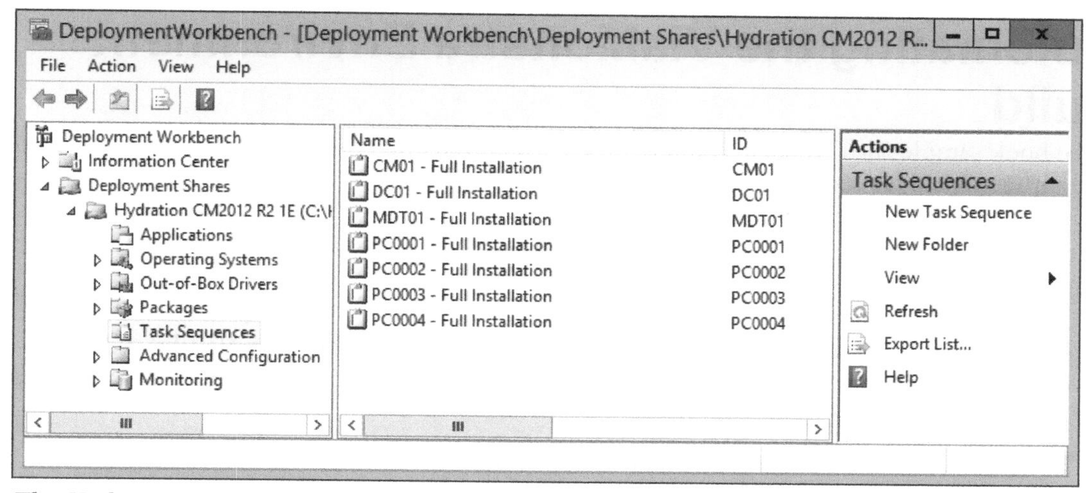

The Hydration deployment share, listing all task sequences.

3. Expand the **Advanced Configuration** node, and then select the **Media** node.
4. In the right pane, right-click the **MEDIA001** item and select **Update Media Content**.

Note: The most common reason for failures in the hydration kit are related to antivirus software preventing the ISO from being generated correctly. If you see any errors in the update media content process, disable (or uninstall) your antivirus software, and then try the update again. Anyway, the media update will take a while to run, a perfect time for a coffee break. ☺

After the media update, you will have a big ISO (HydrationCM2012R2-1E.iso) in the C:\HydrationCM2012R2-1E\ISO folder. Depending on the Windows media version used, the ISO will be about 18–19 GB in size.

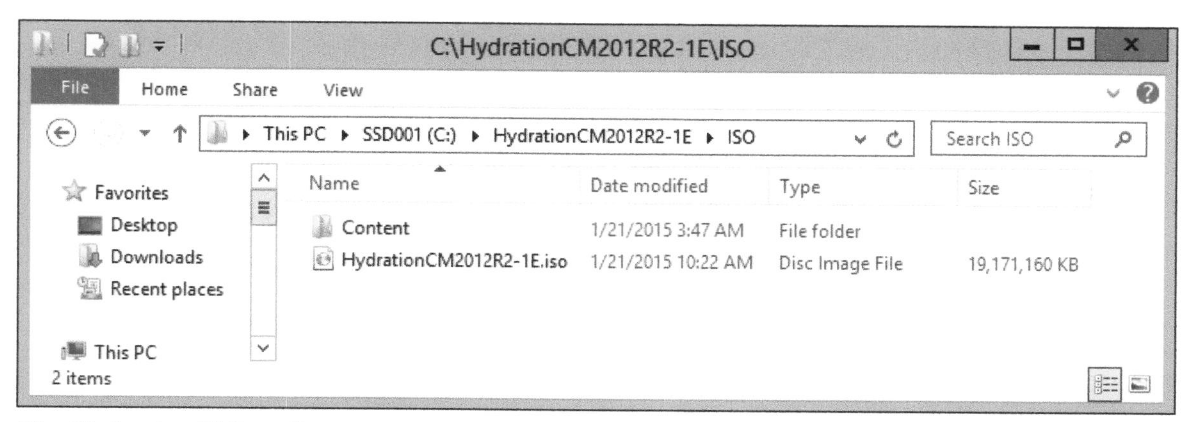

The Hydration ISO media item.

Automating the ViaMonstra Environment Build

In the book sample files, you can find the BUILD-ViaMonstra.ps1 script. This script creates the base virtual machines required for all of the chapters in this book.

Note: The script creates the virtual machines on the disk with the largest volume. If you want to change that, you can modify line 22 in the script.

In this guide, we assume you have downloaded and extracted the book sample files to C:\Labfiles on your Windows Server 2012 R2 Hyper-V host, and that you have already created your hydration ISO.

1. On your **Windows Server 2012 R2 Hyper-V** host, start an elevated (run as Administrator) **PowerShell** command prompt.
2. Create the virtual machines by running the following command:

   ```
   C:\Labfiles\Scripts\BUILD-ViaMonstra.ps1
   ```

Note: The script will start all virtual machines, but you need to complete the build of the **DC01** virtual machine before you can deploy the remaining virtual machines.

3. On **DC01**, after WinPE has loaded, select the **DC01** task sequence.

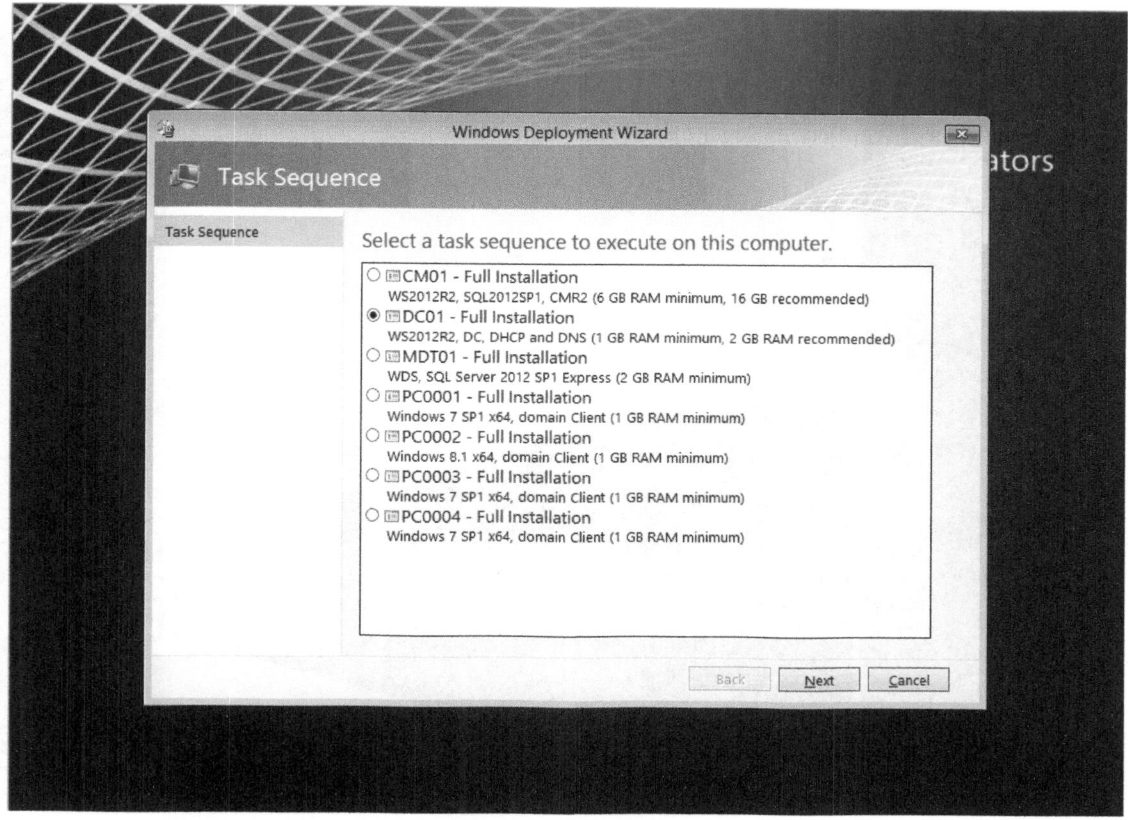

The Task Sequence list showing the hydration task sequences.

4. Wait until the setup is complete and you see the **Hydration completed** message in the final summary.
5. When the **DC01** setup is complete, leave it running and start the setup on the remaining virtual machines.

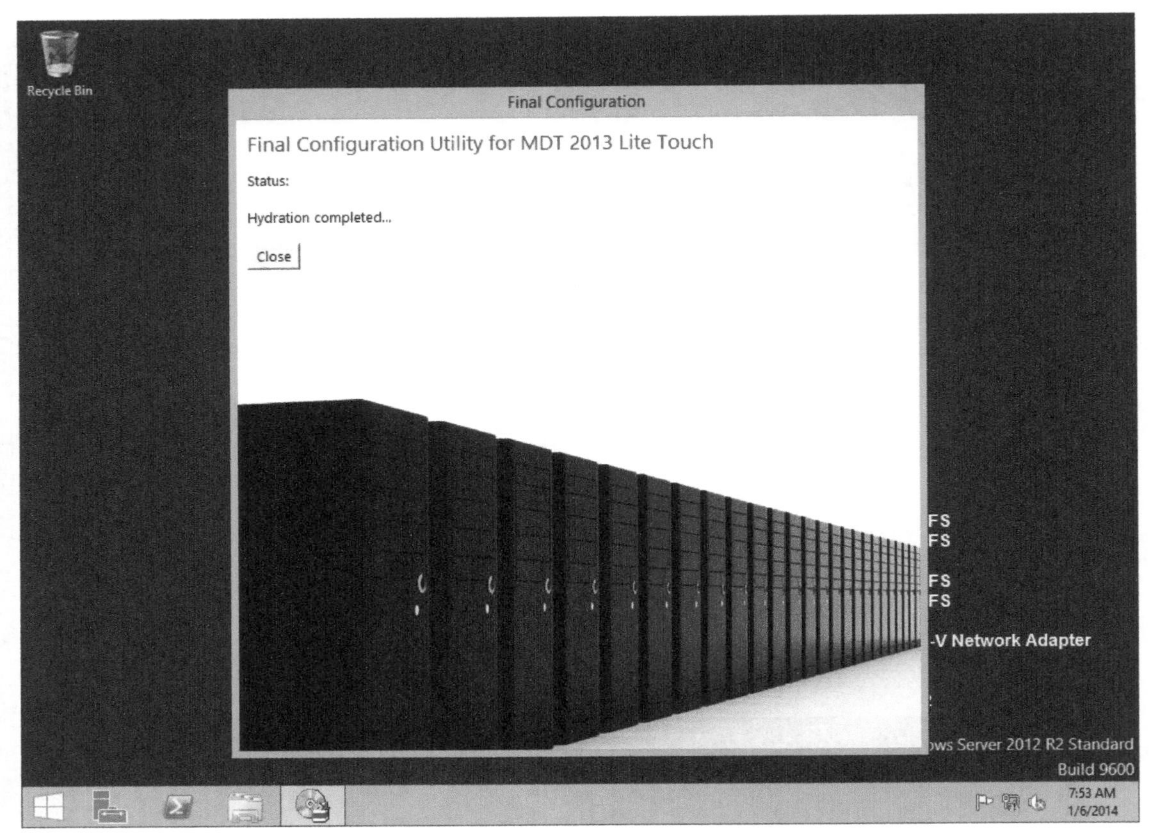

The deployment of DC01 completed, showing the custom final summary screen.

Index

Beyond the Book – Meet the Experts

If you liked their book, you will love to hear them in person.

Live Presentations

Dave frequently speaks at Microsoft conferences around North America, such as TechEd, VeeamOn, TechDays, and MVPDays Community Roadshow.

Émile has presented at the MVPDays Community Roadshow.

You can find additional information on the following blog:

www.checkyourlogs.net

Video Training

For video-based training, see the following site:

www.deploymentartist.com

Live Instructor-led Classes

Dave has been a Microsoft Certified Trainer (MCT) for more than 15 years and presents scheduled instructor-led classes in the US and Canada. For current dates and locations, see the following sites:

- www.truesec.com
- www.checkyourlogs.net

Consulting Services

Dave and Émile have worked with some of the largest companies in the world and have a wealth of experience and expertise. Customer engagements are typically between two weeks and six months. For more information, see the following site:

www.triconelite.com

Twitter

Dave and Émile tweet on the following aliases:

- Dave Kawula: @DaveKawula
- Émile Cabot: @ECabot

Lightning Source UK Ltd.
Milton Keynes UK
UKOW07f1333030316

269547UK00001B/1/P

9 789187 445125